Fighting Fraud

Other Books Authored or Co-Authored

Information Systems Security Officer's Guide: Establishing and Managing an Information Protection Program: May 1998, ISBN 0-7506-9896-9; by Dr. Gerald L. Kovacich; First Edition and July 2003, ISBN 0-7506-7656-6, Second Edition; published by Butterworth-Heinemann (Czech translation of First Edition also available).

I-Way Robbery: Crime on the Internet: May 1999, ISBN 0-7506-7029-0; co-authored by Dr. Gerald L. Kovacich and William C. Boni; published by Butterworth-Heinemann; Japanese translated version published by T. Aoyagi Office Ltd, Japan: February 2001, ISBN 4-89346-698-4.

High-Technology Crime Investigator's Handbook: Working in the Global Information Environment: First Edition, September 1999, ISBN 0-7506-7086-X; co-authored by Dr. Gerald L. Kovacich and William C. Boni; July 2003, and Second Edition; July 2006 ISBN 10: 0-7506-7929-8; ISBN 13: 9-780-7506-7929-9; co-authored with Dr. Andy Jones and published by Butterworth-Heinemann.

Netspionage: The Global Threat to Information: September 2000, ISBN 0-7506-7257-9; co-authored by Dr. Gerald L. Kovacich and William C. Boni; published by Butterworth-Heinemann.

Information Assurance: Surviving in the Information Environment: First Edition, September 2001, ISBN 1-85233-326-X; co-authored by Dr. Gerald L. Kovacich and Dr. Andrew J. C. Blyth; published by Springer-Verlag Ltd (London); Second Edition, ISBN 1-84628-266-7, published in March 2006.

Global Information Warfare: How Businesses, Governments, and Others Achieve Global Objectives and Attain Competitive Advantages: June 2002, ISBN 0-84931-114-4; co-authored by Dr. Andy Jones, Dr. Gerald L. Kovacich and Perry Luzwick; published by Auerbach Publishers/CRC Press.

The Manager's Handbook for Corporate Security: Establishing and Managing a Successful Assets Protection Program: April 2003, ISBN 0-7506-7487-3; co-authored by Dr. Gerald L. Kovacich and Edward P. Halibozek; published by Butterworth-Heinemann.

Mergers & Acquisitions Security: Corporate Restructuring and Security Management: April 2005, ISBN 0-7506-7805-4; co-authored by Dr. Gerald L. Kovacich and Edward P. Halibozek; published by Butterworth-Heinemann.

Security Metrics Management: How to Manage the Costs of an Assets Protection Program: December 2005, ISBN 0-7506-7899-2; co-authored by Dr. Gerald L. Kovacich and Edward P. Halibozek; published by Butterworth-Heinemann.

The Security Professional's Handbook on Terrorism: Establishing and Managing a Corporate Anti-Terrorism Program: To be released in September 2007, ISBN 0-7506-8257-4; co-authored with Edward P. Halibozek and Dr. Andy Jones; published by Butterworth Heinemann.

Fighting Fraud

How to Establish and Manage an Anti-Fraud Program

Dr. Gerald L. Kovacich

AMSTERDAM • BOSTON • HEIDELBERG • LONDON
NEW YORK • OXFORD • PARIS • SAN DIEGO
SAN FRANCISCO • SINGAPORE • SYDNEY • TOKYO
Butterworth-Heinemann is an imprint of Elsevier

Elsevier Academic Press
30 Corporate Drive, Suite 400, Burlington, MA 01803, USA
525 B Street, Suite 1900, San Diego, California 92101-4495, USA
84 Theobald's Road, London WC1X 8RR, UK

This book is printed on acid-free paper. ∞

Library of Congress Cataloging-in-Publication Data
Kovacich, Gerald L.
   Fighting fraud : how to establish and manage an anti-fraud program /
Gerald L. Kovacich.
        p. cm.
   Includes index.
   ISBN 978-0-12-370868-7 (alk. paper)
   1. Commercial crimes.   2. Commercial crimes — Investigation.   3. Fraud —
Prevention.   4. Fraud investigation.   I. Title.
   HV6769.K68 2008
   658.4'73 — dc22

                                                              2007013397

British Library Cataloguing in Publication Data
A catalogue record for this book is available from the British Library

ISBN 13: 978-0-12-370868-7
ISBN 10: 0-12-370868-0

For all information on all Elsevier Academic Press publications
visit our Web site at www.books.elsevier.com

Printed in the United States of America
08   09   10   11   12   13   10   9   8   7   6   5   4   3   2   1

This book is dedicated to all those fraud fighters who combat defrauders and the other miscreants who try to take something of value from others without their permission and without providing the owners with just compensation.

This book is especially dedicated to those whistleblowers who have the guts to stand up when a wrong has been committed!

Quotation*

[T]he modern economic world centers on the controlling corporate organization. . . . Executives of Enron, WorldCom, Tyco and others became the focus of widely publicized criticism, even outrage. Joining the language came the reference to corporate scandals. Avoided only was mention of the compelling opportunity for enrichment that had been accorded the managers of the modern corporate enterprise, and this in a world that approves of self-enrichment as the basic reward for economic merit . . .

. . . Great firms, particularly in energy and mass communications but not so confined, came to dominate the news. In all cases, the situation was the same, as was the result. Management was in full control. Ownership was irrelevant, some auditors were compliant. Stock options added participant wealth and slightly concealed take. . . .

The least expected contribution to the adverse and even criminal activity was the corrupt accounting . . . This provided cover for the devious actions that extended to outright theft. Individuals had long regarded accounting as both competent and honest. . . .

The corporate scandals and especially the associated publicity have led to discussion or appropriate regulation and some action — to positive steps to insure accounting honesty and some proposed remedies, as required, to counter management and lesser corporate fraud . . .

. . . Managers, not the owners of capital, are the effective power in the modern enterprise. . . .

. . . So, as a very practical matter, power passed to the mentally qualified, actively participating management, and it did so irrevocably. The belief that ownership has a final authority persisted, as it still does . . .

. . . The basic fact of the twenty-first century — a corporate system based on the unrestrained power of self-enrichment.

---

* From John K. Galbraith's book, *The Economics of Innocent Fraud: Truth for Our Time.* Houghton Mifflin, Boston. 2004.

Table of Contents

Preface

I must tell you up front that the focus of this book is NOT on investigating frauds, corporations that are responsible in some form for perpetrating frauds, and the like, although some information in that regard is provided.

The emphasis in this book is on *Establishing and Managing an Anti-Fraud Program* for a corporation from an anti-fraud management and leadership viewpoint, with the emphasis on management and leadership.

Although I use the word "corporation" throughout, it also applies to government agencies, nonprofit groups, associations, privately held companies, and any entity that is concerned with the loss of its assets by fraudulent means.

Over the years, many books have been written about fraud in general and also about specific types of frauds. There have also been books written about specific fraud cases dealing with specific corporate frauds.

All of these books, however, for the most part seem to miss one basic fact: namely, the perpetration of a corporate fraud relates to attacking and stealing corporate assets of various kinds. Furthermore, the leadership role of protecting corporate assets has for decades fallen on the shoulders of the corporation's chief security officer (CSO), and it still does today.

That role will be discussed in more detail in the chapters of this book, but suffice it to say here that the corporate CSO has seemed to have abdicated that responsibility — leaving the protection of corporate assets from fraudulent attacks to others both inside and outside the corporation — to auditors and accountants.

This book was written in part to try to change that attitude and to provide justification to begin wresting that leadership responsibility from others and help make a case for justifying why fighting corporate fraud should be one of the primary duties and responsibilities of the CSO, who is indeed the leader for protecting all corporate assets.

This book also seeks to:

- Provide security professionals and others responsible for the protection of corporate assets (e.g., executive management) a roadmap for developing their own anti-fraud program.
- Help them to tailor the program to their own corporate environment.
- Help those who are interested in preventing fraud within their corporations by providing them with an awareness and a better understanding of the threats to corporations by these miscreants.
- Explain how the frauds are costing these corporations a competitive edge in the global marketplace.
- Provide guidance on how to:
  - Establish and manage a corporate anti-fraud program that is both proactive and defensive in nature.
  - Use an aggressive anti-fraud strategic approach under the leadership of the CSO.

This book will also be useful for those accountants, investigators, and auditors, as well as others who work for corporations in the areas of finance, contracts, supply, and the like, and who are interested in indicators of frauds and anti-fraud programs and in viewing the matter from other than an accountant's, investigator's, or auditor's point of view.

Hopefully, they will see that fighting corporate fraud is indeed the leadership responsibility of the CSO and push, pull, and otherwise support the CSO who wants to take on that leadership role.

I want to repeat that this book emphasizes *establishing and managing an anti-fraud program* and how to set up such a program for a corporation. As noted earlier, it is not about investigating incidents of fraud, describing fraud examination functions or incidents of fraud, and the like, except as they relate to the primary objective of establishing and managing an anti-fraud program.

The text consists of three sections and 17 chapters that will provide the reader with a practitioner's guide (a "how-to" book), augmented by some background information to put it all in perspective. The approach used should:

- Enable the reader to understand this global, fraud-threatening environment.
- Immediately put in place a useful anti-fraud program baseline under the leadership of the corporation's CSO.

The format used for this book follows the one I have used in several of my other successful books, primarily because according to many of my readers this format and approach provides basic information in an easy-to-read manner.

Because of similarities between protecting corporate assets from fraud and protecting corporate assets from various other threats agents, I have borrowed the format and some related information from some of my previous books published by Elsevier's Butterworth-Heinemann Publishers. This provides the reader the required information in one book instead of having to read through other books for the information, for example, *The Manager's Handbook for Corporate Security*.

The information provided in this book is the product of decades of experience in fighting fraud-threat agents and of information collected from multiple sources, private, public, governmental, and corporate. This information has been passed on through my professional colleagues as well as through the training and awareness courses offered by various U.S. federal government agencies and the courses and conferences provided by anti-fraud and security-related associations. If I failed to provide specific recognition within the heart of this book for the information they have provided over the years, I apologize in advance for this unintended oversight. After decades in this field, the sources and personal experiences tend to merge and blur.

I hope this book provides you with a basic foundation that will help you build an anti-fraud program and a total assets protection program. I would be very interested in hearing from you concerning your successes and failures in that regard. Also, I welcome all constructive criticism and suggestions on additional topics that you think should be addressed in any further editions of this book. Please send your questions and comments to me through my publisher: Elsevier's Butterworth-Heinemann.

Dr. Gerald L. Kovacich
Whidbey Island, Washington
U.S.A.

Acknowledgments

In taking on any book writing project, success will elude any writer who thinks he or she knows it all. Therefore, it was vitally important for me to be able to call on old friends and professionals to help me meet my specific objectives:

- To provide a book of useful information to help the security professionals and others who are involved in anti-fraud activities to gain information that can be quickly put to use.
- To assist in the protection of corporate assets from the global defrauders of today and tomorrow.

In that context, the following deserve special thanks:

- *Motomu Akashi*, mentor, great friend, and one of the best corporate security professionals ever to have protected a corporate asset, especially in the "Black World"!
- *William C. Boni*, Corporate Vice President and CISO, Motorola Corporation, one of our leading twenty-first-century security professionals.
- *Jerry Ervin*, good friend, former professional crime fighter, information systems security specialist, investigator, special agent, and security guru.
- *Don Evans*, InfoSec Manager, United Space Alliance, who is always there to lend a hand, provide advice to the security "rookies," and support a security conference anywhere, anytime.
- *Edward P. Halibozek*, Vice President of Security, Northrop Grumman Corporation, for his friendship, professional security advice, and his great work as a co-author.
- *Roscoe Hinton*, a very old friend and fellow fraud fighter, Special Agent (recently retired), who was my partner in fighting defrauders who targeted the U.S. government, especially in our investigations

and operations against the defrauders and other miscreants who tried to defraud the Department of Defense and the U.S. Air Force. I hope that we won more than we lost over the years! Thanks Roscoe for the advice and counsel.

- Dr. Andy Jones, Head of Security Technology Research, at the Security Research Centre for British Telecom, United Kingdom; distinguished professor, lecturer, consultant; co-author, good friend, and one of the best of what Britain has to offer to combat high-technology crimes and information systems assets protection.

- Jerry Swick, former senior telecommunications crime investigator, and retired Los Angeles Police Department Lieutenant and co-founder of their computer crime unit. A true crime fighting professional and a good friend.

- All those who work for the *Association of Certified Fraud Examiners* (ACFE) who daily lead the way in supporting the anti-fraud professionals, whether they be auditors, accountants, financial specialists, fraud examiners, security personnel, law enforcement personnel, investigators, corporate or government management — in fact, anyone who is interested in fighting fraud. Thanks especially for your many years of supporting my activities.

- The *American Society for Industrial Security* (ASIS), a security professional organization which has led the way in supporting security professionals. Thanks to them for their continued leadership and support in all they do.

- The *United States Air Force Office of Special Investigations* (AFOSI) for their years of leading the way in the DoD and the federal government in fighting fraud, supporting and providing some of the best anti-fraud training one can ever receive; as well as for being a great place to work as a special agent and fraud investigator.

- The *High Technology Crime Investigation Association* (HTCIA), which has become one of the primary leaders in investigating high-technology crimes, including telecommunications fraud, computer fraud, and various other forms of high technology-related frauds. Thanks to them, law enforcement and security professionals have been working closer together to fight high-technology crimes, including high-technology-related frauds.

Of course, thanks to my better half for over 30 years, Hsiao-yun Kovacich. I must always thank her for many years of support and giving me the "space" I need to research and write. Thanks also for her many hours of researching topics for my writings and for explaining the "thinking Asian mind"!

To the staff and project team of Butterworth-Heinemann — Mark Listewnik, Chris Nolin, Jennifer Rhuda Soucy, Pam Chester, and Kelly Weaver, the very best of professionals! Thanks again for providing great support for another one of my book projects and for having the confidence in me to once again sign me to a book contract!

To those other professionals in the book publishing world of Elsevier's Butterworth-Heinemann, who helped make this book into a successful and professional product. Thanks for your help and professionalism: Melinda Ritchie, Marissa Hederson, and Alisa Andreola.

I also thank you, the readers, who have supported me over the years by attending my lectures and purchasing my books. I hope that my lectures and books have added to your body of knowledge and have helped you to be successful in leading the assets protection efforts of your company or government agency.

Introduction and Premise

This book is an introductory book on the general topic of fraud, with emphasis on fighting fraud through the *establishment and management of a formal anti-fraud program.*

The premise of this book, with which some may agree in whole, in part, or not at all, is based on the idea that today's approach to fighting fraud is not working and that a formal and aggressive anti-fraud program should be in place in all businesses and government agencies.

The leadership role of such a program falls under the duties and responsibilities of the chief security officer (CSO) of the corporation*. That person, or the person by another name, has leadership responsibility for protecting corporate assets from all threat agents whether they are thieves, defrauders, terrorists, or some other sort of miscreant.

It is logical, therefore, that the CSO lead the corporation's anti-fraud program efforts as a standalone program or probably best as an integral part and subset of an overall corporate assets protection program.

There are those who will disagree with this premise. That will be discussed in the last chapter of this book. As you read through this book, please form your own conclusions.

---

* As a reminder (this will be made more than once in this book): the word "corporation" is the catch-all term used in the book to describe any business whether it is a partnership, a corporation, charity, government agency, or the like. However, the anti-fraud program that is to be discussed and used as an example revolves around a corporation.

I

AN INTRODUCTION TO THE WONDERFUL WORLD OF FRAUD

Prior to discussing how to establish and manage a corporate anti-fraud program, it is important to set the stage for that discussion by looking at the environment where today's corporations — businesses — market and sell their products and buy their supplies.

This is important because as we go charging into the twenty-first century, we see that the business environment of the old twentieth century is yes, still there, kind of, sort of, but also rapidly changing in many ways. These changes make it almost impossible to conduct some types of corporate frauds and opens up new possibilities for perpetrating other types of frauds. Furthermore, in many ways, the defrauders of today have taken on a global profile and are no longer relegated to some local area in some small part of the world.

So, in Section I, we set the stage and hopefully provide some logic to help you understand why the corporate anti-fraud program discussed in Section II should be considered and structured (baselined) as proposed. This section is broken down into the following seven chapters:

Chapter 1 The New-Old Global Business Environment
Chapter 2 Corporate Assets, Frauds, and Other Terms — What Are They?
Chapter 3 Fraud-Related Laws
Chapter 4 Corporations Don't Commit Frauds, People Do
Chapter 5 Fighting Fraud — Whose Job Is It Anyway?
Chapter 6 Where There Is a Will There Is a Way — Fraud Schemes
Chapter 7 Fraud Cases and Commentary — Learning by Example

The logic of Section I is that you should first understand the global business environment. After all, that is where you, the leader or team member of the corporate anti-fraud program, must work. Once the basic global business environment is understood, we move on to defining assets and frauds and their related laws. If you don't know what is meant by assets, what frauds are and their associated laws, you will have a difficult time defending corporate assets against attacks from fraud-threat agents. This basic understanding will also help you define a cost-effective process to establish and manage a successful anti-fraud program.

Once we get past the environment, laws, and definitions, it is important to discuss who commits fraud and who should lead the anti-fraud efforts for a business. As you will see, there are different opinions as to who should lead these efforts — there are "rice bowls" at stake anytime one tries to take duties and responsibilities along with their related budget away from another group. It is usually all about bureaucracy and power and not what is best for the corporation.

We will conclude Section I with an introduction to some basic fraud schemes and actual fraud cases that adversely impact corporations and, therefore, the profits and ability to successfully compete in the global marketplace. It is important to understand these threats to corporate assets and some of their modus operandi (MOs) because your anti-fraud program must be able to defend the assets against the fraud miscreants and their attacks.

Once you understand today's corporate and global fraud environment — your working environment — you will be in a better position to design, develop, implement, and manage your own anti-fraud program based not only on the global marketplace and high-technology environment, but also on the fraud-threat agents, their MOs, the specific culture and philosophy of your corporation, and its worldwide facilities.

1

The New-Old Global Business Environment

INTRODUCTION

For those who have responsibility for the protection of corporate assets, it means protecting the assets from all threats — natural and man-made. The emphasis of this book is on the protection of those assets (e.g., information, facilities, equipment, and employees) from fraudulent attacks.

In order to protect corporate assets from fraud, it is vitally important that the security professional and those in business management understand the global business environment in which the corporation will do business; they must also know where the corporate assets are located and how vulnerable they are to attacks by fraud-threat agents.

Some may argue that globalization is another word for internationalization, whereas others may contend that they are different. For our purposes, we will use the meaning stated below. It is best to leave matters relating to such definitions to academicians, whose world is the theoretical world more than the real world — at least the real world of global trade and international frauds.

> Globalization is the term used to describe the changes in societies and the world economy that result from dramatically increased international trade and cultural exchange. It describes the increase of trade and investing due to the falling of barriers and the interdependence of countries. In specifically economic contexts, the term refers almost exclusively to the effects of trade, particularly trade liberalization or "free trade". . . . More broadly, the term refers to the overall integration, and resulting increase in interdependence, among global actors (be they political, economic, or otherwise).[1]

---

[1] http://en.wikipedia.org/wiki/Globalization.

The "globalization" of business has been progressing for centuries. Ever since the first European explorers sought out new worlds, their purpose was to "Christianize the heathens" and trade with or steal from them. On the other side of the globe, Chinese and others were also exploring parts of the world and expanding their trading partners to those in the Middle East and Southeast Asia.

Economic globalization, the business of world trade and the "global marketplace," requires, and always has required, a mostly stable environment. Although in times of crisis and conflict, arms trading does indeed increase, that type of trade is very limited compared to other forms of trading — for example, those goods sought by the general consumers and other businesses. Trade on a global scale has been increasing for centuries, and it is expected to continue to increase, in some areas expanding exponentially and more rapidly than in the past.

As already suggested, in order for trade to flourish, businesses need a relatively stable environment; therefore, when wars break out in a region, as happened so often during the twentieth century, businesses (except for manufacturing and arms trading, of course) suffer. The recent global terrorist trends have adversely affected businesses, including tourism, in areas where the terrorists are the strongest, such as in the Middle East, followed predominantly by other Muslim nation-states or countries with major populations of Muslims, notably, Indonesia, the Philippines, and Malaysia.

You will find that no matter what threat you are protecting the corporate assets from, many of the same safeguards apply. For example, terrorists are currently being financially squeezed as the United States and other nations identify and stop the flow of funds to terrorists. This has led some terrorists to search for other sources of funding, including identity theft, credit card fraud, and other fraud-related schemes. So, it is not an exaggeration to say that your anti-fraud program may not only be protecting corporate assets but also fighting international terrorism.

Fraud-threat agents have in general much less effect on global trade and the marketplace than do terrorists. However, it has had a financial impact on affected corporations through, for example, pirated DVDs. Even the counterfeiting of goods has not slowed down trade with those nation-states such as China where it is prevalent. One finds that as nation-states improve the lives of their citizens and their economies, there is less need for counterfeiting (e.g., books, CDs, DVDs), and it tends to decline over time as in Taiwan.

> Fraud-threat agents are those man-made threats that include people, their schemes, modus operandi, technology supported tools, and the like.

After World War II, trade resumed, increasing around the world, especially trade between the nation-states of Europe and the United States as a result of the Marshall Plan, which the United States implemented to help war-torn Europe rebuild. This rebuilding did not occur in China time because the communists seized control of China in 1949, and of course communism was diametrically opposed to democracy and to private ownership of businesses of the Western world. At the same time, noncommunist nation-states in the Far East, including Japan, South Korea, Thailand, and Taiwan, being capitalist-oriented regimes, began to become successful global trading partners with nation-states around the world. During that process, they regularly violated international agreements, in particular committing copyright violations, product dumping, and the like.

In the twenty-first century, we are witnessing improvements in nation-state relationships — Russia and China have normalized relationships with the United States and Europe, free trade zones have been formed, the European Union has been founded and is flourishing, and Eastern Europe has been liberated from communism, with the result that capitalism has been established in those nations.

In addition, vast and ongoing improvements in communications and in transportation (the ability to ship goods both more efficiently and more rapidly around the world) have led to increased and massive trade and with it dependencies on that global trade. These trade improvements have been brought about in part by ever-increasing improvements in technology, especially high technology driven by the microprocessor.

Current trends also show that an increasing number of nation-states are becoming democratic; the movement toward capitalism is accelerating, and global capitalism is expected to continue growing for the foreseeable future. This trend will drive more global trade, which terrorists do not want to occur, but fraud miscreants love it, for as nations modernize and open up their borders, it provides more opportunities for perpetrating fraud schemes.

Even China has loosened its hold on its people and businesses in recent years and is effectively competing as a global economic power. China is expected to successfully compete in the quest for dominance in the global marketplace in the years to come unless some drastic changes occur in the global trading environment, such as war between Taiwan and China that might include the United States.

GLOBALIZATION OF BUSINESS — BENEFITS TO NATION-STATES

Corporations continue to expand their markets, facilities, and areas of operation around the world, many of which are supported by the nation-states, which benefit from such trades in the following ways:

- Increased employment
- Rise in standard of living
- More tax money to the nation-states
- Ability of citizens to purchase cheaper goods
- Increased trade leverage in the global marketplace
- More global power through economic power

Opponents of globalization maintain that it contributes to the "exploitation of the poor." Others counter that globalization increases business development and expansion, providing employment for those who previously had little hope of finding jobs. Such arguments can be made on both sides of this issue, but one thing is almost certain: globalization will not stop.

EXPANSION OF THE GLOBAL MARKETPLACE AND THEIR AREAS OF OPERATIONS

The global marketplace has expanded over the years from Europe to the Americas and now to Asia. It is expected that future expansions must consider Africa. Although many of Africa's nation-states are presently rather unstable, with the help of more modern nation-states and their global corporations, their situation will eventually change. After all, businesses go around the world to find the cheapest resources, and as Asia becomes more and more modern with ever higher standards of living, Africa may offer the next cheap source of business resources, especially labor. The continent certainly offers some opportunities to become a center for some fraud attacks. One example that comes to mind is Nigeria, but to be fair, it appears to be trying to limit global fraud schemes.

If you look at the some of the attacks perpetrated by fraud-threat agents in Africa, you can see that the threats are already there and ready to wreak havoc on the corporations of the world that dare enter their "domain" and try to be successful. Africa may provide an "excellent test environment" where one can study

- The clash between democratic-minded people
- Corrupt dictators challenged by capitalism and democracy
- Increased adoption of high-technology devices
- Civil wars among the African states and the role fraud-threat agents play in those wars
- The impact of modern nation-states as they support their countries' businesses in the African nation-states
- The actions of miscreants to stop modernization except that which is under their control or to gain from it

> In 1999, Uganda became the first African nation to have more mobile than traditional phones. 30 other African nations followed by 2002. . . . the megacity of Lagos, Nigeria, cell phones were one of the three largest industries there, neck and neck with religion and nutritional supplements.[2]

Africa is a continent worth studying to get some idea of not only what future corporate business will contend with vis-à-vis fraud-threat agents and corrupt governments but also the techniques they may use there and spread to other continents, and vice versa.

Along with that expansion, the increased risks of today's fraud-related miscreants and their attack methodologies and schemes may be frequently encountered for the foreseeable future, and are even likely to increase over time.

What those risks are and how a security professional leading an anti-fraud program for a corporation should deal with them will vary and may depend on such things as

- Types of corporation
- Their locations worldwide
- Their ownership
- Products they produce and market
- Threats to those assets
- Vulnerabilities of the assets protection defenses
- Types of anti-fraud and asset protection controls in place

TYPES OF CORPORATIONS

The types of corporations do not appear to be primary factors when global miscreants use fraud schemes to attack a corporation's assets. In the future this may change, but for now at least the current trend will continue.

CORPORATE OWNERS AND LOCATIONS

The corporate owners are generally the stockholders who may live in various locations in the world. However, their ownership is generally

---

[2] From *Radical Evolution: The Promise and Peril of Enhancing our Minds, Our Bodies — and What it Means to Be Human*, by Joel Garreau, pg. 170. Doubleday and Company, NY. 2005.

believed to be equated to the nation-states where they have their corporate headquarters and other facilities, and not the location of the stockholders. Corporate ownership is so diverse that targeting a corporation owing to its ownership does not seem to be a plausible reason for fraud attacks against them.

Attacks against businesses may be based on their physical locations — local organized crime, local terrorists' cells needing funding, and other local fraud-threat agents. Some nation-states where their businesses are located may have weak laws, a dictatorial or possibly corrupt government, weak criminal justices systems, and so on. These all tend to provide a safer environment for global miscreants, which of course include global or local fraud-threat agents.

With today's high-technology dependencies and vulnerabilities along with our convenient and fast mobility of travel, all types of miscreants can easily move about the world plying their trade. Therefore, a corporation's location may play a role in most non–high-technology, non–Internet-related frauds.

CORPORATE PRODUCTS

The corporations' products may also be a factor in determining whether or not they will continue as targets of fraud-threat agents and other assorted miscreants in the future. Furthermore, it is important to remember that these miscreants may be domestic rather than international threat agents.

As we mentioned earlier, businesses — and global businesses maybe more so — require a stable environment in which to operate. The more chaos, the more difficult it is to successfully do business. However, as businesses expand around the world, many will take more risks and begin operating in foreign nation-states that may not have a stable government and indeed may be the home of one or more groups of miscreants. A prime example is Nigeria and its "have I got a deal for you money schemes." Chaotic internal conditions are ripe for exploitation by fraud-threat agents.

Businesses will take more risks as the global marketplace competition continues to heat up and as they continue to look for cheaper labor, less costly raw materials, and favorable operating conditions, most notably a low tax base. They need these advantages in order to compete and to offer products at lower prices based on lower operating costs. These favorable operating conditions may also be where the criminal justice system is the weakest and, therefore, ripe for exploitation by miscreants of all types, including fraud-threat agents.

It is useful to distinguish economic, political, and cultural aspects of global-ization, although all three aspects are closely intertwined. The other key aspect of globalization is changes in technology, particularly in transport and communications, which it is claimed are creating a global village.[3]

As an anti-fraud professional responsible for the protection of corpo-rate assets, you will continue to find this type of environment for the fore-seeable future. How you will deal with those asset protection needs, defending them against fraud-threat agents' attacks, will offer you some of your greatest challenges.

THE HIGH-TECHNOLOGY FACTOR

The globalization of business is being supported and even driven by the continuing advancements in high technology (that technology based on the microprocessor). Thus, rapid and ever-expanding communications has also advanced the ability of fraud-threat agents to attack those they consider vulnerable to fraudulent schemes. Fraud-threat agents have been using the Internet, e-mails, cellular telephones, and the like to communicate with each other as well as to support their fraud schemes to attack their vic-tims — their corporate targets. They have become quite sophisticated in their use of these high-technology devices and also to take advantage of their vulnerabilities.

As high technology becomes smaller, more powerful, and cheaper, fraud threat-agents will continue to take advantage of the current and future improvements in these devices.

As technology improved, transportation systems such as the sailing ships and ground transportation systems improved. For example, steam engines gave way to diesel and gasoline engines, which has had a positive impact on trade because such improvements increased their speed and size, thus allowing them to transport more products to market faster and more efficiently.

---

[3] Ibid.

The industrialization of nation-states led to expanded and increased trade throughout the world. The advent of modern transportation supported by high technology has allowed today's miscreants to operate far beyond their home territories. Today they operate around the world, and as transportation and communications improve, these fraud-threat agents will acquire additional speed and sophistication in their modus operandi and, therefore, increased ability to not only attack their targets but to do so more effectively, efficiently, and successfully.

A laptop in every pot: A *New York Times* article is provoking an online debate over whether cell phones or laptops are truly the best way to bring the Internet to the world's poor. In-house Microsoft (Research) blogger Robert Scoble agrees with his boss Bill Gates that cell phones are the best way to make Internet access universal: When he travels overseas, he sees everyone reading their phones, not using laptops. David Rothman says he hopes that MIT's cheap-laptop experiment wins out, because it's easier to read on larger screens.[4]

Because corporations depend on high technology, the most advanced high-technology nation-states have become more vulnerable to attacks, and successful attacks at that, than the Third World nation-states, which have little in the way of high-technology infrastructure and therefore, less reliance on it. This state of affairs is expected to continue into the foreseeable future.

At the same time, some previously unaffected nation-states — those not vulnerable to high-technology or other forms of attacks as they do not have that high technology-based infrastructure in place — are becoming more vulnerable to attacks of all sorts, including fraud-related attacks. For example, some nation-states have bypassed the installation of a telecommunications infrastructure based on the telephone landlines and have gone directly to cellular technology for their internal communications needs. Cellular phones are of course more vulnerable to fraud-threat agent attacks than landline telephones. Therefore, this dependency will cause fraud miscreants of the future to increasingly target the corporations and employees who make this infrastructure possible, as well as use that technology in those nation-states.

---

[4] http://money.cnn.com/2006/01/30/technology/browser0130/index.htm?cnn=yes.

Intel: One billion transistors on tiny new chip: Company says it's on track to make fingernail-sized chips by the second half of 2007. . . . it had made the world's first microchip using tiny new manufacturing methods that promise to let the world's top chipmaker make more powerful, efficient processors. The fingernail-sized memory chip is etched with 1 billion transistors that are only 45 nanometers wide — about 1,000 times smaller than a red blood cell, said Mark Bohr, a leading Intel engineer. "It will pack about two times as many transistors per unit area and use less power. It will help future products and platforms deliver improved performance."[5]

NANOTECHNOLOGY

When thinking of protecting corporate assets from fraud-threat agents and their use of high-technology devices as their tools, a security professional must look into the future and see what other vulnerabilities to successful fraud attacks will emerge due to the changes in high technology. In addition, the security professional must also look to these future high technologies for tools to help them defend the corporate assets against fraud-threat agents, and protect them from other threat agents as well.

Some of the most intriguing new high technologies of the future will be based on nanotechnology. According to many government and private scientists, engineers, and business leaders, nanotechnology is the future, and in that future humans will be able to do wondrous things. What is nanotechnology?

Nanotechnology is the understanding and control of matter at dimensions of roughly 1 to 100 nanometers, where unique phenomena enable novel applications. Encompassing nanoscale science, engineering, and technology, nanotechnology involves imaging, measuring, modeling, and manipulating matter at this length scale. . . . A nanometer is one-billionth of a meter; a sheet of paper is about 100,000 nanometers thick.[6]

According to the United States government[7]:

The transition of nanotechnology research into manufactured products is limited today, but some products moved relatively quickly to the

[5] http://money.cnn.com/2006/01/25/technology/intel_chip.reut/index.htm.
[6] http://www.nano.gov/html/facts/whatIsNano.html.
[7] http://www.nano.gov/html/facts/home_facts.html.

marketplace and already are having significant impact. For example, a new form of carbon, — the nanotube — was discovered by <u>Sumio Iijima</u> in 1991. In 1995, it was recognized that carbon nanotubes were excellent sources of field-emitted electrons. By 2000, the "jumbotron lamp," a nanotube-based light source that uses these field-emitted electrons to bombard a phosphor, was available as a commercial product. (Jumbotron lamps light many athletic stadiums today.) By contrast, the period of time between the modeling of the semiconducting property of germanium in 1931 and the first commercial product (the transistor radio) was 23 years.

The discovery of another nanoscale carbon form, C60, the fullerene (also called the buckyball) brought the Nobel Prize in Chemistry in 1996 to Robert F. Curl Jr., Sir Harold W. Kroto, and Richard E. Smalley. It also started an avalanche of research into not only the novel characteristics of C60, but also other nanoscale materials.

Nanoscale science was enabled by advances in microscopy, most notably the electron, scanning tunneling and atomic force microscopes, among others.

The United States and other modern nation-states, as well as global businesses, are racing to take advantage of what the future offers in products and services through the use of nanotechnology. One of the products that is being sought is nano-weapons.

Public Law 108-153; 108th Congress; An Act: To authorize appropriations for nanoscience, nanoengineering, and nanotechnology research, and for other purposes. Be it enacted by the Senate and House of <<NOTE: 21st Century Nanotechnology Research and Development Act.>>. . . . The President shall implement a National Nanotechnology Program. Through appropriate agencies, councils, and the National Nanotechnology Coordination Office established in section 3, the Program shall —

(1) establish the goals, priorities, and metrics for evaluation for Federal nanotechnology research, development, and other activities
(2) invest in Federal research and development programs in nanotechnology and related sciences to achieve those goals; and
(3) provide for interagency coordination of Federal nanotechnology research, development, and other activities undertaken pursuant to the Program.[8]

---

[8] http://frwebgate.access.gpo.gov/cgi-bin/getdoc.cgi?dbname=108_cong_public_laws&docid=f:publ153.108.

Nanotechnology is in just its initial stages of research and development but is rapidly growing. We have all heard of its potential uses to clear blocked arteries, repair human cells, and the like. However, as a security professional responsible for protecting corporate assets from fraud threat-agents, do you see any security issues? Of course there are the nanotechnology devices that may be embedded in an artificial fly or bee that can hover over a computer screen with an embedded video recorder or live video transmitter to capture the information shown on the computer screen, capture data flowing through computer networks or sitting in a room where sensitive discussions are taking place, and transmit that information live around the world through wireless systems.

Let's take that one step further and into the future: look at how the miscreants of the world can use such nanotechnology to destroy anything and anyone at the atomic level. Possible? Yes! Likely? If one has the knowledge and funding, it is quite possible that this may occur. Imagine buildings and people being "eaten away" by nanobots live on television. You can't see them and you can't stop them. Well, hopefully we can stop them but if security and assets protection follows today's trends into the future, the assets protection funding, especially related to defending the corporate assets against fraud-threat agents, is always after the fact and is never ready when needed.

> It appeared that nanotechnology was used to develop an artificial bug that penetrated the high security of the New World Trade Center in New York City and captured the personal information of the majority of the workers with the facility as well as the trade secrets of several corporations within the facility. A previously unknown group claimed credit for the attack and requested one billion dollars to destroy the information they had accumulated. — *Future Newspaper Headline?*

This may sound to you more like science fiction than future science facts. However, many previous science fiction stories have provided a realistic look at the future. We recommend that you research this future high technology and determine for yourself if it offers not only great benefits in the future but also great threats. In the hands of global fraud miscreants who care nothing of culture, societies, people, or their environment such as the world's great cities, the question is not will they use it? The question, rather, is when will they be able to use it? Do you think they really care about what would happen to a corporation, its suppliers, its customers, or its employees once the nano-weapons are unleashed?

Nanotechnology is rapidly approaching, and the question is: Will we be able to defeat these fraud-threat agents in the future to the point where these miscreants will not be able to successfully use such technology against their targeted victims?

How can this technology be used to safeguard corporate assets from successful fraud attacks? For example, can it be used for product certification, and can it be built in to products where only non-pirated or non-counterfeited products will work with certain devices?

HIGH-TECHNOLOGY-RELATED FRAUDS AND OTHER CRIMES[9]

It is important to understand the history of crimes, miscreants' schemes, fraud-threat agents, and the like. The following provides some general insights into the impact of technologies of various types on the protection of corporate assets and the changing business environment threatened by these defrauders and other miscreants.

The global I-Way (Generally known as the Internet) has often been compared to a global highway for information. United States Vice President Gore in his December 1993 speech to the National Press Club commented that "today commerce rolls not just on asphalt highways but along information highways. . . . think of the national information infrastructure as a network of highways, much like the interstates of the 1950s. These are highways carrying information rather than people or goods."[10]

Many other public officials and industry leaders have also used this convenient metaphor. Although the comparison between the physical highways and the digital circuits for communication is not perfect, it nonetheless communicates a useful image. The "highway" metaphor can be especially helpful in better understanding the risks that are part of the I-Way environment.

Using the "information superhighway" metaphor should encourage security and law enforcement professionals to understand that much past experience is, in fact, relevant in this, the information period of the United States' history. The I-Way is intended to communicate in the broadest terms the extended state of connectivity and some of the vast new capabilities arising from the global telecommunications infrastructure.

ADVENT OF THE SUPERHIGHWAYS

In most major Westernized nations, the central governments invested heavily in the middle of the twentieth century to create modern high-speed

---

[9] Excerpts in part taken from the book, *I-Way Robbery: Crime on the Internet* (1999), co-authored with William Boni and printed here with permission from Butterworth-Heinemann (Elsevier).

[10] December 21, 1993. REMARKS BY THE FORMER VICE PRESIDENT, National Press Club Washington, DC.

physical highways. This was seen as a logical progression that would allow the national economies of the country to fully benefit from the potential offered by the invention of the automobile at the end of the nineteenth century. As fascinating as the early automobiles were, their ability to impact national commerce was severely constrained by the lack of paved road networks that would allow them to pass quickly between cities and regions. As recently as the 1930s, it may have required weeks for an auto to traverse the continent from New York to San Francisco, California.

Germany led the way in the 1930s with the *autobahn*; the United States followed with the interstate superhighways. In England they are known as the motorways, and in Italy they are called the *autostrada*. All represented huge capital investments that took decades to complete. In the United States alone, the freeways cost over tens of billions of dollars and took decades to complete. Why did national governments invest billions of taxes in such projects? Because these superhighways facilitated the flow of people, products, and, in time of war, troops and war materials between and among the regions of the nation.

One of the major consequences of these superhighway systems has been the beneficial spread of commerce to many cities. The advantages enjoyed by major metropolitan areas that were serviced by railroad lines, ocean or river ports, and major air terminals were now partially offset by the arterial superhighways of the nation. From mills, factories, fields, and warehouses, businesses created products and their contribution rolled away on trucks, cars, and scooters powered by the internal combustion engine and onto the superhighway system to distant locations. No longer did a business need limit itself to the expense of major transportation hubs.

In general, economists have argued that the superhighway systems contributed to the increased spread of industrial civilization and a generally higher standard of living for more people. Nation-states became a little more homogeneous as the physically mobile population relocated. People became much more mobile.

THE IMPACT OF SUPERHIGHWAYS ON FRAUDS AND OTHER CRIMES

One aspect of the automobile and superhighway system combination that was not anticipated by most citizens was how quickly criminals exploited the new possibilities offered by this combination of technologies. Perhaps the most striking examples can be drawn from the legendary criminals and gangs of the 1930s in the United States. Bank robbers like Bonnie and Clyde, "Ma" Barker, and others, especially Al Capone, exemplified the new breed of vicious criminal. Such criminals exploited submachine guns, combined with the mobility offered by the automobiles and superhighways, to pillage and plunder hapless banks and businesses.

Frequently, the criminals had better guns and cars than the police forces they confronted. Highly motivated by easy access to piles of money, they tended to strike quickly against the poorly protected banks in the smaller towns in the country, machine guns blazing if the hapless local police force made any effort to intervene. Striking quickly, exploiting the element of surprise, they were often successful and typically escaped by automobile and superhighway.

When local police authorities became sufficiently alarmed in one area, the criminals exercised geographic flexibility and traveled down the superhighway to the next unsuspecting small town. The fact that many of these vicious criminals ended up dead did not deter others from committing similar criminal acts in similar ways. They, too, were opportunistically exploiting the environment of their time to engage in their trade. They were the direct heirs to Jesse James and the train bandits who ravaged the Old West in the United States during the post–Civil War era.

In less dramatic but still important fashion, the values, mores, and customs of the advanced nations were irrevocably changed by the combination of the automobile and the superhighway. Dishonor as a means of social control of behavior was weakened by the combination of increased mobility and the folk hero status the public ascribed to the criminals.

Though legal sanctions continued to apply to improper acts even during the advent of the automobile and superhighway, a person who was willing to move on down the superhighway to the next town could perhaps do things that their geographically constrained cousin would never consider. The stereotypical American "cowboy drifter" was now a role nearly anyone in any advanced country could play. If one committed petty theft, frauds, or other crimes locally, one had the option to escape community sanctions via the superhighway to another state and start over again. As with the bank robbers, defrauders and violent offenders found the easy escape by automobile offered continued opportunities to do their evil deeds whether a fraud, rape, murder, or other offense.

The deeds of these criminals were often widely reported through newspapers and radio broadcasts. This broadcasting of their exploits sometimes made them into "folk heroes." As part of this romantic exaggeration, they were portrayed as "Robin Hoods." Law enforcement was often portrayed as incompetent, lacking funding, knowledge, and jurisdiction to effectively pursue these criminals.

Throughout much of the United States' history, security and law enforcement responsibilities have primarily been a local affair. Training, scientific equipment, and technology such as radios or high-powered pursuit vehicles were nonexistent or in very short supply in the 1930s, and good detectives were as likely to break a case through physical or psychological coercion of suspects as through more professional police investigations. In such a world the high-powered weapons, mobility, and use of the superhighway by criminal gangs were often a winning combination.

In the late 1800s the Pinkerton Detective Agency was successful in obtaining contracts to safeguard railroads as a direct result of law enforcement's geographic limitations during the 1870s. In a similar fashion, the gang wars in Chicago and elsewhere in the 1930s resulted in a little known United States federal government organization receiving a mandate to confront the crime problems of that time. The United States Federal Bureau of Investigation found itself tasked to be the lead agency to confront the wave of violence that local security and law enforcement professionals were unable or unwilling to confront. With some degree of success, federal law enforcement was able to prevail over the machine gun-toting robbers of the 1930s.

A SHORT HISTORY OF FRAUDS AND OTHER CRIMES VIA THE I-WAY

Let's look back at some examples of the "ages past." These examples are greatly simplified, but they support the idea that over the centuries the environment has changed, but criminals remain the same, committing crimes for the same reasons that they have always committed crimes.

During the Agricultural Age (up to about 1745 in the United States according to the Tofflers),[11] robbers stole money from banks, stores, and people, and escaped on foot or on horses. Particularly in the "colonies," criminals were limited to areas where they could walk or run to and/or away from apprehension. Using horses, they could make faster getaways! The only knowledge they required was how to ride a horse; where to go to get the money, goods, or other valuables they planned on stealing; and a plan for the crime.

If they could not afford a horse, they could always steal one. So the horse was one of the tools used to support committing the crime. This, coupled with their other basic tools of a good fraud scheme and a plan, meant they were ready to commit their frauds.

With the advent of the Industrial Age (about 1745 to 1956 in the United States according to the Tofflers) came the automobile, which greatly enhanced the robbers' ability to steal or defraud a person or business. Robbers still robbed and defrauders still committed frauds, but now they were able to expand their crime areas because through the automobile they could travel farther in less time. Also, they could get away faster and hide farther away from the crime scene.

So, the automobile did for the robbers, defrauders, and other miscreants in this age what the horse did for them in the earlier age: it expanded their crime areas; they also were able to get away farther and faster.

The advent of the superhighways exponentially increased the criminals' opportunities. No longer required to use dirt or country roads and

---

[11] The Tofflers discuss this topic in their numerous books. It is suggested that the reader do a "search" online for their books and read those that may help better understand our history.

two-lane highways, the automobile coupled with the superhighway greatly expanded their crime area. As before, criminals used this "new technology" and enhanced environment to help commit the same types of frauds they had always committed and for the same reasons. In this case, as in days past, they purchased their method of transportation — this time the car — or they stole one. They still needed a fraud scheme as their weapon and a plan.

SUPERHIGHWAY FRAUDS AND OTHER CRIMES TO I-WAY ROBBERIES

So why is all this history relevant to the security and law enforcement professional in dealing with the fraud and other crime challenges raised by the I-Way? Let's compare the environment of the 1930–1940s in the United States with the I-Way world of the 1990s:

1930–1940s
- Mobile criminals (automobiles + superhighways)
- Weakest targets selected for exploitation
- Employment of advanced technology (machine guns and commando tactics)
- Sequential attacks against targets of opportunity
- Local security and law enforcement poorly equipped for response
- Geographic limitations on investigations and response
- General decline in effectiveness of social controls due to mobility technology (superhighways and automobiles)
- U.S. federal government intervention via FBI (stop the bank robbers and bootleggers)

1990s–Present
- Mobile criminals (modems + I-Way)
- Weakest targets subject to exploitation
- Advanced technology (vulnerability scanners, information warfare tactics)
- Sequential attacks against targets of opportunity
- Local security and law enforcement poorly equipped for response
- Geographic limitations (national borders) on investigations and response
- General decline in effectiveness of social controls due to global mobility technology (microcomputers and I-Way)
- U.S. federal government intervention via FBI (stop the I-Way robbers, defrauders, and hackers)

When viewed in perspective, one can see that the I-Way defrauders and other miscreants of the Information Age have much in common with the superhighway robbers of the Industrial Age. Based on these considerations, security and law enforcement professionals should therefore understand that little has really changed over the years. Therefore, the problems, issues, and approaches to dealing with them will be very similar. We must emphasize that what did not work before will not work now, and what worked before may or may not work in the present. Law enforcement and security professionals should learn from history and use the appropriate methods and techniques.

One overwhelming distinction is obvious. Whereas in the earlier era the U.S. federal government could respond to citizens' concerns about rampant lawlessness by empowering the FBI to enforce U.S. laws, that is not the case today.

The I-Way is global in scope and is growing fastest in nations and continents that are not likely to take direction from the United States and where the United States has no jurisdiction. How will security and law enforcement professionals of a nation influence the global response necessary to confront the more serious risks that the I-Way will create? In the absence of a global "I-Way Patrol," each individual nation's response is likely to fall short of effectively addressing the complete spectrum of criminal threats.

At a news conference held after an all-day meeting at FBI headquarters of the Justice Ministers of the G-8 countries (the largest industrialized countries in the world) in December 1997, former United States attorney general Janet Reno said, "Criminals no longer are restricted by national boundaries. . . . If we are to keep up with cybercrime, we must work together as never before."[12] The news release from this important meeting went on to list the following areas where these major nations have agreed to collaborate:

- Assign adequate number of properly trained and equipped law enforcement personnel to investigate high-tech crimes.
- Improve ways to track attacks on computer networks.
- When extradition is not possible, prosecute criminals in the country where they are found.
- Preserve key evidence on computer networks.
- Review the legal codes in each nation to ensure that appropriate crimes for computer wrongdoing are proscribed and that the language makes it easier to investigate the crimes.
- Establish close cooperation with the private sector to develop new ways of detecting and preventing computer crimes.
- Make increased efforts to use new communications technologies, such as video teleconferencing, to obtain testimony from witnesses in other nations.

---

[12] "Nations Band Together Against Cybercrime" Reuters 10 Dec 97.

These are essential steps, even if they are general in nature. However, the past track record of nations cooperating in such efforts has evidenced little past success. Therefore one should not be overly optimistic about the future based only on these actions. The global reach of the I-Way and the difficulties of obtaining jurisdiction over perpetrators represent one of the greatest challenges in dealing with I-Way robbers. To the extent that the collaboration of the G-8 nations ultimately extends to the other nations of the globe, perhaps under the broader auspices of the United Nations or other agencies, organizations can have increased confidence that even the most sophisticated I-Way robbers may ultimately face prosecution.

As law enforcement has adapted its methods and incorporated new technology to combat frauds, private organizations also have adopted various strategies to combat risks to their interests. It is likely that many organizations, confronted with increasing risks from the I-Way, will choose to respond as the railroad industry did in the 1880s in the United States.

At that time the railroads, frustrated by the largely ineffective nature of geographically limited law enforcement, engaged the Pinkerton Detective Agency to help protect corporate interests against the James gang and similar highly mobile criminal gangs. It is possible, indeed likely, that many large organizations will choose to engage the resources of private sector specialists (cyber-sleuths or digital detectives) to help them resolve I-way-enabled frauds directed against them. This may happen because the limited resources in the public sector are directed to larger or more serious crimes, or simply because public agencies will generally take longer to complete an investigation owing to the many competing priorities.

I-WAY ROBBERY — ITS PREVALENCE

Over the years, there have been dramatic increases in frauds and other crimes via the I-Way. Why the dramatic increase in such reports and apparent losses? Many factors have contributed to this trend, but in large part, these trends have developed because the I-Way makes every organization's system an on and off ramp, which puts computer systems at greater risk than ever before. With the rapid pace of growth in the I-Way, there are simply more computer systems that are more accessible than ever to more people in more places on the planet.

Because the I-Way connected computers and networks contain more valuable information and other valuable assets (including digital forms of money), they are thus more important to businesses and government agencies than ever before.

The same applies to the I-Way for the I-Way robbers, because the information that travels the I-Way and their ability to share methods, tools, and techniques is also one of their most important assets. Many tools and utilities are freely available to virtually anyone with a modem and I-Way access. There are perhaps thousands of public sites and an unknown number of private bulletin boards and chat areas in which the most clandestine and capable I-Way robbers, defrauders, and other miscreants in the underground share tools, techniques, and methods of defeating security measures. With a vast array of tools to draw from, is it at all surprising that penetrations are becoming more common?

THERE IS NO I-WAY PATROL TO STOP I-WAY ROBBERS

It will come as no great surprise to security and law enforcement and professionals that criminals are willing to make the effort to transition their trade to the I-Way. Recall the classic comment by convicted bank robber Willy Sutton, who, when asked why he robbed banks, told his interviewer "Because that's where the money is!" Following that comment, *where* is the money in today's global economy? As almost every high school student now knows, it is in computers, wire transfer networks, and the global I-Way itself. It would be totally unrealistic to expect Willy's heirs to change their chosen profession merely because computers and networks are supplanting tangible cash in commerce.

Although computer fraud has existed for decades, some experts believe that computer technology today is roughly where automotive technology was in 1905 and that we have not yet seen the full extent of computer-related crime.[13] Jonathan Winer, deputy assistant secretary of state in the international narcotics and law enforcement arm of the State Department, has said: "We have created an information superhighway without speed limits and without traffic controls."[14] Many public and private sector representatives have expressed significant concern over the ability of criminals to use the I-Way to launder money and commit other crimes.[15]

GLOBAL CONNECTIVITY VIA THE I-WAY = GLOBAL EXPOSURE TO ATTACKS BY FRAUD-THREAT AGENTS AND OTHER MISCREANTS

It is vital that security and law enforcement professionals recognize how radically different this new environment is. As recently as the late 1980s, the most common form of nonemployee computer crime probably involved a teen-ager in the local telephone dialing area using a "war dialer"[16] to try to emulate the movie *War Games.*

In the 1980s, a company could protect itself against a wide range of risks with relatively inexpensive security technology. In today's era of

---

[13] Tuesday, September 15, 1998, 9:47 AM, NewsBits Reuters.
[14] Ibid.
[15] Ibid.
[16] Ibid.

global connectivity and access one should not assume that what was sufficient for simpler times will suffice for the present. Those organizations that choose to ignore their increasing vulnerability and trust haphazard security measures may well suffer serious losses. Potential I-Way robbers are not likely to ignore forever poorly protected on ramps that have valuable assets.

An I-Way robber is no more likely to ignore an easy network-firewall penetration any more than his distant relative in the 1930s would have passed an unlocked bank vault. Just as banks and businesses in the past had to harden their facilities, hire trustworthy guards, and install video surveillance cameras and alarms to safeguard their cash vaults, today's "digital data vaults" require enhanced protection. When organizations fail to invest adequately in protection, they run the risk of damage or loss of their key assets.

Any successful anti-fraud program must include controls to protect the corporate assets made accessible due to the I-Way and its corporations' on and off ramps, as well as internal corporate networks. It must also take into account the continuous changes in high technologies that often open corporations' assets to new fraud schemes.

CAPABILITIES AND LIMITATIONS OF LAW ENFORCEMENT

If tidal waves of criminal enterprise are about to overwhelm the I-Way and impact this new commercial medium, what can we expect from the "I-Way patrol"? Unless things change drastically, it would seem not much. First, every security and law enforcement professional must understand that, at present, no single, central organization has the responsibility and capability to patrol and protect the global I-Way; there is not (at least not yet) a global "I-Way patrol." The reasons are readily apparent considering the current state of planetary political organization.

The nation-state remains the primary organizing unit for most of the Earth's population, and it is unlikely any country would tolerate an international I-Way patrol with jurisdiction to seize and prosecute suspects or even proven perpetrators of activity that is criminal in another country. The uproar that arose in Mexico when U.S. government agents seized and prosecuted a physician affiliated with a drug cartel for his involvement with a U.S. Drug Enforcement agent's murder provides a real-world example of the consequences of unilateral transborder law enforcement. However, to put these matters in a little different perspective, imagine the uproar in the United States if a non-United States police force had authority to arrest U.S. citizens because they posted comments that were considered sacrilegious to another country's religious/spiritual leadership.

Rather than create a global I-Way patrol, it is more reasonable to expect updated extradition treaties as probably the best short-term answer to the problems of obtaining jurisdiction over I-Way robbers. For example, note that Argentina initially declined to extradite to the United States a young man who admitted he hacked into a number of U.S. government systems via the I-Way, including NASA's systems. Although this was a criminal act under relevant United States statutes, he had not violated any laws of his homeland. Although he ultimately gave himself up to authorities and pled guilty to the charges, his surrender was done voluntarily.

The inconsistencies in legal language, statutes, and codes from country to country are just one of the major problems associated with policing the global I-way. In the absence of well-developed international agreements and treaties, and lacking any sort of I-Way patrol or even common policing standards, it is likely that organizations will be subject to criminal activities originating in another country. If this situation arises, there may be no local authority able or willing to pursue a criminal investigation against the I-Way robbers.

CHALLENGES TO SECURITY PROFESSIONALS AND OTHERS

The I-Way has brought with it many new challenges to the security professional. Just learning the vocabulary and technical terms arising from the I-Way is a significant issue. Some also look at the challenges from the I-Way robbers, fraudsters, spies, and terrorists as something completely new. Looking closer, we find little that is truly new from the I-Way robbers. Few of the basic techniques or objectives of these criminals have changed. What is actually new is the *environment* in which they operate.

It is now the Information Age, and all business and government agencies that operate today inhabit a technology-driven environment. It is the microprocessor-based, network-intensive environment alone that is new. Make no mistake: the "bad guys" and "girls" still have the same motives, opportunities, and rationalizations for committing their frauds and other crimes.

Today's generation of criminals is still committing crimes and frauds for precisely the same reasons that they and their predecessors have always committed crimes: it is how they choose to earn their livelihood. However, to be successful in the Information Age, they must now commit crimes in the contemporary business environment. With the rapid growth of the I-Way and I-Way Commerce (also known as Electronic Business in some parts of the world), I-Way robbers must operate with knowledge of the I-Way.

Criminals are attempting to do what they have always done: to steal, defraud, and subvert others for personal, corporate, national, and/or political gain. The methods they use are largely the same, and they only change when the I-Way environment requires them to change to achieve their objectives.

If we really think about it, do we have any reason to believe criminals, that is, defrauders, really are much different today than they were in the days of Jesse James? Even in a world featuring computers, coupled with the digital, virtual I-Way, and the increased use of I-Way commerce, "cyber defrauders" still have the same objectives: to take someone's money or other assets and to convert them for their personal benefit. However, no longer bounded by physical locations or very much by time, the I-Way now allows them to have global mobility and to escape in nanoseconds.

CASE STUDY 1

As the chief security officer for the XYZ Corporation, your boss told you that next year the corporation will be expanding its business, which includes the manufacturing of their widgets, into Nigeria. You are told that since you have primary responsibility for leading the corporation's assets protection efforts, you must tell executive management what needs to be done to protect the corporate assets en route to Nigeria and in-country at their new satellite location.

Executive management is concerned with protection of corporate assets and has heard many negative stories about the massive numbers of frauds being perpetrated out of Nigeria. So, they have a serious concern about establishing a facility there. However, they must do so inasmuch as the Nigerian government has offered favorable tax benefits as well as other incentives to build a factory there, and such a facility would help the corporation to achieve a more competitive position in the global marketplace.

So now what do you do? No, you don't leave the corporation, for you need the job and medical benefits, and it also pays well. The first step, of course, would be to contact those involved, probably a project team, who are responsible for successfully making this event happen. You should then become a member of that project team.

As a member of that project team, you should also consider the following:

- Develop and brief the team on an assets protection operational plan, which includes an anti-fraud aspect, equipment, and people, for moving the assets to Nigeria.
- Include the following subsets:
  - An operational security plan
  - A transportation plan
  - An executive protection plan
  - An employee protection plan
  - A budget plan
- Determine whether a new building will be constructed or whether a current building will be used instead. In either case, a facility physical

security plan to include physical security survey must be completed. Construction, supply, and logistics frauds are a major concern here.

- With employees traveling to Nigeria prior to the operation of the new facility, include a travel security plan that encompasses awareness of current and past fraud schemes against individuals.
- Conduct research on Nigeria, its culture, customs, society, and such.
- Learn to speak the local language as much as possible.
- Coordinate with your nation-state's government agencies, such as the U.S. Department of State and the U.S. Embassy in Nigeria, to determine the fraud-threat environment.
- Coordinate with the local authorities — local police, and government security personnel stationed in the area of the corporation's proposed facility; identify localized fraud schemes; profile defrauders and the like.
- Be actively involved in this project.

These are part of just a high-level outline as to what should be considered for implementation, to include the anti-fraud aspects. Can you identify other major tasks to ensure that a successful facility is established?

CASE STUDY 2

As the CSO of an international corporation, how would you go about determining the corporation's position in the global marketplace, its visibility to threat agents, and the vulnerability of the corporate assets to these fraud miscreants?

One approach would be to:

- Talk to the corporation's business office staff.
- Talk to the corporation's marketing and sales staff.
- Search the Internet for information on the corporation, its competitors, and its global visibility.
- Talk to the corporation's public relations staff.
- Talk to the corporate auditors.
- Review corporate security department's history of investigations and inquiries.
- Talk to the corporate ethics director.
- Search the Internet for fraud schemes and cases that may impact or apply to the corporation.

By taking these steps, you can begin to build a corporate profile and begin to answer the above question.

SUMMARY

Corporations are increasingly operating in a global marketplace and are therefore more susceptible to fraud-threat agent attacks anywhere in the world.

Corporations will continue to expand their global operations driven and supported by high technology. Although high technology is a crucial factor in lowering operating costs and increasing profits, it also makes corporate assets more vulnerable to all types of attacks. To date, many fraud-threat agents have used high technology as both tools and targets. The trend is expected to continue into the future.

Careful study of the information presented in this chapter and other publicly available data concerning a short history of globalization and frauds reveals several common themes:

- Globalization will continue.
- Computer/network-enabled frauds are a rapidly growing component of global fraud statistics.
- No one in business, government, or academe really knows the full extent or the complete nature of frauds that have already been committed or are happening at this moment.
- We can conclude that, although the I-Way and information access enabling technologies like the Web browser–server combinations are creating more complex environments, we should not expect that complexity alone will protect valuable resources against losses.

Criminals over the ages have proven themselves highly adaptable, and they already appear to be capable and willing to exploit globalization and technologies for their benefit.

As with the criminals, security professionals and law enforcement officers have all been challenged to adapt, learning in earlier ages to ride horses, drive automobiles, and now exploit the computers and networks to combat the latest generation of "digital desperados."

2

Corporate Assets, Frauds, and Other Terms — What Are They?

INTRODUCTION

To discuss how to fight frauds related to corporations and how to establish and manage an anti-fraud program for any business, for example, a corporation, it is important that we begin with a basic understanding of terminology. In this case, it is important to define the basic fraud-related terms. We will use those terms and definitions that are generally accepted throughout the security, auditing, and fraud examiner's professions,[1] and that means those terms that are legally defined. After all, those are about the only definitions that can be used in a court of law or any other legal proceeding.

Why is terminology so important? It is important because if you do not use legally defined terms and establish an anti-fraud program that includes investigations and inquiries into fraud allegations based on those terms, you may find that you cannot accomplish prosecution support or other forms of disciplinary action that are based on improper elements of proof. Remember: elements of proof for frauds are derived from the definitions of fraud terms.

---

[1] This is also important since many of the readers may be reading about frauds for the first time, and this will make it more convenient than having the reader rummage through books, articles and Internet sites to determine what is meant by what I've said, e.g. definitions.

In defining the general term *fraud* and providing samples of various forms of frauds, let's begin with a basic understanding of what a fraud is or what some forms of fraud actually are. It is also vitally important that you understand the "elements of proof" of the various types of frauds, for you must provide evidence that the identified fraud miscreant actually perpetrated a fraud and did not just make a mistake.

> In matters of fraud, proving "intent" is the key ingredient. Therefore, any anti-fraud program must provide controls and such that facilitate that proof.

Human errors often occur since we human beings are not perfect. It is often difficult to determine if someone just made a mistake or in fact intended to commit a fraudulent act. In all cases, proving "intent" is vital. By the way, one cannot perpetrate a fraud by mistake.

This "proof of intent" is vital in conducting:

- Fraud inquiries (where corporate policies or procedures have been violated but not civil or criminal laws)
- Investigations (where one or more civil, e.g., regulation, or criminal laws has been violated)

It is also vital when establishing your corporate anti-fraud program. Do you know why? Think about it. If you don't have policies, procedures, and processes in place that can help show that the employee violated some corporate or governmental laws or regulations and did so *knowingly*, it will be much more difficult, if not impossible, to show that the employee *intended* to defraud the corporation.

DEFINITION OF GENERAL FRAUD[2]

Fraud is generally defined as:

- A knowing misrepresentation of the truth or concealment of a material fact to induce another to act to his or her detriment.

---

[2] The definitions cited were reprinted from *Black's Law Dictionary*, Eighth Edition, Bryan A. Garner, Editor In Chief; published by West Publishing Company, St. Paul, MN; with permission of Thomas West.

- A misrepresentation made recklessly without belief in its truth to induce another person to act.
- A tort arising from a knowing misrepresentation, concealment of a material fact, or reckless misrepresentation made to induce another to act to his or her detriment.
- Unconscionable dealing; especially contract law, and the unfair use of the power arising out of the parties' relative positions and resulting in an unconscionable bargain.

Actual Fraud is defined as:

- A concealment or false representation through a statement or conduct that injures another who relies on it in acting.

It also comprises three elements:

- Fraud in fact
- Positive fraud
- Moral fraud

> In the case of an "actual fraud," you want to be able to prove these three elements and to have policies, procedures, and processes in place to provide controls that will show that it was in fact an actual fraud that an employee, supplier, customer, or others committed and it was their intent to do so.

It is also vitally important that the person committing the actual fraud did so

- Knowing what the corporation's policies, procedures, and processes were; and that the fraudster
- Knew that those policies, procedures, and processes were to be followed at all times, ideally by so attesting to this knowledge in writing — which is a key process in your anti-fraud program.

This consideration is important because in the U.S. judicial system today, it generally must be shown that the person perpetrating the fraud against the corporation, especially an employee or someone who has a business working relationship with the corporation, was aware of the policies, procedures, and processes that were violated and/or knew that such actions were against corporate policy, procedures, or civil or criminal laws.

In the United States, an investigator, fraud examiner, or security professional cannot rely on the expression "ignorance of the law is no excuse" to help "make the case" against the defrauder. In fact, there are some indications that the alleged defrauder must also be told in advance when making them aware of anti-fraud policies and procedures to follow the consequences of his or her actions of not following the "rules". It is especially important in these days of "It's not my fault!" where personal responsibility seems to have taken an extended holiday.

Remember that unless you are a lawyer and feel confident in defining a fraud and how to go about identifying the elements of proof, you should coordinate with the corporate legal staff and get their input when such legal issues arise. It will not only save you time and possible embarrassment but will help ensure that your actions do not cause a lawsuit against the corporation, which may have not otherwise been contemplated by the "offended party."

It may also to help ensure that your employment is not terminated over such matters. Also remember that "anyone can sue anyone over anything." However, with the proper anti-fraud program elements in place, you have a better chance of ensuring that the fraud miscreant does not successfully win his or her lawsuit.

Even though the preceding and succeeding definitions apply to the United States and possibly some other countries, most modern countries have similar laws that basically require the same elements of proof. However, a global corporation must know the specific fraud-related statutes in each country and take these statutes into consideration when developing and managing an anti-fraud program for a global business.

Fraud, in law, general term for any instance in which one party deceives or takes unfair advantage of another. Any means used by one person to deceive another may be defined as fraud. For example, if a person represents himself or herself as the agent of a business with which he or she is unconnected and causes another to make a contract to the other party's disadvantage or injury, the first party is guilty of fraud.

Furthermore, if, in making a contract, a person obtains an unjust advantage because of the youth, defective mental capacity, or intoxicated condition of the other party to the contract, he or she is guilty of fraud.

In a court of law, it is necessary to prove that a representation was made as a statement of fact; that it was untrue and known to be untrue; that it was made with intent to deceive and to induce the other party to act upon it; and that the other party relied on it and was induced to act or not to act, to his or her injury or damage.

In equity, fraud includes any act, omission, or concealment involving a breach of legal or equitable duty or trust, which results in disadvantage or injury to another. An example of fraud in this sense is the act of an insolvent who contrives to give one creditor an advantage over the others. Fraud can also be constructive, that is, deemed fraud by interpretation. The sole difference in the case of constructive fraud is that no dishonest intent need be adduced. It arises from a breach of duty, such as the breach of a fiduciary relationship in which a trust or confidence has been betrayed.[3]

SPECIFIC FRAUD DEFINITIONS

Each of the various types of frauds has its own definition that incorporates the general definition of fraud but also includes specifics related to various types of fraud. Following are some of the basic types of frauds that every security professional or fraud fighter should know:

- Civil Fraud: An intentional but not willful evasion of taxes. The distinction between an intentional (i.e., civil) and willful (i.e., criminal) fraud is not always clear, but civil fraud carries only a monetary, noncriminal penalty.
- Criminal Fraud: Fraud that has been made illegal by statute and that subjects the offender to criminal penalties such as fines and imprisonment.
- Fraud Feasor: A person who has committed fraud; also termed defrauder.
- Fraudulent Act: Conduct involving bad faith, dishonesty, a lack of integrity, or moral turpitude.

In addition and depending on your corporate environment (e.g., financial, manufacturing), you should also have a basic understanding and definitions of the following types of frauds[4]:

- Bank Fraud
- Bandkruptcy Fraud
- Constructive Fraud
- Extrinsic Fraud
- Fraud in Law
- Fraud in Inducement
- Fraud on the Community
- Fraud on the Court
- Fraud on the Market
- Fraud on the Patent Office
- Insurance Fraud
- Intrinsic Fraud
- Long-firm Fraud
- Mail Fraud
- Promissory Fraud
- Wire Fraud
- Fraudulen Alienation
- Fraudulent Banking
- Fraudulent Conveyance

---

[3] Microsoft Encarta Encyclopedia Standard 2004.
[4] These terms are from Black's Law Dictionary as noted earlier.

CORPORATE ASSETS

When discussing corporate fraud, we are talking about some fraud miscreant illegally gaining access to or fraudulently impacting a corporate asset or assets. Therefore, it is important to understand what an asset is and the various types of assets. After all, the objective of an anti-fraud program is to protect corporate assets from fraud.

In order to develop, establish, and maintain a viable anti-fraud program, you must know what assets are and the role your specific corporate assets play in your anti-fraud program, as well as their value to some *fraud feasor* or *defrauder*.

Yes, I am sure you have the general idea of what an asset is; however, it is important to know what an asset is in legal terms and also the various types of assets. After all, you don't want to develop an anti-fraud program based on what you think an asset is and discover your hard work is for naught when your corporation goes to court to get that asset back and ensure the perpetrators are held accountable. (This is a nice way of saying that they are found guilty and imprisoned or that a monetary punishment is exacted against them.)

With that in mind, the following definitions are provided concerning "assets":

- <u>Asset</u>
  - An item that is <u>owned</u> and has <u>value</u>
  - The entries on a balance sheet showing the items of property owned, including cash, inventory, equipment, real estate, accounts receivable, and goodwill
  - All the property of a person (especially a bankrupt or deceased person) available for paying debts or for distribution

If you want to show that someone defrauded the corporation of one or more of its assets, you must be able to show that the asset or assets were owned by the corporation and that the asset or assets had value.[5]

Please keep this consideration in mind when you develop and manage an anti-fraud program. If you cannot show that the corporation owned the asset and that it had some value to the corporation, then it may not meet the legal definition of an asset. Your anti-fraud program must ensure that

---

[5] The information provided here and throughout this book are based on my investigative and security experiences over 45 years. I am not a lawyer nor do I have a law degree. It is important that what you read be taken in that context. Each incident is somewhat different, and the corporate legal staff and/or prosecutor must be in the coordination loop to ensure all legal requirements such as the elements of proof are met.

there is documentation to show both. Some basic asset definitions are as follows:[6]

- Capital Asset: Long-term asset used in the operation of a business or used to produce goods or services, such as equipment, land, or an industrial plant (also termed fixed asset).
- Commercial Assets: The aggregate of available property, stock in trade, cash, and other assets belonging to a merchant.
- Intangible Asset: Any nonphysical asset or resource that can be amortized or converted to cash such as patents, goodwill, and computer programs, or a right to something, such as services paid for in advance.
- Real Asset: An asset in the form of land. Loosely, any tangible asset. Also termed hard asset.
- Tangible Asset: An asset that has a physical existence and is capable of being assigned a value.

Other asset terms you may need to know, again depending on your corporate products and environment, are as follows:[7]

- Accrued Asset
- Admitted Asset
- Appointive Asset
- Assets by Descent
- Asset in Hand
- Asset Under Management
- Current Asset
- Dead Asset
- Earning Asset
- Equitable Asset
- Frozen Asset
- Hidden Asset
- Illiquid Asset
- Individual Asset
- Legal Asset
- Mass Asset
- Net Quick Assets
- Net Asset
- Nominal Asset
- Nonadmitted Asset
- Nonprobate Asset
- Personal Asset
- Premarital Asset
- Quick Asset
- Wasting Asset
- Asset Acquisition
- Asset Allocation
- Asset-Coverage Test
- Asset-Depreciation Range

OTHER TERMS AND DEFINITIONS

Some other terms and definitions that will be used throughout this book and must be known in order to establish and manage a successful anti-fraud program for your business are as follows:[8]

---

[6] These definitions also taken from Black's Law Dictionary.

[7] Ibid.

[8] These are general definitions taken from various sources over the years.

- Policy: A course of action; a program of actions adopted by an individual, group, or government, or the set of principles on which they are based; shrewdness or prudence, especially in the pursuit of a particular course of action.
- Procedures: The established methods for doing something.
- Processes: A series of actions taken toward a particular aim; treatment or preparation of something in a series of steps or actions.
- Plans: Schemes for achieving objectives; a method of doing something that is worked out usually in some detail before it is begun and that may be written down in some form or possibly retained in memory.
- Projects: Tasks or schemes that require a large amount of time, effort, and planning to complete; an organized unit of work.
- Formal Project Plan: A formal project that is documented in writing and includes the combination of tasks to be accomplished to meet a specific objective or objectives, has a beginning and an ending date, and will take more than 30 days to complete. It may or may not have specific resources identified and allocated to it. It is monitored by management on a periodic basis.
- Informal Project Plan: A plan that may or may not meet the criteria of a Formal Project Plan with the exception that it will not take more than 30 days to complete and will not be formally monitored by management.

Some of these definitions may or not apply to your particular working environment. However, they are presented here to assist you in developing and managing your anti-fraud program. Specifically, they provide a baseline on which you can build such a program by incorporating into it the various types of assets that apply to your working environment. It also ensures that your anti-fraud and assets protection policies, procedures, processes, plans, and projects provide for any needed successful disciplinary action, civil lawsuits, or criminal prosecutions.

CASE STUDY

As the leader for your corporation's anti-fraud program, you are asked to provide material to be used as part of a total assets protection awareness briefing to be given to new employees of the corporation as part of their orientation into the corporation's working environment.

These monthly new-hire briefings will be given by a staff member of the Human Resources Department who is not familiar, in detail, with the anti-fraud program. The time spent on the anti-fraud topic will be limited to three slides or about five minutes.

What informational slides would you provide for that briefing?

At the International Widget Corporation (IWC), the anti-fraud program leader provided the following slides:

1.   A summary chart of IWC's anti-fraud program
2.   A summary chart of the definition of what IWC considers a fraud and employees' reporting requirements
3.   A summary chart citing policy references and the names and contact numbers for yourself and others who could provide additional information on the IWC anti-fraud program.

What information would you provide the awareness briefing person in your three slides?

SUMMARY

In order to build a successful anti-fraud program as part of or separate from a corporate assets protection program, one must know what a fraud is and the various types of frauds. It is also important to know what an asset is and the various types of assets that you must consider in building your anti-fraud program for your particular corporation and its working environment.

You must define the elements of proof required to "prove" that a fraud has occurred against your corporation, and you must be able to support any wanted disciplinary action, civil lawsuits, and/or criminal prosecution. After all, if your anti-fraud program does not provide the necessary policies, procedures, processes, plans, and projects, you may lose corporate assets and not be able to successfully do anything about it.

3

Fraud-Related Laws

INTRODUCTION

When fighting fraud where the corporation is the "victim," it is important to keep in mind the laws that may apply. After all, when you are defending the corporation against fraudulent attacks, you also want to be in a position to support corporate disciplinary action of employees and to support the civil or criminal prosecution of the fraud miscreants, whether they are employees or outsiders.

It is vitally important that your corporate anti-fraud program have in place those policies, procedures, and processes leading to controls that not only help mitigate fraud-threat agent attacks but also provide for the elements of proof required to prove that a fraud has occurred. In addition, your program should provide reasonable controls that would assist in identifying the fraud-threat agent.

> The element of fraud which tends to stymie successful prosecution is the obligation to investigate. It falls on potential investors or customers to fully investigate a proposal before any money exchanges hands. Failure to take appropriate measures at the time of the proposal can seriously weaken a fraud case in court later. The accused can claim that the alleged victim had every opportunity to discover the potential for fraud and failed to investigate the matter thoroughly. Once a party enters into a legally binding contract, remorse over the terms of the deal is not the same as fraud.[1]

If you, in coordination with the corporate legal staff, cannot identify a law that has been violated, it may not be a fraud in legal terms but may possibly be just a violation of corporate policy. If it is a violation of corporate

---

[1] http://www.wisegeek.com/what-is-fraud.htm.

policy, disciplinary action may be justified against corporate employees, but obviously the corporation would not be in a position to discipline non-corporate employees. The corporation may, however, be in a position to take some civil action against the attackers (e.g., suppliers, customers). For example, the violation may be one related to a breach of contract only.

FRAUD COULD INFLATE COST OF TERRORIST ATTACKS Officials are gearing for a possible wave of insurance fraud that will inflate the financial cost of the recent terrorist attacks, warns the Coalition Against Insurance Fraud, a Washington-based watchdog. "Disasters inevitably attract scam artists who try to exploit emergency conditions for profit. The only question is how much insurance fraud will occur, and how much it will cost policyholders," said Dennis Jay, the coalition's executive director. Most scams will involve phony or inflated claims. But crooks also could peddle fake, overpriced or unneeded "terrorism" or "travel" coverage to jittery consumers, Jay said. Insurers likely will pay most basic attack-related claims upfront, then revisit the suspicious claims when the emergency subsides, Jay said. Anti-fraud agencies and insurers in the New York region already are setting up coordinated anti-fraud operations to root out scams as early as possible. Investigators have uncovered several suspicious claims, but still are probing whether they're true scams. Personal and commercial lines are vulnerable to fraud. It may take weeks, however, before officials can estimate the seriousness of the fraud problem. Suspicious commercial claims that are large and complex could take longer to detect, Jay noted. . . . Only a small fraction of claims will be phony, but even a tiny portion of the huge overall claim volume could mean millions of stolen dollars, Jay said. Officials are preparing for insurance scams such as these: Fake death, Business interruption, Commercial property, Workers compensation, Personal property, Padded repairs, Phony auto claims, Backdating of policies. and Phony, overpriced or unneeded insurance.[2]

SOME U.S. FEDERAL FRAUD-RELATED LAWS[3]

The following are some of the primary federal anti-fraud laws in the United States:[4]

---

[2] http://www.insurancefraud.org/releases_2001.htm#060701.

[3] It is important to note that these are not all of the possible laws on which a corporation may support prosecution against attackers but just a sampling. As always when it comes to legal matters, close coordination must be maintained with the corporate legal staff and reliance on them for guidance. However, such laws should be considered when establishing and managing your corporation's anti-fraud program.

[4] http://www.access.gpo.gov/uscode/title18/parti_chapter47_.html.

- Sec. 1001. Statements or entries generally
- Sec. 1002. Possession of false papers to defraud United States
- Sec. 1003. Demands against the United States
- Sec. 1004. Certification of checks
- Sec. 1005. Bank entries, reports, and transactions
- Sec. 1006. Federal credit institution entries, reports, and transactions
- Sec. 1007. Federal Deposit Insurance Corporation transactions
- Sec. 1008, 1009. Repealed
- Sec. 1010. Department of Housing and Urban Development and Federal Housing Administration transactions
- Sec. 1011. Federal land bank mortgage transactions
- Sec. 1012. Department, of Housing and Urban Development transactions
- Sec. 1013. Farm loan bonds and credit bank debentures
- Sec. 1014. Loan and credit applications generally; renewals and discounts; crop insurance
- Sec. 1015. Naturalization, citizenship or alien registry
- Sec. 1016. Acknowledgment of appearance or oath
- Sec. 1017. Government seals wrongfully used and instruments wrongfully sealed
- Sec. 1018. Official certificates or writings
- Sec. 1019. Certificates by consular officers
- Sec. 1020. Highway projects
- Sec. 1021. Title records
- Sec. 1022. Delivery of certificate, voucher, receipt for military or naval property
- Sec. 1023. Insufficient delivery of money or property for military or naval service
- Sec. 1024. Purchase or receipt of military, naval, or veterans' facilities property
- Sec. 1025. False pretenses on high seas and other waters
- Sec. 1026. Compromise, adjustment, or cancellation of farm indebtedness
- Sec. 1027. False statements and concealment of facts in relation to documents required by the Employee Retirement Income Security Act of 1974
- Sec. 1028. Fraud and related activity in connection with identification documents and information
- Sec. 1029. Fraud and related activity in connection with access devices
- Sec. 1030. Fraud and related activity in connection with computers
- Sec. 1031. Major fraud against the United States
- Sec. 1032. Concealment of assets from conservator, receiver, or liquidating agent of financial institution
- Sec. 1033. Crimes by or affecting persons engaged in the business of insurance whose activities affect interstate commerce

- Sec. <u>1034</u>. Civil penalties and injunctions for violations of section 1033
- Sec. <u>1035</u>. False statements relating to health-care matters
- Sec. <u>1036</u>. Entry by false pretenses to any real property, vessel, or aircraft of the United States or secure area of any airport

RELEVANT CONSUMER PROTECTION LAWS FOR FRAUD IN THE UNITED STATES

Consumer protection laws are designed to protect all consumers, the gullible as well as the shrewd. The fact that a false statement may be obviously false to those who are trained and experienced does not change its character or take away its power to deceive others less experienced. Our consumer protection laws were enacted for the protection of the people, many who are trusting and naive about the wolves of the business world that come dressed in lambs' clothing.[5]

A FEW EXAMPLES OF U.S. FEDERAL ENFORCEMENT OF FRAUD-RELATED LAWS, APPROACH AND ACTIONS

The U.S. Department of Justice conducts both criminal and civil litigation in combating telemarketing fraud. United States Attorneys' Offices throughout the country, as well as the Fraud Section of the Criminal Division of the DOJ, have successfully prosecuted many criminal cases against fraudulent telemarketers. The Office of Consumer Litigation of the Civil Division of the department, which conducts both civil and criminal litigation in consumer-related cases, has also prosecuted telemarketing fraud cases.

Under federal law, state attorneys general have been given broad power by the U.S. Congress to combat telemarketing fraud. For example, a state attorney general can file lawsuits in federal court and shut down fraudulent telemarketers through national injunctions so as to prevent companies from moving on under a different name after being banned in one state.

Federal mail and wire fraud charges, which had a five-year maximum penalty, now carry an additional five years for telemarketing fraud or an additional ten years if ten or more senior citizens are targeted.

In a typical telemarketing fraud indictment that a federal grand jury would return, the Department of Justice includes charges under criminal statutes such as wire fraud (18 U.S.C., sec. 1343), mail fraud (18 U.S.C.,

---

[5] http://www.crimes-of-persuasion.com/Laws/US/criminal_laws.htm.

sect. 1341), and conspiracy to engage in wire and mail fraud (18 U.S.C., sect. 371). Each of these statutes carries a maximum term of imprisonment of five years.

The court holds that to sustain a conviction for wire fraud, a fraudulent telemarketer need not personally call victims to incur criminal liability for a "co-schemer's" use of telephones to cheat them.

Mail and wire frauds have a unique characteristic in that each is complete when the mail or wire has been used. Just the existence of the scheme plus the use of the mail or an interstate wire to further the scheme will suffice. Each completed call is therefore a separate, completed fraud offense, even if the money was not sent in.

MAIL FRAUD STATUTES (CONDENSED AND PARAPHRASED)

Title 18, United States Code, Section 1301. Importing or transporting lottery tickets

Whoever brings into the United States a ticket, gift enterprise, or similar scheme for sale or interstate transfer, or offers prizes dependent on chance, or any advertisement of such a scheme, shall be fined under this title or imprisoned not more than two years, or both.

Section 1302. Mailing lottery tickets or related matter

Whoever knowingly deposits in the mail, or sends or delivers by mail:

Any letter or such concerning any lottery, gift enterprise, or similar scheme offering prizes dependent in whole or in part upon lot or chance or any payment for the purchase of any ticket or part thereof shall be fined or imprisoned not more than two years, or both; and for any subsequent offense shall be imprisoned not more than five years.

Section 1303. Postmaster or employee as lottery agent

Any employee of the Postal Service who knowingly delivers any letter advertising any lottery, gift enterprise, or similar scheme shall be fined under this title or imprisoned not more than one year, or both.

Section 2326. Senior Citizens Against Marketing Scams Act

In addition, under a statute enacted in 1994 as part of the Senior Citizens Against Marketing Scams Act (18 U.S.C., sect. 2326), federal courts can impose an additional term of up to five years' imprisonment where the mail, wire, or bank fraud offense was committed in connection with the conduct of telemarketing.

They can impose an additional term of imprisonment of up to ten years' imprisonment if the offense targeted persons 55 and older or victimized ten or more persons 55 and older. A similar enhancement can be added to the bank fraud sentence.

Convicted individuals must also be ordered to pay full restitution to their victims.

Title 39, United States Code, Section 3005. False Representations; Lotteries

(a) Upon evidence that any person is engaged in conducting a scheme or device for obtaining money through the mail by means of false representations, or is engaged in conducting a lottery, gift enterprise, or scheme for the distribution of money, the Postal Service may issue an order that:

(1) directs the postmaster of the post office at which mail arrives to return such mail to the sender appropriately marked as in violation of this section;
(2) forbids the payment by a postmaster to the person of any money order or postal note and provides for the return to the remitter; and
(3) requires the person or representative to cease and desist from engaging in any such scheme, device, lottery, or gift enterprise.

Section 1341. Frauds and Swindles

Whoever, having devised or intending to devise any scheme to defraud, or to sell any counterfeit or spurious security, sends by the Postal Service, or by any private or commercial interstate carrier, or receives any such thing, shall be fined or imprisoned not more than five years, or both.

If the violation affects a financial institution, such person shall be fined not more than $1 million or imprisoned not more than 30 years, or both.

Section 1342. Fictitious Name or Address

Whoever, for the purpose of promoting, or carrying on any such scheme or any other unlawful business, uses a fake name or address shall be fined or imprisoned not more than five years, or both.

Section 1345. Injunctions Against Fraud

The attorney general may commence a civil action in any federal court to rejoin such violation.

MONEY LAUNDERING

Because the owners and operators of telemarketing schemes often use the proceeds to further the scheme — for example, to pay the costs of their telemarketing business activities, such as payment of salaries and rent and purchases of "leads" and "gimmie gifts" — the Department has increasingly included charges under the federal money-laundering statutes (18 U.S.C., sects. 1956 and 1957).

Each of these latter statutes carries a maximum term of imprisonment of 20 years and 10 years, respectively, and provides the department with a basis to obtain criminal forfeiture of the telemarketers' property. In some cases they will even, as appropriate, use RICO (Racketeer Influenced and Corrupt Organization) charges.

FINANCIAL INSTITUTION FRAUD (BANK FRAUD)

In cases where fraudulent telemarketers have misled banks when they applied for merchant accounts to process victims' credit card charges, the department has also charged the telemarketers with financial institution fraud (18 U.S.C., sect. 1344). That statute carries a maximum term of imprisonment of 30 years.

CIVIL LITIGATION

Telemarketers sometimes engage in unfair practices that may not rise to the level of criminal violations but nevertheless harm consumers. In such cases, the Office of Consumer Litigation frequently initiates civil litigation at the request of the Federal Trade Commission (FTC).

These cases seek enforcement of FTC rules that govern the conduct of telemarketers, such as the Telemarketing Sales Rule, or rules that directly apply to telemarketers or the Franchise Rule, and rules that regulate the practices of anyone, including telemarketers, selling franchise opportunities.

These enforcement actions serve several purposes. First, they obtain court orders that prohibit misrepresentations and require the telemarketer to comply with the pertinent FTC rule. This frequently results in firms going out of business. Firms that remain in business tend to provide more complete and accurate information to potential customers. Second, these actions may obtain civil penalties or consumer redress from violators, forms of monetary deterrence that can also benefit victims.

Third, the individuals who are subject to orders in these cases risk charges of civil or criminal contempt of court if they violate the court orders. The Office of Consumer Litigation and the FTC, through "Operation Scofflaw," have sought and obtained terms of imprisonment against individuals who violate such orders.

U.S. TREASURY COLLECTION

In many cases involving fraud, the FTC receives judgments against the defendants so that they will attempt to collect on these with the goal of returning money to the victims. Collection is often difficult, however, because the defendants do not have identifiable assets subject to seizure. So, the FTC recently began working with the U.S. Treasury for assistance in collecting these judgments.

The Treasury's Financial Management Services Division is able to use its collection expertise to aggressively collect amounts owed by fraudulent telemarketers.

In cases where Treasury is unable to collect after diligent effort, it will report to the Internal Revenue Service that the uncollected debt should be treated as income to the defendant, subject to taxation.

SECURITIES VIOLATIONS

By successfully advocating in the General Assembly for a change making securities violations felonies, attorney generals can initiate a policy of criminally prosecuting securities violators rather than handling them administratively.

ROLE OF PHONE COMPANIES

A federal law requires phone companies to discontinue or refuse services to businesses that use their lines to transmit gambling information. The law has been used primarily to stop bookmaking operations but has shut down lottery operations as well.

EUROPEAN FRAUD-RELATED LAWS

The European Union (EU) and individual European nations are also concerned with fighting frauds. They define fraud as: "Deliberate deception used for unfair or illegal advantage."[6]

In Europe, Interpol, Europol, and the EU share information in order to help prevent, investigate, and prosecute frauds. The EU has established the OLAF (or Office Européen de Lutte Anti-Fraude) or "European Anti-Fraud Office" with fighting fraud that includes "protecting the interests of the European Union, to fighting fraud, corruption and any other irregular activity, including misconduct within the European Institutions, in an accountable, transparent and cost-effective manner." In so doing, OLAF reports to the European Parliament.

OLAF fulfills its mission by conducting, in full independence, internal and external investigations. It also organizes close and regular cooperation between the competent authorities of the member states in order to coordinate their activities. OLAF supplies member states with the necessary support and technical know-how to help them in their anti-fraud activities. It contributes to the design of the anti-fraud strategy of the European Union and takes the necessary initiatives to strengthen the relevant legislation.

> The objective of the OLAF is to protect the interests of the European Union, to fight fraud, corruption, and any other irregular activity, including misconduct within the European's institutions. In pursuing this mission in an accountable, transparent and cost-effective manner . . .[7]

EU FIGHT AGAINST FRAUDS

The EU's OLAF is set up:

- To provide an independent investigative service.
- To "Carry out all the powers of investigation conferred on the Commission by Community legislation and the agreements in force with third countries, with a view to reinforcing the fight against fraud, corruption and any other illegal activity affecting the financial interests of the European Community."

---

[6] See http://europa.eu.int/comm/justice_home/glossary/glossary_f_en.htm and the subsequent footnotes relative to EU's anti-fraud program, from which this section is liberally quoted.

[7] Ibid.

- "To consolidate this independence, the Office is subject to regular control of its investigative function by a Supervisory Committee, made up of five outside persons independent of the Community Institutions, who are highly qualified in the areas of competence of the Office. At the request of the Director-General or on its own initiative, the Supervisory Committee will deliver opinions to the Director-General concerning the activities of the Office, without however interfering with the conduct of investigations in progress."

- "In close cooperation between the Commission services and the member states, the Committee also issues guidelines for national authorities and reference documents on Fraud and other irregularities. It elaborates the Annual Report of the Commission, as provided under Article 280 of the EC Treaty, an overview of Community and national action and initiatives, including an image of case reporting and of the trends of fraud and other irregularities throughout the EU."

- "OLAF, in cooperation with its national partners (investigation services, police, legal and administrative authorities, etc.) does its best to counter the criminals and the fraudsters, who did not wait for the opening of the borders to organize their illicit activities at international level. OLAF is to some extent the engine of the 'Europe of legality' against the 'international nature of criminality; harmful to Community interests."

- "To this end, OLAF can carry out administrative investigations inside the institutions (see EC Decisions 1999/394 and 1999/396), the bodies and organs of the Community, in the event of fraud harmful to the budget of the EU. It is also responsible for detecting the serious facts, linked with the performance of professional activities."

- "OLAF comprises some 280 agents, including the nonstatutory personnel; the total number of staff should rise to 330 persons towards the end of 2002. The investigators of OLAF, like all the other officials and Community servants, work in the exclusive interest of the Communities. They have to discharge their functions and do their work while keeping only in mind the interests of the Communities, without taking instructions from any government, authority, organisation or person independent of the institution. To achieve these specific tasks, the majority of the personnel of OLAF have however a solid professional experience gained in the national investigation, police and judicial services, in the area of investigations concerning complex fraud cases, in the analysis and evaluation of information, or in activities of support or development of policies in the area of the fight against fraud."

- "OLAF is therefore neither a 'secret service,' nor a police force. It is rather the legal instrument for administrative investigation with which the European Union has been equipped by the

Commission, to guarantee better protection of Community interests and compliance with the law against attacks from organized crime and fraudsters."[8]

ASIA AND FIGHTING FRAUD

Asian nation-states are also concerned with the crimes perpetrated by both internal and international miscreants. Although their emphasis seems to be more on combating illegal drugs, trafficking in women and children, money laundering, and terrorism, they are also concerned with fighting fraud.

One of the primary bodies for fighting such criminal activities is the Association of Southeast Asian Nations (ASEAN). At the inaugural meeting of the association hosted by the Philippine government in December 1997, it issued a declaration establishing a framework for cooperation among the ASEAN members in combatting "transnational crime."

The Declaration provided the following initiatives for regional cooperation on tackling transnational crime:[9]

1. Hold discussions with a view to signing mutual legal assistance agreements, bilateral treaties, memorandum of understanding or other arrangements among member countries.
2. Consider the establishment of an ASEAN Centre on Combating Transnational Crime (ACTC), which will coordinate regional efforts against transnational crime through intelligence sharing, harmonization of policies and coordination of operations.
3. Convene a high-level ad-hoc Experts Group within one year to accomplish the following with the assistance of the ASEAN Secretariat:
   a. ASEAN Plan of Action on Transnational Crime
   b. Institutional Framework for ASEAN Cooperation on Transnational Crime
   c. Feasibility study on the establishment of ACTC
4. Encourage member countries to consider assigning Police Attaches and/or Police Liaison Officers in each other's capital in order to facilitate cooperation for tackling transnational crime.
5. Encourage networking of the relevant national agencies or organizations in member countries dealing with transnational crime to further enhance information exchange and dissemination.
6. Expand the scope of member countries' efforts against transnational crime such as terrorism, illicit drug trafficking, arms smuggling,

---

[8] http://europa.eu.int/comm/dgs/olaf/mission/mission/index_en.html.
[9] http://www. aseansec.org/5640.htm

money laundering, and traffic in person and piracy, and to request the ASEAN secretary general to include these areas in the work program of the ASEAN Secretariat.

7.   Explore ways by which the member countries can work closer with relevant agencies and organizations in Dialogue Partner countries, other countries, and international organizations, including the United Nations and its specialized agencies, Colombo Plan Bureau, Interpol, and such other agencies, to combat transnational crime.

8.   Cooperate and coordinate more closely with other ASEAN bodies such as the ASEAN law ministers and attorneys general, the ASEAN chiefs of National Police, the ASEAN finance ministers, the directors-general of Immigration and the directors-general of Customs in the investigations, prosecution, and rehabilitation of perpetrators of such crimes.

CASE STUDY

As in all wars, the war in Iraq offers many challenges, and one of them is the potential for fraud. The following case[10] is but one example showing that when it comes to matters of fraud, the waters are often very murky:

> The Virginia courtroom, just outside of Washington, D.C., was set to try what should have been a simple matter of whether or not Custer Battles, an upstart security company, based in McLean, Virginia, had defrauded its customers by as much as $50 million. By the end of the hearing last week, a perplexed judge was asked to decide whether the United States government controlled Iraq's oil revenues that were used to pay the company.

> "The funds that were used were Iraqi funds, not U.S. funds," said veteran Washington lawyer John Boese. . . . The fact that CPA was in temporary possession of the money and distributed it does not form a basis for a false claim.

> . . . , the attorney for the plaintiffs claimed . . . that the U.S. largely controlled the Coalition Provisional Authority (CPA) that was running Iraq at the time and was clearly understood to be "a government entity" by the U.S. Congress when approving the $87 billion funding package in November 2003 for reconstruction and military spending in

---

[10] See article, "Iraq Contractor Claims Immunity from Fraud Laws; Seized Oil Assets Paid for Offshore Overbilling" by David Phinney, Special to CorpWatch, December 23, 2004.

Iraq. . . . Custer Battles[11] has been accused of illegally inflating costs on plum contracts in 2003 to protect the Baghdad International Airport as well as for a massive program that replaced Iraq's currency.

. . . the lawsuit under the False Claims Act, reinvigorated by Congress in 1986, which is considered a key weapon in fighting contract fraud. It allows federal courts to award financial incentives to people in the private sector to step forward and assist the government in recovering the money, if they have evidence of wrongdoing."

As the chief security officer (CSO) for such a company:

- How would you react to the above?
- Would you try to get involved?
- If so, in what manner would you try to get involved? For example, would you offer investigative assistance to the company's legal staff?
- How would you feel working for such a company?

As the CSO, what things must you consider? An example of some things to think about are as follows:

It seems that in today's corporate world, it is not unusual to be working for a company that has been accused of perpetrating a fraud. Normally, your anti-fraud program should address such types of frauds; however, in the "real world" it generally will not.

One reason that you will have a difficult time selling such a program or a particular part of such a program is that corporate frauds are often committed at the highest levels of a corporation, and any attempt to conduct an inquiry to prove or disprove rumors of fraud or specific allegations will cause a quick end to your professional career in that company. Remember that these are the same executives who must approve your corporate anti-fraud program.

If you have a basis for believing that such frauds are being perpetrated within your corporation, you can become a "whistleblower." If so, no matter if you are right or wrong, your career at that corporation will be in jeopardy as corporate executives will find some way to get rid of you — "reorganization" is sometimes used to "squeeze" someone out of the corporation.

Although it is not right to take this punitive action, it unfortunately happens more often than one may realize. Furthermore, any chances of your joining another corporation will be minimal because of the stigma attached to your name. Consequently, your chances of obtaining a similar job may be in jeopardy.

---

[11] This case is an example of the complications of fraud matters, and in no way are we implying the guilt or innocence of the contractor.

It is a sad commentary on today's corporate world that ethics and honesty are good as long as you don't "rock the boat." The following is an example of what may happen when you become a whistleblower:

"BLOWING THE WHISTLE" ON DEFRAUDERS CAN BE DANGEROUS

Los Alamos whistleblower beaten outside bar: A Los Alamos lab whistle-blower scheduled to testify before Congress was badly beaten in an attack outside a Santa Fe bar. . . . in a hospital recovering from a fractured jaw and other injuries, . . . wife and his lawyer believe the attack was designed to keep him quiet . . . assailants told her husband during the attack early Sunday that "if you know what's good for you, you'll keep your mouth shut.". . . . has a pending lawsuit against the University of California alleging whistleblower retaliation.

He had been scheduled to testify before the House Energy and Commerce Committee later this month about alleged financial irregularities at the nuclear weapons lab. . . . the 52-year-old lab employee got a telephone call late Saturday night — after he was already in bed — wanting to meet with him at a Santa Fe bar about 45 minutes from their home. . . .

husband told her the man never showed up, but as he was leaving the topless bar's parking lot, a group of men pulled him from his car and beat him. . . . sued the university in March, alleging that after they uncovered management failures, university and lab managers tried to make their jobs miserable so they would quit. . . . had been voicing complaints about lab management for years. He testified in a 1997 deposition that the chief of the lab's audit division "didn't want to see certain things put in reports," including "unallowable costs" and "embarrassment to the university."[12]

This is an example of how dangerous such activities can be. Whistleblowers are vital, but they may pay a heavy price.

SUMMARY

Nations-states around the world are concerned with fraudulent activities within and directed toward their corporations. Many nation-states have banded together to form associations, such as EU and ASEAN, to combat international crimes, including frauds. Generally, the most developed nation-states have more comprehensive laws, one reason being the fact that they are the most targeted.

---

[12] http://www.cnn.com/2005/US/06/07/whistleblower.beaten.ap/index.html

It is important to be familiar with the associations, treaties, and laws relative to fraudulent matters in every nation-state where your corporation has offices. Furthermore, your corporate anti-fraud program should consider such laws and design a corporate anti-fraud program that will help prove or disprove allegations against the applicable laws of the nation-states where the corporate facilities are located.

4

Corporations Don't Commit Frauds; People Do

INTRODUCTION

According to John Galbraith, "the word capitalism has been replaced by the term 'the Market System'. . . . Those who most enjoy their work . . . are all but universally the best paid. . . . Low wage scales are for those in repetitive, tedious, painful toil. Those who least need compensation for their effort, could best survive without it, are paid the most. The wages, or more precisely the salaries, bonuses, and stock options, are the most munificent at the top, where work is a pleasure."[1]

If you agree with Galbraith, and let's assume for the sake of discussion that you do, then consider this: It should only be "those on the bottom" who should consider perpetrating frauds since they who are least likely to enjoy their work and are paid the least, while at the same time they are trying to enhance their lifestyle.

Some may see perpetrating a fraud or other type of crime as the only way out of their current predicament. They are also the ones who may generally have the least amount of education and the least amount of experience in a job or profession that can help propel them to the "good life". But other reasons may also be involved; these will be discussed throughout this chapter.

ARE DEFRAUDERS A PRODUCT OF THEIR ENVIRONMENT, OR IS IT IN THEIR GENES?

If you agree with Galbraith's comments, then why is it that history, especially the recent history of U.S corporations and their executive

---

[1] From John K. Galbraith's book, *The Economics of Innocent Fraud: Truth for Our Time.* Houghton Mifflin, Boston. 2004.

management, has shown that apparently many frauds are committed at the higher levels of corporate management? Is it:

- Just plain ole human nature at work?
- All about power?
- About seeing how much money you can amass?
- Based on how a person was raised, or is it more in the genes derived from the defrauder's ancestors?
- All of the above?
- None of the above?

Criminologists from all over the world have made a lifetime study of the reasons humans commit frauds and other crimes. The debate goes on and will probably continue much as the chicken and the egg "controversy" is forever. There are those who say it is based on your "inherited DNA," but then they can't explain it when the child of alcoholic, drug using, or criminal parents turns into a model citizen. There are those who believe that an individual's criminal behavior is based on his or her environment; again, however, they are unable to explain why some people raised in crime-ridden housing projects become model citizens.

Is it, as some believe, that we are reincarnated in each life to learn and experience new things and by doing so, over many thousands of lifetimes, eventually enter Nirvana or become "one with the Universe"? If that is the case, then we have no choice as to our fate in each lifetime.

Obviously, at least in this lifetime, we won't know. However, some theories have been floated that may help us understand the criminal mind and thereby put us in a better position to thwart their fraud attacks.

SOME CRIMINOLOGY THEORIES

Throughout history, many theories have been proposed as to why people commit crimes. It is important for the security professional to have a basic understanding of these theories as a baseline for protecting corporate assets from fraud-threat agents and other criminals. This of course then holds true for protecting the assets from defrauders through a comprehensive corporate anti-fraud program. "Know your enemy" is a good adage to remember and one that is quite often not thought about or not contemplated enough by the corporations' anti-fraud professionals.

> Do people commit crimes because (1) it is their fate, (2) it is God's will, (3) they are a product of their environment, or (4) they inherited bad genes? Or (5) is society to blame?

Is there a method for identifying potential defrauders and other criminals by their physical features (e.g., thin fingers and bushy eyebrows)? Don't laugh. Since at least medieval times, such ideas have been advanced. And you know what? We still don't really know why some people commit frauds and other crimes while those in similar circumstances do not. However, there have been, and still are today, theories on why people commit frauds and other crimes.

Some of the theories of crime, punishments, and why people commit crimes can be summarized as follows:

- Spiritual:[2] People commit crime due to some "other worldly powers." These people believe that they were inflicted with natural disasters as punishments for their past deeds.
- Naturalism:
  - Criminal actions are free-will choices.
  - Criminal actions are caused by factors beyond the person's control.
  - Criminal actions are so designated by criminal law where certain actions and/or people are designated as criminal. In other words, the law defines the criminal act and therefore defines as a criminal anyone who violates that act.
- Realism: Nation-states have the power derived from God to govern their people and to punish them for wrongdoing.
- Classical/Neo-Classical/Idealism: Cesare Beccaria wrote in 1764 that reforms were needed to make the criminal justice system more rational and logical in lieu of what he perceived to be the personal justice meted out by judges and the harshness of the punishments.
- Utilitarianism: The actions of human beings are motivated by self-interest; morality should be judged based on the usefulness to society. Criminals should be reformed through hard labor.
- Positivism: Criminals have specific characteristics that are different from those of others; a thief may be identified by bushy eyebrows, large lips, sharp vision, mobile eyes, long and slender fingers.[3]
- Existentialism: Human beings are free to make their own choices and are not bound by heredity, social conditions, morality, or the like.
- Analytical: There are two forms of society according to Emile Durkheim:
  - A society with a high degree of homogeneity based on a more primitive, mechanical form of society and a low division of labor; laws keep humans from deviating from society's norms

---

[2] These theories and others can be found in *Theoretical Criminology*, Third Edition, by George B. Vold and Thomas J. Bernard, published by Oxford University Press, 1986, New York; and *History of Criminology: A Philosophical Perspective* by David A. Jones, published by Greenwood Press, 1986, New York.

[3] Ibid, Page 82, Jones

- A society with a greater homogeneity of values and a higher division of labor. Durkheim also argued that
  - Some percentage of crime in a society is natural; without which society would be unhealthy
  - "No living being can be happy or even exist unless his needs are sufficiently proportioned to his means."[4]

These and related theories consider crime causations based on poverty, economic inequality, social controls, learned behavior, ecology of crimes, and the like.

As a security professional, remember that you are defending the corporate assets against defrauders. It would behoove you to learn more about the theories of criminology and consider such theories when developing your corporate anti-fraud program. After all, you are defending the corporate assets, and the defenses should incorporate controls that mitigate the attacks of fraud-threat agents. Therefore, knowing something about their makeup helps provide fraud-threat agent profiles.

FRAUD-THREAT AGENTS

Let's look at the fraud-threat agents, their profiles, motivations, inhibitors, capabilities, amplifiers, and catalysts. First, however, let's take a moment to discuss human errors or accidents vis-à-vis fraud.

HUMAN ERRORS — ACCIDENTS

Being human, we naturally will make mistakes. So, does human error fall under the category of natural threats and are we humans to be considered "natural threat agents," or do we fall under the category of "man-made" threats?

There is no law or rule that says that you must treat it as one, the other, both or neither. However, human error is a threat to corporate assets. For example, by downloading a program, joke, or photo from some Web site to your corporate computer in your office, you may also download and initiate some form of malicious code such as a worm or a virus. Such malicious codes attack valuable corporate assets and may cost the corporation in terms of cleanup costs, public image, lost revenue, and the like. You didn't mean to do it. It was an accident.

Yes, corporate assets must be protected from such incidents. However, when it comes to fraud and fraud-threat agents' attacks against corporate assets, one thing should be perfectly clear: *It is not possible to accidentally, unintentionally, or mistakenly perpetrate a fraud!*

---

[4] Durkheim, *Suicide*. Translated into English in 1952. Extracts at http://www.mdx.ac.uk/www/study/xdur.htm.

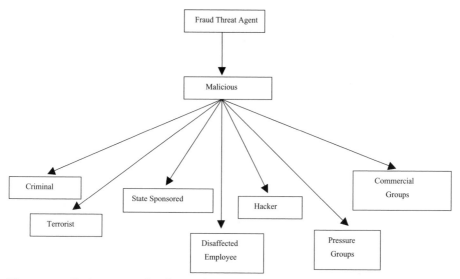

Figure 4-1. Various types of malicious fraud-threat agents.

So, when someone is identified as having attempted or successfully perpetrated a fraud, and says it was a mistake or an accident, give the person no credence. The only mistake he or she may have made was perpetrating the act in the first place and subsequently getting caught.

MAN-MADE OR MALICIOUS FRAUD THREATS

Man-made or malicious fraud threats take many forms, with new types of fraud threats being identified all too often.[5] However, these fraud threats can all be categorized into general groupings.[6] (See Figure 4-1.)

In order for a malicious fraud threat to exist (is there any other kind than malicious?), there must be an agent who will implement the threat, and that agent must have the motivation, capability, and opportunity to do so.

POTENTIAL FRAUD-THREAT AGENTS

A malicious threat agent can be generated from any number of groups. This is not meant to be an exhaustive list of potential sources or groupings of

---

[5] The information in this section is based on the work of Dr. Andy Jones, my previous co-author, colleague, and friend and modified here to specifically address the fraud threat agents.

[6] Ibid.

malicious threat agents, for these will change over time as technology, society, education, national and international politics, culture, and a host of other factors change and have an effect.

Malicious Threat Agent — State Sponsored

State-sponsored malicious fraud threats may take any form, such as attacks against financial systems in order to modify public perception or cause instability in the country and cause or prevent the country from taking other actions. Characteristically, this group will be risk averse and will be conservative in its actions, making great efforts to evade identification.

Most information on nation-states is readily available from open sources. The limiting factor in this information is that it may be dated. To be effective, a fraudulent attack sponsored by a nation-state must have:

- The technology to mount the attack against financial institutions
- The telecommunications, Internet, and power supplies to allow the attack to take place and to sustain it
- Sufficient personnel resources with an adequate level of education and skill to mount and maintain the attack

Each country will have specific cultural drivers. These drivers will impact why and how fraudulent attacks are conducted. The impact of each type of attack will vary, and the likelihood of each must be considered separately.

Malicious Threat Agent — Terrorists

Terrorist activity may be linked to criminal activity, and as malicious fraud-threat agents, terrorists may operate as individuals or in groups. Terrorism requires funding to be effective, and given that terrorists operate outside of normal national and international laws, they will commonly resort to criminal activity to generate funds that will support their activities in addition to any direct terrorist related actions.

Qualitative information on terrorist organizations is not, for the main part, readily available from open sources. Although generic information from external sources will be available, accurate and in-depth information is not normally available in a form that can be verified except where it is released or disseminated from national resources that will probably be hostile to the "terrorist" organization. Therefore, security professionals will have a difficult time preparing for fraudulent attacks by terrorists. However, they undoubtedly will employ the same basic attack techniques as any other defrauders will use. After all, their goal is basically financial: to support their terrorist activities that will cause economic chaos in nation-states they consider their enemies.

For a terrorist-sponsored attack to be effective, as noted earlier, it may also be necessary to have the technology available to mount the attack, as well as the telecommunications, Internet connectivity, and power supply that will allow the attack to take place. If one of the required outcomes of the attack requires that it be sustained, then a sufficient depth of personnel resources with an adequate level of education and skill must also be available. Each terrorist group will have specific drivers, which may be religious, cultural, ethnic, political, or any number of others.

A good generic resource for information on terrorism and terrorist groups can be found at *The Juris*,[7] a publication that provides a large number of links to give specific information on particular groups and to resources that provide general information on terrorism.

Terrorist groups are affected by a wide range of factors that will influence their motivation and ability and the likelihood that they will be able to successfully carry out a fraud attack. The sources of this information will be varied, but the most likely sources will be those that concentrate on the terrorist organizations or the media, which are likely to have up-to-date information.

Malicious Threat Agent — Pressure Group

Pressure groups will tend to have a specific focus or cause that they support and maintain. Recent history has shown that such groups, whether they are secular or religious, have learned that they can achieve results by exerting influence on peripheral targets rather than on a direct attack on the primary target. In order to hurt their targeted corporation, they may also resort to attempts to hurt the corporation financially.

Qualitative information on pressure groups is not, for the main part, readily available in the public domain from open sources. Although generic information from external sources will be available, accurate and in-depth information is not normally available in a verifiable form inasmuch as these are not accountable organizations.

To launch an effective attack, the pressure group must have the requisite technology. It is assumed that the group would have the telecommunications, Internet connectivity, and power supply sufficient for the attack to take place. If the required outcome of the attack is that it is sustained, then the pressure group must also have sufficient personnel resources with an adequate level of skill. Each pressure group will have specific drivers, which may be religious, cultural, ethnic, political, or any number of others.

---

[7] See www.law.duq.edu/pdf/juris

Because of the range of organizations included in this group and because they have varying degrees of legitimacy and history, identifying specific sources of information for the various aspects of the pressure group cannot easily be done. For detailed information on a specific pressure group, it is necessary to examine the information sources specifically related to that group. The details available on a pressure group will be variable over a period of time as it becomes more or less active.

Pressure groups are affected by a wide range of factors that will influence their motivation and ability and the likelihood of carrying out an attack. The objective of a threat agent sponsored by a pressure group may be to cause a corporation to declare bankruptcy and otherwise hurt its public image and thus its stock prices. The impact of each type of fraud attack will vary, and the likelihood of each must be considered separately in light of the organization's aims and target.

Malicious Threat Agent — Commercial Group

A threat agent that acts on behalf of a commercial group will tend to have one of a small number of objectives, including damaging the interests of competitors to influence small nation-states. This group will generally be risk averse and conservative in its actions and will go to great lengths to evade identification. For a fraud attack sponsored by a commercial group to be effective, it is necessary that the group have the requisite resources.

If the required outcome of the attack requires that it be sustained, the group must also have sufficient personnel resources with an adequate level of skill. Each commercial group will have specific drivers, but these will be predominantly financial or competitive gain.

Qualitative information on the capability of a commercial organization to carry out an attack is not generally available in the public domain from open sources. Although very specific and detailed information will be available on many aspects relating to the commercial concern, specific information with regard to its capability to pose a fraud threat will only be generated from analysis of the organization or from information on past activity as it becomes available. To avoid identification, the commercial group may outsource such fraud attacks to "mercenaries."

A successful attack that is sponsored by a commercial organization requires that the group have the needed technology, notably, the telecommunications, Internet connectivity, and power supply.

If the required outcome of the attack is that it be sustained, then the organization must also have sufficient personnel resources with an adequate level of skill. The driver for a commercial organization to mount an attack will be the desire to gain a commercial advantage in the marketplace, for example, by reducing the competitor's ability to operate efficiently in the marketplace.

A wide range of factors will affect the commercial group's motivation and ability and the likelihood of carrying out an attack. The impact of each type of fraud attack will vary, and the likelihood of each must be considered separately in light of the organization's perceived aims and target.

Malicious Threat Agent — Criminal

Criminal activity poses a fraud threat to corporations and is the type of fraud threat most often discussed. These criminals attack in order to

- Gain access to a computer network in order to defraud someone of resources (money or property).
- Prevent the detection or investigation of other criminal activity.
- Gain information that will enable them to commit other frauds.
- Gain access to personal information that will enable them to commit other fraud crimes, such as identity theft.

Because the descriptor "criminal" covers an enormous range of activities extending from financial gain to murder, drug smuggling, trafficking, and sex offenses, it is not possible to present any generic characteristics. However, our main concern is their classification as a fraud-threat agent.

For the purposes of the present work, the threat agent, whether a defrauder or a group of defrauders, will generally have one of a small number of objectives. This group, like the others already discussed, will generally be risk averse and conservative in its actions and will make every effort to evade identification.

This defrauder group, like the others discussed, requires the necessary resources to mount an effective attack. Having resources is not normally an issue for these criminals because they tend to be "cash rich" and do not have to account for their funds. If the attack outcome needs to be sustained, they must also have sufficient personnel resources with an adequate level of skill. Each defrauder or defrauder group will have specific drivers, mostly financial or competitive gain.

Any form of usable information on a criminal organization's ability to carry out an attack is not generally in the public domain from open sources. Law enforcement and national intelligence agencies invest a vast effort to gather this type of information and usually have only limited success, though some inference can be made over a period of time as the effects of the group's actions become apparent.

This defrauder or defrauder group may also require the technology and level of skill needed to mount an effective attack. It is assumed that the telecommunications, Internet connectivity, and power supply are available to allow the attack to take place.

If the required outcome of the attack is that it be sustained, then the organization must also have sufficient depth of personnel resources with an adequate level of skill. The driver for a defrauder or defrauder group will be financial gain or influence. This may not be apparent from the form of an attack.

It is difficult to deal separately with each factor that may contribute to a defrauder or defrauder group's capability to pose a threat; however, considerable information is available from which the individual elements that are required can be extracted. Defrauders or defrauder groups are affected by a wide range of factors that will influence their motivation and ability and the likelihood of carrying out an attack.

A fraud-threat agent may be sponsored by a criminal group such as an organized crime group. The impact of each type of fraud attack will vary, and the likelihood of each must be considered separately in light of the criminal group's perceived aims and target.

Malicious Threat Agent — Hacker

The hackers' normal objectives are to demonstrate to their peers that they have a level of skill that will gain them status or cause visible damage to a system simply "because they can." Other reasons may include their desire to gain access to a system in order to utilize its resources, either for the processing capability or to cover other activities. Inasmuch as the basis of this group is technical capability rather than a specific motive or pressure, the type of attack that may be mounted will not be based on the impact to the system owner but rather on the real or perceived benefit to the perpetrator.

For the hacker's fraud attack to be effective, the hacker needs the requisite resources. This is not normally an issue for a hacker group because they have support from their peers. If the required outcome of the attack requires that it be sustained, the hackers must also have sufficient personnel resources with an adequate level of skill. Each hacker group will have specific drivers, but these will be predominantly for self aggrandizement or revenge. All the same, one cannot discount the fact that some hackers are used to commit fraudulent acts.

Any form of usable information on the hacker group's ability to carry out a fraud attack will, if it is available, be in the public domain from open sources. Law enforcement and national intelligence agencies make only limited attempts to gather information on these groups, and owing to the groups' transient nature, they have had only limited success. Some inference can be gathered over a period of time as the effects of the hacker group's actions become apparent.

To be effective in their fraud attack, the hacker group needs the appropriate level of skill, and it is assumed that the group will have the telecommunications, Internet connectivity, suitable technology, and power supply sufficient to allow the attack to take place.

If the required outcome of the attack is that it be sustained, then the group must also have sufficient depth of adequately skilled personnel. The drivers for a hacker group to mount an information attack will vary, with the main drivers ranging from curiosity to financial gain to revenge.

It is difficult to deal separately with each factor that may contribute to the capability of a hacker or hacker group to pose a threat; however, considerable information can be extracted from the individual elements. Hacker groups are affected by a wide range of factors that will influence their motivation and ability and the likelihood of carrying out a fraud attack.

The impact of each type of fraud attack will vary, and the likelihood of each must be considered separately in light of the hacker organization's perceived aims and target.

Malicious Threat Agent — Disaffected Staff

A disaffected staff member will be seeking to cause damage to the image or structure of the organization or to extract value in the form of funds or property of some value. Indicators of potential disaffected staff can be isolated, and a number of identified case histories can be used to identify significant common factors from these case histories.

Any form of usable information on the capability of a disaffected staff member to carry out a fraud attack will be in the public domain from open sources, providing it has been made available by the employing organization. Information that is held by law enforcement and national intelligence agencies is not likely to be made available in reasonable time because it will potentially be required for prosecution.

To carry out a fraud attack, a disaffected staff member needs to possess the appropriate level of skill. The drivers for the disaffected employee to mount an information attack will be varied, with the main ones ranging from financial gain to revenge using fraudulent attack techniques.

Malicious Threat Agent — Subversive Organizations

A staff member who belongs to a subversive organization will probably not be known to the organization by which they are employed. Membership in a subversive organization will become an issue when the fraud-related aims and objectives of the employing organization are in conflict with those of the subversive organization or when the subversive organization can further its own fraudulent aims using the information, facilities, infrastructure, or influence provided by the employing organization.

Indicators of this type of threat agent will be difficult or impossible to identify because the motivation of the perpetrator will not be clear and it will be difficult to determine his or her membership in the organization. It is clear that some organizations will be more prone to this type of fraud-threat agent than others — for example, large and high-profile international corporations, which are the types of organizations that can leverage significant influence and favor.

Any form of usable information on the effect of subversive or secretive organizations on a corporation with regard to their ability to carry out a fraud attack will not likely be in the public domain unless it has already been made available. Information that is held by law enforcement and national intelligence agencies is not likely to be made available because it will have been gathered either as part of an investigation for subsequent criminal prosecution or as intelligence for reasons of national security.

For a fraud attack undertaken by a subversive within an organization to be effective, it is necessary that such subversives possess the appropriate level of skill. The drivers for a subverted staff member to mount a fraud attack will vary, with the main ones being the desire to gain influence and financial rewards to help support their organization.

In these cases, it may not be the individual or group that poses the most significant element of threat, but instead the organization is the target of their attention. The most likely reason for this fraud-threat agent to mount an attack on an organization would be to gain funds and/or financially harm the corporation.

CAPABILITIES

An organization or an individual's capability to mount a fraud attack and to sustain it at an effective level will vary with the complexity, resources, and sophistication of both the attacking force and the target. It may be sufficient for fraud attackers to mount an attack at any level in order to achieve their objective, but a high level of sophistication may be needed over a long period for the attack to have a significant effect.

To be effective, a malicious fraud-threat agent must have the capability to conduct and sustain an attack. The constituent elements of "capabilities" are detailed in Figure 4-2.

To be able to carry out an attack, a malicious threat agent must have the necessary means, skills, and methods. In some cases, these agents must also have a sustainable depth of capability in order to achieve their aims.

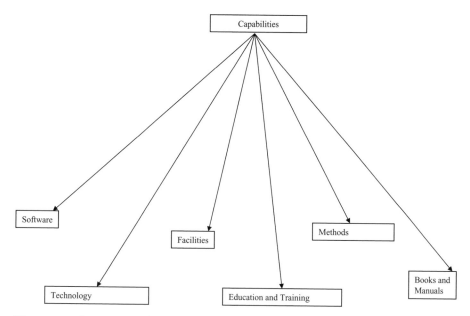

Figure 4-2.   Components of malicious fraud attack capabilities.

MOTIVATION

The motivation to carry out a malicious attack may arise from any number of situations. Some commonly accepted motivational drivers are political, secular, personal gain, religion, revenge, power, terrorism, curiosity, and the like.

The motivation of the fraud-threat agent is a subjective area influenced by a wide range of factors dependent on the originating threat agent. The preceding motivational factors are not intended to be a comprehensive list, but rather to indicate the range of potential drivers. In some cases, a number of these drivers will act together to influence the threat agent (see Figure 4-3).

Fraud-Threat Agent Motivators

The factors and influences that motivate a threat agent are diverse and may operate either singly or in unison. Although a range of groupings of threat agent motivators can be easily generated, the reason that each of the factors would come into effect and the degree to which they would influence the threat agent are subject to many varying influences.

The primary groupings of threat agent motivators are detailed in the following listing, together with a general description, but no further

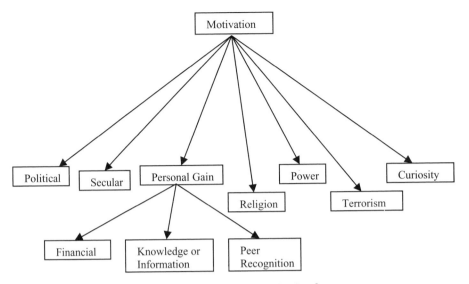

Figure 4-3. Components of the fraud-threat agent motivation factors.

analysis of this subject area will be undertaken here. The main motivational factors are:

- Political. Where the motivation is for the advancement of a political cause, it may be because the threat agent wishes to further the cause of the political organization or their own position within the political grouping. The outcome may be an attack on a political party's Web site or the denial of service of a resource, particularly during the period running up to an election.
- Secular. If the threat agent's motivation is to support his or her secular beliefs, it is possible that the agent's level of action is quite high. A person who is supporting his or her own secular beliefs will be likely to pursue an attack to a final conclusion.
- Personal Gain. A number of aspects have been grouped together under this general descriptor, as individuals are motivated by different rewards and gains. Three types of gain have been identified. The first is financial gain, through which the threat agent will gain money, goods, or services upon carrying out the attack. This may be direct gain through using stolen credit card numbers, or it may be indirect gain through being paid to carry out the attack. The second type of gain is the acquisition of knowledge or information. In this area the benefit that the threat agent may seek is in the information itself or the knowledge that is gained in obtaining access to the information. The third type of personal gain is in the form of recognition by the threat agents' peers. As a result, the threat agent may gain status

among his or her peers or get access to additional information or resources as a result of having demonstrated certain abilities.

- Religion. This is one of the more regularly observed motivational factors. Religious conflicts are among the most common, and as a result it is expected to be a major motivational factor for a threat agent. Attacks on these types of targets are common, given the number of conflicts that are occurring at any point in time, as well as the profile of the varied religions and an attacker's ability to identify not only the religious artifacts but also the assets of the adherents of that religion (in a number of cases, it is possible to tell an individual's religion from his or her name).

- Power. If an individual seeks to gain power or to demonstrate already attained power, he or she may choose to demonstrate his or her capability through an attack on an information system.

- Terrorism. A relatively new phenomenon, cyberterrorism has not yet been conclusively observed. Conversely, the terrorists' use of information systems is well proven.

- Curiosity. Curiosity is a strong and difficult factor in quantifying motive. Because it is normally unfocused and will only be directed at the target in question while the curiosity lasts, it is difficult to predict or to determine when the threat agent will have sated his or her curiosity.

The elements that provide the motivation for an individual or a group to carry out an attack will be highly variable and subjective. What constitutes motivation to one individual or group may not affect another similar group in the same way. The following elements are general indicators only. (No attempt has been made to quantify or value the effect of the preceding factors on the threat agent as this is outside the scope of the project.)

ACCESS

In order for threat agents to carry out a fraud attack on corporate assets, they must have access to those assets, either directly or indirectly. By indirectly, we mean that the defrauder causes someone to take some action that will support the defrauder's attack. Furthermore, in today's high-technology and microprocessor-driven world, such attacks can likely be accomplished through electronic access (via other networks).

A defrauder may, for example, use "social engineering" techniques — that is, try to talk someone into doing what the defrauder wants them to do or provide the defrauder with the information needed to assist in perpetrating the fraud. Using such methods as posing as someone else, gaining information through normal discussions with the person having that information, and getting that person to talk about their jobs, company, and so on, the defrauder can often successfully receive the information needed.

> Without direct or indirect access to corporate assets, a fraudulent attack cannot be successful.

CATALYSTS

A catalyst is required to cause a fraud-threat agent to select the target and the time at which the attack will be initiated. The catalyst could be something that affects either the target or the threat agent.

The causal factor in a fraud-threat agent's decision on whether and when to carry out an attack on corporate assets may be as a result of an event, such as publicity for a organization with which the agent has a disagreement, or perhaps the start of an armed conflict between the agent's country and an opponent. Another factor may be the defrauder's circumstances, and any change (perhaps in location, social grouping, employment, or financial status) may affect the defrauder's ability or desire to carry out an attack.

An attack may also be triggered by the advent of a new technology, which makes what was previously not achievable a possibility (see Figure 4-4).

The catalyst may be either real or perceived. Examples of catalysts are a change in the employee's employment status or a negative change in the employee's financial condition (see this chapter's case study for a more detailed example).

The main groupings of threat catalysts have been identified as:

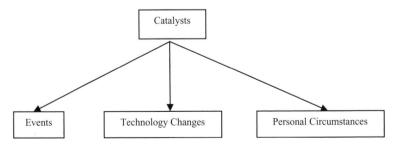

Figure 4-4.   Components of the fraud-threat agent catalysts.

- <u>Events</u>. An event may be related to the attacker or to the target, either directly or indirectly. An event that influences the threat agent might be a personal experience or exposure to news that triggers predetermined actions. An event that affects the target might be a research and development success that might change the value of the company and damage a competitor who may want to "get even."
- <u>Technology Changes</u>. A change in technology occurs at approximately nine-month intervals, and as a result, new uses for technology become apparent, and shortcomings in the technologies in use become understood in the wider community. This constant technology churn can be the catalyst for fraud-threat agents to carry out an attack as they see an opportunity developing.
- <u>Personal Circumstances</u>. The fraud-threat agent's personal circumstances may change as a result of exposure to information that affects his or her values or beliefs. Alternatively, the change might come as a result of the actions of others, such as the agent's being fired from his or her job, thereby opening the time needed to conduct a fraud attack, and having the motivation of revenge against the former employer. Another alternative may be an elevation in position or peer regard and a desire to demonstrate one's skills.

INHIBITORS

A number of factors (effectors) will inhibit a fraud-threat agent from mounting an attack either on a specific target and/or at a specific time. Again, these factors may affect either the target or the threat agent. An example may be the perception that the targeted corporate assets are well protected and that any attempt to attack them will be quickly detected.

A range of factors will both inhibit and assist a fraud-threat agent in perpetrating a successful attack. These factors have been labeled as inhibitors and amplifiers. The inhibitors are identified in Figure 4-5.

An inhibitor will either prevent a fraud-threat agent from carrying out a successful attack or minimize the impact of a successful attack or reduce a threat agent's inclination to initiate an attack. These inhibitors constitute the heart of any anti-fraud program and are often called anti-fraud defenses; in some cases they are called controls. These inhibitors include:

- <u>Fear of Capture</u>. If threat agents have the perception that, if they initiate an attack, they are likely to be identified and captured, this perception will act as a deterrent and will inhibit the perpetrator.
- <u>Fear of Failure</u>. If the threat agents believe that they are likely to fail in their attempt to conduct an attack, this belief may deter them from trying. This effect will be further enhanced if they are sensitive to the

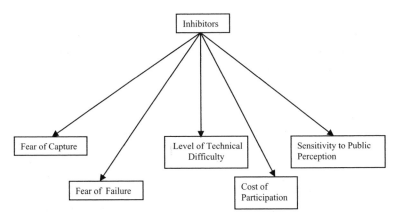

Figure 4-5. Components of fraud-threat agent attack inhibitors.

opinions of others and believe that the failure will become known to them.

- Level of Technical Difficulty. If the defenses of a target that has been identified by a fraud-threat agent are shown to be difficult to overcome, then this will, in most cases, reduce the likelihood of the threat agent attacking the system as the threat agent will search for a less challenging target. In some cases, this situation may be inverted as the threat agents will attack the most difficult of targets to prove or demonstrate their skills and abilities.
- Cost of Participation. If the cost of undertaking the attack is too high, the fraud-threat agent will be deterred from initiating the attack. The cost may be in terms of finances or of the appropriate equipment or of time or information.
- Sensitivity to Public Perception. If the target that the threat agent has selected is one that would gain the threat agent disfavor in the eyes of the public, this may act as a deterrent. An example would be an attack on the military resources of your own country during a conflict or an attack on a respected charity. The threat agent's sensitivity to public feelings may inhibit the action.

A threat inhibitor will be any factor that decreases the likelihood of either a fraud attack taking place or an attack being successful. The factors may be either real or imagined. Examples of inhibitors may be publicity relating to individuals being prosecuted or investigated for attempting to break into a corporate network or a change in the state of the security of a system in order to perpetrate a fraud.

Threat inhibitors will, in a manner similar to threat amplifiers, be a mixture of transient and longer term influences. As a result, the sources of information on these threat inhibitors will be varied. The added dimension relating to these influencing factors is that some are real and others are perceived.

Other Issues That May Inhibit Fraud Threats

- Law Enforcement Activity. If the laws within the target country or the country from which the fraud-threat agent is operating are strong and relevant and have been tested in the courts and shown to be effective, and if the law enforcement community is seen to be aggressive in its application of the law, these, too, will act as an inhibiting factor.
- Target Vulnerability. If the targeted assets that the fraud-threat agent has identified are perceived to be in a well-protected state or if the assets are thought to be protected by a variety of devices, the fraud-threat agent will likely be deterred from undertaking the attack.
- Target Profile. If the target is less attractive to the threat agent than those in similar organizations, the likelihood of an attack may be lessened.
- Peer Perception. If the consensus of opinion of the fraud-threat agent's peers is that the target would be "poor" for reasons of ease of access, resulting in no peer acknowledgment for a successful attack, or because the business of the target receives the peer's support, then the likelihood of an attack will decrease.

AMPLIFIERS

A number of factors will encourage a fraud-threat agent to mount an attack against a particular target. Again, these factors may affect either the target or the fraud-threat agent. An example may be the perception that the targeted corporate assets are not well protected and that an attempt to attack it will not be detected.

The types of effectors that will amplify or increase the possibility of a successful attack are varied but will include factors such as peer pressure. In this amplifier, fraud-threat agents may also have a desire to be well regarded by their peers. Their desire is to gain the recognition and respect of their fellow miscreants and peers through the demonstration of their skills, and this will strengthen their resolve to carry out the attack.

The fraud-threat agent's level of education and skill will improve his or her confidence and increase the likelihood of success. The amount of access to the information that the fraud threat agent needs in order to mount a fraud attack will increase the possibility of a successful attack. (See Figure 4-6.)

A threat amplifier is any factor that increases the likelihood that an attack will either take place or will be successful. The factors may be either real or imagined. Examples of amplifiers may be discussion among defrauders of the discovery of a new method for penetrating the security of a particular corporate target.

Threat amplifiers may be a mixture of transient and longer term amplifiers; as a result, the sources of information on these will be varied. There is an added dimension with these influencing factors in that some are real and some are perceived.

Of the factors that were identified, the following were considered to be the most significant:

- Peer Pressure. Threat agents may be more likely to carry out an attack if they feel that to do so will enhance their prestige or status within their peer group. Particularly within system-hacking circles, elevated status and regard by other hackers will gain the individual access to information and resources that they did not have before and will also achieve one of their aspirations of increased status within the community.
- Fame. In all social groupings, a proportion of the defrauders will seek to be recognized for the actions they have undertaken. These actions may have been good or bad, but the attacker's desire to be recognized for his or her skill and daring will be quite high.
- Access to Information. If an individual or a group believes that they will gain access to useful information, either as a direct result of carrying out a fraud attack or as an indirect reward for it, they will, in

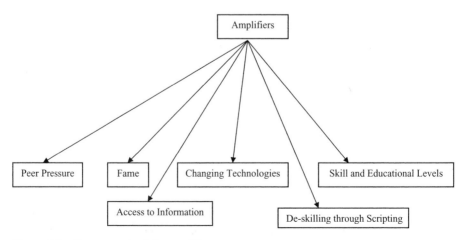

Figure 4-6. Components of the amplifiers.

some cases, be more inclined to carry out the attack. This access to information may be the primary motivation for the attack or a secondary benefit.

- Changing Technology. As technology develops, a recurrent theme that has also developed is the release of a new technology, its acceptance into common use, discovery of weaknesses in the technology, and finally exploitation of the weaknesses for illicit purposes.
- De-Skilling Through Scripting. As new techniques to subvert the security of systems are understood, the more skilled attackers, most particularly those from the hacking community, will write scripts that will automate the attack. As these techniques become available to the less skilled users who could not carry out the attack without the automated tools, the number of people who could conduct an attack is increased. Such attacks may be the basis for perpetrating frauds.
- Skill and Education Levels. As the general level of education with regard to technology increases and the use of technology becomes almost ubiquitous and as the skill level with regard to the use of new technologies increases, so the number of people who have an understanding of the technology and ways to carry out fraud-related attacks will rise.

Other Issues That Will Amplify Fraud Threats

- Law Enforcement Activity. If the laws within the target country or the country in which the fraud-threat agent is operating are perceived to be weak or not relevant to the types of activity that the attackers are using; or if the laws that are being used have not been tested in the courts or have been tested and been shown to be ineffective; or if the law enforcement community is seen to be reluctant in its application of the law — any of these alternative scenarios will act as an amplifying factor.
- Target Vulnerability. If the targeted assets identified by the fraud-threat agent are perceived to be in a poorly protected state or if they have vulnerabilities that come into effect through no fault of the security professionals or corporate management, the likelihood that the fraud-threat agent will undertake the attack will be amplified.
- Target Profile. If the target profile is more attractive to the threat agent than those of similar organizations, this will amplify the likelihood of an attack.
- Public Perception. If the public is largely opposed to the organization that the target represents (e.g., large oil corporations that are perceived to be gouging their customers through artificially high prices), then the likelihood of a threat agent carrying out an attack will be increased.

FRAUD-RELATED FACTORS FOR ATTACKING SYSTEMS

In today's high-technology environment, one must have a working knowledge of computer systems and include the use of these systems in any defense against fraud-threat agent attacks because certainly the fraud-threat agents will use such tools if they can help perpetrate a successful fraud attack on corporate assets.

In order for a fraud-threat agent to mount a successful attack on a system, at least two system-related factors must be present:

1. In order to have an effect, there must be an exploitable vulnerability in the system for the threat agent to utilize. For a vulnerability to be exploitable, it must be known, or there must be an expectation that it will be known, to the threat agent, and the threat agent must have sufficient access to the system to affect the attack. The vulnerability may exist in the hardware, the operating system software, or the applications software.
2. The target system must be important enough to the defrauder that the loss of it or a degradation in its availability, confidentiality, or integrity would support the defrauder's successful attack to defraud the corporation or other entity.

RELATIONSHIP OF THREAT ELEMENTS

The potential for a fraud-threat agent to pose an actual fraud threat through such things as an information infrastructure will be influenced by a number of factors. For the threat agent to pose a real threat to an information infrastructure, the agent must posses a capability and must also be able to gain either physical or electronic access.

The potential impact of such a threat agent will be influenced by its level of capability. The threat agent will be influenced by factors that will inhibit his or her ability to form a threat and will be strengthened by other factors. In addition, some type of catalyst will cause the agents to act, depending on their motivation. The components of "threat" that apply to a malicious threat and their interrelationships are detailed in Figure 4-7.

CASE STUDY

In this chapter, it was pointed out that motivation and opportunities play a major role in fraud-threat agent attacks or the potential for their attacks. The topic of threat agents can be discussed and written about for volumes; however, the preceding provides the corporation's chief security officer (CSO) or other security professionals with at least an overview of the topic.

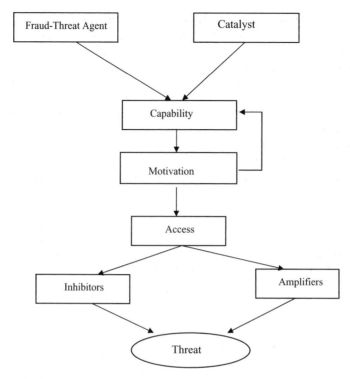

Figure 4-7. Threat components and their relationships.

As a CSO, what do you think you need to understand about fraud-threat agents? The following information may help you answer that question:

In order for a CSO to be able to mount an adequate, cost-effective defense of company assets, the CSO must understand all the types of fraud threats against the company. Furthermore, he or she must also understand the mind of these defrauders. One must understand as much as possible how these miscreants think and why they think, act, and react as they do.

Remember that first and foremost it is the human factor that is involved in all these threats and it is the human miscreants that the CSO, other security professional, or others charged with defending the corporate assets against fraud-threat agent attacks must understand. This point cannot be overemphasized, especially since it is precisely the human factor and how the miscreants think that are usually lacking in the CSO's quest to build a successful assets protection program and specifically an anti-fraud program as a standalone corporate program or as a subset of the corporate assets protection program.

The security professional, though "required" to be knowledgeable in international politics, business, marketing, finance, management, leadership, auditing, high technology, social science, psychology, and the like, must also have a good working knowledge of criminology.

Being a corporate security professional and especially a CSO is a very challenging job, and to be successful, one must have much more than just a background and experience in fighting fraud attacks and attackers. In fact, that is one of the major problems with many security professionals. Their backgrounds are usually planted firmly in basic assets protection, with the priority being given to physical security, when in fact the primary threats are rooted more in the human factors associated with the threat agents such as the defrauders.

> Understanding the human factors is at least as important, if not more important, than understanding when and how to install alarms, physical access controls, and the like.

The security professional must first of all understand the fraud threats and then use a holistic and systematic approach to finding the solution to mitigating the threats. Some threats may be completely eliminated, some may be mitigated to provide for the least amount of risks, while others may be such that the security professional can only hope and pray that the company's assets will not be threatened by the defrauders. However, it seems that there are always some of "them" around.

According to the Association of Certified Fraud Examiners and members of the criminology profession, three requirements are present when considering the human threat agent. They are the same regardless of the type of attack to be launched.

- Motive: If one is not motivated to attack a system, that person will not attack; therefore, that person is not a threat.
- Rationalization: One must be able to rationalize the attack. For example, many devoutly religious people have committed one or more crimes. If they were that religious, how could they commit such a crime when they also believe that they would go to hell and suffer eternal damnation for such crimes? They must rationalize in their minds that what they were to do was not in violation of God's law or God would forgive them. If they could not rationalize or justify it to themselves, they would not commit the crime. The rationalization need not be logical or make any sense to anyone else, but the attacker must believe it.

- Opportunity: The final part of this triad is opportunity. Those who are motivated and can rationalize an attack, but know there is no opportunity to commit or successfully commit that attack or no opportunity to commit that crime without getting caught, will not commit the crime.

When discussing this triad, it is important to remember that as human beings we will all probably commit a fraudulent act under the "right" circumstances. An internal employee of the company may be a model employee; however, if the employee's circumstances changed for the worse, elements of the triad would come into play and an employee once not considered a threat would become a threat. For example:

You have a family with kids growing up and getting ready for college; you have a mortgage, car payments, and the normal other bills; you worked for a company for about 25 years; and you are about 54 years old. You were called into the boss's office one Friday and told the company was downsizing and was terminating your employment. However, because the company was terminating over 500 people, the federal law required that you be given 60 days notice. You knew that you would have difficulty finding another job, especially at your age, and besides that your skills were somewhat outdated, not in great demand. You didn't know how you would make it. You knew that the college money for the kids would have to be used to survive. You also knew that you'd have to sell one car as you couldn't afford two. You were also concerned about other finances. In other words, in about 60 days, you knew that your entire world would be turned upside down and you didn't know how you would survive. Gloomy enough for you? It happens every day. Sometimes by the thousands!

For most people, that would be enough to start thinking somewhat negatively about the place where they work and the managers, company president, et al. However, to really push you over the edge, let's say the next morning you get up for work and read in the business section of the paper that the company you work for was having greater sales than ever and had record profits. You read on to learn that because of that, the company president was getting a $2.5 million bonus and the executive managers were getting $1 million each for saving the company so much money over the years and for increasing sales and profits.

You are now motivated to get what you can from that company in the next 60 days. You deserve it. You gave them your "blood, sweat and tears" for 25 years, and they are where they are today partly because of you. And what did they give you? The boot! So now you have the motive and the rationalization. Some people use violence (e.g., the post office worker kills the manager who yelled at him). Others use fraud, theft, and whatever opportunity gives them; while yet others steal and sell sensitive company information and destroy or modify company information and systems.

The triad "bar" is higher for some than for others. However, it is now a matter of survival, a basic and extremely strong human trait. You and your family must survive. You are not about to have your house repossessed, as well as your car, and be one of the homeless out there. Add to that a little revenge, frustration, and hostility at not being able to find another job as day 60 approaches.

Yes, we all have our limits. As a security professional, keep the triad in mind as you build the corporate anti-fraud program. It is important to know the culture and atmosphere of a company, and as the CSO, you must be tuned into the changes caused by downsizing, restructuring, mergers, and the like, for they often create additional fraud-threat agents.

As a CSO for a major international corporation, what policies, procedures, plans, processes, and/or projects would you put in place to mitigate the fraud threats based on the preceding scenario?

SUMMARY

Today's security professionals are faced with many threats, and one of the biggest and fastest growing of these threats is the fraud-threat agents. Once these agents were either internal or in some way associated with the corporation (e.g., supplier); because of such interfaces as the Internet and other businesses' networks, as well as the new global market environment where the corporation is now connected, the threats of frauds and thus the number of fraud-threat agents has grown. It appears that internal fraud threats may be equally matched by the external threats — or even exceed the internal threats.

Today's security professional must understand these internal and external (e.g., global) fraud threats to the company's assets. These fraud threats are categorized as malicious fraud-threat agents.

5

Fighting Fraud — Whose Job Is It Anyway?

INTRODUCTION

Many corporations' managers, employees, stockholders, and government oversight agencies (e.g. the U.S. Securities and Exchange Commission) continue to struggle with the unprofessional, unethical, and/or downright criminal conduct perpetrated by miscreants from inside and outside corporations. These activities include the fraudulent escapades of corporations' executive management, lower-level management, other employees, suppliers, customers, and anyone else who can see a selfish, though illegal, gain for themselves at the expense of the corporation or others.

The ever-increasing frauds perpetrated by people on corporations, internally and externally, will continue as the "What's in it for me? I deserve it! You owe me!" attitudes prevail. A combination of greed, lack of ethics, integrity, and honesty; as well as short-sighted executives, and also a lack of coherent, holistic, and proactive corporate anti-fraud programs, are some of the root causes of the fraud problems facing corporations today.

> It is not necessary to change. Survival is not mandatory. — *W. Edwards Deming.*[1]

The ferreting out of frauds within a corporation has been and generally remains the responsibility of various departments within a corporation. These may include security staff investigators, outside CPA firms, internal auditors, external auditors, the corporate ethics director, and

---

[1] http://en.thinkexist.com/quotes/w._edwards_deming/2.html.

basically anyone else corporate management deems to be the "logical" place to saddle a department with this responsibility. They are often scattered responsibilities throughout a corporation with either little or no delegated cohesive, consolidated leadership responsibility, nor a comprehensive, holistic anti-fraud program.

ROLE OF EXECUTIVE MANAGEMENT

The owners of a corporation or other entity expect management to be responsible for all that goes on within that corporation, including safeguarding the interests (e.g., assets) of that corporation. After all, that is why they were hired and why they get the "big bucks!"

Sadly, some of the most outrageous frauds perpetrated in the last decade, at least within the United States (although these corporations have offices, influence, and impact around the world), have been done by executive management.

> It is the responsibility of all levels of management, as well as all employees, suppliers, and others who have access to corporate assets to protect those assets from fraud.

Executive management, has taken advantage of their positions and have perpetrated frauds that have had major financial impact on their corporations, employees, and stockholders. There is no excuse for such behavior, which is done for purely selfish reasons. One would think that their millions of dollars in salary, stock options, bonuses, "golden parachutes," and other perks would leave them content. However, as we have seen, this is not the case.

Executives are sometimes able to perform such devious and fraudulent acts in collusion with others such as outside accounting, CPA, or auditing firms, which assist in rationalizing or twisting some financial or accounting procedures in favor of the corporation and executive management in order to hold on to their lucrative corporate contracts worth often millions of dollars.

The major questions that should be answered by executives — some of whom may perpetrate frauds — relative to an anti-fraud program include the following.

- Will corporate executive management approve and support a corporate anti-fraud program?
- If not, why not? Are they afraid of getting caught with their hands in the corporate assets cookie jar?

- If they will support a corporate anti-fraud program (e.g., budget), will they allow it to be sufficiently proactive and have sufficient controls in place to identify indicators of frauds by corporate executives?
- Will executive management support oversight of their activities to include looking for fraud indicators related to their actions?
- Will they support a strong corporate ethics program?
- Will they support a strong "whistleblower" policy that encourages the reporting of fraud indicators, anonymously without management trying to identify the whistleblower and easing them out of the corporation?

These are just a few of the key questions that will determine the quality and success of a corporate anti-fraud program. If executive management does not support a proactive anti-fraud program, you may wonder why. Some executives rationalize that they already have that in place by having an ethics program, auditors, outside CPA firm oversight, SEC oversight, or other such positions.

They may even maintain that by establishing a corporate anti-fraud program, they are implying or saying to the world that they need one because frauds permeate the corporation. They also say that such a formal program would be a "public relations disaster" as they would then have to explain that they are just trying to help safeguard the owners' assets and that they are not aware of any frauds within the corporation. In some respects they may be correct in what they say. However, are such excuses adequate and logical to explain away a formal corporate anti-fraud program?

Other complications that arise are due to the laws, rules, regulations, and policies that are so complex, such as those relating to accounting procedures, tax procedures, and the like, that they are often subject to interpretation that may be stretched past their logical limits. Thus, they become indicators of frauds, but it is difficult to prove intent and not just one interpretation of what is required.

So, what should executive management do? Approaching this issue from a corporate assets protection viewpoint, giving the interests of the corporate owners the highest priority, a corporation's executive management should support such a program both in spirit and with budget. Without the approval and budgetary resources support, as well as other types of executive management support, such a program is doomed to failure.

Executive management generally will not directly say no to an anti-fraud program but will instead rationalize that such a formal program is not needed. Executives will base that decision on their use of internal and external auditors, a corporate ethics specialist, external CPA firm, SEC oversight, and the like as being their anti-fraud program.

Would a corporate anti-fraud program identify fraud indicators relative to the actions of executive management? If the program was an ideal program, possibly maybe, maybe not. That is probably not the answer you would want to hear, but it is a realistic one.

> No matter what happens in a corporation, ultimately the protection of assets, although they may be delegated for day-to-day responsibility to the CSO, rests with the executive management and cannot be delegated away to others.

ROLE OF CORPORATE MANAGEMENT

Other corporate managers will of course take their direction from executive management. In any anti-fraud program or even a general assets protection program, corporate managers have the responsibility for supporting the protection of corporate assets from frauds and other crimes, as well as protecting those assets so that they are controlled and used only as stated in corporate policies.

Corporate managers are also responsible for ensuring that all corporate employees, customers, suppliers, associates, subcontractors, and any others who have access to corporate assets do so in accordance with corporate policies. Hopefully, that will include those policies supported by procedures, plans, processes, and projects of a corporate anti-fraud program.

Currently, some management of corporations lack corporate loyalty, for they want to know what is in it for them. Based on this and other short-term views by corporate managers, is it any wonder why corporate employees feel no loyalty to the corporations? This feeling is compounded by the many corporate layoffs of employees that take place as the easy way to save corporate assets, primarily money. Those who survive the cuts see that many in management positions get ridiculously huge bonuses for saving the corporation money through layoffs.

> The Twenty-first Century Management Motto: I am as loyal as you pay me. Someone pays me more, I will be more loyal to them. So, what's in it for me?

One vice president of a large international corporation told his management staff that they should look for savings in all areas of their department and that included laying off employees and finding ways to merge departments, even if by doing so the managers eliminated their own positions. They were told that they should do so for the good of the corporation!

Wouldn't that be a wonderful thing to do — for the good of the corporation? Can you imagine going home and telling your spouse that the kids will not be going to college, or your mortgage will not be paid in the future as you just eliminated your own job for the good of the corporation?

Do you think that the vice president will do that too? Actually, it may be possible as long as the "golden parachute" is attached to his or her back. Such attitudes by corporate managers make many employees ill at ease and cause them to begin making contingency fraud plans (e.g., "If I am going to be laid off, I am going to get even before I leave").

ROLE OF THE CORPORATE EMPLOYEES

The role of all corporate employees is to safeguard the corporate assets under their control and to do so in accordance with management direction and corporate policies, which hopefully include those requirements as stated in a corporate anti-fraud program.

That would include reporting violations of such policies as when fraud indicators are identified. Such responsibility must be told to the employees and is generally done so through security awareness and training programs that include anti-fraud briefings and possibly e-mail anti-fraud messages, pamphlets, posters, and the like.

ROLE OF THE ETHICS DIRECTOR

Over the years, may corporations, especially in the United States, have seen the need to establish a position, staff, and/or department of ethics. This need has arisen as individuals have become more, well, unethical.

The workforce that was once loyal to the corporation has gradually found that their loyalty is not reciprocated by the corporation. In fact, many in corporate management quietly discourage long-term employees from remaining as they are paid more due to their corporate longevity. Moreover, as they get older, they may require more time off for medical treatment and the corporate medical benefits will increase, making the long term employee an expensive corporate asset.

Add to that the need to "cut corners" to save money in a very competitive global environment and the decline in general morality, for example, "Why shouldn't I get my share? The means may be fraudulent but the gains are what counts."

An ethics specialist is therefore mandated in many corporations. How much they actually accomplish will be a factor of their budget, management support, and executive management direction for zero tolerance of unethical behavior — at all levels within the corporation.

Based on their primary duties and responsibilities, should they lead a corporate anti-fraud program? The answer is maybe, depending on the structure and culture of the corporation. It is my belief that they are part of the anti-fraud program team but not its leader unless that leader is also the corporation's chief security officer (CSO).

ROLE OF THE AUDITOR

Corporate internal auditors (those who are employees of the corporation and are paid directly by the corporation) are hired to internally audit corporate departments for compliance with corporate and government policies, laws, regulations, and the like.

Although some may argue that there may be a few exceptions out there in the corporate world, auditors basically look for compliance and if it looks good on paper, they are usually satisfied if one plus one equals two.

> Remember that "corporate fraud" means the frauds perpetrated against a corporation or other business-related entity by individuals within and/or external to a corporation. It does not mean frauds perpetrated exclusively by "corporations." Fraud is a "people business."

The accountants and/or auditors (who often have an accountancy background and experience) can provide a good supporting role in combating corporate fraud. However, although they have been receiving some training and gaining some experience in dealing with frauds over the years, they approach it from an auditor's viewpoint and not as part of leading an assets protection program that includes a proactive anti-fraud program.

No offense is intended to auditors or others, for they are just doing what they have been trained to do in the manner in which they were trained. Frauds are perpetrated by people, and therefore, one's anti-fraud training, education, and experience should focus in part on understanding people in general, as well as defrauders and their motivations. This aspect is not emphasized to auditors in their auditing and accounting education.

In addition, most people do not like confrontation, nor do they like dealing with hostile people. Even security and law enforcement professionals do not like hostile encounters. However, the training and experiences of security and law enforcement professionals place them in a better position to successfully deal with people in confrontational situations.

Should the manager of the audit department also be the leader of a corporate anti-fraud program? The answer is no, for several reasons, including those stated earlier. For example, this would include compliance with the corporate anti-fraud program, as well as the audit staff writing the anti-fraud program and its policies, and perhaps also many of its processes, procedures, and such.

This would represent a conflict of interests inasmuch as they themselves approve what they have written and implemented; they also serve as the auditors to determine whether what they did was the correct thing to do and supports compliance with other corporate policies, government oversight laws, regulations, and so on.

> Today's auditors have been filling the vacuum left by the security specialists who have not taken responsibility for total assets protection, for example, protecting corporate assets from defrauders. Consequently, auditors are even becoming involved in fraud-related investigations and establishing anti-fraud programs!

ROLE OF THE FRAUD EXAMINER

A fraud examiner (certified fraud examiner) is a rather recent "profession," and for many it is an additional duty or responsibility. It is the focus of the Association of Certified Fraud Examiners (ACFE).[2] ACFE has a certification program that certifies individuals as fraud examiners if they pass an extensive examination and have a certain amount of experience.

A CFE may have the background of a federal, state, local, international, or foreign law enforcement professional, such as a detective, private investigator, accountant, auditor, or professional security personnel. The basic criterion is that the CFEs are in some way involved in fighting fraud.

Although CFEs do play a vital role in combating frauds, they generally have another and primary responsibility — auditor for a corporation. Therefore, they fall into those categories discussed earlier and are not in a position of authority or have primary leadership responsibility for protecting corporate assets, unless they are also the chief security officer (CSO) for a corporation.

---

[2] See http://www.acfe.com.

The authority for assets protection falls on the corporation's CSO, with all its accompanying duties and responsibilities. Assets protection leadership has been delegated to the CSO by corporate management.

ROLE OF THE CHIEF SECURITY OFFICER (CSO)

The corporation's CSO and staff of security professionals have for the most part shirked their professional anti-fraud responsibilities, much as they have evaded their duties and responsibilities with regard to information systems security (InfoSec). As with the InfoSec assets protection needs, corporate security professionals must take a lead role in combating corporate frauds — those that occur to or within their corporation. Until corporate security professionals begin to lead the corporation's anti-fraud efforts, the fraud problems of corporations will continue to fester and more often than not will continue to cost the corporations their profits and their poor public relations images — as it has in the InfoSec sector.

After all, what are we talking about here? We are talking about protecting the corporate assets from the fraud-threat agents. Security professionals are in a position to defend the corporation against this threat to the corporate assets, just as they are with defending the corporate assets (i.e., people, physical holdings, and information) from thieves, terrorists, and the many other threat agents.

The role of the corporate security professional is to lead a protective assets protection program whether it is formal or informal. The program is more than just a checklist of duties to be performed and responsibilities to be met. It is a commitment to the management and employees of a corporation to provide a safe and secure work environment.

A safe and secure work environment reduces the chances of disruptions to the business. Disruptions (which can be in many forms), breaches of security, and loss of information or physical assets can degrade the quality of the work environment and negatively impact the profitability of the corporation. The CSO has the lead in this protective role. Security professionals in the security department provide their skills and effort in support.

Because the security professionals are involved with all departments within a corporation, they should have some of the best overall knowledge as to the state of the corporation as it relates to employee morale, corporate projects, and problems within various departments. They also know basically what is going on throughout the corporation. If the security staff is out and about the corporation as they should be, they will probably have a better understanding of the state of the corporation than anyone else in the corporation, including the CEO. Therefore, they are in a better position to view poor assets protection processes, which leave assets vulnerable to frauds by those employees they see who are, for example, disgruntled.

The CEO hears what managers tell the CEO, and the security staff sees and hears what those doing the hands-on jobs are saying about their work. Therefore, the security staff can provide an overall idea of the state of security within the corporation and its vulnerabilities to frauds. However, they may also be able to provide nonsecurity help to various departments. For example, if someone is dealing with a problem and trying to figure out how to solve it, a member of the security staff may know of others within the corporation who had that problem and how to solve it. That problem solving may also be able to better secure assets from frauds, or at least the employee may "owe" the security professional a favor and repay that favor in some way, for example, identify fraud threats or vulnerabilities in anti-fraud defenses.

WHY THE CORPORATE SECURITY PROFESSIONAL?

Global markets, uniqueness of product, diversity of the workforce, customers, and a rapidly changing technological environment make the anti fraud task incorporated into an anti-fraud program more complex. Understanding how a business works is necessary, but not sufficient, for providing an appropriate level of anti-fraud protection. It takes more than just an understanding of the business to develop and implement a successful anti-fraud program; it also takes an understanding of fundamental security principles, people (human nature), and fraud schemes.

These are the basic reasons security professionals should manage the task of providing an anti-fraud program for a corporation. Do you want an auto mechanic to do brain surgery on your daughter? No, of course not. So, executive management should not take the anti-fraud program role lightly.

Investigators approach fraud from, naturally, an investigative viewpoint — solve the crime. Fraud examiners specialize in fraud-related matters; however, few come from outside the audit or investigative professions. Furthermore, within a corporation they are usually investigators (they react to fraud allegations) or auditors (they look for compliance). All serve in a reactive role. They are normally not in a leadership position responsible for protecting corporate assets — defending the assets against frauds; a proactive (offensive) as well as a defensive posture is needed. While some CSOs may also be a certified as fraud examiners, that is only a side benefit. Regardless, the duties and responsibilities of a CSO clearly call for the CSO to lead the corporate assets protection efforts, and anti-fraud program is part of that effort.

CASE STUDY

As the CSO for a global corporation, what department manager do you believe has the *leadership* responsibility for protecting corporate assets from fraud-threat agents? It is the auditors, security staff, ethics director, human resources specialist, or another department manager?

The case is made in this chapter for making that responsibility part of the CSO's duties and responsibilities, inasmuch as the CSO has leadership responsibilities for assets protection and that means from any threats, including fraud-threat agents.

SUMMARY

The responsibility for establishing and managing a specific corporate anti-fraud program is generally nonexistent, although many professionals within a corporation have a "piece of the anti-fraud action." These include the security staff, security investigators, ethics specialists, accountants, auditors, general management, legal staff, human resources personnel, executive management, and employees.

The duties and responsibilities for leading the corporate assets protection effort fall on the shoulders of the corporation's CSO and security staff. It is therefore logical that they be responsible for establishing and managing — and leading — the corporation's anti-fraud program.

This leadership role would include responsibility for establishing an anti-fraud program and establishing and leading a corporate anti-fraud team, which would include all those team members responsible for some part of the tasks related to fighting fraud such as ethics director, management, auditors, human resources specialists, and legal specialists.

6

Where There Is a Will There Is a Way — Fraud Schemes

INTRODUCTION

In discussing fraud schemes, we are also covering their history because these schemes have already been tried — usually more than once and often successfully. By understanding fraud schemes of the past, we can learn from them and develop an anti-fraud program that will identify controls and provide better defenses to protect corporate assets.

When developing a corporate anti-fraud program, we must also project these same schemes into the future and look at future technology, business changes, and environmental changes to determine whether such fraud schemes will be eliminated through the installation of improved technologies or other changes, or actually make the corporate assets even more vulnerable to these fraud schemes.

We must also "think outside the box" by incorporating future technology advances, looking into the minds of future defrauders, and brainstorming fraud schemes of the future that are not even possible today — or at least not tried as far as we know. The schemes of future fraud-threat agents must then also be considered in the establishment and management of a corporate anti-fraud program.

> A proactive corporate anti-fraud program would be a welcome change from today's mostly reactive approach!

For once, the security professionals and others should try to prepare now to meet the future fraud-threat agents so that their defenses will already be in place when these defrauders attempt to attack corporate assets. Now that would be a welcome change!

TYPES OF FRAUD SCHEMES

Defrauders in the past have used many types of fraud schemes. The following are just a few of those that have been identified. Obviously, the many types of fraud schemes that have been perpetrated, even in just the twentieth and twenty-first centuries, are too numerous to be provided here.

The objective of identifying some fraud schemes here is to give you an idea of what challenges lay ahead of you in fighting fraud and to provide at least some glimmer of the types of fraud schemes your corporate anti-fraud program must consider if you are to successfully defend the corporate assets against fraud attacks.

You may not agree with the categories identified, and you should remember that the list is not all inclusive. However, no matter what your corporation's products and/or services are, your corporation will more than likely be in the position of a victim to some fraud-threat agents' schemes. For example, even though your corporation may not be in the financial field, it will have financial transactions and a financial department. It may produce widgets, but it will also in all probability use the Internet and other telecommunications to conduct business.

When developing your corporate anti-fraud program, you should research the corporation's overall organizational structure and then identify the fraud schemes that may be used against each of the corporation's functions and departments. For example, employment fraud would be a primary concern for the Human Resources Department, which must be wary of employee applicants who provide false education and experience information and perhaps even impersonate another person.

> CNN.com on April 27, 2007 asked the following: "Have you ever lied on a resumé?" The answer was "Yes 15% and No 85%". This means that a percentage of your employment applicants may not be trustworthy.

Some may categorize the fraud schemes presented in one way or another. However, such schemes often overlap, which may make it more difficult to categorize them in one category only. For example, should you categorize an ATM fraud scheme as one under banking, financial, computer, telecommunications, or technology fraud schemes?

How you establish a set of fraud scheme categories should be based on what seems the most logical method to you as the developer of a corporate anti-fraud program. Suffice it to say that fraud schemes should be categorized and that all relevant information for each fraud scheme should be placed in a database as part of a corporate anti-fraud program. Furthermore, subsets should be established using a logical dataset naming convention so that the fraud schemes can be sorted in a variety of ways.

> Wells Fargo will never send unsolicited e-mail that requires our customers to provide personal or account information. Any unsolicited request for Wells Fargo account information you receive through e-mails, Web sites, or pop-up windows should be considered fraudulent and reported immediately. (Wells Fargo Online)

The rest of this chapter is devoted to identifying and discussing various fraud schemes that may be applicable to your corporation. A word of caution is needed here. No matter what your corporation does as far as products and/or services, you should not discount a fraud scheme because you do not think it applies to your corporation. Some examples are cited to support this view.

FINANCIAL

Under this category you should consider such matters as those related to your corporation's finance department. Also under this category one can add "Banking" and categorize all fraud schemes related to banking.

Note: Some of the schemes presented may be considered legitimate — for example, requests for information and requests for actions; however, they may also be used for fraud attacks.

Through use of the Internet as a fraud-threat agent tool, one can send out blanket e-mails such as the following:

- Dear JPMorgan Chase & Co. Member, We recently reviewed your account and suspect that your JPMorgan Chase & Co. account may have been accessed by an unauthorized third party. Protecting the security of your account is our primary concern. Therefore, as a preventive measure, we have temporarily limited access to sensitive account features. To restore your account access, we need you to confirm your identity. To do so we need you to follow the link below (link deleted by author) and proceed to confirm your information: Thank you for your patience in verifying your account information. Sincerely, JPMorgan Chase & Co. Customer Service

- We regret to inform you that the primary e-mail for your e-bay account was changed on April 10, 2005. If you did not authorize this change, please contact us using the link below: **click here and reenter your account information. Please do not reply to this e-mail. This mailbox** is not monitored, and you will not receive a response. **For assistance, log in to your e-bay account and click the Help link located in the top right corner of any e-bay page. Regards, Safeharbor Department e-Bay, Inc,** The e-Bay team. This is an automatic message. Please do not reply.

- Unauthorized access to your PayPal account! We recently noticed more attempts to log in to your PayPal account from a foreign IP address. If you accessed your account while traveling, the unusual log in attempts may have been initiated by you. However, if you are the rightful holder of the account, please visit Paypal as soon as possible to verify your identity: You can also verify your account by logging into your PayPal account at (deleted by author). If you choose to ignore our request, you leave us no choice but to temporarily suspend your account. We ask that you allow at least 72 hours for the case to be investigated, and we strongly recommend that you verify your account in that time. Thank you for using PayPal! PayPal Email ID PP315

- Dear Bank of the West customer, We recently noticed one or more attempts to log in your Bank of the West account from a foreign IP address, and we have reasons to believe that your account was hijacked by a third party without your authorization. If you recently accessed your account while traveling, the unusual log in attempts may have been initiated by you. However if you are the rightful holder of the account, click on the link below and submit, as we try to verify your account. (In case you are not enrolled, use your Social Security Number as User Name and the first 6 digits of Social Security Number as Password): The log in attempt was made from: . . . If you choose to ignore our request, you leave us no choice but to temporarily suspend your account. We ask that you allow at least 48 hours for the case to be investigated, and we strongly recommend not making any changes to your account in that time. If you received this notice and you are not the authorized account holder, please be aware that it is in violation of Bank of the West policy to represent oneself as another Bank of the West account owner. Such action may also be in violation of local, national, and/or international law. Bank of the West is committed to assist law enforcement with any inquiries related to attempts to misappropriate personal information with the Internet to commit fraud or theft. Information will be provided at the request of law enforcement agencies to ensure that perpetrators are prosecuted to the fullest extent of the law. Please do not respond to this e-mail as your reply will not be received. For assistance, log in to your Bank of the West account and choose the "HELP" link. Thanks for your patience as we work together to protect your account. Regards, The Bank of the West Corp. Copyright © 2005. All rights reserved.

- Subject: Amazon Payments Billing Issue — Greetings from Amazon Payments. Your bank has contacted us regarding some attempts of charges from your credit card via the Amazon system. We have reasons to believe that you changed your registration information or that someone else has unauthorized access to your Amazon account. Due to recent activity, including possible unauthorized listings placed on your account, we will require a second confirmation of your identity with us in order to allow us to investigate this matter further. Your account is not suspended, but if in 48 hours after you receive this message your account is not confirmed we reserve the right to suspend your Amazon registration. If you received this notice and you are not the authorized account holder, please be aware that it is in violation of Amazon policy to represent oneself as another Amazon user. Such action may also be in violation of local, national, and/or international law. Amazon is committed to assist law enforcement with any inquiries related to attempts to misappropriate personal information with the intent to commit fraud or theft. Information will be provided at the request of law enforcement agencies to ensure that perpetrators are prosecuted to the full extent of the law. To confirm your identity with us click here: (address deleted by author) After responding to the message, we ask that you allow at least 72 hours for the case to be investigated. E-mailing us before that time will result in delays. We apologize in advance for any inconvenience this may cause you, and we would like to thank you for your cooperation as we review this matter.

  Thank you for your interest in selling at Amazon.com. Amazon. com Customer Service . . . this message and any files or documents attached may contain classified information. It is intended only for the individual or entity named and others authorized to receive it. If you are not the intended recipient or authorized to receive it, you are hereby notified that any disclosure, copying, distribution, or taking any action in reliance on the contents of this information is strictly prohibited and may be unlawful. If you have received this communication in error, please notify us immediately, then delete it from your system. Please also note that transmission cannot be guaranteed to be secure or error-free.

- From: Subject: CommonWealth Central Credit Union Online Multiple Password Failure. CommonWealth Central Credit Union is devoted to keeping a safe environment for its community of consumers and producers. To guarantee the safety of your account, CommonWealth Central Credit Union employs some of the most advanced security measures in the world, and our anti-fraud units regularly screen the CommonWealth Central Credit Union database for suspicious activity. We recently have discovered that multiple computers have attempted to log into your CommonWealth Central Credit Union

Online Banking account, and multiple password failures were presented before the logons. We now require you to revalidate your account information to us. If this is not completed by . . . we will be forced to suspend your account indefinitely, as it may have been used for fraudulent purposes. We thank you for your cooperation in this manner. In order to confirm your Online Bank records, we may require some specific information from you. Click here or on the link below to verify your account (address deleted by author). Thank you for your prompt attention to this matter. Please understand that this is a security measure meant to help protect you and your account. We apologize for any inconvenience. If you choose to ignore our request, you leave us no choice but to temporarily suspend your account. CommonWealth Central Credit Union Security Team

Interestingly, often the receivers of these messages do not have an affiliation with the senders. When some of these corporations were contacted via separate e-mails, they advise that they do not conduct business this way and did not send out such e-mails.

Also note the similar patterns between these messages. For example:

- They provide the e-mail address that you are to go to instead of allowing you to go to the entities' Web site on your own.
- They imply they will need personal information such as account number and social security number.
- They threaten to cut you off from their services.
- They want you to wait awhile to give them a chance to investigate, and they ask you not to change anything until then (yeah, so they can clean out your account, steal your personal information, or make major charges to it, etc.)

When you read such things, you may wonder why anyone would answer them if they do not have an account with that business. Hopefully, most do not, but some may do so without thinking. Those who may have accounts with these businesses more than likely will answer these e-mails and provide the requested personal information. Such information would allow the defrauder to then use the information of identity theft and other types of frauds.

Why would any miscreants think they could get away with such schemes, especially if the receiver does not have an account with the business? It's simple: do a major broadcast to e-mail addresses across the Internet and see how many reply. After all, if you get one reply that allows you the defrauder to perpetrate some fraud schemes, it will be worth it. Besides, sending such messages is not costly.

Are such defrauders in fear of getting caught? Not very likely as tracking them down is difficult, requiring cooperation that is not easily forthcoming from various law enforcement agencies. In addition, these defrauders may be living in a foreign country where there is no law enforcement jurisdiction or the amount involved is not sufficient to have law enforcement even take an interest.

And such things as the following do not help:

Info on 3.9 M Citigroup customers lost. . . . Computer tapes with information about consumer lending lost by UPS in transit to credit bureau. . . . EW YORK (CNN/Money) — Citigroup said Monday that personal information on 3.9 million consumer lending customers was lost by UPS while in transit to a credit bureau — the biggest breach of customer or employee data reported so far.[1]

If your employees receive such an e-mail, and they may do so at work through no fault of their own, you would want this information reported to you and also you want to be sure to incorporate such a scheme into your employee fraud awareness program and, through coordination with your information technology department (IT), have this e-mail address blocked as part of the corporation's e-mail filtering process.

Why you may ask? In many cases, the receivers of such messages do not even have an account with this financial institution, and by going to their identified link, you are identifying yourself to the defrauders. In addition, in all probability they will ask for your personal information such as full name, social security number to "prove" your identity, and your account number.

When such e-mails are brought to your attention, you should call the security department of the financial institution or e-mail them the received message asking them to verify it. You may or may not be surprised to receive replies stating that they did not send out such a message. When contacting them, do NOT use a Web site or e-mail addresses supplied by the potential defrauder's e-mail.

CREDIT CARD SKIMMING[2]

The U.S. Secret Service and others warn of credit card skimming. A waiter or waitress (or others) at a restaurant or other place of business uses a magnetic card reader and slides your credit card through it on the way to the cash register or credit card machine — or at another convenient time.

---

[1] http://money.cnn.com/2005/06/06/news/fortune500/security_citigroup/index.htm?cnn=yes.

[2] Broadcast on the History International Channel's World Justice Program, February 23, 2006.

The "skimmer card reader" may then be taken, as an example, to someone in a car parked nearby and loaded into a computer. It is then sent via e-mail to contacts anywhere in the world. From there, it is used to make fraudulent copies of your credit card or otherwise used to get cash and/or make purchases. This may happen while you are finishing your coffee awaiting the credit card slip to sign!

If you are using a corporate credit card, this kind of fraud will obviously impact your corporation. So, it behooves you to determine whether corporate employees use corporate credit cards and to see that there are controls in place to help prevent such a fraud-threat agent attack using this fraud scheme.

Furthermore, such schemes should be incorporated into an employee fraud awareness briefing for all employees but, if you prefer, at least those who use such a corporate credit card. For general dissemination it may help employees protect their own credit cards; prevent them for being misused; and possibly give them a reason to want to perpetrate a fraud or other crime against the corporation in order to pay such debts caused by the fraudulent use of their personal credit card.

As part of your corporate anti-fraud program, you would want to know the processes in place for obtaining such a corporate credit card, as well as the process for monitoring its use, for example, reconciling the credit card bill with the credit card expenses of the employee using the card.

MORTGAGE FRAUDS[3]

According to an article in *Fortune* magazine, the number of reported mortgage frauds increased from under 10,000 reported cases in 2003 to almost 40,000 in 2006. The reported losses inceased from just over $.2 billion in 2003 to about $1 billion in 2006, with 2005 reportedly having losses of over $1 billion.

Three of the known schemes are as follows:

- **Rent-to-steal:** A renter shows up who seems to have all the right documentation to qualify. It's a deal! . . . the renter (using an alias with fake or stolen identification) goes to the local court and files a false "satisfaction of loan" document complete with your forged signature, forged bank officers' signatures, and bank seals. . . . con artist is able to go to lenders and take out new loans on the property — often taking out several, practically simultaneously, in your name. . . . renter vanishes and three or four banks are claiming title to your home.

---

[3] http://money.cnn.com/popups/2006/fortune/fraud/3.html.

- **Straw-man swindle:** Con artists use a "straw man" or "straw buyer" to purchase a property . . . uses a false identity. . . . The straw buyer gets a mortgage on the property. Then the straw buyer signs the property over to the huckster in a quitclaim deed, relinquishing all rights to the property as well as the underlying mortgage. The straw buyer gives the huckster the mortgage proceeds, taking a small cut — usually 10% — for himself. The huckster doesn't make any mortgage payments and often even pockets rent from unsuspecting tenants until the property falls into foreclosure. Usually the straw man, not the mastermind, is arrested for fraud.
- **The million-dollar dump:** A con artist looks for a low-end, rundown house for sale. He approaches the seller and says he's willing to pay the full asking price — but only if the seller will . . . [give] a bigger mortgage than the house is worth. So if the owner agrees to relist the house at, say, triple the price, then the buyer can apply for a bigger mortgage. The swindler, using a false identity, takes out the super-sized mortgage, pays the seller, and pockets the remainder. The house usually ends up in foreclosure.

After reading these schemes, you may think none of them applies to your corporation. However, they may apply without your even knowing it. For example, let's say that your corporation in no conceivable way has anything to do with any type of mortgage financial dealings. Does it take out mortgages on property or sell property such as an old office building or manufacturing facility? Would such schemes as the mortgage frauds described in the foregoing then be possible?

What if one of your employees was a victim to such a mortgage scheme and got deeply in debt and saw no way out? Might that employee revert to perpetrating some fraud against his or her employer, the corporation that employs you to protect the corporate assets?

If you assume that one or more of these schemes apply to your corporation as being a potential victim, what will you do about it? The obvious answer of course is to incorporate controls, awareness training, and proactive actions into your corporate anti-fraud program.

COMPUTER AND TELECOMMUNICATIONS FRAUDS

Computers have become so integrated into the business environment that computer-related risks cannot be separated from normal business risks. There is such an increased trust in computers for safety-critical applications (e.g., medical) that there is increased likelihood that attacks or accidents can cause deaths.

In addition, the use and abuse of computers have become widespread, with increased threats of frauds. Individual privacy is at risk owing to large databases containing personal information, which is available to many unauthorized people due to poor information protection programs.

A computer and technology fraud is defined as: "Any falsification or embezzlement accomplished by tampering with computer programs, data files, operations, equipment, or media, and resulting in losses sustained by the organization whose computer system was manipulated; knowingly accessing or otherwise using a computer, without authorization or exceeding authorization, with intent to commit a fraudulent act."[4]

In the 1970s, computer frauds were rarely reported because the companies or government agencies did not want the public to lose confidence in either them or computers. Frauds were generally large dollar amounts and spectacular. Perpetrators generally were computer specialists: programmers, computer operators, data entry personnel, systems analysts, and computer managers.

In the 1980s, the type and frequency of computer fraud changed owing to the personal computer, telecommunications advancements, and networking. Perpetrators generally were workers under stress, suffering from financial or personal problems; disgruntled employees; bored; tempted by curiosity; and challenged. This was also the time of the hacker.

In the 1990s–2000s, international crime and frauds are developing as a result of increased international networking. Also, the technologies of the private branch exchange (PBX) and cellular phones brought with them the telecommunications defrauders and other miscreants that have increased as the technology became cheaper, more powerful, more globally connected, and more widely used, while being vulnerable to fraud-threat agent attacks.

Computer and telecommunications perpetrators of frauds generally are the same as in the past but now include more international defrauders and other miscreants.

The basic techniques used in manipulating computer and telecommunications systems that may support fraud-threat agents' attacks include:

---

[4] U.S. FBI definition.

<u>Viruses and Worms</u>: These represent a set of instructions that propagate themselves through computers and that deliberately perform functions unwanted by the user.

<u>Trojan Horse</u>: Covert placement of instructions in a program causes the computer to perform unauthorized functions but usually still allows the program to perform its intended purpose. This is the most common method used in computer-based frauds and sabotage.

<u>Trap Doors</u>: When developing large programs, programmers tend to insert debugging aids that provide breaks in the instructions for insertion of additional code and intermediate output capabilities. The design of computer operating systems attempts to prevent this from happening. Therefore, programmers insert instructions that allow them to circumvent these controls. Fraud-threat agents can take advantage of these trap doors.

<u>Salami Techniques</u>: This technique involves the theft of small amounts of assets from a large number of sources without noticeably reducing the whole. In a banking system, the amount of interest to be credited to an account is rounded off. Instead of rounding off the number, that fraction of it is credited to a special account owned by the perpetrator.

<u>Logic Bombs</u>: This computer program is executed at a specific time period or when a specific event occurs. For example, a programmer would write a program to instruct the computer to delete all personnel and payroll files if his or her name were ever removed from the file.

<u>Data Diddling</u>: This technique involves changing data before or during entry into the computer system — for example, forging or counterfeiting documents used for data entry; and exchanging valid disks and tapes with modified replacements.

<u>Scavenging</u>: This method includes obtaining information left around a computer system, in the computer room trash cans, and so on.

<u>Data Leakage</u>: Through this technique, information is removed by smuggling it out as part of a printed document, encoding the information to look like something different, and taking it from the facility.

<u>Piggybacking/Impersonation</u>: Physical access is one method used. For example, the fraud-threat agent follows someone in through a door with a badge reader; electronically uses another's user id and password to gain computer access; or taps into the terminal link of a user to cause the computer to believe that both terminals are the same person.

<u>Simulation and Modeling</u>: The computer is used as a tool or an instrument to plan or control a criminal act.

Wire Tapping: The fraud-threat agent taps into a computer's communications links to be able to read the information being transmitted between computers and between computers and terminals.

With regard to telecommunications today, the criminals use stolen authorization codes to hide illegal activities such as frauds. The majority of telecommunications frauds are accomplished using a computer as the weapon of choice. This method should come as a surprise to no one.

Phreakers (those hackers who attack telecommunications systems as their first choice) hack for active long-distance authorization codes on telecommunications switches. They also look for network access numbers, phone numbers, and other types of authorization codes. Once they enter, they may establish a fraudulent account for their use and the use of fellow phreakers. However, they are not above stealing codes from wallets and purses or perpetrating telephone scams via social engineering.

Other techniques include shoulder surfing by which defrauders watch the person using the telephone and see what numbers are being dialed. Once they obtain PINs or authorization codes, they sell them or give them to friends. Many are sold to call-sell operators, who use them to sell overseas, toll-free calls for approximately $20 per call, usually with no time limit. They also will set up independent three-way calls for the same purpose.

The four major types of telecommunications crimes/frauds taking place today are relative to: (1) computer dial-up systems, (2) cellular phones, (3) voice mail boxes, and (4) electronic mail.

Dial-ups are defined as those systems that can be accessed through a computer with a modem to a computer that has a modem. Hackers or phreakers will use a war dialer, social engineering, or other techniques to help them gain access to computers and telephone switches.

These "hack-attacks" are also perpetrated against pay phones, sometimes called "fortress fones" because of their construction. They are also called "single-slot coin telephones." These telephones are hacked to gain free long-distance calls, worldwide. Two pieces of equipment that can be used are:

- Blue Boxes, which imitate tones of telephone switching equipment, tell the switch the call was aborted, but actually allow unrestricted dialing (outward dialing); and
- Black Boxes, which tell the switch the phone is still ringing when it is not, allowing calls to go through (receive calls). In the United States possessing these boxes constitutes a felony.

Hackers and phreakers trade information via e-mail and through Web sites. They are used for trading information, such as dial-up information (e.g., user ids, passwords; credit and ATM card information), as well as how to build hacking tools (e.g., Blue Boxes).

The fraud associated with private branch exchanges alone has forced some U.S. companies into bankruptcy or out of business. Those businesses that are not prepared could face the same end — not to mention the destruction to the national economy that could be caused by these criminals or even by disgruntled employees.

Cellular phones are one of the recent types of technology that has been widely used to perpetrate frauds and other crimes. Criminals often use this tool because on many occasions the call cannot be traced back to them.

Electronic mail is the process of sending and storing written communications through computer networks. Using e-mail through such systems as Internet does provide vulnerabilities in that the true sender of the message can be disguised. Examples of such uses were discussed under the heading Financial earlier in the chapter.

The e-mail method can work well to assist in the economic sabotage of a business. In addition, because a sender's identity can be disguised, sensitive business information can be safely sent forward to an unauthorized address.

Computer and telecommunications defrauders can be organized crime members, white-collar workers, drug dealers, people in debt, people wanting revenge, greedy people — anyone, under the right circumstances.

ATM FRAUDS

In this age of information, financial institutions and their customers increasingly rely on computers and their associated technology to conduct financial transactions. One of the most popular systems is the Automatic Teller Machine (ATM).

The number of ATMs has increased rapidly in the last decade and continues to grow. Their networks are evolving internationally, providing ATM access to millions of people throughout the world.

With the increase in computers, networks, and ATMs comes an increase in criminals who take advantage of this new technology for personal gain. Therefore, the access to ATMs internationally causes more criminals to be able to access more systems from more locations. Also in wide use is the Electronic Funds Transfer System (EFTS), a computerized system that affects the transfer of information necessary to conduct financial transactions.

When we talk about ATM frauds, we are talking about a crime, whether prosecuted or not, that would *not* have occurred but for the presence of the ATM system.

Two basic types of complaints can be indicators of fraud: (1) customer-initiated and (2) bank-initiated.

The customer-initiated complaints include the following:

1. Unauthorized withdrawals where the customer claims the debits were not authorized.
2. Shortage of dispensing funds from the ATM where the customer claims there is a discrepancy in the amount requested from the ATM and the amount that the customer received.
3. Customer claims that the amount deposited was not credited to the customer's account.
4. Customer claims that the amount received was less than the amount posted on the monthly statement.
5. Customer claims that the deposit credited to the account was incorrect.
6. Other claims that are customer–initiated.

The bank-initiated complaints include the following:

1. Bank claims that the check deposited is uncollectible.
2. Bank personnel open the deposit envelope only to discover nothing inside.
3. The deposited checks were stolen or were fraudulent checks.
4. The customer initiated a withdrawal that caused an overdraft.
5. Other claims that are bank-initiated.

Once these complaints are made, it is sometimes difficult to determine who is at fault, and because the banks generally want to maintain good public relations with their customers and the community, they usually assume the customer is being truthful — unless proven otherwise.

Potentially fraudulent incidents can be divided into two basic categories: withdrawal-related and deposit-related.

Withdrawal-related incidents include:

1. The customer's ATM card was lost or stolen.
2. The customer made the withdrawal, but didn't remember it at the time.
3. The customer made the withdrawal with the intent to defraud the bank.
4. The ATM system malfunctioned, causing the error.

Deposit-related incidents include:

1. The customer deposited an empty envelope in the ATM.
2. The deposit was made into the wrong account.
3. The deposit was different from that keyed into the ATM.
4. The deposit was different from that noted on the deposit envelope.
5. The customer deposited a stolen or fraudulent check.
6. The customer deposited an uncollectible check.
7. There was confusion and no error existed.

8.   The bank posted the incorrect amount.
9.   The bank posted the deposit to the wrong account.
10.   A person other than the customer made a bad deposit.

Lost or stolen ATM cards are the biggest problem for both customers and banks. It is also the most common method for perpetrating a fraud, or at least claiming that is the reason for the discrepancies in the customer's account. The ATM card's major problem is their theft, followed by lost cards and the customer's claim that he or she never received the cards through the mail system.

Most cards that are lost or stolen are in the home, followed by the retail store, car, place of employment, the street, school, and miscellaneous other locations.

Most of the stolen cards are not the target of the thief but are located in the customer's wallet or purse, which is the thief's target. Unless it is an organized ATM and credit card criminal ring, the thief does not usually target the ATM card itself.

When a customer loses possession of his card, the time it takes for that loss to be discovered plays a crucial role in whether or not that card will be used for fraudulent purposes. Another critical factor is the location of the loss and whether or not the PIN was also compromised. If the card is lost in a high-crime area, one can almost certainly assume that the card will be used to attempt to perpetrate a fraud. Many customers choose not to remember, or cannot remember, their PIN; therefore, they write it down in a convenient location — on the card itself!

Studies have shown that potentially fraudulent withdrawals can, and are, made by different categories of people, including the customer, his or her spouse or children, a boyfriend or girlfriend, another relative, or someone not related to the customer, but known to the customer, such as a neighbor.

When analyzing the potentially fraudulent incident, it should first be determined whether or not there was a loss, a customer loss or a bank loss. or whether both the customer and bank suffered a loss. This finding is important because if there was no loss, then the problem is less serious and may lead to identifying a problem in the process rather than determining that a fraud has taken place.

It has been noted that the bank denies customer claims for one or more of the following reasons:

1.   The customer withdraws the claim.
2.   The customer was confused and after discussions with banking officials determines the claim was not valid.
3.   The customer still has his ATM card in his possession.
4.   The customer gave his PIN to another.
5.   The customer claimed the PIN was protected and was still in possession of his card.

6.   The customer cannot or refuses to provide details relative to the loss or transaction.
7.   The bank does not have any record of the transaction.
8.   Other miscellaneous reasons.

What are some of the vulnerabilities or weaknesses in the ATM system that makes fraud possible? The following are a few of the most common ones:

1.   The account was established with intent to defraud.
2.   The ATM card was stolen from a vendor, processing center, or storage.
3.   The ATM card and/or PIN was stolen through the mail system.
4.   The ATM card was stolen from the mailbox.
5.   Cash or checks were stolen from the deposit envelope.
6.   The ATM card was not protected from family or friends.
7.   The customer misrepresented himself.
8.   An active ATM card was accidentally left in the machine.
9.   The customer deposited an empty envelope.
10.   The customer deposited a fraudulent check.
11.   The customer made an offline overdraft.
12.   The customer falsely reported a transaction problem.
13.   A physical attack was made on the ATM.
14.   A robbery took place at or near the ATM.
15.   There was a wiretap on communications links.
16.   Manipulation of the ATM and/or its system software took place.
17.   Theft of account information occurred.
18.   Account and/or transaction information was manipulated.
19.   Other miscellaneous items.

As the improvement and use of computers and telecommunications systems increase, one can expect more threats from sophisticated, international defrauders and other criminals. The technology defrauder (techno-defrauder) of the future not only has the potential to steal great amounts of money through the weak systems, but also the opportunity to blackmail companies with the destruction of their automated information, not to mention sophisticated terrorist threats.

Note: the information on ATM Fraud was taken from several old U.S. government documents no longer available and whose sources have been lost, as well as the author's personal experiences.

CLICK FRAUD

Click fraud[5] occurs in pay per click online advertising when a person, an automated script, or a computer program imitates a legitimate user

---

[5] http://en.wikipedia.org/wiki/Click_fraud.

of a Web browser clicking on an ad for the purpose of generating a charge per click without having actual interest in the target of the ad's link. Click fraud is the subject of some controversy and increasing litigation owing to the advertising networks being a key beneficiary of the fraud whether they like it or not.

Use of a computer to commit this type of Internet fraud is a felony in many jurisdictions, for example, as covered by Penal Code 502 in California in the United States and the Computer Misuse Act 1990 in the United Kingdom.

Click fraud has brought arrests with regard to malicious clicking in order to deplete a competitor's advertising budget.

In 2004, a California man created a software program that he claimed could let spammers defraud Google out of millions of dollars in fraudulent clicks. Authorities said he was arrested while trying to blackmail Google for $150,000 to hand over the program.[6]

According to the Click Fraud Network (CFN), "the costs for pay-per-click search advertising have skyrocketed. Click fraud is a significant problem that needs to be addressed. Over 70% of search advertisers are worried about this threat to search campaign ROI" (Return on Investments).[7]

The CFN identified five signs of click fraud:

1. Your pay-per-click campaign costs are continuing to rise while your online sales are not meeting expectations.
2. Your conversion rate for paid search is lower than the conversion rate for your free listings.
3. The cost-per-click for each of your best performing search terms has been steadily increasing.
4. You suspect your competitors are deliberately driving up your costs by generating fraudulent clicks.
5. You do not have a tool in place that is specifically designed to catch click fraud.

Click fraud is a perfect example of a scheme that could not have been perpetrated in the past. The primary reason is that the technology was not

---

[6] Ibid.

[7] http://www.catchclickfraud.com/?campaign=google&adgroup=CCF.

available or was being used in such a manner that could not even provide for the idea of such a fraud scheme.

This is also an example of why every corporate anti-fraud program must provide processes to keep up with high-technology developments, new fraud schemes, and also brainstorming sessions to identify ways to perpetrate new frauds. Based on the information developed, the anti-fraud program would then be updated to provide defenses against such attacks even before some fraud-threat agents tried such attacks.

CLIP-ON FRAUD[8]

Tele-defrauders and other criminals are always looking for innovative ways to steal telephone service. They are driven by the free services and by the prospects of the profit to be derived from the illegal activity. A vast majority of tele-abuse is committed through Customer Premise Equipment. Defrauders and other miscreants will continue to take advantage of the vulnerabilities of unsecured PBXs and communications networks.

Although it is essential that network risk management strategies continually be considered, let's not forget some of the old and tried fraud methods. Clip-on fraud, which was prominent in the 1970s and ebbed in the 1980s, may be making a comeback. It is unknown exactly how much clip-on fraud has cost corporations, such as telecommunications corporations, but hundreds of thousands of dollars in illegal calls are currently being rung up.

Typically, the way clip-on fraud works is as follows: a tele-defrauder will attach a butt phone to the copper connectors in a "b-box," which is generally located on a sidewalk. The b-box serves as a junction for the phone lines to hundreds of homes and businesses in a particular area. Once inside the b-box, the tele-defrauder clips on to the phone lines and finds the dial tone. A newer variation of clip-on fraud involves the use of a cordless telephone and a portable battery. After the base station is connected to the terminals in the b-box, the phone moves with the tele-defrauder, allowing him to operate in a secure location 200' to 300' from the terminal, reducing the possibility of detection. In more sophisticated cases, the phone line's dial tone is forwarded to a nearby pay phone. In either scenario, after having established a base of operation, the call-sell operation begins where people line up to pay for calls.

The vast majority of clip-on fraud cases have occurred in Southern California with its vast immigrant population. The tele-defrauders have a

---

[8] Information based on a discussion between the author and Jerry Swick, former senior investigator — MCI and retired Los Angeles Police Department Lieutenant, Computer Crime Unit.

ready market of people wanting to make inexpensive international calls to their friends and families. This fraud occurs primarily on the weekends in light industrial or commercial areas.

Clip-on fraud activity shows up as direct dial calls on the customers' bills. When the customers receive their bill, they are confused and do not realize they have been victimized. A company in Los Angeles racked up more than $30,000 in fraudulent long-distance calls not realizing that tele-defrauders clipped on to their phone lines from a b-box located blocks from their location. Moreover, to make matters worse, the company's ability to conduct business was affected because their lines were tied up. It is important to note that the FCC has ruled that clip-on fraud that can be proved to be on the local exchange carrier's end of the demarcation line is the responsibility of the local exchange carrier (LEC). This ruling establishes an important precedent when trying to resolve billing issues.

Clip-on fraud is a complicated problem and is not easily detected. The users and carriers are at risk and should consider some basic security measures. The LECs are upgrading security at the b-boxes in the affected areas. Monitoring for suspicious activity on the network and international call blocking are among the practical attempts to get a handle on the problem.

Most importantly, users should check monthly bills for any unauthorized calls. It is clear that no one solution will prevent clip-on fraud from occurring. A company should tailor security measures to the way they conduct business, as what works for one may not work for all. A collaborative effort on the part of both local and long-distance carriers as well as the customer is very important.

When developing your corporate anti-fraud program, be sure to look at the various computer and telecommunications schemes to determine which ones may apply to your corporation. Then ensure that your anti-fraud program includes controls and other defenses in place to mitigate the risk of such fraud-threat agent attacks. This would include an evaluation of the corporate processes in place in dealing with the uses of these technologies.

SECURITIES FRAUDS

Securities fraud (e.g., stock fraud) affects many corporations and obviously their owners, the corporate owners (stockholders).

Since the Crash of 1929, securities fraud has affected the average investor more and more. Retirees, single parents, and people saving for their children's educations lose their life savings to fly-by-night con men. . . . What is securities fraud? In most cases, it's nothing more than stealing. Sure, the securities laws contain a more technical definition. But

*when investors are enticed to part with their money based on untrue state-
ments, it's securities fraud — and it's illegal.*[9]

The schemes to inflate or deflate stock prices for personal or corporation gain is not new. However, such schemes seemed to have increased
during the last years of the twentieth century and into the twenty-first
century.

There have been security frauds related to "penny stocks," hedge
funds, mutual funds, and the like. The schemes and actions taken against
them are too numerous to mention here. As with all fraud schemes, by
using an Internet search engine one can find numerous sites that discuss
this fraud scheme as well as many more that have not been mentioned in
this chapter.

EMPLOYMENT APPLICATION FRAUDS

Today's job searchers must aggressively compete for jobs. This fierce competition pits applicant against applicant, with each applicant's formal
education and experience being the baseline for qualifying for a job
interview.

With such fierce competition, many applicants falsify their experiences and education, sometimes claiming to have a graduate degree when
they do not. The applicant hopes that the corporation does not have a
policy with related procedures and processes in place to verify their education and experience claims.

If your corporation does not have such a process and one that can be
considered incorporated into an anti-fraud program, you do so at your
corporation's peril. Think about it. If the employee will falsify such records
and rationalize it, how strong are their moral and ethical beliefs to stop
them from perpetrating additional frauds on the corporation and in doing
so being able to rationalize it?

One security professional at a major international corporation, who
had a system in place to interview an applicant's character references,
check credit records; and verify previous employment and education,
stated that about 15% of all applicants included false information on their
application (personal interview with author).

IDENTITY THEFT SCAMS

We have heard the many horror stories about identify thefts and identity
scams. Therefore, there is little need to discuss them in depth in this

---

[9] http://www.fool.com/specials/2000/sp000223fraud.htm.

chapter. However, to make the point that fraud-threat agents are continuously trying various old and new fraud schemes to separate people and corporations from their assets, the following vignette is offered:

A new identity theft scam is being perpetrated on unsuspecting victims. In this scam, the scammer calls the residence or office number of the victim and identifies him/herself as an officer or employee of the local court of jurisdiction. The scammer announces to the victim that he/she has failed to report for jury duty, and that a bench warrant was issued against them for their arrest. The victim's reaction is one of shock and surprise, which places them at an immediate disadvantage and thus much more susceptible to the scam. The victim will rightly deny knowledge of any such claim, that no jury duty notification was ever received.

The scammer shifts into high gear, reassuring the victim of the possibility this is all "just a misunderstanding" or "some sort of clerical error" that can be straightened out on the phone. All they need to do is "verify" their information with a few simple questions. Any reluctance on the victim's part and the scammer will threaten that the failure to provide the information will result in an immediate execution of the arrest warrant.

The scammer obtains names, social security numbers, and dates of birth, and will solicit credit card or bank account numbers claiming these will be used by their credit bureau to "verify" the victim's identity. Family members who receive these calls are especially vulnerable to coercion. Threats against the victim's career, should he/she be arrested and now have a criminal record, are frightening and persuasive.[10]

Although such a scheme may not have direct implications for the corporation, as with other more personal-related schemes, such attacks may cause employees to consider perpetrating frauds against the corporation to recoup their losses. Often they see no way out other than to take such action. They may also do so out of fear that their corporation may be notified and consider them a "security risk" and mark them for a layoff at the first opportunity.

If the employee were to bring his or her problems to someone in the corporation, what would be the reaction of your corporation? How would that reaction impact the corporation's protection of assets and the anti-fraud program?

"NIGERIAN SCAM"

The Scam operates as follows: the target receives an unsolicited fax, email, or letter . . . containing either a money laundering or other illegal proposal OR you may receive a Legal and Legitimate business proposal

---

[10] The author received this via email and the sender wanted to remain anonymous.

by normal means. Common variations on the Scam include "overinvoiced" or "double invoiced" oil or other supply and service contracts where your Bad Guys want to get the overage out of Nigeria (Classic 419); crude oil and other commodity deals (a form of Goods and Services 419); a "bequest" left you in a will (Will Scam 419); "money cleaning" where your Bad Guy has a lot of currency that needs to be "chemically cleaned" before it can be used and he needs the cost of the chemicals (Black Currency 419); "spoof banks" where there is supposedly money in your name already on deposit; "paying" for a purchase with a check larger than the amount required and asking for change to be advanced (cashier's check and money order 419); fake lottery 419; chat room and romance 419 (usually coupled with one of the other forms of 419); employment 419 (including secret shopper 419); and ordering items and commodities off "trading" and "auction" sites on the web and then cheating the seller. The variations of Advance Fee Fraud (419) are very creative and virtually endless, so do not consider the above as an all-inclusive list!

At some point, the victim is asked to pay up front an Advance Fee of some sort, be it an "Advance Fee", "Transfer Tax", "Performance Bond", or to extend credit, grant COD privileges, send back "change" on an overage cashier's or money order, whatever. If the victim pays the Fee, there are often many "Complications" which require still more advance payments until the victim either quits, runs out of money, or both. If the victim extends credit on a given transaction etc. he may also pay such fees ("nerfund" etc), and also stiffed for the Goods or Service with NO Effective Recourse.

Quoted from http://home.rica.net/alphae/419coal/. See that site for more details.

This fraud scheme has been around for some time, but it is interesting to look at all its many recent "variations on a theme." It began in the early 1990s in West Africa by miscreants there who began by sending out about 30,000 letters a week. They identified their potential fraud victims through country telephone books. It has gotten so bad now that this fraud scheme has gone from letters to faxes to e-mails. The Criminal Code in Nigeria identified this scheme as a fraud under Law 419, the so-called 419 scheme — taking money under false pretenses.

For some of the victims the old adage "If it is too good to be true, it usually is" never crossed their minds as they accepted the offers. At least three victims were reportedly murdered when they went to Nigeria to collect their money.

This "419" fraud scheme is somewhere between Nigeria's third to fifth largest industry! It apparently all began in the 1980s–1990s when the Nigerian economy collapsed and some out of luck people turned to this fraud, also known as an Advanced Fee Fraud. It has grown to such a large global scale that the U.S. Secret Service set up a task force in Lagos in 1995 mostly to address the issues associated with this scam. Some of these fraudsters have since moved on to drug trafficking.

This is one type of fraud that leads to the death of its victim, and obviously this type of scheme should be part of a corporate anti-fraud program and be included in the fraud awareness briefings to employees. After all, many of these e-mails are received at work. Furthermore, the protection of corporate assets includes corporate employees as one of the corporation's most valuable asset groups.

The number of e-mails sent out relative to this type of fraud can be done easily and cheaply from anywhere in the world to anyone in the world. As a result of improved Internet and e-mail technologies, the defrauders no longer even need to pay for stamps or long-distance telephone calls to fax machines around the world.

ACCOUNTING FRAUD SCHEMES

There are many type of accounting fraud schemes.[11] Following are just some of them that may apply to your corporation and must be considered in any successful corporate anti-fraud program:

On-Book Frauds

On-book frauds are those that occur within a corporation or other entity. It includes illicit payments or activities that are recorded, generally in some disguised manner, in the corporation's regular books and records. Some examples include payments to a phony vendor generated by fictitious charges to travel, entertainment, or other miscellaneous accounts.

On-book frauds are normally detected at the point of payment. For example, if a payment is made to a fictitious vendor, the fraud might be discovered by examining the addresses of all vendors. The address for a fictitious vendor may match up with either a post office box or an employee's address.

Off-Book Frauds

Off-book frauds normally occur outside the accounting mainstream and, therefore, no audit trail is likely to exist. Generally, for an off-book fraud to occur, the corporation usually has unrecorded vendor rebates or significant cash sales.

---

[11] Some of this information was provided by ACFE as incorporated into their training courses, and is stated here with their permission, as well as U.S. government anti-fraud courses and the author's personal investigative experiences.

Some examples of off-book frauds include bribery and kickbacks. Off-book frauds are typically proved at the point of receipt; that is, the initial "red flag" will appear with regard to the receipt of illicit funds. For example, if an employee has suddenly purchased a new car and a new home, but the employee's salary has not changed, then one might conclude that the employee has received wealth from an outside source. If there is no logical explanation for the increased wealth, and irregularities are suspected, further investigation may be recommended to determine the source of the possible outside income.

Cash

Cash is the focal point of many accounting entries. Cash, both on deposit in banks and petty cash, can be misappropriated through many different schemes that include:

— Skimming
— Voids/Under-rings
— Swapping checks for cash
— Alteration of cash receipt tapes
— Fictitious refunds and discounts
— Journal entries
— Kiting

Skimming

Skimming is the process by which cash is removed from the entity before the cash is recorded in the accounting system. This is an off-book scheme; receipt of the cash is never reported to the entity. A related type of scheme is to ring up a sale for less than the actual sale amount. (The difference between the actual sale and the amount on the cash register tape can then be diverted.) This is of particular concern in retail operations (for example, fast food restaurants) in which much of the daily sales are paid by cash, and not by check or credit card.

Voids/Under-Rings

There are three basic voids/under-ring schemes.

- The first is to record a sale/cash receipt and then void the same sale, thereby removing the cash from the register.
- The second, and more common, variation is to purchase merchandise at unauthorized discounts.
- The third scheme, which is a variation of the unauthorized discount, is to sell merchandise to a friend or co-conspirator utilizing the

employee's discount. The co-conspirator then returns the merchandise for a full refund, without regard to the original discount.

Swapping Checks for Cash

One common method in which an employee can misappropriate cash is to exchange his or her own check for cash in the cash register or cash drawer. Periodically, a new check is written to replace the old check. This process can be continued such that, on any given day, there is a current check for the cash removed. This is a form of unauthorized borrowing from the company. Obviously, if it is the company policy that cash drawers or registers must be reconciled at the conclusion of each day and turned over to a custodian, then this fraud scheme is less likely to be committed. However, if personnel are allowed to keep their cash drawers and only remit the day's receipts, then this method of unauthorized borrowing is allowed to continue.

Alteration of Cash Receipts Documentation

A lack of segregation of duties can create an opportunity for that employee to misappropriate company funds. For example, if the same person is responsible for both collecting and depositing the cash receipts, then this person has the ability to remove funds from the business for his or her own personal use and conceal such theft through the deposits. This is often the case in smaller organizations in which there are few personnel to divide the daily operations between. A variation of this scheme is to mutilate or destroy the cash receipt documentation in order to thwart any attempt to reconcile the cash deposited with the cash receipts.

Fictitious Refunds and Discounts

Fictitious refunds are those in which the employee enters a transaction as if a refund were given; however, no merchandise is returned, or no discount is approved, which substantiates the refund or discount. The employee misappropriates funds equal to the fictitious refund or discount. This scheme is most prevalent in the retail/merchandise industry.

Journal Entries

Unauthorized journal entries to cash are not as common as the preceding schemes. This type of scheme may be easier to detect because its method of concealment is more obvious. The typical journal entry scheme involves fictitious entries to conceal the theft of cash. If the financial statements are not audited or reviewed, this scheme is relatively easy to employ. However, for larger businesses with limited access to journal entries, this concealment method may be more difficult to use. Generally, fraud schemes that involve journal entries to cash are more likely in financial institutions where there are numerous, daily entries to the cash account.

Kiting

Kiting is the process whereby cash is recorded in more than one bank account, but in reality, the cash is either nonexistent or is in transit. Kiting schemes can be perpetrated using one bank and more than one account or between several banks and several different accounts. Although banks generally have a daily report that indicates potential kiting schemes, experience has shown that they are somewhat hesitant to report the scheme until such time as the balance in their customers' accounts is zero.

There is one important element common to check kiting schemes: all kiting schemes require that banks pay on unfunded deposits. This is not to say that all payments on unfunded deposits are kiting schemes, but rather, that all kiting schemes require that payments be made on unfunded deposits. In other words, if a bank allows its customers to withdraw funds on deposits on which the bank has not yet collected the cash, then kiting schemes are possible. In today's environment whereby customers are utilizing wire transfers, kiting schemes can be perpetrated very quickly and in very large numbers.

Accounts Receivable — Four Basic Schemes

There are four basic accounts receivable schemes:

— Lapping
— Fictitious sales with corresponding accounts receivable
— Diversion of payments on old written-off accounts
— Borrowing against accounts receivable

Lapping

Lapping is the recording of payment on a customer's account sometime after the payment has been received. The term lapping is used to describe a method of concealing a defalcation, wherein cash received from a customer is originally misappropriated by the employee, and, at a later date, cash received from another customer is credited to the first customer's account.

The second customer's account is credited still later by cash received from a third customer. This delay of payment applications (credits) continues until it is detected, the cash is restored, or it is covered up by credit to the proper customer and a fictitious charge to operating accounts.

The basic lapping scheme operates as follows: the employee has misappropriated company funds through customer A's account (for example, by diverting a cash payment or issuing a refund payable to the employee). In order to conceal the misappropriation, the employee must now record payments to customer A's account. When customer B makes a payment, the employee posts the payment to customer A's account. When customer C makes a payment, the employee posts it to customer B's account, and so on. Often the employee will falsify documents to conceal the misappropriation of the funds in a lapping scheme.

Fictitious Accounts Receivable

Generally, the motive for adding fictitious accounts receivable to the records is to disguise fictitious sales. There are two primary motives for fictitious accounts receivable:

— Meet sales quotas, or "window-dressing" the company
— Receive sales-based compensation

Diversion of Payments on Old Written-Off Accounts

Another internal fraud scheme in the accounts receivable is the diversion of payments on old or slow-paying accounts. In this scheme, once an account has been written off, the employee has the opportunity to collect the receivable and divert the funds to himself or herself, because companies typically do not keep track of old, written-off accounts receivable.

Often old accounts receivable are assigned to a collection agency for collecting. These agencies typically are paid on a percentage of the collected amounts. Fraud schemes can be perpetrated by these collection agencies if the company does not monitor the method by which the agency receives old accounts and the collection process itself.

The assignor company needs to assure itself that the collection agency is being assigned only truly old accounts and not good accounts that can reasonably be expected to pay within the normal course of business. In addition, the company needs to be sure that the collection agency cannot compromise the indebtedness such that collections are not reported to the company. This would allow the collection agency to compromise indebtedness for its own collection and not remit amounts owed the company.

Borrowing Against Accounts Receivable

Infrequently, employees will use the company's accounts receivable as collateral for their own personal loans. This is similar to schemes in which employees use the company's investments for the same purpose. This scheme is described in more detail in another subsection of the present work.

BRIBERY AND CORRUPTION

When talking about bribery and corruption (e.g., illegal gratuity), we are talking about giving or receiving (or offering or soliciting) something of value in order to influence some official act. The illegal gratuity is basically giving or receiving (or offering or soliciting) something of value for performing some official act.

There is also the fraud scheme associated with kickbacks — giving or receiving anything of value to influence a business decision, without the employer's knowledge or consent. The scheme is also known as commercial bribery.

CONFLICTS OF INTEREST

Conflict of interest schemes are related, for example, to a corporate employee taking an interest in a transaction that can be or is adverse to the interest of the corporation or other entity. These conflicts of interest may result in fraud schemes associated with:

— Gifts, travel, and entertainment
— Cash payments
— Checks and other financial instruments
— Hidden interests
— Loans
— Payment of credit card bills
— Transfers at other than fair market value
— Promises of favorable treatment

PURCHASING — FOUR BASIC CATEGORIES

There are four basic categories concerning fraud schemes related to purchasing:

1. Fictitious invoices
2. Overbilling
3. Checks payable to employees, including duplicate payments
4. Conflicts of interest

Fictitious Invoices

Fictitious invoices are invoices that are not represented by a legitimate sale and purchase (e.g., a vendor that does not exist).

Overbilling

Overbilling is a fraud scheme concerning the submission of an artificially inflated bill that has been submitted to the corporation for payment, with the overpayment diverted or paid to one or more employees or accomplices.

Checks Payable to Employees, Including Duplicate Payments

Checks that are payable to employees (including duplicate payments) relate to employees creating payment to themselves by circumventing the control system, such that company payments are diverted to themselves or to companies they control. In addition, duplicate payments may be submitted, and as processes are not set up to catch duplicates, an employee overrides the system controls. Often the person with authority to override controls is a supervisor or manager, who is in a position to defraud the corporation.

Conflicts of Interest

Conflicts of interest can occur when an employee has an economic interest in a transaction that adversely affects the company. As is true of all of these fraud schemes, several may be used simultaneously to perpetrate the fraud.

INVENTORY

Most frauds perpetrated in inventory and warehousing seem to involve:

— Theft of goods
— Personal use of goods
— Charging embezzlements to inventory

Theft of Goods

This is simple theft that can be perpetrated by an employee who has access to that inventory worth stealing. Methods include hiding the item in their clothing, placing it in garbage cans to recover later, and placing the items in other opened boxes that are being shipped out of the security enclosure. Computer software and hardware are some of the major theft items in today's modern businesses and government agencies.

Personal Use of Goods

An employee states that he or she is just going to "borrow" the item. A hand receipt is not used or tracked, and soon everyone forgets the item had been borrowed.

Charging Embezzlements to Inventory

Since inventory accounts are generally not reconciled until the end of each year, it is a simple matter to charge embezzlements to these accounts. Embezzlements are often concealed through the use of an expense or inventory account. This is because at the conclusion of each fiscal year, the expense accounts are closed to retained earnings (or fund balance).

Therefore, the audit trail becomes very obscure or even disappears at the conclusion of each year. Inventory accounts are often used as the concealment account for large embezzlements because the account balances are large enough to accommodate the entries required to conceal large losses.

INVESTMENTS AND FIXED ASSETS

Internal fraud schemes using investment assets are generally perpetrated by employees who are "borrowing" or using the asset for their personal benefit.

Investments

The three basic investment fraud schemes have to do with:

1. Use as collateral
2. Borrowing on earned interest
3. Avoidance of other losses or expenses

Use as Collateral

Using corporate assets as collateral relates to those assets used by employees who have the ability to "use" company investments without detection and can "borrow" the asset for their personal use.

Borrowing on Earned Interest

Borrowing on earned interest is a fraud scheme relating to corporations with cash on deposit. If controls are inadequate, an employee may have the ability to "borrow" the cash for personal use.

Avoidance of Other Losses or Expenses

Employees may have the ability to use company assets, in particular liquid assets, for unauthorized purposes such as to avoid other losses or expenses.

PAYROLL AND PERSONAL EXPENSES

The primary fraud schemes under payroll and personal expenses include:

— Ghost employees
— Overtime abuses
— Withholding tax schemes

Ghost Employees

Ghost employees are fictitious employees on the payroll employee list or in the payroll computerized database. Obviously, no services are received in exchange for payment to the nonexistent employee.

Overtime Abuses

Overtime abuses include such things as corporate employees charging and getting paid overtime when they did not perform the overtime work. Another type of overtime fraud scheme would be for employees to work overtime when no overtime work was required.

Withholding Tax Schemes

Withholding tax schemes include "borrowing" trust account taxes from a corporation until required for deposit. The person in the corporation that does the payroll "borrows" the money.

PROCUREMENT/CONTRACTS

One of the major and most lucrative areas for defrauders is in the procurement and contract areas.

In order to be able to bid on a contract, the bidder must be "responsible and responsive." This means that they provide a bid that addresses the contract specifications and not some they decided to make up and/or add. Furthermore, they must have the capability to actually do the work according to the contract's specifications.

There are various types of contracts, and although they all have some things in common, they also share some differences. Contracts can be fixed price, fixed price plus, cost plus, and the like.

These contracts can also cover anything and everything that a corporation wants to outsource to allegedly save money. The word "allegedly" is used here because sometimes the corporation ends up paying more for the services or products outsourced than if they did it "in-house".

Some fraud schemes include:

—   Using cheaper materials than what the contract called for.
—   Buying into a contract by providing a low bid and then coming up with ways to increase the contracts' costs and thus the defrauders' profits; for example, a painting contract in which the contractor proposes adding a sealer before painting, even though one may not be needed, nor is it in the original painting contract.
—   Not meeting contract specifications; for example, a roofing job requiring asphalt with clean rock of certain sizes being added when dirty rocks are used in sizes including those out of specifications with the contract.

Many of the procurement and fraud schemes will include other fraud schemes; for example, a construction contract's corporate inspector may receive kickbacks to look the other way when specifications are not being met.

TELEMARKETING FRAUD

When you send money to people you do not know personally or give personal or financial information to unknown callers, you increase your chances of becoming a victim of telemarketing fraud.[12]

Warning signs: What a caller may tell you:

—   "You must act 'now' or the offer won't be good."

---

[12] This scheme and subsequent schemes of this chapter are quoted from the FBI web site: http://www.fbi.gov/majcases/fraud/fraudschemes.htm.

— "You've won a 'free' gift, vacation, or prize." But you have to pay for "postage and handling" or other charges.
— "You must send money, give a credit card or bank account number, or have a check picked up by courier." You may hear this before you have had a chance to consider the offer carefully.
— "You don't need to check out the company with anyone." The callers say you do not need to speak to anyone, including your family, lawyer, accountant, local Better Business Bureau, or consumer protection agency.
— "You don't need any written information about their company or their references."
— "You can't afford to miss this 'high-profit, no-risk' offer."

ADVANCE FEE SCHEME

An advance fee scheme occurs when the victim pays money to someone in anticipation of receiving something of greater value, such as a loan, contract, investment, or gift, and then receives little or nothing in return.

The variety of advance fee schemes is limited only by the imagination of the con artists who offer them. They may involve the sale of products or services, the offering of investments, lottery winnings, "found money," or many other "opportunities." Clever con artists will offer to find financing arrangements for their clients who pay a "finder's fee" in advance. They require their clients to sign contracts in which they agree to pay the fee when they are introduced to the financing source. Victims often learn that they are ineligible for financing only after they have paid the "finder" according to the contract. Such agreements may be legal unless it can be shown that the "finder" never had the intention or the ability to provide financing for the victims.

COMMON HEALTH INSURANCE FRAUDS

Medical Equipment Fraud

Equipment manufacturers offer "free" products to individuals. Insurers are then charged for products that were not needed and/or may not have been delivered.

"Rolling Lab" Schemes

Unnecessary and sometimes fake tests are given to individuals at health clubs, retirement homes, or shopping malls and billed to insurance companies or Medicare.

Services Not Performed

Customers or providers bill insurers for services never rendered by changing bills or submitting fake ones.

Medicare Fraud

Medicare fraud can take the form of any health insurance frauds. Senior citizens are frequent targets of Medicare schemes, especially by medical equipment manufacturers who offer seniors free medical products in exchange for their Medicare numbers. Because a physician has to sign a form certifying that equipment or testing is needed before Medicare pays for it, con artists fake signatures or bribe corrupt doctors to sign the forms. Once a signature is in place, the manufacturers bill Medicare for merchandise or service that was not needed or was not ordered.

LETTER OF CREDIT FRAUD

Legitimate letters of credit are never sold or offered as investments. Legitimate letters of credit are issued by banks to ensure payment for goods shipped in connection with international trade. Payment on a letter of credit generally requires that the paying bank receive documentation certifying that the goods ordered have been shipped and are en route to their intended destination.

Letters of credit frauds are often attempted against banks by providing false documentation to show that goods were shipped when, in fact, no goods or inferior goods were shipped.

Other letter of credit frauds occur when con artists offer a "letter of credit" or "bank guarantee" as an investment wherein the investor is promised huge interest rates on the order of 100 to 300% annually. Such investment "opportunities" simply do not exist. (See Prime Bank Notes for additional information.)

PRIME BANK NOTES

International fraud artists have invented an investment scheme that offers extremely high yields in a relatively short period of time. In this scheme, they purport to have access to "bank guarantees" that they can buy at a discount and sell at a premium. By reselling the "bank guarantees" several times, they claim to be able to produce exceptional returns on investment. For example, if $10 million worth of "bank guarantees" can be sold at a

2% profit on ten separate occasions, or "traunches," the seller will receive a 20% profit. Such a scheme is often referred to as a "roll program."

To make their schemes more enticing, con artists often refer to the "guarantees" as being issued by the world's "Prime Banks," hence the term Prime Bank Guarantees. Other official sounding terms are also used such as Prime Bank Notes and Prime Bank Debentures. Legal documents associated with such schemes often require the victim to enter into nondisclosure and noncircumvention agreements, offer returns on investment in "a year and a day," and claim to use forms required by the International Chamber of Commerce (ICC). In fact, the ICC has issued a warning to all potential investors that no such investments exist.

The purpose of these frauds is generally to encourage the victim to send money to a foreign bank where it is eventually transferred to an off-shore account that is in the con artist's control. From there, the victim's money is used for the perpetrator's personal expenses or is laundered in an effort to make it disappear.

While foreign banks use instruments called bank guarantees in the same manner that U.S. banks use letters of credit to insure payment for goods in international trade, such bank guarantees are never traded or sold on any kind of market.

THE PONZI SCHEME

A Ponzi scheme is essentially an investment fraud wherein the operator promises high financial returns or dividends that are not available through traditional investments. Instead of investing victims' funds, the operator pays "dividends" to initial investors using the principal amounts "invested" by subsequent investors. The scheme generally falls apart when the operator flees with all of the proceeds or when a sufficient number of new investors cannot be found to allow the continued payment of "dividends."

This type of scheme is named after Charles Ponzi of Boston, Massachusetts, who operated an extremely attractive investment scheme in which he guaranteed investors a 50% return on their investment in postal coupons. Although he was able to pay his initial investors, the scheme dissolved when he was unable to pay investors who entered the scheme later.

PYRAMID SCHEME

Pyramid schemes, also referred to as franchise fraud, or chain referral schemes, are marketing and investment frauds in which an individual is offered a distributorship or franchise to market a particular product. The real profit is earned not by the sale of the product, but by the sale of new distributorships. Emphasis on selling franchises rather than the product eventually leads to a point where the supply of potential investors is exhausted and the pyramid collapses. At the heart of each pyramid scheme there is typically a representation that new participants can recoup their original investments by inducing two or more prospects to make the same investment. Promoters fail to tell prospective participants that this is mathematically impossible for everyone to do, since some participants drop out, while others recoup their original investments and then drop out.

CASE STUDY

If an employee came to you and stated that she had just received a strange e-mail advising her that she had the opportunity to receive millions of dollars and she thought it was too good to be true, what would you do?

Of course, depending on the contents of the e-mail, the corporate culture, and your anti-fraud program reporting requirements and follow-up actions, you might want to consider the following:

- Thank the employee for reporting the matter and advise the employee not to take any action and you will get back to her with more information.
- See if you can trace the e-mail to the sender.
- Do an Internet search for that and similar fraud schemes that may apply, and collect all pertinent information.
- Contact local, state, or federal law enforcement authorities who work on fraud matters and determine if they have heard of such e-mails being circulated.
- If so, obtain full details from them.
- As applicable,
  - Update the anti-fraud program database of fraud schemes.
  - Update the employee awareness briefing based on the collected information.
  - Send out an e-mail broadcast fraud alert so that all corporate employees are aware of this fraud scheme and what to do about it.
  - Update fraud scheme defenses and be sure that controls are in place to stop such e-mails (e.g., firewall, e-mail filters block e-mails from this address).
  - Update the fraud-reporting metrics management system to show this employee's reporting of the fraud scheme. (See Chapter 13) as an indication of the cost-benefits of an anti-fraud program awareness briefing policy.
  - Contact the employee and thank the employee for her conscientious efforts.

SUMMARY

Fraud schemes of one kind or another have been around since the first human tried to obtain the assets of another through fraudulent means. The days of the snake oil salesmen of the Wild West continue. However, today's fraud-threat agents are much more sophisticated, as are their fraud schemes. They are also more global, and the successfully perpetrated frauds often provide higher rewards than ever before, thanks to modern technology such as the cheap use of the Internet.

One must be ever-alert for new fraud schemes and learn the lessons of others who have fallen victim to the fraud schemes of old, as well as those of today. A database of fraud schemes should be part of any anti-fraud program.

One thing about fraud schemes, as the old adage states: "Where there is a will, there is a way"! It is often amazing how ingenious defrauders are at coming up with new fraud schemes.

One must also begin now to establish an aggressive and proactive anti-fraud program that will incorporate assets defenses and controls in order to protect the corporate assets from future fraud scheme attacks.

7

Fraud Cases and Analyses — Learning by Example

INTRODUCTION

This chapter presents actual fraud or fraud-related cases along with the author's commentary. Some of the cases presented are new, and others are a year or two old. However, don't let their dates of occurrence fool you, as many are still being tried today, albeit maybe with a little different "twist." The point is to understand the modus operandi, try to theorize the defrauders' rationales and profiles, and then learn from them.

Once you become familiar with the fraud schemes of Chapter 6 and read through the actual fraud cases discussed in this chapter, you should be in a better position to move on to Section II of this book, which discusses the establishment and management of a corporate anti-fraud program, based on the fraud-threat agents' mindsets and attack schemes.

Many of the cases cited are related to our use of high technology. That is understandable as today's and definitely tomorrow's high-technology environment provides the ability to perpetrate old fraud schemes in a new environment with new tools and to perpetrate new fraud schemes in this our modern information-driven and information-dependent world supported by the microprocessor-based high technology.

ACTUAL FRAUD AND FRAUD-RELATED CASES

The cases provided are in no particular order of importance and are used to provide a general awareness of the "talent" of various defrauders and/or some of their modus operandi.

It is important to remember that we know of these fraud cases because they were <u>not</u> successful in that someone found out about them. As Honore de Balzac so correctly stated: *The secret of a great success for which you are at a loss to account is a crime that has never been found out, because it was properly executed.*

One never knows how many successful frauds are committed around the world on a daily basis. The scary part is, of course, the fact that since they are successful, we do not know about them. Compounding this fact is the fact that most corporations and other entities have little or no formal anti-fraud program, one that is proactive and not just reactive.

PHISHERS AND TAXPAYERS

The following is an example of a fraud scheme showing another use of e-mail, Web sites, and technology to perpetrate a fraud where none was possible only a few years back.

> **A British Internet-security firm is warning people to not get hooked by an e-mail scam promising tax refunds from the U.S. Internal Revenue Service.** The e-mails, known as a "phishing" scam in technology speak, exploit a loophole allegedly built into the real IRS Web site, according to the firm, but instead of getting money back from the government, those biting on the scam could be giving away the contents of their bank accounts. . . . Phishing scams have been around for years and their success usually hinges on the perceived legitimacy of the e-mails, which often include official logos and language. Typically, they ask for personal information like Social Security or bank account numbers. Making the scam even more effective is that the address appears legitimate — an extension of the www.govbenefits.gov site — but the site is bogus.
>
> It appears real because the phishers have found a flaw in the design of the IRS Web site, one that allows them to "bounce" people to the fake site, according to Sophos, a company that tracks malicious Internet programs. . . . The IRS is contesting this claim, saying its site is completely secure. "Any Web vulnerabilities exploited by this scam are not caused by the IRS site," said an e-mail from an IRS representative, who added that no changes have been made to the site as a result of this scam. In a written statement, the IRS reminded taxpayers that it doesn't send unsolicited e-mails, it will never ask for personal or financial information via e-mail and there is no special form to obtain tax refunds.[1]

---

[1] http://edition.cnn.com/2005/TECH/internet/11/30/phishing.irs/index.html.

Commentary: A typical government or corporate response is to say their site is "completely secure." This is impossible! No Web site and nothing on the Internet can be guaranteed to be safe. Why is that? It is because there are inherent vulnerabilities in high-technology hardware and software. After all, that should be expected since they were developed by human beings and human beings are far from perfect. Should we expect otherwise from man-made things?

A good point to remember is that most corporations or government agencies will never ask for personal information over the Internet. If you find one that does and it is a legitimate site, stay away from that business because they may not adequately protect vital information such as your credit card or social security number. Of course, this does not include businesses operating in a secure mode asking for your credit card information for some purchase you are making. However, even in those instances, be sure you are shopping on a legitimate site that uses encryption (e.g., see the little yellow lock on the Web site page when you are about to do business on line).

Unfortunately, even in those cases where the information seems to be secure, you have no guarantees, as some hackers have in the past broken into shopping Web sites and set up false home Web sites that collect your information and then may ask you to log in again as your information was incorrectly entered. You may think it is a typo when it is not. The second login will then take you to do the legitimate Web site.

FRAUD BY CORPORATE EXECUTIVES

Adelphia founder sentenced to 15 years[2] NEW YORK (CNN/ Money) — The founder of Adelphia Communications was sentenced Monday to 15 years in prison . . . for his role in a multibillion-dollar fraud that led to the collapse of the nation's fifth-largest cable company . . . deals the father and son were convicted of helped drive Adelphia into bankruptcy. . . . The sentencing comes as prosecutors have achieved some big wins in their fight against corporate corruption. Three days ago a New York state jury convicted former Tyco CEO Dennis Kozlowski and CFO Mark Swartz on charges that they looted the manufacturing conglomerate of $600 million.

In March, a federal jury in New York found former WorldCom CEO and co-founder Bernard Ebbers guilty on charges related to an $11 billion accounting scandal at the telecommunications giant, now known as MCI. WorldCom filed the largest bankruptcy in U.S. history just a

---

[2] http://money.cnn.com/2005/06/20/news/newsmakers/rigas_sentencing/index.htm?cnn=yes

month after Adelphia went bankrupt. . . . conspiring to hide $2.3 billion in Adelphia debt, stealing $100 million, and lying to investors about the company's financial condition.[3]

Commentary: In the United States and other "modern" nation-states, we have seen the rise of massive amounts of frauds perpetrated by corporate executives. It seems to be a combination of quests for more power, selfish greed, and little regard for the impact of their massive frauds on the stockholders and employees, many of whom have lost all their savings, retirement opportunities, and such.

Some of the frauds are made possible because there are times when not only collusion occurs, thereby negating many controls in place based on separation of functions, but also perhaps due to more and more complicated regulations. Furthermore, new fraud-related laws make new fraud crimes possible. As legislatures such as the U.S. Congress seem to be more and more involved in micro-legislating, the laws seem to become more complicated and full of ambiguities.

Such types of frauds by corporate executive management are very difficult to deter and detect. After all, when you have the combination to the corporate assets safe, how can an accountant, auditor, chief security officer (CSO), or others identify such frauds and take action to stop them? Who wants to be the first to accuse a CEO or other member of the corporate executive management team of being defrauders?

If you do so, you do so at your personal and professional peril. For even if you are right, as some whistleblowers have found out, you will eventually be not only out of work but maybe even sued by these powerful defrauders. After all, they have massive amounts of funds to use for their lawyers. Do you? Even if they don't have a chance to win, they will make you pay a financial price as well as add massive amounts of stress to your life and the lives of your loved ones.

As for new employment, good luck! Other managers will not hire you just because you are a very honest and brave person. No, they will not hire you because they are concerned that you may again blow the whistle based on some of their actions, even if they can be legitimately explained. Here

---

[3] All individuals listed in this chapter were listed as they appeared in the footnoted and edited article. However, the readers must understand that this does not imply that they have been finally found guilty as there are appeals that take place and the persons cited may actual by subsequently be found not guilty. The information provided in this chapter is for education purposes only so that the CSO or other individual who wants to build a anti-fraud program can learn for these cases and ensure that their anti-fraud program incorporates "lessons-learned" from these cases in the form of controls and other defensive measures as well as proactive measures.

in the United States, we compound the reporting dilemma as we are often brought up being told "Don't be a fink!" "Don't be a tattletale!"

So, you may be right, but you will pay a price. If you have bills and family, and want your current career and profession to continue and not have to move to a deserted island and eat raw fish and drink coconut milk the rest of your life, you must really think about your actions. That is a very sad thing to have to state, but that is life in today's environment — and maybe always was and will be.

FOREIGN EXCHANGE TRADING FRAUD

Allied probes $750 million fraud . . . LONDON, England (CNN) — Allied Irish Banks has suspended nearly all foreign exchange trading and has opened an investigation into a suspected fraud totalling an estimated $750 million at a U.S. subsidiary, . . . an American in his 40s who had worked at the bank for seven years. "Allied Irish Banks, p.l.c. is undertaking a full investigation into foreign exchange trading operations at the Baltimore headquarters of its U.S. subsidiary Allfirst," a news release from AIB said on Wednesday. "This decision follows the uncovering by Allfirst management of suspected fraudulent activities by one trader who has since failed to report for work."

The married father has been a "respected member of his local community,". . . . "He has never given anybody any reason to believe from his performance and his job until now that he was an unusual individual in any way." Indications of suspected fraudulent activity in the foreign exchange trading area at Allfirst were discovered during a management review within the treasury division of the subsidiary, . . . the losses arose on a series of unauthorised transactions in a number of foreign currency contracts. . . . the alleged fraud as "complex," where the trader required varying amounts of cash for different reasons at different times of the year. Alarm bells sounded over sums. . . . Ultimately, it was the increase in the amount of cash that he was requiring that set off the alarm bells.[4]

Commentary: Such scams have been around for some time. One of the common, yet unexpected, aspects of such frauds is identifying who the fraud-threat agents are. For example, in this case it was a "married father and a respected member of the community." This points out that anyone can be a defrauder, even those who appear to be good workers. A potential fraud indicator is a person who seems to always be working late, on weekends and doesn't take vacations. In one such case, the "sweet, little old

---

[4] CNN televised story—2002.

lady" who worked for a small company doing their accounting functions and of course with no separation of functions defrauded the company out of more than $1,000,000 over 30 years!

As an anti-fraud leader, beware of good workers! Maybe a sad thing to say but history has shown that many defrauders appear to be the hardest workers, coming in early, staying late, and so forth.

KATRINA WASTE AND FRAUDS

Auditors: Katrina waste could top $2 billion: Story Highlights

- Waste after Hurricane Katrina could top $2 billion, government auditors say;
- Wasteful spending already has been tabbed at $1 billion
- $500,000 worth of contracts have been awarded without little or no competition; . . . Federal investigators have already determined the Bush administration squandered $1 billion on fraudulent disaster aid to individuals after the 2005 storm. Now they are shifting their attention to the multimillion dollar contracts to politically connected firms that critics have long said are a prime area for abuse.[5]

Commentary: When anti-fraud defenses are circumvented in the name of getting aid to victims quickly, the chances for frauds naturally go up. It is a "Catch-22" for the government agencies: either respond slowly and be sure controls are in place to minimize fraud or get aid quickly to victims and worry about the potential for fraud later. It is difficult to go out for bids on contracts using generally accepted processes, including anti-fraud defenses, which are inherently slow while people are in need of immediate help.

ORGANIZED CRIME AND CYBERCRIME

Cybercrime More Widespread, Skillful, Dangerous Than Ever eWeek. com . . . malware hunters infiltrate black hat hacker forums, chat rooms and newsgroups, posing as online criminals to gather intelligence on the dramatic rise in rootkits, Trojans and botnets. . . . well-organized mobsters have taken control of a global billion-dollar crime network powered by skillful hackers and money mules targeting known software security weaknesses. . . . "There's a well-developed criminal underground market that's connected to the mafia in Russia and Web gangs and loosely affiliated mob groups around the world. They're all involved

---

[5] http://www.cnn.com/2006/US/12/26/katrina.waste.ap/index.html

in this explosion of phishing and online crime activity,". . . . Just two years after the Secret Service claimed a major success with "Operation Firewall," an undercover investigation that led to the arrest of 28 suspects accused of identity theft, computer fraud, credit card fraud and money laundering, security researchers say the mobsters are back, with a level of sophistication and brazenness that is "frightening and surreal." . . . A law enforcement official familiar with several ongoing investigations showed eWEEK screenshots of active Web sites hawking credit card numbers, Social Security numbers.[6]

Commentary: Although still slow to react and especially now when, at least in the United States and some other nation-states, law enforcement and intelligence resources are directed primarily at antiterrorist activities, some investigative agencies are trying to stem the tide of frauds perpetrated internationally and nationally by these miscreants.

SECURITIES FRAUD IN CYBERSPACE

L.A. pair charged over cyberfraud . . . The FBI charges that two L.A. men artificially inflated stock price by posting false information on Internet bulletin boards. . . . Two men have been charged in federal court here with conspiracy to commit securities fraud for allegedly artificially inflating a company's stock price by posting false information about the firm in Internet bulletin boards.[7]

Commentary: The Internet has become a great and cheap tool through which rumors and other modus operandi can lead to frauds that were nonexistent a few years ago or that reflect the ability to do so on a grander scale.

COMPUTER HARD DRIVES LEAD TO FRAUDS

Dead disks yield live information . . . Identity thieves are gleaning personal information from scrapped computers. A hard drive from a personal computer that a man had thought he had disposed of properly yielded highly personal letters relating to his financial affairs including details of bank accounts and insurance claims. All of which is potential gold dust for the UK's fastest growing crime trend, identity theft. As the university's forensic team conducted the research, it peeled back the layers on the disk. Web searches, phone numbers of employees, email

---

[6] http://www.foxnews.com/story/0,2933,191375,00.html
[7] ZDNet News, December 15, 1999

conversations with family friends and details of their daughter's boy-friends — all spilled onto the university computers. There was enough data for a would-be identity thief to garner more information by ringing up those people identified and "socially engineer" more relevant details. . . . "Impersonation and bribery are used to get inside informa-tion ranging from car registration details to bank records." Being care-less with personal information also breaks the Data Protection Act, . . . a point forcibly made by a spokeswoman for the Information Commis-sioner. The company, which has a worldwide workforce of 58,000 and sales of €14.7 bn, had again disposed of hard drives from computers that contained highly detailed company information including personal details on staff payroll, internal contact details, internal planning and strategy documents, written warnings to staff plus copies of invoices and orders.[8]

Commentary: It is amazing how many people and those in responsible positions in corporations allow their computer systems to be disposed of without wiping out the data of their hard drives. This is especially impor-tant these days where the hard drives are so massive and can literally hold all the information of a corporation on one drive.

Not that many years ago, miscreants were involved in "dumpster diving" to gather corporate information. By that, I mean literally go into the trash containers outside corporations looking through the garbage for information that can help them commit identity frauds and break into computers. Now, they just have to buy or otherwise obtain the old comput-ers of corporations and get more information than they ever could have from the dumpsters.

DEBT-COLLECTING FRAUDS

Debt "counselors" hit for $100 M scam: FTC settles with agencies that promised consumers free debt counseling, but took their money any-way . . . Regulators announced settlements Wednesday with three debt-counseling agencies that they said had bilked consumers out of more than $100 million, a scam they said was becoming increasingly common. The three companies promised to help consumers manage their debts but in fact only made their problems worse, the Federal Trade Commis-sion said. Clients paid thousands of dollars to keep bill collectors at bay, but instead saw their debts, interest rates and late fees increase as the companies did little to help, . . . Some consumers were forced to declare bankruptcy when the companies told them to stop paying their

---

[8] http://technology.guardian.co.uk/weekly/story/0,,1840396,00.html

bills but then didn't negotiate on their behalf, . . . "All three companies lied about who they were, what they could do for consumers and how much they charged,". . . . The companies agreed to give back a total of more than $25 million to consumers, and two are in the process of being shut down. None of the owners face jail time as the FTC does not have criminal authority.[9]

Commentary: As modern-day consumers continue to buy, buy, buy and charge, charge, charge their goods to their multiple credit cards, some reach a point of financial crisis. One cannot expect them to be able to get out of their debts by themselves. After all, they didn't have enough sense to use financial planning; therefore, they often have little chance of knowing how to get out of debt.

These consumers are ripe for the defrauders who take advantage of their "stupidity" and their financial naiveté. Remember that these people are also desparate and are also corporate employees who may have access to valuable corporate assets.

GOVERNMENT CONTRACTING FRAUD

Defense contractor . . . paid $1 million in bribes . . . A defense contractor admitted Friday that he paid a California congressman more than $1 million in bribes in exchange for millions more in government contracts. Mitchell Wade pleaded guilty in U.S. District Court to conspiring with former Rep. to bribe the lawmaker with cash, cars and antiques, and to help him evade millions of dollars in tax liability. . . . entering his plea to charges that carry a maximum prison sentence of 20 years. . . . quit Congress last year after he pleaded guilty to taking bribes from Wade and others. Wade, former president of defense contractor. . . . in Washington, also acknowledged making nearly $80,000 in illegal campaign contributions in the names of . . . employees and their spouses to two other members of Congress, who were not identified. The lawmakers apparently were unaware the donations were illegal, according to court papers. Prosecutors also laid out a second, separate conspiracy in which Wade was alleged to have paid bribes to a Defense Department official and other employees in return for their help in awarding contracts to his company. . . . pleaded guilty to this scheme as well. The Pentagon employees were not named in court filings.[10]

Commentary: This is an old fraud and has been around for many decades. Many defrauders take advantage of government agencies due to the massive

---

[9] CNN Money, 30 March 2005; also see http://www.ftc.gov

[10] http://www.usatoday.com/news/states/2006–02–24-contractor_x.htm

amount of contracts and money that is available. Often the oversight for such contracts is handled by government employees whose salaries pale in comparison to the money being made by contractors and the money available for bribing these government employees.

In addition, many of these government employees may be overseeing numerous contracts and cannot be everywhere at once. Their lack of experience and training in how to properly do their job and how to look for fraud indicators adds to the lure of this lucrative fraud area. By the way, this also applies to other corporate employees who oversee other types of corporations and their contracts.

FRAUD-THREAT AGENTS CAN BE ANYONE IN ANY POSITION

> **Dish washer "raids USA's richest":** A trainee waiter and dish washer has been arrested for swindling millions of dollars after "cloning" the identities of 200 of America's richest people.... spent his spare time surfing the internet,... allegedly defrauding millions of dollars from some of the most protected and high-powered figures in the US.... described him as supremely talented at obtaining the credit card details and stockbroker accounts... operated a complex series of PO boxes, untraceable mobile phones and virtual voicemail services to clone the identities of 200 celebrities he picked from the Forbes magazine list of the "Richest people in America...."

> When he was eventually arrested, police found lists of home addresses, National Insurance numbers, telephone and brokerage account details and bank balances for his famous victims scrawled beside their entries in the magazine's list. He even knew the bank account passwords and mother's maiden names of some of the tycoons he targeted and had fake corporate papers, writing paper and stamps from respected financial firms.... The alarm was raised because the transfer would have put... account into debt.... Detectives investigated and found that more than 29 post office boxes had been taken out in the name of tycoons and rich stars in New York into which cash and cheques were delivered.... employed prostitutes and cab drivers to collect the fraudulent packages that were often sent to non-existent addresses.[11]

Commentary: The ingenuity of these miscreants is truly amazing at times, and one must admire their innovative approaches to committing frauds. Sometimes one wonders what such defrauders could accomplish if they

---

[11] http://www.thisislondon.com/dynamic/news/story.html?in_review_id=372288 &in_review_text_id=318092

would set their minds to honest pursuits! Never underestimate the potential for some employees or others to commit fraudulent acts based on their positions or perceived level of intelligence.

> Identity theft: Usually, a scam involves the theft and use of someone's credit card information. In more serious cases, a victim's entire identity is absconded with, and the criminal gets new credit cards and loans in the victim's name. Obviously, this can be a nightmare for the unwitting person who must deal with credit issuers and reporting agencies. . . . victims find themselves "in the position of having to prove they didn't do something."[12] *(The credit card may be a corporate or government agency credit card!)*

U.S SECURITIES AND EXCHANGE COMMISSION (SEC) FIGHTING FRAUD

SEC Conducts "Pump-And-Dump" Net Stock-Fraud Sweep . . . The Securities and Exchange Commission (SEC) today took action against 33 companies and individuals accused of engaging in "pump-and-dump" microcap stock schemes that brought in illegal profits of more than $10 million. The SEC brought the actions after conducting its fourth nationwide Internet fraud sweep, in which it searched the Internet for misleading and illegal messages on Web sites, electronic newsletters and Internet message boards touting more than 70 thinly traded microcap stocks. Pump-and-dump operators typically use such venues to generate enthusiasm for a particular small stock, which artificially inflates the shares' value. Once the stock has reached a certain valuation, the fraudsters sell off or "dump" their shares for a profit, leaving bamboozled investors holding essentially worthless stock.

The SEC said the perpetrators of the schemes targeted in its sweep pumped up the total market capitalization of their stocks by more than $1.7 billion before unloading them on the market. The commission said many of the fraud perpetrators appeared to have no securities industry experience whatsoever: one was a bus mechanic, while another turned out to be a student moonlighting as a chauffeur. Other parties implicated in the stock scam included foreign-based individuals and entities that used the Internet to reach US investors, the SEC said.[13]

---

[12] http://www.usatoday.com/tech/2001–08–03-net-dangers.htm
[13] http://findarticles.com/p/articles/mi_m0NEW/is_2000_Sept_6/ai_65024697, Newsbytes News Network, 6 September 2000.

SEC . . . action brings the total number of Internet fraud cases filed by the SEC to 180. The commission conducted previous sweeps . . . which dealt with the fraudulent touting of publicly traded companies through the Internet. . . . the SEC conducted a sweep to uncover sales of bogus securities over the Internet.[14]

Commentary: Government agencies such as the SEC are overworked, understaffed, and overwhelmed by the job they have to do when it comes to deterring and investigating potential frauds. Sadly, the matter can probably only get worse as legislative bodies seem to make more detailed and more complicated laws as frauds are discovered. The government agencies don't help as they spew out regulations by the hundreds. Add to that the ability of international fraud-threat agents to attack corporate assets anywhere in the world from anywhere in the world.

FRAUD IN SCHOOL SYSTEMS

Eleven indicted in school corruption probe . . . Eleven people, including teachers and school secretaries, were indicted Thursday on fraud and theft charges in a continuing FBI probe of corruption in the city's school system. Those indicted included three employees of the school system's credit union, accused of stealing nearly $150,000 by withdrawing money from accounts of customers who were dead or had moved. Two insurance brokers were also accused of paying kickbacks to a school system administrator in return for contracts.

More than a dozen people have pleaded guilty, or agreed to do so, to charges of fraud and bribery in various schemes that have bled millions from the city's school system, considered one of the country's worst. Twenty-four people have been indicted this year . . . indictments came days after schools Superintendent Anthony Amato announced that the system faces a multimillion dollar deficit — and blamed the deficit partly on years of theft by its workers.[15]

Commentary: If you name a business or public entity or even a job description, you will no doubt be able to find someone somewhere in one of these entities (e.g., schools) perpetrating a fraud. After all, where there are valuable assets that someone wants or wants to convert into cash, there will be

---

[14] Ibid; also see http://www.sec.gov
[15] http://www.cnn.com/2004/EDUCATION/12/17/schools.corruption.ap/index.html

a way to do it. As many rationalize; "I am not stealing from anyone, just a corporation, just a public entity. Besides, they are insured." As in the case just cited, frauds can have a devastating effect on an entity's budget. Frauds may also be perpetrated for other than financial gain, even for altruistic reasons. (e.g. The "Robin Hood" rationale.)

DEAD SOLDIERS AND E-MAIL SCAMS

U.S. warns of online schemes that make reference to Iraq: WASHINGTON (AP) — Federal authorities are investigating two e-mail scams, including one targeting families of troops killed in Iraq, that claim to be connected to the Homeland Security Department. The scams "are among the worst we have ever encountered," Michael J. Garcia, director of the department's Immigration and Customs Enforcement bureau, said Friday. Both of the online pleas for help — and money — link themselves to the bureau. In one scheme, e-mail sent to families of U.S. soldiers killed in Iraq includes a link to the bureau's Web site. The e-mail seeks to recover money from a friend of the slain soldier.

In the other, the e-mail identifies itself as being sent by a federal agent trying to track down funds looted from the Iraqi Central Bank by one of Saddam Hussein's sons. The e-mail also links to the bureau Web site and asks for confirmation of the recipient's address by urging, "There is a very important and confidential matter which I want us both to discuss."

. . . The bogus e-mails resemble the so-called "Nigerian letter." In that persistent scam, victims are told they will receive money, often from the "Government of Nigeria," after paying a fee often characterized as a bribe to that government.[16]

Commentary: All fraud-threat agents are bad; however, it seems that many sink to the bottom of the food chain. These slime bags and scum of the earth who take advantage of the families and friends of fallen soldiers should be sentenced to long prison terms, or worse sentences which I won't mention here (*Hint:* Sometimes torture is a good thing!). Their types of frauds are the most despicable of frauds.

ANOTHER EXAMPLE OF INSIDER FRAUD

Emulex Fraud Suspect Was Former Internet Wire Employee The FBI said today that the Los Angeles man arrested for posting a bogus press

---

[16] http://www.goldstarwives.org/iraq-email-scam.htm, Associated Press 18 February 2005.

release that sent shares of Emulex Corp. stock plummeting last Friday was a former employee of the Internet wire service that distributed the fraudulent information. . . . charged him with securities and mail fraud for earning more than $225,000 in short trades after sending the bogus release via e-mail to Internet Wire, his former employer. . . . investigators were able to trace the release back . . . because the e-mail included language that suggested the author had a familiarity with the procedures used at Internet Wire, and that the message represented that the company's sales department had already reviewed and approved the release. . . .

The FBI said a recording of . . . stock trading records indicate that he executed a series of short sales of 3,000 shares of Emulex stock at prices between $72 and $92 per share. During the following week, Emulex's stock prices rose to more than $100 per share. After issuing the bogus release Friday morning, the bureau said . . . executed trades to cover earlier short sales losses by buying 3,000 shares of Emulex, yielding a profit of more than $50,000. Later in the day, . . . purchased an additional 3,500 Emulex shares on a margin account at $52 per share, for a total expenditure of $180,000. Three days later, he sold those shares for a profit of $186,000.[17]

Commentary: Stock-related frauds are not only common but often cause major problems for the targeted corporations. Sometimes such frauds cause the corporation or other entity to declare bankruptcy. This type of fraud scheme has happened so often that the SEC and others have been able to more rapidly identify these frauds and are in a better position to take action faster than before, often aided by computer monitoring programs that would identify some of these types of potential fraud indicators.

The computer can be used as a weapon by defrauders, but it can also be used by investigators and others who fight fraud. Unfortunately, it seems the fraud fighters don't seem to take advantage of these high-technology tools as much as the defrauders do.

EXECUTIVE MANAGEMENT AND ACCOUNTING FRAUD

Enron's whistle blower details sinking ship: . . . Enron's most prominent whistle blower Sherron Watkins . . . described a company that increasingly became mired in accounting fraud in 2001, prompting her to send an anonymous letter to Enron founder Kenneth Lay in August warning him that the company "had a hole in the ship and we're going to sink."

---

[17] Newsbytes News Network, 31 August 2000.

Watkins, a former vice president at Enron, testified that in mid-2001 she began investigating Enron's relationship with LJM (a special purpose entity designed to take high-risk poor-performing assets off Enron's balance sheet) and was increasingly alarmed as it became apparent that the relationship didn't stand up to accounting scrutiny. . . .

She went on to predict that Enron "will implode in a wave of accounting scandals."[18]

Commentary: It is interesting to note that no matter what the government, auditing, or accounting oversight, some frauds go undetected unless a whistleblower, usually from the inside of the corporation or entity, steps forward. That takes real courage as the life of the whistleblower will change drastically and generally not for the good, when the first alarm of a potential fraud is sounded.

MERCHANDISE RECEIPT AND EXCHANGE FRAUD

Ex-White House aide admits to fraud . . . A former top White House aide who was arrested on a theft charge admitted to a store investigator he fraudulently returned merchandise that he didn't buy, according to charging documents . . . a former domestic policy adviser to President Bush, made fraudulent returns worth at least $5,000 at Target and other stores in the Washington suburbs on 25 different occasions. . . . he stopped . . . outside the company's Gaithersburg store after . . . allegedly received a refund for items using a receipt from an earlier purchase. . . . had receipts from previous purchases at Target stores and admitted to . . . that he was committing fraudulent returns," . . . According to authorities, . . . would buy items and take them to his car, then return to the store, pick up identical items from store shelves and take them to the return desk, presenting his original receipt.[19]

Commentary: Not so surprisingly, anyone in any position at work or in life is susceptible to perpetrating frauds if the circumstances are right. However, it is still surprising to learn of the fraud-threat agent's profile, and one wonders why on earth someone would perpetrate such a fraud. This is especially true for those whose monetary reward is so small.

A scarier thought is what national security secrets does this person know, and if he is so desperate to perpetrate a $5,000 fraud, what would he do for $10,000 or more in bribes?

If your corporation is involved in retail merchandising or even if your corporation has a company store for employees, such a fraud scheme must be considered when developing an anti-fraud program.

---

[18] http://money.cnn.com/2006/03/15/news/newsmakers/enron/index.htm
[19] CNN, 14 March 2006.

CLICK FRAUDS

> **FBI, SEC Probe Web Sites Offering Large Returns Looking at Ads** . . . Federal investigators are examining Web sites . . . autosurf pages that promise to pay members simply for viewing advertisements. The FBI and SEC are taking a closer look at these sites that bear a similarity to the famous Ponzi scheme, where investors are lured in by promises of lavish returns, but are paid with the money from future investors, rather than money earned from a legitimate business activity. . . . offers free membership, but only pays users who have upgraded, investing in $6 increments, with a maximum of $6,000. . . . the FBI has elevated Internet crime to its third-highest priority. . . . In 2004, the FBI's Internet Crimes Complaint Center fielded 207,000 complaints, up 66 percent from the year before, though most were not related to investment scams. Still, the agency notes that many people who are conned out of small sums would be unlikely to report the crime.[20]

Commentary: This is another example of the use of today's Internet and high-technology devices as tools to perpetrate old fraud schemes. Fraud-threat agents will use the tool available and the opportunity presented to attack assets. When developing an anti-fraud program, be sure to include these "oldies but goodies" fraud schemes and project them into the future, incorporating the future technology that will be common and available to them.

MORTGAGE FRAUD

> **FBI warns of mortgage fraud "epidemic"** . . . Seeks to head off "next S&L crisis": Rampant fraud in the mortgage industry has increased so sharply that the FBI warned . . . of an "epidemic" of financial crimes which, if not curtailed, could become "the next S&L crisis." . . . Assistant FBI Director . . . said the booming mortgage market, fueled by low interest rates and soaring home values, has attracted unscrupulous professionals and criminal groups whose fraudulent activities could cause multibillion-dollar losses to financial institutions.
>
> . . . In one operation, six individuals were arrested Thursday in Charlotte, charged with bank fraud for their roles in a multimillion-dollar mortgage fraud, officials said. The two-year investigation found fraudulent loans that exposed financial institutions and mortgage companies to $130 million in potential losses, . . . some organized ethnic groups are becoming involved in mortgage fraud schemes, but he declined to identify the groups.

---

[20] http://online.wsj.com/article/SB113953819846670333.html

Officials said mortgage fraud is one prominent aspect of a wider problem of fraud aimed at financial institutions. The FBI said action has been taken against 205 individuals in the past month in what it described as the "largest nationwide enforcement operation in FBI history directed at organized groups and individuals engaged in financial institution fraud."

In addition to mortgage fraud, "Operation Continued Action" also targeted loan fraud, check kiting, and identity theft as major problems. In one check-kiting scheme in Binghamton, New York, the operator of a recycling business wrote in excess of $1 billion in worthless checks over a 14-month period, officials said. Not all of the checks were cashed.[21]

Commentary: This is yet another example of innovative fraud-threat agents operating in any environment where they can attack and gain control of some form of corporate or other entity's assets. It is also another illustration of an old fraud scheme that must be considered when developing an anti-fraud program. If you don't think it applies to your corporation, please be sure before you ignore this or any other fraud scheme. You may be surprised by the kinds of activities your corporation or its subsidiary may be involved in.

GOVERNMENT CONTRACTORS AND FRAUD

Former Air Force buyer jailed over Boeing deal: . . . The U.S. Air Force's former No. 2 weapons buyer was sentenced to nine months in prison on Friday after telling the court she had given Boeing Co. a rival's secret data and inflated weapons deals to ingratiate herself with the company, her future employer. The disclosure . . . could spark a new round of ethical, legal and business headaches for the Chicago-based aerospace giant, the Pentagon's No. 2 supplier after Lockheed Martin Corp . . . she had agreed to a higher price than she thought was appropriate for what became a $23.5 billion plan to acquire modified Boeing 767 aircraft as refueling tankers. "The defendant did so, in her view, as a 'parting gift to Boeing' and because of her desire to ingratiate herself with Boeing, her future employer," according to a statement of facts she signed.[22]

Commentary: This is another example of an old type of contract fraud. There are literally thousands of such types of frauds perpetrated for many, many decades. If your corporation has any type of contracts with businesses

---

[21] http://www.cnn.com/2004/LAW/09/17/mortgage.fraud/index.html
[22] Reuters, 02 October 2004.

or government agencies, and obviously it does, one must definitely consider such fraud schemes in an anti-fraud program.

> One SEC commissioner reckons that Internet fraudsters are scamming more than $1 billion (#600 million) a year from investors worldwide. "These people," he says, "want your money and they recognise that the Internet provides them with anonymity. With the press of a button, they can get bogus information out to millions of people 24 hours a day." Because the Internet reaches all of us, and is essentially an unregulated marketplace, these warnings should also be taken seriously in Britain.[23]

FRAUDS AND MICROSOFT SOFTWARE

Fraudster Snares Microsoft Certificates; Users Warned ... Software titan Microsoft Corp. [NASDAQ:MSFT] today warned that two of its digital certificates were erroneously issued to an imposter seeking to trick users of Microsoft products into running harmful programs. . . . The certificates could be used to sign executable content under the Microsoft name, enabling the attacker to "create a destructive program or ActiveX control, then sign it using either certificate and host it on a Web site or distribute it to other Web sites," Verisign said.[24]

Commentary: Here again we have innovative miscreants using today's high-technology tools to help perpetrate some unauthorized activities. Such types of actions can easily be used to support some fraud schemes.

Y2K-RELATED FRAUD

FTC Nabs Mining Co Pitching Y2K-related Fraud: . . . The Federal Trade Commission secured court backing to stop a California businessman from using year 2000-related fears to con investors into buying stocks and options in his mining company. . . . agreed to stop marketing investments in the gold mining company as an option ahead of a financial breakdown related to the change in the millennium.[25]

---

[23]   16 August 1999, infowar.com.

[24]   Newsbytes News Network, 22 March 2001. Also see http://www.microsoft.com/technet/security/bulletin/MS01–017.asp

[25]   Dow Jones News Service, 17 November 1999.

<u>Commentary</u>: Although the Y2K crisis is well behind us, the fraud scheme used here is still valid — using fear tactics to manipulate the thinking of potential fraud victims to act in a certain way conductive to the fraud-threat agent being successful.

Fear, and especially financial fears, is a strong motivator that often drives the intended fraud victims to take actions conducive to perpetrating a successful fraud. These defrauders know that and use human nature to their advantage. That is why as a fraud fighter developing an anti-fraud program, you, too, must understand human nature and the thinking and fear processes of victims, as well as the defrauders.

If a fraud-threat agent used fraud scheme tactics but the targeted victims did not act to help the fraud to succeed, then the "good guys" win. The potential fraud then is not successful. That is why it is imperative that any anti-fraud program include an employee awareness program so that potential victims or fraud targets do not facilitate the fraud attacks.

DATA STORAGE CONDUCIVE TO FRAUD-THREAT AGENTS

> **Google's long memory stirs privacy concerns:** . . . When Google Inc.'s 19 million daily users look up a long-lost classmate, send e-mail or bounce around the Web more quickly with its new Web Accelerator, records of that activity don't go away. In an era of increased government surveillance, privacy watchdogs worry that Google's vast archive of Internet activity could prove a tempting target for abuse. Like many other online businesses, Google tracks how its search engine and other services are used and who uses them. Unlike many other businesses, Google holds onto that information for years. Some privacy experts who otherwise give Google high marks say the company's records could become a handy data bank for government investigators who rely on business records to circumvent Watergate-era laws that limit their own ability to track U.S. residents.[26]

<u>Commentary</u>: As corporations and government agencies continue to compile information on employees, consumers, and the like, owing in part to more powerful and cheaper high technology, we are all more vulnerable to fraud-threat agents obtaining that information and using it to perpetrate one or more frauds.

Is it too late to protect private information, or is the genie out of the bottle and can't be put back in? One corporate executive once said, "There is no privacy. Get over it!" I tend to agree with that statement. However, we can still put controls and anti-fraud processes in place that will help protect the privacy of employees and corporate sensitive information as best we can.

---

[26] Reuters, 3 June 2005.

ANOTHER EXAMPLE OF CLICK FRAUD

> **Google settles "click fraud" case:** . . . Google Inc. has agreed to pay up to $90 million to settle a lawsuit alleging the online search engine leader overcharged thousands of advertisers who paid for bogus sales referrals generated through a ruse known as "click fraud." The proposed settlement, announced by the company Wednesday, would apply to all advertisers in Google's network during the past four years. . . . The total value of the credits available to advertisers will be lower than $90 million because part of that amount will be used to cover the fees of lawyers who filed the case last year in Arkansas state court.
>
> . . . Google makes virtually all of its money from text-based advertising links that trigger commissions each time they are clicked on. Besides enriching Google, the system has been a boon for advertisers, whose sales have been boosted by an increased traffic from prospective buyers. But sometimes mischief makers and scam artists repeatedly click on specific advertising links even though they have no intentions of buying anything. The motives for the malicious activity known as click fraud vary widely, but the net effect is the same: advertisers end up paying for fruitless Web traffic.
>
> The lawsuit alleged Google had conspired with its advertising partners to conceal the magnitude of click fraud to avoid making refunds. . . . The company's shares fell $10.57 to close at $353.88 on the Nasdaq Stock Market, then shed another $2.11 in extended trading.[27]

Commentary: Click fraud! Who would have "thunk" it? When it comes to fraud-threat agents, once again the old adage, "Where there is a will there is a way!" seems to apply. Although stated more than once, I'll state it once again: your anti-fraud program must consider old and new fraud schemes, incorporate today's and tomorrow's high technology as tools for perpetrating frauds, and build an anti-fraud program with the controls and defense against such attacks.

In addition, be sure to incorporate proactive fraud surveys to aggressively look for fraud indicators and, where found, follow up with an aggressive and immediate inquiry to prove or disprove that a fraud has taken or may take place.

PYRAMID SCHEMES MOVE ON TO THE INTERNET

> **Internet company settles pyramid scheme claim** . . . An Arizona company that sells "Internet malls" — Web sites with links to retail-

---

[27] CNN, 9 March 2006.

ers — will pay $5 million back to its customers to settle charges that it operated an illegal pyramid scheme, . . . charged more than $100 for each mall, the FTC said, and claimed that customers would make substantial income on the deal if they continued to recruit more participants. Customers received commissions if visitors clicked links on their site and made purchases at the stores. . . . Explanations on the site state that the company blames some of its members for "unscrupulous" conduct, which led to the federal investigation.[28]

Commentary: I am being redundant, but hopefully repetition will help drive home the main points. This is another example of an old fraud scheme being used in today's and probably tomorrow's high-technology, information-dependent, and information-driven world.

In the . . . Financial Director, . . . was quoted in an article on computer fraud . . . detailed the method of dealing with internal fraud: "The first thing that you do is to make sure that you do not disclose to the internal . . . that he has been discovered. You then monitor what he does to discover where the money or information is going." On the subject of whether or not a victim should bring civil proceedings or rely on criminal proceedings, . . . "Limited police resources mean that there is at least a risk of action not being taken. The police have different priorities and, in the end, a victim will have to decide what is important to him."[29]

PREPAID CELLULAR PHONE FRAUD

Ex-Verizon employee charged with fraud . . . A former Verizon Wireless employee was indicted by a federal grand jury Thursday on charges he stole more than $20 million from the company's prepaid cellular telephone service. . . . indicted on 10 fraud and money laundering counts. As a customer service representative, . . . had access to a password-protected Verizon computer account in which the company kept a record of prepaid cell phone minutes. Customers on the plan could buy cards on which were printed 15-digit personal identification numbers. They would then call a telephone number to activate the prepaid minutes to make a telephone call. . . . alleged to have copied more than $20 million worth of the 15-digit numbers and sold them on his. . . . He continued accessing the Web site and copying the numbers even after he left the company.[30]

---

[28] CNN, 27 March 2001.
[29] Reuters.
[30] Associated Press, 13 August 2004.

Commentary: This is another example of a fraud scheme that is continually being modernized and is keeping up with the high technology and the vulnerabilities they present. Any successful anti-fraud program will continually be updated and will consider what "modernization vulnerabilities" come with the new high technology or processes now in place or those that will be in place in the future — including new services and products that your corporation may offer or use.

Does your corporation use prepaid telephone cards? If not, are you sure, or are you just taking someone's word for it who may or may not really know? If such cards are used, what controls are in place and how do you know they are working? Who monitors their usage and accompanying bills?

IDENTIFYING INTERNATIONAL CORRUPTION

U.S. spies on corruption overseas—Listening devices used to compile data on who is bribing who . . . The U.S. intelligence community uses electronic eavesdropping to maintain and update a top secret database of international bribery cases, according to new reports by the State and Commerce departments and senior U.S. officials. The information is being used extensively as leverage to help American companies compete abroad and is being matched by similar efforts on the part of U.S. economic competitors. . . . THE DATABASE built by U.S. intelligence agencies contains the names of foreign companies that offer bribes to win international contracts and is reported to list hundreds of contracts worth hundreds of billions of dollars that over the past 14 years went to the biggest briber rather than the highest bidder.

The database is developed mainly through electronic eavesdropping, say U.S. intelligence officials. Such eavesdropping, called communications intelligence or COMINT, is at the center of the "Echelon" controversy. European parliamentarians, among others, are accusing the United States of massive electronic spying for commercial purposes, using a worldwide network of spy sites linked by ferret software known as Echelon.

Under a U.S. law known as the Foreign Corrupt Practices Act (FCPA), the U.S. Department of Justice can bring criminal charges against American companies making payments to foreign government officials in order to obtain or retain business. Companies, officers, and directors risk expensive and disruptive investigations, criminal and civil sanctions, and private lawsuits if they fail to take the steps necessary to avoid prohibited payments.[31]

---

[31] Reported by Robert Windrem, an investigative reporter for NBC News, 21 July 2000.

<u>Commentary</u>: It seems that the saying, "Hello, I am with the government and I am here to help you," comes to mind. It would behoove a CSO to contact his or her local FBI or other entity and determine how such a program might negatively and positively impact your corporation. Will such government representatives talk to you about it or even acknowledge that such a program exists? That may depend more on your personal than official relationship with the person or persons you contact.

This revelation may come as a surprise to some, but not all government employees are honest. Some even perpetrate frauds, as one earlier example shows. Perhaps the government person collecting such information may use it for personal gain. After all, the government is not the best payer in the world.

In the United States, you may be able to obtain at least some limited information if you discuss it as part of the corporation's responsibilities under the Economic Espionage Act. Of course, as the CSO with responsibility for the anti-fraud program, you may have a better chance of succeeding if you are a retired FBI agent — but not always.

CREDIT CARD INFORMATION THEFTS AND FRAUDS

MasterCard: Only 68,000 at "higher" risk in breach: . . . Credit card users, don't fret. Only a small fraction of the 13.9 million credit card accounts at MasterCard that were exposed to possible fraud were considered at high risk, the company said Saturday. MasterCard International Inc. . . . said only about 68,000 of its card holders are at "higher levels of risk." And while those 68,000 should closely examine their credit or debit card accounts, customers do not have to worry about identity theft, . . . which processes credit card and other payments for banks and merchants. . . .

The incident appears to be the largest yet involving financial data in a series of security breaches affecting valuable consumer data at major financial institutions and data brokers. Only about 13.9 million of the 40 million credit card accounts that may have been exposed to fraud were MasterCard accounts. It was not immediately clear how many of the other accounts were considered at high risk. Under federal law, credit card holders are liable for no more than $50 of unauthorized charges. Some card issuers, including MasterCard, offer zero liability to customers on unauthorized use of the card.[32]

<u>Commentary</u>: Only 13.9 million exposed out of 40 million. Wow! What were the other accounts? That sure makes us all feel better, doesn't it? The

---

[32] Associated Press, 17 June 2005. http://www.usatoday.com/money/perfi/credit/2005–06–17-mastercard-security-breach_x.htm

corporations involved always seem to rationalize such thefts as having little or no impact on consumers or others. I would ask them to prove it. Prove that it does not impact your financial situation or privacy instead of the consumer victims having to prove they have been harmed.

What can a fraud-threat agent do with "only" 13.9 million MasterCard accounts chock full of great information that can be used to help perpetrate multiple types of frauds?

The way to mitigate this terrible lack of protection is to hold the corporation responsible liable and to impose punitive damages based not on whether or not you as an individual were actually harmed but only on the fact that your personal information was not adequately protected. Furthermore, such damages should be very large to help deter such lack of assets protection. That is the only way to get the attention of corporations — by hurting their profit margins. For example, maybe for each account even exposed to compromise, each card holder gets a mandatory $5,000.

When that happens, profits will decline, and stockholders with declining stock value and dividends will demand action. If not, they will also continue to suffer as a result of the lackadaisical attitude of those responsible for protecting these assets — let's start with the CEO.

Will this happen? I doubt it. One just has to look at the massive lobbying campaigns now in effect between corporations and legislatures. Would this proposal for supporting legislation be met by an onslaught of corporate lobbying from many types of corporations? No doubt about it!

HACKERS, CRACKERS, PHISHERS, OH MY!

Crackers Snag Credit-Card Info . . . Three teenagers claim to have stolen approximately 8,000 electronic invoices for online credit-card orders placed over the past two years through a Web electronics retailer. "This shows a disgusting lack of security on the Internet," said one of the crackers, who provided a sample of the data to Wired News this week to support the claim. "Thank God we aren't poor people, or con artists. . . . [We did this] purely for fun." . . . He said the group installed software that allowed them to pilfer 4.3 MB worth of archived credit-card orders and a 15 MB Microsoft Office inventory database. The cracker supplied Wired News with a file that contained copies of 583 credit-card orders for computer equipment purchased online. . . .

The teenagers, all Americans, said they launched their attack by uploading a File Transfer Protocol server program known as *Serv-U* to the Dalco server. With the program's default directory set to the target machine's hard drive, and the program running in the background, the crackers said they were able to browse the directories and steal the data. "It was rather clever," boasted the cracker in an interview conducted over Internet Relay Chat, a global and largely anonymous text-based chat network. He said that what he called ... poorly configured Windows NT 3.5 server allowed his team to gain high-level administrator access to the unencrypted databases. He said on Thursday that he had since erased all of the data from his own machine without passing it on to anyone, but could not speak for the others.[33]

Commentary: Maybe this is an "oldie" but it is still a "goodie." Yet, again we have a case of potential fraud-threat agents taking advantage of the vulnerabilities of high technology. Although the software may evolve, history has shown that, while programmers may close some security loopholes, they often open up new ones. So, it is just a matter of time before defrauders discover these new vulnerabilities and take advantage of them.

URBAN LEGENDS AND FRAUDS

You can look up anyone's driver's license for free on the Internet ... This is really scary. ... Now you can see anyone's Drivers License on the Internet, including your own! I just searched for mine and there it was, picture and all.[34]

Commentary: Urban legends appear on the Internet all the time and people pass them around as if they were all true. It is also truly amazing how fast they travel. The author has on more than one occasion received the same urban legend from different people at least three times in one day.

It seems that no one cares to ever check out the information to determine if it is true. This can easily be done by using a search engine and then going to one of the several sites identified for discussing "urban legends." This example is not really a "fraud" per se but is provided just to show how fast information, bogus information, can travel around the world in an instant to probably millions of Internet users who may then take some action based on the bogus information. As noted earlier, such falsehoods can have major impacts on the stocks of corporations and support the perpetrations of various types of frauds.

MEDICAL RESEARCH FRAUD

School sorry over stem cell fraud: Seoul University issues apology after panel findings. ... One day after a panel investigating the work of

---

[33] http://www.wired.com/science/discoveries/news/1998/10/15665. 16 October 1998.

[34] Paraphrased from material on various urban legend Web sites.

disgraced South Korean scientist . . . found that he faked claims of cloning human embryonic stem cells, the Seoul National University has issued a public apology. University president . . . said . . . fraud was "an unwashable blemish on the whole scientific community as well as our country" and a "criminal act in academia," according to the Associated Press. . . . resigned last December after colleagues accused him of deliberately fabricating data in his cloning research.[35]

Commentary: As general ethical conduct seems to continue to decline, it has an impact on the very fiber of our societies. One part of society that can least afford fraudulent conduct is in the area of medical research. Such research has a direct bearing on our health and therefore our lives. Millions of precious medical research dollars can be wasted due to fraudulent conduct by those involved in such research.

One wonders about the extent to which medical research frauds are perpetrated on an annual basis all over the world. One must assume that no country or corporation doing medical research is immune to these and other types of frauds.

Projecting such thinking into medical research identifying disease cures, one also wonders whether anyone with a medical condition has or will be crippled, suffer, or even die because some fraud delayed the cure. Many more examples could be cited here, but suffice it to say that a successful fraud may actually be a contributing factor in our deaths.

CORRUPTION AND THE WAR IN IRAQ

Rumsfeld: Corruption hurting Iraq: Administration proposes $439 billion Pentagon budget. . . . Continued corruption in Iraq could damage efforts to create a democracy there, Defense Secretary Donald H. Rumsfeld said Tuesday, adding that it is up to the Iraqis to seize control and take more responsibility for their country. "It's true that violence, corruption and criminality continue to pose challenges in Iraq" and are "so corrosive of democracy," he told members of the Senate Armed Services Committee. "It's critically important that it be attacked and that the new leadership in that country be measured against their commitment to attack corruption," he added. Rumsfeld provided no specific examples. But there have been recent allegations that some revenue from Iraq's slowly rebuilding oil industry have been siphoned to help finance the insurgency there. Rumsfeld added that "our awareness of corruption is increasing," because coalition officials are doing more to investigate those problems within the government.[36]

---

[35] http://edition.cnn.com/2006/HEALTH/01/10/skorea.stemcell/index.html
[36] Associated Press, 7 February 2006.

Commentary: This is another example of and a sad commentary concerning the damage frauds can do. In this case, it may even be responsible for the deaths of innocent civilians and the allies' soldiers. Often, people look at fraud as just a white-collar crime in which big government and major corporations are the only victims, no people actually get hurt, and they (corporations) can afford it and have insurance, and on and on.

COMMENTS ON IDENTITY THEFTS AS A VEHICLE TO FRAUD

Identity theft is a part of today's digital landscape, and in today's environment individuals are nearly helpless to protect themselves either from the theft and abuse of their identity or to repair the damage done by an identity theft. Identities are stolen by the hundreds of thousands, if not millions at a time and can be distributed over the Internet in a matter of hours and the information can be used for fraudulent purposes by a criminal with impunity. None of the currently deployed solutions including encryption, public key infrastructure, digital certificates, secure sockets, etc., are effective in preventing identity theft and abuse.[37]

Commentary: Identity theft and related frauds have exploded with the acceleration of high technology and as prices of high-tech goods have become lower and lower, resulting in increased vulnerabilities. Such successful attacks against employees may have an adverse impact on these employees' behavior and motivation, leading them to perpetrate a fraud to offset their financial losses as a fraud victim, where that motivation to commit a fraud did not exist before the theft.

LOBBYISTS AND CORRUPTION

Lobbyist to plead guilty to fraud, other charges . . . agrees to cooperate with federal prosecutors, . . . Former high-powered lobbyist . . . guilty . . . to corruption, fraud and tax evasion charges in a deal with federal prosecutors, a source close to the negotiations. . . . the former lobbyist may have thousands of e-mails in which he describes influence-peddling and explains what lawmakers were doing in exchange for the money he was putting into their campaign coffers. . . . Prosecutors accused . . . of conspiring to "corruptly offer and provide things of value, including money, meals, trips and entertainment, to federal public officials in return for agreements to perform official acts" benefiting . . . and his lobbyist partner. . . . The government alleged that between January 2000

---

[37] news@infowar.com

and April 2004, . . . and the lobbyist "would falsely represent to their clients that certain of the funds were being used for specific purposes.[38]

Commentary: Corrupt politicians — this should come as no surprise. How would such news impact your corporation and an anti-fraud program? What if your corporation's management was paying the lobbyists? How would you know? If you found out, what would you do? These are serious questions and bear serious consequences depending on the action or non-action that you take. As stated earlier, whistleblowers pay a price. Are you willing to pay that price?

INTERNET SCAMS ARE INTERNATIONAL

UK: Investors Warned About U.S.-Style Internet Scams: UK investors have been told to watch out for American-style "pump and dump" Internet scams, in which false information is circulated with a view to forcing up share prices. . . . This particular electronic crime has two elements, international regulators believe. Having bought cheap shares in a lesser-known company, the fraudster generates false publicity as to its value in an effort to pump up the share price. He then dumps the shares and cashes in, leaving investors out of pocket.

The Internet is a perfect medium for attracting potential investors. Perpetrators of such frauds require little more than a credible website, some links to fictitious articles concerning the company's prospects and false share tips disseminated via Internet news groups. The U.S. Securities and Exchange Commission (SEC) has a team of more than 200 people monitoring the Internet for signs of abuse. They carry out regular sweeps, working with the SEC's Office of Internet Enforcement.[39]

Commentary: This is another example, albeit on a more global scale, of the use of today's high technology to support a fraud scheme.

FAKING A MEDICAL CONDITION

Prosecutors: Man Faked Retardation for Nearly 20 Years to Scam Government Out of $111,000: For nearly 20 years . . . his mother has collected disability benefits on his behalf. In meetings with Social Security officials and psychologists, he appeared mentally retarded and

---

[38] http://us.cnn.com/2006/POLITICS/01/03/abramoff.plea/index.html

[39] *The Times*, 11 May 1999.

unable to communicate. His mother insisted he couldn't read or write, shower, take care of himself or drive a car. But now prosecutors say it was all a huge fraud, and they have video. . . . contesting a traffic ticket to prove it. "He's like any other person trying to get out of a traffic ticket," Assistant U.S. Attorney Norman Barbosa said Tuesday . . . indicted in September on charges of conspiracy to defraud the government and Social Security fraud, and the case was unsealed Tuesday. . . . The benefits cited in the indictment totaled $111,000.[40]

Commentary: This is another amazing example of defrauders using any opportunity to perpetrate a fraud. What if the mother was a corporate employee? Of course, if found guilty, she might be fired, but even before that, shouldn't some anti-fraud processes be in place to see what corporate assets she had access to and what controls are in place to protect them?

Are there any fraud indicators relative to her access and use of the corporate assets? Shouldn't your anti-fraud program have processes in place that allow a further check into this corporate employee's access to corporate assets?

INTERNET FRAUD SWEEP

New Jersey Charges Nine in Internet Fraud Sweep . . . The New Jersey attorney general's office filed civil charges against nine people on Monday as part of an Internet fraud crackdown that uncovered bogus sales of company stocks, Beanie Baby toys and the impotence drug Viagra. "On the Internet, fraud is just a mouse-click away," Mark Herr, director of the New Jersey Attorney General's Consumer Affairs Division, said in announcing the charges. He said the cases were the first in the state involving "significant cyber-fraud." Five people were named in a nine-count complaint charging them with sales of 531,898 shares of unregistered stock in (a corporation) a phony e-commerce services company. . . . The complaint alleged more than 350 investors were bilked of $850,000 that the defendants took for personal use and which were not used for legitimate business purposes. None of the defendants was registered with the state's Bureau of Securities or the National Association of Securities Dealers.[41]

Commentary: High-technology tools combined with the innovation of fraud-threat agents continue to lead to new fraud schemes and more sophisticated use of old fraud schemes.

---

[40] http://www.foxnews.com/printer_friendly_story/0,3566,234657,00.html
[41] Reuters, 16 November 1999.

ATM FRAUD

Thieves net $100,000 in WaMu ATM scheme . . . Group used fake keypads and bank-card slots in New York branches to steal from bank accounts. . . . A sophisticated group of thieves used technical trickery to steal ATM card information — and over $100,000 — from customers at two New York City Washington Mutual branches. The thieves rigged fake keypads and bank-card slots onto ATMs to gather card information and encoded the information on new cards, police say. They then used the new, fraudulent cards for withdrawals from approximately 50 Washington Mutual accounts at other ATM locations. . . . Images of the suspects were recorded on the bank's security cameras.[42]

Commentary: ATM frauds continue to occur; however, it is believed they are occurring at a slower rate than when the ATMs first came into use. It is probably still more likely that an ATM customer will be mugged at an ATM than a fraud-threat agent will take advantage of the vulnerabilities of ATMs.

Recently, some have said that the encrypted software used to facilitate ATM transactions may not be secure. This may be the case, but for all but the most sophisticated miscreants, they are probably secure. For those with a Ph.D. in computer science, can we consider any high-technology device secure?

We should never consider any high-technology device, any controls, or any portion of any anti-fraud program to be able to stop 100% of all fraud-threat agents or to thwart all fraud schemes. All we can ever expect is that the levels of risks will be made as low as possible and that for the remainder, we can hope for the best. As some movie dialogue once went: "Hope? We are hanging on hope?" The answer is that when all is said and done, "Yes, we are." Our hope is based on the philosophy of risk mitigation and not risk elimination.

SOCIAL SECURITY SCAM

The Social Security Administration (SSA) has warned of a new e-mail scam in which recipients are asked to update their personal information or risk having their Social Security "account" suspended indefinitely. Recipients are then directed to click on a link in the e-mail that takes them to a Web site designed to look like the SSA's Web site. Among the pieces of information recipients are asked to give are: Name, Address, Date of Birth, Social Security Number, Credit Card Number, and/or Bank Account Number.[43]

---

[42] http://money.cnn.com/2006/01/06/news/atm_fraud/index.htm?cnn=yes
[43] *AFOSISA Global Alliance* magazine, Summer 2006.

Commentary: This is a typical scam, and one can tell by the detailed, personal information requested that the SSA, other government agencies, or private agencies for that matter would not ask for. When you go online to transact business and a credit card or other personal information is requested, you must always check the Web site address to be sure you are at the proper Web site address and not one that looks like the legitimate address. You may also want to use your search engine to find the Web site you are interested in. Never click on a Web site that is noted in an e-mail to you and then transact business. Yes, it may be legitimate, but why take the chance? Just search for that business's or government agency's Web site and then go to it. You still may end up on a bogus site, but your chance of going to the legitimate site is better.

STAMP FRAUD

Spanish Police Raid Auction Houses in Stamp Fraud Probe . . . At least four people have been arrested in raids by Spanish police as part of an ongoing fraud investigation involving two prominent stamp collection companies. . . . The companies . . . are accused of defrauding nearly 200,000 mostly retired investors in a pyramid scheme involving overvalued stamps . . . subject of a Barron's magazine investigation, which found that its stamps were likely overvalued and that proceeds from sales to new investors were being used to pay returns to other investors. Barron's also reported that Lloyd's of London, insurer to the tune of $1.5 billion, might pull their backing over the allegations of improper practices.[44]

Commentary: There are probably as many different types of fraud targets and victims as there are pyramid–Ponzi schemes. The greed of the fraud victims is a major contributor to successful frauds. How will you try to deal with the human greed issue as part of your anti-fraud program? One view is that you discuss the potential negatives of perpetrating a fraud as part of the employees' awareness program, put controls in place to minimize the opportunities for frauds, and conduct aggressive fraud surveys looking for fraud indicators and employees who are not following procedures that impact the potential for frauds to occur.

The idea is to take away one or more of the following:

* *Opportunities* to perpetrate a successful fraud
* Employees' *motivation* to commit a fraud and/or
* Any *rationale* that an employee may use for committing the fraud — this is probably the most difficult task because humans can rationalize anything regardless of the facts.

---

[44] http://www.foxnews.com/printer_friendly_story/0,3566,194804,00.html

An interesting book about Ponzi who is "credited" with the Ponzi scheme is author Mitchell Zuckoff's book, *Ponzi's Scheme — The True Story of a Financial Legend*. It is an interesting read and helps one to understand how such a fraud can occur, even when one seems to have no real intention to perpetrate a fraud — at least at first.

BANKER AND IDENTITY THEFT

Russian bank chief jailed for identity theft . . . A Russian bank chief, who coordinated an international identity theft operation, has been jailed for six years . . . helped run a criminal gang, which stole millions of pounds from British, American and Spanish account holders. The fraudsters used stolen credit card numbers to create false identities to purchase expensive electronic equipment and other goods, which they then resold on eBay. Police believe the global campaign could have spanned a decade.[45]

Commentary: Identity theft is a tempting fraud-related crime as one can commit this crime from other nations, often with impunity. Of course, all types of crime are rampant in Russia today, so the existence of identify theft there should not be surprising, even from a banker!

ACCOUNTING FIRM FRAUD

New York attorney general accuses accounting firm of fraudulent business practices by steering customers into IRA accounts. . . . filed a lawsuit Wednesday against the accounting firm . . . sending the company's shares plunging. . . . stock tumbled nearly 8 percent in mid-morning trade on the New York Stock Exchange following the news.

. . . accused the financial services firm of fraudulent business practices by steering approximately 500,000 customers into IRA accounts, that were "virtually guaranteed" to lose money. Those customers who opened the Express IRA accounts were often burdened by unadvertised account fees, making it difficult to grow their savings.[46]

Commentary: If you can't trust a major accounting firm to identify improper procedures in a corporation, within their own corporation and the like,

---

[45] SC Magazine, 19 December 2006. http://www.scmagazine.com/uk/news/article/610317/russian-bank-chief-jailed-identity-theft
[46] http://money.cnn.com/2006/03/15/news/companies/spitzer_hr/index.htm?cnn=yes

who can you trust to identify frauds? The answer is you can't trust anyone. Under the right circumstances, anyone will perpetrate a fraud — even you or me. You may say you would never do that and yes, you may be the exception. However, there may be circumstances that provide you with the opportunity, motive, and rationale to do so.

Have you ever in your lifetime taken something of value from another without reimbursing that person for what you took? Maybe you just didn't put the 50 cents in the coffee collection can when you took that cup of office coffee. Petty? Maybe. Wrong? Of course. So how did you rationalize that theft? No change? No money? The price is too high and you only pay for every third cup? Yes, rationalization is an interesting human phenomenon. Actually, you can see that it can work at all levels of thefts or frauds.

Never say never is good advice. After all, as we often find, we are surprised when we learn that the father or mother and pillar of the community or the little ole lady and grandmother is a major defrauder. We are astounded! How could he or she do that? I would never have suspected such a person.

You will find that each one of us may have what we consider to be a valid reason, a rationale as to why we would attempt to perpetrate a fraud, even if we are God-fearing, church-going, part-time Sunday School teachers. Human nature is interesting to study and important for you to try to understand as you go about developing a successful anti-fraud program. Remember: corporations don't commit frauds — people do.

What human beings are made of and what constitutes our ways of thinking are often neglected areas of consideration when we set about to protect corporate or other entities' assets from defrauders or other miscreants. However, it is probably our most important consideration when we are developing an anti-fraud program. We must also understand the thinking of fraud-threat agents. Too often we concentrate on controls almost in a vacuum; however, for controls to work, they must be based at least in part on the potential fraud-related thinking and actions of the employees.

Ex-Tyco CEO was sentenced to $8\frac{1}{3}$ to 25 years in prison Monday for his part in stealing hundreds of millions of dollars from the manufacturing conglomerate.[47]

---

[47] CNN Money, 19 September 2005

LAWYERS AND MEDICAL RIP-OFFS

Today's human beings are in general living longer and healthier lives than ever before. At the same time, we humans are messing up this earth with toxic chemicals and other man-made inventions. Although maybe not a fraud in all cases per se, the following provides the potential for fraud:

> **The $40 Billion Scam: How slick lawyers have turned a genuine health crisis into a ripoff you won't believe** . . . So far, at least 79 companies have filed for bankruptcy due to asbestos litigation alone, and 60,000 workers have lost their jobs. About 8,400 companies with facilities nationwide have faced lawsuits. Meanwhile, insurance companies are out $59 billion through 2005, with $34 billion paid out in cases and another $25 billion locked away in reserves. Those costs get passed along to consumers and companies as higher premiums and eventually prices for thousands of products and services.
>
> And what about those plaintiff lawyers behind the flood of lawsuits?
>
> "I would estimate their fees are north of $20 billion," says Brickman (A professor of law at the Cardozo School of Law at Yeshiva University in New York), who has exhaustively researched the scandal over 16 years. "The bottom line is that in mass torts, fraud works."[48]

These diagnoses were driven by neither health nor justice. They were manufactured for money. *U.S. District Judge Janis Jack.*

ANOTHER MENTION OF THE "NIGERIAN" SCAMS — VARIATIONS ON A THEME

Last but certainly not least is the topic of the Nigerian type of scams floating around the Internet. There are so many versions of this type of fraud that citing them all would double the size of this chapter!

The basic premise of this fraud scheme is that someone somewhere will reply to the e-mail and then be convinced either to send money or visit a certain place in order to collect money. As previously mentioned in Chapter 6, this is a dangerous fraud scam.

If you have not received any of these types of e-mails, you must not have any e-mail connections!

---

[48] "The Legal Scam You Pay For," *Reader's Digest*, January 2007, p. 74

CASE STUDY

You are beginning the development of your corporation's anti-fraud program. What processes would you consider integrating into your program based on the fraud cases cited in this chapter?

For this case study, no sample answer is given. All that information and hints of what to do are found throughout the commentaries associated with the cited cases.

Hacker attack at UCLA affects 800,000 people:

- UCLA says hacker invaded database for more than a year.
- Info exposed on about 800,000 students, faculty, staff.
- Data included Social Security numbers, birth dates, and addresses.
- UCLA: No evidence any data have been misused.[49]

SUMMARY

Thousands, if not millions, of frauds that have been perpetrated over the centuries. Ever since one human being wanted to have something of value belonging to another human being without providing just compensation and the owner's agreement, fraud schemes have been used to illegally gain that asset or assets.

With the ever-increasing role of high technology in our world many new frauds have sprung up, and many old ones have been identified, which have been brought into the twenty-first century through the use of the high-technology tools with all their vulnerabilities.

The examples provided do not even come close to identifying each type of fraud scheme that has been tried. Such an endeavor would take lifetimes and probably still not be completed. However, the examples do give some idea as to what the fraud fighter is up against, and they also help the fraud fighter develop a successful anti-fraud program based in part on the fraud schemes and identified types of frauds noted in this chapter.

---

[49] Associated Press via CNN, 12 December 2006.

II

ESTABLISHING AND MANAGING AN ANTI-FRAUD PROGRAM

Section I introduced you to the world in which businesses operate on a global scale; discussed the impact of high technology on businesses and frauds; and presented some fraud laws, schemes, and cases to help you gain a basic awareness of the fraud threats against your corporation's or other entity's assets.

Section II is the heart of this book. It provides you with a basic anti-fraud program guide on which you can build a program specific to your corporation's needs. It is not all-encompassing but is a guide to help get you started in defending your corporation's assets from fraud-threat agents.

This section begins with an introduction to the fictitious International Widget Corporation (IWC). This international corporation provides you with a model that you can use to build your anti-fraud program. It is especially useful for those of you who do not as of yet work for a corporation as a leader in establishing and managing a corporate anti-fraud program or have responsibility for assets protection.

This method has been used in the past, and readers have commented favorably on the usefulness of providing such a fictitious corporation.

The subsequent chapters explain how to begin to develop an anti-fraud program and manage it, including getting direct and indirect support of others within the corporation.

Section II's chapters are as follows:

Chapter 8 The International Widget Corporation
Chapter 9 Establishing an Anti-Fraud Program
Chapter 10 Managing an Anti-Fraud Program
Chapter 11 Winning through Teaming

The title of each chapter provides you with some idea as to what will be covered in this section.

As a reminder of what was stated in the Preface, the emphasis of this book is on *establishing* and *managing* an anti-fraud program in order to fight fraud. Therefore, you can expect this section to emphasize management techniques, teamwork, and liaison approaches that are useful when you begin to establish an anti-fraud methodology for your corporation (e.g., budget) and generally work with others within an international corporate environment.

8

The International Widget Corporation

INTRODUCTION

The International Widget Corporation (IWC) is a fictitious international corporation that you as the chief security officer (CSO), or another who has responsibility to lead an anti-fraud effort, can use to develop an anti-fraud program. It is also a model to help the fraud fighter think about how to defend corporate assets against global fraud-threat agents and their schemes.

This method (using a fictional corporation as a model) is used to assist the new CSO by providing a more practical model for a corporate anti-fraud program, as well as provide information that may also prove useful to experienced CSOs. In other words, it represents more of a "real-life" approach using real scenarios. The scenarios and the actions taken are based on actual situations that can be found in today's modern business environments.

You are encouraged to build an anti-fraud program based on IWC. One word of caution, however: the approach used is provided in a simplistic form. Even so, the basics provided will at least provide some assistance in your more complex environment — at least that is the goal.

IWC BACKGROUND INFORMATION

The IWC CSO must understand the business and processes of IWC if a quality, cost-effective, corporate anti-fraud program is to be developed for IWC. Part of that process requires the CSO to identify those key elements of IWC's history and business that must be considered in developing the IWC anti-fraud program, as well as consider IWC's organizational structure. (See Figure 8-1.)

The following is a summary of IWC's business environment (italics on page 168 are added to identify the key phrases that the CSO must take into consideration when building the anti-fraud program.):

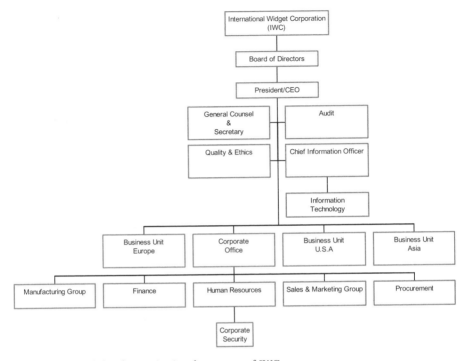

Figure 8-1.   High-level organizational structure of IWC.

IWC is a high-technology corporation that makes high-technology widgets. In order to make these widgets, it uses a proprietary process that has evolved over the five years that IWC has been in business.

The proprietary process is the key to IWC's success as a leader in the manufacturing of high-technology widgets. The process had cost millions of dollars to develop. The protection of the high-technology widget process is vital to IWC's survival.

Computers are used to control the robots used in the manufacturing of widgets. Over the years, the use of robots has drastically reduced costs by eliminating many of the human manufacturing jobs. This automated manufacturing process is the pride of IWC and is considered one of its "crown jewels." Without this automation, IWC could literally no longer produce the widgets, not only because of the cost factors, but also because the manufacturing requires such small tolerances to make the products that humans could not manufacture today's widgets.

IWC is in an extremely competitive business environment. However, based on changes in technology that allow for a more efficient and effective operation through telecommunications and networks, it has found that it must network with its global customers and subcontractors. Furthermore, IWC continues to look for new ways to replace employees with robotics or other ways of creating efficiencies to lower the number of employees that IWC must employ. It currently has low profit margins and any frauds will adversely impact that margin.

To provide for maximization of the high-technology widget process, IWC shares or interfaces its networks with its subcontractors, who must also use IWC's proprietary processes. The subcontractors, under contractual agreements, have promised not to use or share IWC's proprietary information with anyone. They have also agreed to protect that information in accordance with the security requirements (which include those defenses that assist in protecting the assets against threat agents) of their contract with IWC. (*Note*: All contracts that include the sharing of IWC assets should include asset protection specifications and address liability issues.)

Because of today's global marketplace, IWC has expanded its operations to include some manufacturing plants, coupled with small marketing and sales forces in Europe and Asia. This expansion took place in order to take advantage of the lower manufacturing and operational costs available outside the United States. In addition, this approach enables IWC to take advantage of political considerations; the corporation is looked upon as a local enterprise, thus gaining at least some political support to make marketing and selling easier in the countries where they are located.

Currently, a small manufacturing plant is located in the Dublin, Ireland, area and consideration is being given to opening up a plant outside of Prague, Czech Republic, within the next one to two years. Once that plant is operating as expected — with at least 25% lower operating costs than those in the Dublin plant — the plan is to close the Dublin plant and use Prague as the European home manufacturing base.

In order to take advantage of the Asian market and the cheap labor and overhead costs in China, IWC has decided to move its Asian plant from Taiwan to China (PRC) within a year. The China plant will be located outside of Guangzhou. The IWC executives hotly debated the decision to open the plant in China. In order to open the plant in China, the Chinese government requires IWC to share its technology and assets and to do so as a joint partner with a Chinese firm known as "Lucky Red Star."

The concern over this joint venture is that by sharing the "crown jewels," IWC's assets and proprietary processes could subsequently be used to compete against IWC on a global basis, and, moreover, with the Chinese government's support. The IWC executives were concerned that they might eventually be priced out of business. In the end, however, the executives decided that these business risks must be taken if IWC had any hopes of expanding its sales throughout Asia and leveraging the cheaper manufacturing costs in China and the Czech Republic. IWC will consider eliminating the manufacturing plant within the United States sometime within the next three to five years, after the European and Asian operations have proved successful.

Because of the many potential counterfeiting schemes, copyright violations, and such, IWC is also concerned about increased attacks against the corporate assets, especially its "crown jewels," as well as more fraud-threat agents' attacks.

KEY ELEMENTS FOR THE CSO TO CONSIDER

On the basis of this background information on IWC, the IWC CSO should keep the following key elements in mind:

1. IWC is a *high-technology, multibillion dollar, highly visible, global corporation:* IWC uses and is dependent on information and computer-based processes. Such technology is vulnerable to a multitude of different attacks, including those by fraud-threat agents. This makes the IWC assets protection and anti-fraud programs of vital importance. Its locations, visibility, and economic power make it a prime target for fraudsters.
2. IWC *uses a proprietary process:* Information relative to the proprietary process is one of the most valuable assets within IWC, and it must be protected at all costs from all threats, including the use of fraud schemes to gain access to this process.
3. *The proprietary process is the key to IWC's success and vital to company survival:* The number one priority of the assets protection and anti-fraud programs must be to ensure that this process receives the highest protection. It is therefore a priority for the CSO to ensure that the current anti-fraud mechanisms are in place and that they are adequate.
4. IWC is *in an extremely competitive business:* To the CSO, this means that the potential for use of fraud schemes is a factor to consider in establishing the anti-fraud program.
5. IWC is *networked with its customers and subcontractors; subcontractors must also use IWC's proprietary process, under contractual agreements:* When the CSO builds the IWC anti-fraud program, the customers' and subcontractors' interfaces to IWC entities must be a key anti-fraud concern.
6. Because of today's global marketplace, IWC has over the last several years expanded its operations to include some *manufacturing plants, coupled with a small marketing and sales force in Europe and Asia.* The European and Asian plants must also be considered when developing the IWC anti-fraud program. The program must be global in nature, but it must also consider the risks and fraud threats to its assets based on working in a foreign environment. For example, the amount and type of local frauds, as well as the society and culture of the foreign nations, must also be factored into the anti-fraud program.

7.   Because of the foreign plants, *key executives will also be traveling extensively to the foreign locations.* Therefore, the threats posed by defrauders must be factored into any foreign travel briefings to these executives and to all other corporate employees who will be traveling overseas, even if for vacation.

GETTING TO KNOW IWC

Since the CSO is new to IWC and the widget industry, the CSO, in the first week of employment, will walk around the entire company, see how widgets are made, learn what processes are used to make the widgets, and watch the process from beginning to end.

The CSO will want to know as much as possible about the company. It is very important that the CSO understand the inner workings of the company. In fact, before being interviewed and finally hired as the CSO, the CSO applicant researched and studied all possible information about IWC and the widget industry. This knowledge proved very useful in the job interview process

Many new CSOs sit through the general in-briefing given to new employees, learn some general information about the company, and then go to their office. They start working and may not see how the company actually operates or makes widgets. They seldom see or meet the other people who participate in hands-on protection of the IWC's vital assets from fraud-threat agents and others. These people include users of automated systems on the factory floor, human resources personnel, quality control personnel, legal staff members, auditors, procurement personnel, contract personnel, financial specialists, purchasing and contract specialists, in-house subcontractors, and other non-IWC employees.

When asked why they don't walk around the plant or understand the company processes, the normal reply is: "I don't have the time. I'm too busy 'putting out fires'!" The answer to that dilemma is take a time management course; manage your time better; and make the time!

A CSO cannot provide a service and support-oriented anti-fraud program without an understanding of the company, its culture, and how its products are made. If you want to spend your time "putting out fires," do it right and join the fire department because you won't be a successful CSO.

The CSO should know how the manufacturing processes operate, how manufacturing is supported by other company elements, how employees use IWC assets, the problems they are having doing their jobs because of assets protection — security — constraints, and whether or not they are even following the IWC assets protection policies and procedures. As the CSO is acquiring this knowledge, he or she should be cognizant of the potential for various fraud attacks.

While the CSO is learning about the corporation and how things are done, employees should also be asked how well they think the assets they use are protected from fraud attacks and what they consider some of the processes' weaknesses.

All the IWC anti-fraud and related assets protection policies and procedures neatly typed and placed in binders will simply be ignored if they get in the way of employees doing their primary functions or do not help defend against fraud attacks.

The IWC CSO understands that one cannot see all these things from the office or cubicle. The CSO can only do the job well by walking around the areas where the people are working and actually using IWC assets, and by talking to all levels of employees from corporate management to the custodians. In addition, the new CSO should ensure that all members of the security staff, as well as all other corporate employees belonging to the anti-fraud team leadership group, take the same approach to their jobs.

IWC'S BUSINESS PLANS

The CSO must have an understanding of business and business competition on a global scale. Prior to developing an anti-fraud program, the CSO must also read and understand the IWC plans, which include the corporation's Strategic Business Plan, Tactical Business Plan, and Annual Business Plan. These plans are outlined at the executive management level and are passed down to all IWC departments. The management of the departments then makes input into the plan outline, after which this information is integrated at the executive management level. From there, the plans are passed down to the IWC departments, who will develop their own plans to support the overall IWC plans (see Figure 8-2).

STRATEGIC BUSINESS PLAN

IWC has developed a proprietary, Strategic Business Plan (IWC SBP), which describes IWC's strategy for maintaining its competitive edge in the design, manufacture, and sale of high-technology widgets. That plan sets the baseline and the direction that IWC will follow for the next seven years. It is considered IWC's long-range plan. It was decided that any plan longer than seven years was not feasible owing to the rapidly changing environment created by technology and IWC's competitive business environment.

The IWC SBP sets forth the following:

- The expected annual earnings for the next seven years.
- The market-share percentage goals on an annual basis.

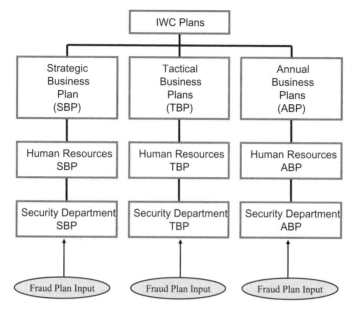

Figure 8-2. Structure of the IWC business plans.

- The future process modernization projects based on expected technology changes bringing faster, cheaper, and more powerful computers, telecommunications systems, and robotics.
- IWC expansion goals.
- IWC's acquisition of some current subcontractor and competitive companies.
- The requirement that a mature anti-fraud program can protect IWC's valuable assets, especially its proprietary information and processes, while allowing access to these assets by its international and national customers, subcontractors, and suppliers.

The CSO must understand the IWC SBP because the corporate security SBP must be integrated into the next level of SBP and provide the strategies necessary to support the IWC SBP. This includes the anti-fraud elements of such an effort.

TACTICAL BUSINESS PLAN

IWC's proprietary Tactical Business Plan (IWC TBP) is a three-year plan and sets more definitive goals, objectives, and tasks. The IWC TBP is the short-range plan that is used to support IWC's SBP. IWC's successful implementation and completion of its projects is a critical element in meeting IWC's goals and objectives.

The IWC TBP also calls for the *completion* of an anti-fraud program that can protect IWC's proprietary and sensitive information and processes as well as other assets, while allowing access to them as needed under contractual agreements with national and international customers, subcontractors, and suppliers. In addition, it is expected to be able to integrate new, secure processes and the like, with *minimum* impact on schedules or costs.

Key Elements of IWC's TBP

The IWC TBP must itself also be protected from fraud-threat agents in a similar fashion as the IWC SBP.

The CSO must always remember that some of the IWC assets, such as its information, are time-sensitive and that the global marketplace is always dynamic. That is, its value to defrauders and others is time-dependent and changes as global market conditions change. Thus, its anti-fraud defense requirements may decrease over time and also be less costly. This is a key factor in protecting any information: *It should be protected using only those methods necessary, and only for the time period required, based on the value of that asset over time.*

> The CSO must consider that the IWC anti-fraud program must contain processes to reevaluate the anti-fraud defensive mechanisms used to protect IWC assets so that it is only protected for the period required.

As was true with the IWC SBP, the CSO must understand the IWC TBP because an IWC security TBP must be developed to integrate security services and support into the IWC TBP. The corporate security TBP should identify the goals, objectives, and tactics necessary to support the IWC TBP. These must include the establishment and maintenance of a proactive anti-fraud program.

A key point that should not be overlooked can be found by comparing portions of the IWC SBP and the IWC TBP. The IWC SBP states that "[i]n addition, it is expected that the anti-fraud program will be capable of supporting the integration of new customers, subcontractors, plants, processes, hardware, software, networks, etc. while maintaining the required level of threat agent defenses without impact to schedules or costs."

The IWC TBP includes a similar statement: "In addition, it is expected that the anti-fraud program will be capable of supporting the integration of new customers, subcontractors, plants, processes, hardware, software, networks, etc. while maintaining the required level of anti-fraud defenses with minimal impact to schedules or costs."

The interpretation can be made that the CSO has three years to establish a viable anti-fraud program with minimal impact on schedules and costs. After that three-year period, it is expected that the anti-fraud program will *not* impact schedules or costs. As the new CSO, you must determine if that goal of zero impact is possible. (*Hint*: There will always be some impact. The goal should be to minimize that impact.)

As the new CSO, this potential conflict should be immediately brought to the attention of upper management for clarification and interpretation. The apparent conflict may have been caused by the selection of a poor choice of words. However, it may be that the IWC management meant what they said. It is then up to you as the IWC CSO to meet that objective or have the sentence clarified and changed.

IWC'S ANNUAL BUSINESS PLAN

IWC also has a proprietary Annual Business Plan (IWC ABP) that sets forth its goals and objectives for the year. The IWC ABP defines the specific projects to be implemented and completed by the end of the year. The successful completion of these projects will contribute to the success of IWC's Tactical Business Plan and Strategic Business Plan.

IWC's ABP called for the hiring of a CSO to establish an anti-fraud program that would provide for the protection of IWC's valuable assets from fraud-threat agents, while allowing access to the assets by its customers, subcontractors, and suppliers. This obviously seems like an impossible challenge, but it is not one that is unusual for corporate executives to demand or require.

The CSO will also be responsible for managing the corporate security organization. The CSO will report to the executive vice president of Human Resources (HR). The executive vice president of HR reports directly to IWC's chief executive officer (CEO).

IWC AND THE HISTORY OF ITS CSO

At one time, IWC had only a professional physical security program made up of alarm systems, badge readers, and a guard force. Its program was accomplished under a guard force, outsourcing contract as overseen by the IWC Contracts and Procurement Office. This office also oversees its separate access badge reader contract and its alarm system contract. Ultimately, however, the IWC executives determined that they needed a professional CSO and organization to meet their ever-increasing security requirements as they expand worldwide and mature as a corporation.

IWC's executive management agreed that a CSO position should be established and that the CSO hired should lead the IWC's assets protection program. Because IWC had previously been a victim of fraud attacks, the CSO was also charged with establishing an anti-fraud program and managing the corporate security organization. However, no consensus was reached as to where in IWC the CSO reported. The new CSO did understand, however, that no assets protection program could be successful unless it included an anti-fraud program as part of the overall assets protection program.

Some members of executive management recommended that the CSO report to the director of auditing. However, the director of auditing advised that the auditing department was strictly responsible for determining IWC's compliance with applicable state, federal, and international laws and company policies and procedures. The director felt that the auditors' limited scope and functions would adversely limit the CSO in establishing and managing an assets protection program as well as the anti-fraud program.

The director of auditing also argued that a conflict of interest might present itself if the CSO were to establish corporate anti-fraud policies and procedures — albeit with management support and approval — while at the same time having another part of that organization (the audit group) determine not only compliance with those policies and procedures, but also if they were adequate.

The CSO and the corporate security department were also considered for inclusion in the Information Technology Department (IT) since IWC was an information-based and high technology-supported corporation whose major assets were computer-based. The reasoning was that the majority of assets that required protection were IT supported, regardless of whether they were protected from defrauders, thieves, or other miscreants.

Since the information systems security (InfoSec) organization was under IT, it made sense to place all of security under IT. However, the executive vice president of IT strongly objected. That offer was tabled pending the hiring of the CSO. They reasoned that the CSO and the vice president of IT could meet later, discuss relevant anti-fraud defensive issues, and decide the best approach to be used by the IT Department.

Also considered as the "home" of the CSO and the corporate security organization was the Finance Department, which also reported directly to the CEO. Both of these were not considered "practical" by the vice president of finance and the CEO.

Following a survey taken of other corporations similar to IWC, it was determined that the majority of the corporate security departments in those corporations were part of the Human Resources departments. Thus, it was finally decided that the CSO position and organization should be established within the HR Department. Apparently, no one else seemed to want to be responsible for the function, but also it seemed a logical positioning based on the survey.

A CSO was hired; however, due to the lack of progress in developing an anti-fraud program and the loss of some valuable corporate assets as a result of successful fraud attacks, the other CSO was fired and the new CSO (you, the reader) was hired. During the interview process and again after being hired, the new CSO determined why the CSO position was formed and why it reported where it did in the IWC organizational structure.

During the interview process, the new CSO applicant laid out an anti-fraud program baseline that helped the executive management team select you as the new CSO as no other applicant or past CSO ever discussed providing an anti-fraud program and for making the case as to why one would be necessary, but as a subset of the assets protection program. Such an IWE anti-fraud program made a great deal of sense to the management team, especially after the CSO (when an applicant for the position) provided examples of the types of fraud threats, schemes, and fraud successes that had taken place against other corporations and other entities.

The new CSO's understanding of how this position ended up where it did provides some clues as to the feeling and inner workings of IWC's management vis-à-vis the CSO and the anti-fraud program. This information will be useful both when the CSO begins to establish IWC's anti-fraud program and when the CSO requests support from these corporate executives. It also provides the CSO with some insight into what type of support the CSO's organization may receive from these executives. The circumstances surrounding the firing of the previous CSO also helped the new CSO understand what must now be considered the number one priority: the establishment of the IWC anti-fraud program.

Here is an example of the use of this information: Knowing that no major, logical department within IWC wanted the corporate security, responsibility could be leveraged. That means that those department heads might not mind supporting corporate security and the anti-fraud program, but they did not want to have too much responsibility for that effort. This provided the CSO the possibility of being a strong leader without concerns that the departments identified would want to absorb some of the security functions into their departments. Thus, a more centralized, CSO-directed anti-fraud program could probably be established. As with any position within a corporation, office politics played a major role in this endeavor, as did informal information channels, such as the flow of gossip. To be successful, the CSO must understand the "game" of office politics, power, and "back-channel" information flows.

Furthermore, it is clear that the director of auditing would support the anti-fraud program but had some concern as to how well the auditors would support the CSO leading the anti-fraud program. The CSO assumed that from the auditing standpoint, the audit manager would probably agree to be part of an anti-fraud team but would not want any responsibility for writing the assets protection and the anti-fraud program policies and procedures.

When the CSO decides how to establish assets protection and anti-fraud policies and procedures, he or she must keep in mind what departments should be involved in a particular part of that development and "buy-in" process.

KEY ELEMENTS OF IWC'S ANNUAL BUSINESS PLAN

The CSO must also develop a corporate anti-fraud program annual business plan. That plan must include goals, objectives, and projects that will support the goals and objectives of IWC's ABP and include those associated with defending the corporate assets against defrauders and other miscreants.

ANTI-FRAUD PROGRAM PLANNING

The main philosophy running through this chapter should be obvious: As a service and support organization, the IWC security department and the IWC anti-fraud program must include plans that support the corporation's business plans.

The CSO should be able to map each major business goal and the objective of each plan to key anti-fraud program projects and functions. When writing the applicable anti-fraud program plan, the CSO will also be able to see which functions are not being supported. That may or may not be a problem. However, the mapping will allow the CSO to identify areas where required support to the plans has not been identified in the CSO's plans.

The CSO can then add tasks where increased anti-fraud support is needed. Following this procedure will show management how the anti-fraud program is supporting the business. When mapping the anti-fraud program plan probably through the assets protection plan to the business plans, the CSO should summarize the goals because they will be easier to map.

IWC'S DEPARTMENTS OF PRIMARY IMPORTANCE TO THE CSO

Since the IWC Security Department is a service and support organization, all the IWC departments and personnel are important to the CSO. However, the CSO must work closely with several departments and rely on them to successfully provide anti-fraud program service and support. In addition, several are an integral part of helping to ensure that the anti-fraud program is successfully implemented and managed. At IWC, these departments are:

- *Ethics Department*: This small organization reports to the CEO and is managed by a director. This organization is responsible for working with the training department to provide ethics training to the employees. In addition, it manages the IWC Ethics Hotline. The Ethics Hotline was established to receive complaints and conduct inquiries into allegations of wrongdoings by the employees or others who may be associated with IWC. The complainants may remain anonymous if they so choose. If they provide their names, that information is kept IWC-Private.

  If an allegation is received that requires more detailed inquiry possibly involving evidence, more in-depth interviews, and interrogations, the ethics director provides that information to the CSO's manager of investigations. The manager of investigations works directly for the CSO, conducts the inquiries, and reports the results back to the director of ethics, who is defined as the internal customer for such matters. The director of ethics chairs a monthly ethics meeting whose members include the CSO's representative (manager of investigations), legal representative, Human Resources representative, and the manager of audits

- *Audit Department*: IWC's Audit Department is similar to other corporate audit departments. The auditors in this department have the primary responsibility for conducting audits to ensure that IWC is operating and that its employees are performing their duties, in accordance with applicable federal, state, and local laws, as well as corporate policies and procedures. The audit manager and the CSO share information of mutual interest.

- *Legal Department*: This department is responsible for performing all common duties associated with any corporation's legal department, including providing advice and assistance to the CSO as requested or deemed appropriate.

- *Employee Relations, Human Resources Department*: This organization within the Human Resources Department, as the name implies, deals with employee issues such as employee complaints about their managers, providing guidance to managers relating to employee discipline.

The structure of IWC is no different from that of most other corporations. The corporate environment (or corporate office) differs from that of a business unit. The corporate environment has a strategic outlook, managing the overall business performance and strategy of the company. The focus is on the strategic direction of the enterprise, making the company profitable and producing shareholder value. The IWC corporate office generally does not develop and deliver products and services. That is done by its business units, although they maybe co-located, as they are at IWC.

In support of its vision, a corporate office will establish the overall strategy for the company determining the type and scope of business. The corporate office will also develop policy, provide performance and compliance oversight, and exercise its fiduciary obligations to the board of directors and the shareholders. The corporate office usually does not get involved in the daily operations of a business unit. However, there are exceptions or conditions such as poor performance, at which time the corporate office will intervene in the operation of a business unit.

A business unit functions much differently from a corporate office. It operates in an environment where goods and services are designed, developed, produced, and delivered. It is a tactical operation in support of the company business strategy, and its day-to-day focus is on getting the product out. Typically, many different business units operate independently of each other and report to a corporate office (see Figure 8-1). Each business unit has different strategic objectives that fit into the overall company strategy.

IWC, like every company, regardless of size, has its own special culture. Some companies encourage competition between business units. Here rivalries as well as aggressive behavior are encouraged and rewarded. In other companies, teamwork is advocated. "Social scientists tell us that cultures are built upon behavioral 'norms' which are defined as a set of expectations on how people will behave in a given situation."[1] The culture of a company can differ between the corporate environment and the operations environment just as much as it differs between companies. Subcultures within an organization exist, which may differ significantly from the larger organization. Understanding the company culture is essential for a successful anti-fraud program.

IWC VISION, MISSION, AND QUALITY STATEMENTS

IWC requires that all those in IWC management perform certain management, albeit sometimes bureaucratic, tasks. Like many of today's modern corporations, IWC has developed vision, mission, and quality statements using a hierarchical process. IWC directed that the statements should link all levels in the management and organizational chain. The statements of the lower levels should be written and used to support the upper levels and vice versa.

---

[1] Golin, Mark, et al, "Secrets of Executive Success" (Emmaus, PA: Rodale Press), 1991.

Most employees seem to regard such "statements" as part of just another management task that is somehow supposed to help all employees understand their jobs — or whatever. However, these statements are often developed in "employee team meetings," get printed, are placed on walls, and are soon forgotten. Confidentially, many managers feel the same way, and that is probably why managers present them as just another task to be performed by or with employees.

This is unfortunate, for these statements are a good idea inasmuch as they set a direction and philosophy for everyone at IWC, at all organizational levels. When presented with the right attitude, they can be used to focus the employees on objectives and give them a better understanding of why they are there doing what they are doing. IWC's vision, mission, and quality statements are as follows:

Vision Statement

In many of today's businesses, management develops a vision statement. The vision statement is usually a short paragraph that attempts to set the strategic goal, objective, or direction of the company. IWC has a vision statement and requires all organizations to have statements based on the IWC corporate statements.

What Is a Vision? A vision statement is a short statement that is:

- is clear, concise, and understandable by the employees;
- is connected to ethics, values and behaviors;
- states where IWC wants to be (long term);
- sets the tone; and
- sets the direction for IWC

IWC's Vision Statement: *IWC's vision is to maintain its competitive advantage in the global marketplace by providing widgets to our customers when they want them, where they want them, and at a fair price.*

Mission Statement

Mission statements are declarations as to the purpose of a business or government agency.

IWC's Mission Statement: *Design, manufacture, and sell high-quality widgets, thereby expanding our global market shares while continuing to improve processes in order to meet customers' expectations.*

Quality Statement

Quality is what adds value to a corporation's products and services. It is what your internal and external customers expect from you.

IWC Quality Statement: *To provide quality widgets to our customers with zero defects by building it right the first time.*

PLANS

Plans are generally thought of as a logical series of tasks, functions, and thoughts written down in order to accomplish some future objective. In the case of IWC, it is like any small, medium, or large corporation. It has business plans, hiring plans, marketing plans, and the list goes on. The CSO also must develop plans to ensure that an IWC assets protection program and anti-fraud program can be successfully established and managed as part of its service and support to the corporation.

Since the SBP is a seven-year plan, the specifics of how to get there are not defined in sufficient detail to assist the CSO in also stating generalities. Keeping in mind the service and support functions and the "parasite on the profits" philosophy, the CSO's SBP statement related to this particular goal is as follows:

- *Establish and manage a cost-effective IWC Anti-Fraud Program that will provide the minimum amount of anti-fraud defenses conducive to an acceptable level of risk and thus contributing to the IWC goal of IWC 7% average annual profit increase for the next seven years.*

Remember that the Corporate Security Department goals must integrate into the Human Resources Department goals and SBP and then to IWC. This is part of the "balancing act" that a CSO must do as the IWC Security Department is under the Human Resources Department. Therefore, the goals must support the Human Resources goals. At the same time, the CSO is responsible for the IWC anti-fraud program for the entire corporation that is broader in scope than just Human Resources goals.

The CSO works in a world of office politics where often security is given a bad name. These goals help show that the CSO and the Corporate Security Department are "team players" and doing their part to support the IWC goals. As the CSO, also remember that if you do not agree with someone, they often say that you are not a "team player." This should be a warning to you to conform to someone's beliefs or be considered a possible adversary. If this comes from a peer, be wary. If it comes from your boss, be very concerned, and in fact, it is imperative that a one-on-one meeting be held to discuss the matter.

> The real beauty of these two supporting IWC SBP goals is this: You come across, as you should, like a team player ready to sacrifice and do your part to meet the IWC goal.

Based on the minimum amount of anti-fraud defenses conducive to an acceptable level of risk is a key term. What is considered the acceptable level of risk is an *executive management decision* and should be based on risk analyses conducted by members of the Corporate Security Department in conjunction with various other IWC staff members who can contribute to the individual analyses.

The executive management's decisions relative to risk will include deciding which of the various options presented along with the value of the assets and their anti-fraud defensive costs versus risk should be implemented. Thus, the executive management's decisions are a factor in the cost of protection. Therefore, the CSO can fall back on the position that the executive management decisions assisted in whether or not the CSO met this SBP goal. In other words — "It's not my fault!" This approach is sometimes necessary in dealing in the world of office politics. It is sad but also a matter of survival. You must weigh the risks of using such a position if it becomes necessary. As the saying goes, "Damned if you do and damned if you don't."

The CSO should try to have the minimal amount of budget and staff conducive to getting the job done. The CSO should try to get performance and thus raises and bonuses tied more to successfully getting the job done at least cost consistent with the protection of the assets. The job of the CSO is challenging, but it can also be a fun job.

OTHER IWC PLANS AND CSO SUPPORT

Using the approach as discussed above, the CSO must integrate anti-fraud program SBP, TBP, and ABP goals into the CSO's assets protection goals, HR goals, and the IWC overall goals.

CASE STUDY

As the new CSO, how would you go about developing anti-fraud-related vision, mission, and quality statements?

One approach would be to:

* Identify the IWC statements.
* Identify the HR statements.

- Identify the previous Security Department statements.
- Develop anti-fraud-related statements that support the above statements.
  - Discuss the development of statements with your boss.
  - Establish a project team with selected members of the security department representing all the security department organizations to draft statements and coordinate them with all security department personnel for input.
  - Have the project team finalize statements.
  - Have the CSO modify as appropriate and approve the statements.
  - Submit the statements to the CSO's boss for approval.

SUMMARY

The reader can use the fictitious global corporation, IWC, to build an anti-fraud program.

Many corporations set their goals and objectives in planning documents such as strategic, tactical, and annual business plans. These plans are key documents for the CSO to read and use to determine the corporation's future directions.

These plans are also key documents that the CSO may be able to use to determine what is expected from the CSO and the anti-fraud program. The plans should also be used as the basis for writing service and support anti-fraud plans, as separate documents or as sections that are integrated into the identified corporate planning documents.

The decision process of the IWC executive management in determining which department the CSO and the corporate security organization belong to provides some key information that the CSO should use in establishing the anti-fraud program and related security organization. It helps identify potential "power plays" by managers and provides a glimpse at the corporate political environment.

The CSO must look at IWC from a global perspective and consider political, technological, economic, and global competitive factors, fraud-threat agents, and similar topics around the world. This broad scope is required when developing an anti-fraud program for IWC that will meet the worldwide needs of the IWC, now and into the future.

9

Establishing an Anti-Fraud Program

INTRODUCTION

With this chapter we begin what is the heart of this book: establishing and managing an anti-fraud program. The International Widget Corporation (IWC) will be used as the corporation for which an anti-fraud program is to be established and managed. If you are working for a corporation, you can of course substitute your corporation for IWC so that you can build a realistic model that works in your environment.

IWC's assets (i.e., people, facilities, information, and equipment) are valuable and must be consistently protected by all IWC employees, contracted personnel, associate companies, subcontractors — in fact, everyone who has authorized access to these assets. They must be protected regardless of the environment in which they are located, for example, in IWC facilities in foreign countries.

A corporate chief security officer (CSO) is responsible for ensuring that these assets are protected and does so by establishing and managing a formal assets protection program. Such a program must protect the corporate assets from the various threats, both national and international. As a subset of that program or as a standalone program, depending on the corporate culture and needs, is the anti-fraud program. For our purposes, such a program is a subset of the corporate assets protection program at IWC. (See Figure 9-1.)

In order to provide anti-fraud defenses and related protection measures, those individuals who have authorized access to the IWC assets must:

- Be aware of the details of the IWC anti-fraud program, at least as it applies to them.

Anti-Fraud Program Drivers

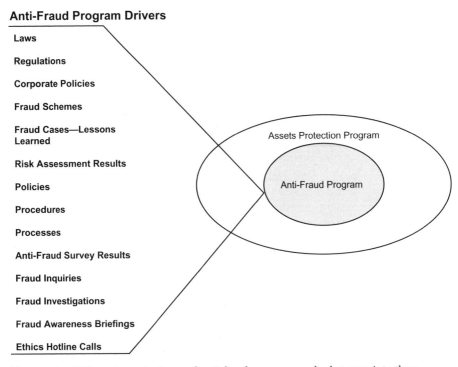

Laws

Regulations

Corporate Policies

Fraud Schemes

Fraud Cases—Lessons Learned

Risk Assessment Results

Policies

Procedures

Processes

Anti-Fraud Survey Results

Fraud Inquiries

Fraud Investigations

Fraud Awareness Briefings

Ethics Hotline Calls

Assets Protection Program

Anti-Fraud Program

Figure 9-1. IWC assets protection and anti-fraud programs and what goes into them.

- Receive guidance as to the policies, procedures, processes, and plans relating to the anti-fraud program.
- Understand how to apply anti-fraud defensive measures.
- Understand why such anti-fraud measures are required.
- Understand at least basic fraud schemes.
- Know how to rapidly report potential fraud threat agent attacks and vulnerabilities.

When IWC's CSO decided that a policy document was needed, the IWC CSO drafted one for the IWC CEO to sign, after coordinating it with the VP of HR, for subsequent distribution to IWC employees and all others with access to IWC assets. It was also done to fulfill that requirement as stated in the IWC plans (e.g. IWC Strategic Business Plan).

The type of policy document that you as the CSO draft will depend on your corporate culture and the type of format that the CEO prefers to use. This format and "wording" can be found in other CEO-signed documents that were sent out to the IWC employees and also by discussing the draft with your boss and the CEO's secretary, who will know how the policy document should be worded for the CEO's signature.

It is imperative that the CEO state his or her support for the anti-fraud program and does so in writing. The difficulty is to have such a policy approved and made available to all employees, associates, and others without it seeming that such a program was necessary owing to the perception of "massive frauds" taking place within the corporation. As is true of most policy documents, office politics plays a very important role.

IWC'S ANTI-FRAUD PROGRAM

The CSO knew that, to successfully protect IWC's assets from fraud-threat agents, formal guidelines and directions had to be provided to the IWC employees. There also had to be some formal processes for ensuring that the IWC assets are protected from fraud-threat agents in an effective and efficient manner — in other words, "good and cheap."

It was obvious to IWC's management and the CSO that to do otherwise would cause employees to protect assets as they saw fit, or not protect them at all. Such was almost the case now at IWC, and the CSO knew that there was an urgent need to quickly establish an anti-fraud program based on the history at IWC of successful and unsuccessful attacks by fraud-threat agents.

The IWC anti-fraud program would be developed taking into consideration and/or incorporating:

- Reasons for the anti-fraud program, including its drivers such as laws and regulations.
- IWC vision, mission, and quality statements.
- Legal, ethical, and best business practices.
- IWC's strategic, tactical, and annual business plans.
- IWC's assets protection program to include its related strategic, tactical, and annual security plans, policies, and procedures as directed by the IWC CSO.
- The corporate security department's vision, mission, and quality statements.
- Current anti-fraud related policies, procedures, and processes.
- Other anti-fraud related documents.

The IWC anti-fraud program cannot be developed in a vacuum if it is to work. The input of others is a necessity as the program, if not done correctly, may adversely impact IWC's business. Remember that the CSO's security department and functions must be service and support driven. Furthermore, they are an overhead function; thus they take away from IWC's profit base.

As part of that endeavor, the anti-fraud program must be integrated into the IWC assets protection program and must support the IWC business plans. It then follows that the plans call for certain actions to protect IWC's vital assets.

Remember what is being discussed here are the plans, processes, policies, and procedures that are established, implemented, and maintained (kept current) as they apply to all IWC departments. This should not be confused with the security department's internal plans, policies, and procedures (e.g., work instructions, processes, and such that apply strictly within the IWC security department).

As the CSO, one of your first tasks is to obtain a copy of the IWC assets protection program document (hopefully there is one). If none is available, should one be developed prior to developing an anti-fraud program as a subprogram to that assets protection program? At IWC, a formal assets protection program does exist.

Within your corporation, you may find that:

1. There is no such document.
2. The one now in use is not really current and needs updating.
3. To your shock and amazement, the IWC assets protection program documents are current and excellent.

Of the three options, which would you prefer and why? Actually, there are benefits to all the options. The one you choose will probably be based on where you are coming from and where you are going (e.g., your education, experience, and what you would like to see in such a plan).

Option number one has some benefits. If there is no such document as the IWC assets protection program by any name, one can "do it right the first time" and develop one that meets IWC's needs using your own tried and true methods. However, the less experience you have, the more difficult it will be to do it right the first time.

If you are new to the corporate CSO position, it may be doubly difficult and a real problem. No, not a problem, because you are now in a management position; therefore, these are not called problems. They are called "challenges."

Having an assets protection plan that has been approved by executive management has some benefits, of course. "Approve it?" you say. "Why does anyone have to approve it? I am the CSO, the security professional, the expert in the business. I know what I am doing. I don't need any non-security people out there playing amateur assets protection expert." That may have worked in the past, maybe in the times of the hunter-gatherer period, but not now. Teaming is now the latest approach in corporate management. One reason for that is of course so that no one is responsible and yet everyone is in it together and, therefore, all our responsible. "It's not my fault!", "We all agreed," and "It's not my responsibility!" are what generally follows when something goes wrong.

Here's the issue: as the CSO, you are going to establish an anti-fraud program that will impact everyone and everything in IWC in one form or another, since the IWC assets permeate all levels of IWC and IWC cannot function without them. You are the new CSO at IWC and really don't have a good handle on how anti-fraud assets protection policies and procedures impact the IWC business of making widgets.

You may have a great way to protect a certain type or types of assets, but find that if it were implemented it would slow down production. That is not a good idea in the competitive, fast-paced, global marketplace in which IWC competes for business. That may get you a warning first but then fired (as was the case of the last CSO?), or it may increase costs in other ways (impeding employees' productivity is a cost matter also).

The second option also has some good advantages, especially for the CSO who has less experience in the profession and/or less experience at IWC. The advantage is that you have a framework on which to build. But as with option number one, some caution is advised, especially when building on that framework, basically changing it to how you envision the final assets protection program and anti-fraud program baselines.

Option number two allows you, as the new CSO, the opportunity to see what executive management has authorized to date. In other words, you know how much "protection" the executive management of IWC will allow at what expense to productivity, costs, and so forth. This will help you decide how to structure your anti-fraud program: you will not likely receive any additional budget to incorporate an anti-fraud program into the overall IWC assets protection program since IWC is continually looking for ways to save money and increase productivity.

If you increase assets protection defenses by adding a more formal and aggressive anti-fraud program, it must provide sound, convincing business reasons why that should happen. In this cause, you have an edge because of the previous loss of IWC assets to fraud-threat agents, which led in part to the firing of the former CSO. In addition, the CEO is supportive in that both the Strategic Business Plan (SBP) and Tactical Business Plan (TBP) have assets protection/anti-fraud goals, and those plans had to be approved by the CEO prior to implementation.

The CSO can make a case for the anti-fraud program as part of the "new and improved" assets protection program. Thus, the assets protection program already has high visibility and at least some executive management support. However, that "honeymoon" may not last long if you require protection mechanisms that are not backed by sound business sense.

Option number three is great if you are new to the CSO position and/ or lack confidence or experience in assets protection and anti-fraud program development. However, caution is also needed here because IWC assets were lost and the former CSO was fired. The questions you must get answered are as follows:

- Did the assets protection processes — and for our purposes those specifically related to an anti-fraud program or lack thereof as set forth in the IWC assets protection program — leave a vulnerability or vulnerabilities that allowed the fraud threat agents to take advantage of it?

- Was the assets protection or anti-fraud aspects of it not the issue but someone or a group failed to follow proper procedures?
- Was the CSO just not the right person for the job at IWC? (If this is the case, find out why so that you don't make the same mistake, assuming you want to work for IWC for more than a year or two.)

As the new CSO, you should get the answers to these questions and then determine the best way to integrate an anti-fraud program into the overall assets protection program for IWC. You of course want to determine whether the assets protection program can be modified and enhanced to mitigate future fraud-threat agent attacks. The benefit of a current assets protection program is that it has received the concurrence of executive management — but remember that it may be a bad plan. After all, what does executive management know of assets protection and anti-fraud matters except what the CSO tells them, aside from "common-sense" knowledge?

Let us assume that there is an IWC assets protection program but none of it addresses fraud-related matters such as fraud-threat agents and defending the assets against their schemes. Furthermore, it is not up to date.

So, the IWC must start from the beginning to build an anti-fraud program. Actually, that may not be entirely true. If you are an experienced CSO, you have brought knowledge and experience to the IWC CSO position, and that includes fighting frauds.

> There generally are some assets protection plans, policies, procedures, and processes that can be used to support an anti-fraud program or be modified to fit into an anti-fraud program.

It would be cost-effective if assets protection plans, policies, and processes can be used in part in building the anti-fraud program. It would be a more effective and efficient method to implement since the employees and others are already aware of how, at least in general, to protect IWC assets from general threats. It may just be a matter of gathering applicable plans, policies, procedures, projects, and processes together for analysis as part of establishing the anti-fraud program baseline.

In addition, over the years the IWC CSO has swapped and collected assets protection and anti-fraud plans from other security professionals that may prove useful. Several words of caution are in order:

- Never take another's assets protection program documents (or any documents) without approval of the appropriate corporate authority because such plans may be considered and marked as corporate-confidential, corporate-private, corporate-proprietary, and the like. There is an ethics issue here.

- Remember that the other assets protection and anti-fraud plans may be outdated and/or not meet the needs of IWC (e.g., different corporate culture or environment).

ANTI-FRAUD PROGRAM PROJECT PLANNING

Using formal project management techniques, the CSO decided to establish an anti-fraud program project team. The CSO must either select a project lead, lead the team, or have the group select its own project lead. If the CSO's security organization has one or more staff members experienced in anti-fraud matters (e.g., Certified Fraud Examiner [CFE]), one of those specialists may be the natural one to head up the project team.

Other team members should include members within the IWC security organization who are responsible for each of the assets protection functions of the security organization — for example, investigator, assets protection education, and awareness specialist. Although someone who was a CFE may appear to be the best person to lead the project team, that also depends on the individual's leadership abilities, project management skills, interpersonal relations skills, knowledge of IWC office politics and culture, and the like. These qualities hold a higher priority in the project lead selection process than the credentials of just a CFE.

> One should not automatically assign the anti-fraud program project's leadership role to anyone who does not also have project management and leadership skills, which include the skills related to teaming with others to meet specified goals.

These team members would not be used full time on the project but represent the various security — assets protection — functions and provide input as deemed appropriate by the project team leader. If no one met the criteria for such an important position as the project leader, then the CSO may have to take on that responsibility.

Generally speaking, the CSO should not be taking on such jobs as the project will take time away from the overall duties of the CSO position. However, both the CSO and the entire security department's reputation will be positively or negatively affected by the results of this project and the eventual establishment and management of the IWC anti-fraud program. The IWC CSO, being new to the job, is especially busy with the normal CSO activities; however, the CSO may not have a choice, even though the use of micro-management techniques should be avoided in all but under the most vital and necessary circumstances.

The IWC CSO decided to use only specialists from the security department at this time to speed up the draft of the baseline anti-fraud program's primary document — the document that contains the requirements, processes, plans, policies, and procedures. To do otherwise, for example, adding auditors, IT staff, human relations specialists, ethics specialists, legal staff, and so on, would invariably cause so much time in discussions and arguments over the relative restrictiveness of policies that the outcome could be a slowdown or committee analysis-paralysis. The CSO determined that coordination would be done upon security's finalization of the draft document.

Let's now assume that there is an overall IWC assets protection plan in place with outdated portions. The CSO, who has already read the document and does not agree with some of the requirements in it and sees other requirements that are obviously lacking, should first meet with the security specialists currently responsible for the assets protection program and the maintenance of the assets protection document and that person's manager. The assumption is that someone in the current security organization has responsibility for the assets protection program — or equivalent plan or program.

The main purpose of the meeting would be to determine why it is not current and discuss the rationale for all the requirements stated in the document. It may be that some portions were deleted due to executive management objections. These must be identified because it is of little use to update the plan and program if it is to meet resistance and rejection when it is briefed to and coordinated with executive management, unless the CSO strongly believes that some requirements should be added and makes a case for such changes to executive management.

The CSO must decide whether or not to:

- Update the overall IWC assets protection program to include its plans, policies, procedures, and processes and set the anti-fraud program aside until that is completed.
- Update the assets protection program and the anti-fraud program in parallel.
- Update the anti-fraud program as the highest priority while maintaining the overall assets protection program's status quo.

If you were the IWC CSO, what would you do?

If you decide to hold the anti-fraud program project in abeyance pending completion of the update of the assets protection program, you may find that the anti-fraud program may be delayed a year or more, or worse yet, you may never get to it due to the need to constantly update the overall assets protection program and related plans, policies, procedures, and processes.

Would this be prudent knowing that IWC has been the target and victim of fraud threat agents in the past and may still be a target of fraud-threat agents?

If you decide to do both as projects in parallel, would there be:

* Some chaos as a result of changes being made to the overall assets protection program which may impact the anti-fraud program while the anti-fraud program project team is working with outdated assets protection plan information?
* How much rework of the anti-fraud program would then be required later — for example, the anti-fraud program would be out of date as the assets protection program plans, policies, procedures, and processes were updated?

If you want to maintain the status quo of the assets protection program and develop the anti-fraud program, remember that vital aspects of the assets protection program would also apply to the anti-fraud program and such aspects may be outdated. Therefore, you would be building the initial anti-fraud program baseline on outdated assets protection program. Thus, the anti-fraud program would have to be updated as soon as the assets protection program was brought up to date. This may not only cause some confusion among those who have to comply with both programs, but may also incur additional costs. If nothing else, employees will incur costs in lost productivity as they learn the new policies, procedures, processes, and such that apply to how they protect the IWC assets from all miscreants, including the fraud-threat agents and their schemes.

The CSO has decided to establish two project teams and to work both projects in parallel. The other two options were considered as leaving the assets at too great a risk to all the various miscreants who may target one or more assets of IWC. Furthermore, since some of the assets protection criteria will also be used in the anti-fraud program, or at least have some influence on it, they both must be expedited and thus must be developed together.

If two project leaders and the team members have been identified, the CSO must be actively involved since there must be constant communication between the two project leads if both projects are to be successful. The CSO would do this by receiving periodic status reports from both project team leaders.

The CSO must ensure that neither project leader operates in a "project vacuum," and they must share information on a regular basis — at least weekly. Neither can view their project as more important than the other's.

To begin the project, the CSO will explain the objectives of both projects at one of the CSO's regular security managers' meetings and again at one of the expanded staff meetings. The IWC CSO will also require that both project team leaders and project team staff members' managers brief the CSO on a weekly basis as to their progress, issues, and such.

Once the projects are well under way and appear to be going smoothly, at least as they relate to communications between the two project teams, the CSO may want to be briefed only every other week and then maybe once a month. It will all depend on the progress and lack of conflicts between the two project teams.

IWC ANTI-FRAUD PROGRAM PROJECT MANAGEMENT AND PLANNING

It is important to have a formal project plan to manage such a vital program. At IWC, the CSO and staff perform two basic types of work: (1) level of effort (LOE) and (2) projects. LOE is the day-to-day routine operations such as physical access control, awareness briefings, guard patrols, and investigations.

Projects are established in which some tasks related to the assets protection plan initial updates; in addition, the anti-fraud program project must be completed, but they are not ongoing tasks. It is imperative that the CSO, the CSO's managers, and the project leads be intimately familiar with and experienced in both project management and time management.

The IWC CSO has established a criterion as to whether or not some task or tasks should be a project. Projects must have:

- A stated objective (generally in one clear, concise, and complete sentence)
- A beginning date
- An ending date
- Specific tasks to be performed to successfully meet the objective
- A project leader
- Specific personnel to complete each task
- The stated date as to when each task will be completed

The IWC CSO has directed that a project plan be used to manage the anti-fraud program development, as well as the update assets project plan and program. Using Figure 9-2 as an example, let's develop a project and fill-in-the-blanks for major portions of the chart for an anti-fraud program:

SUBJECT: The project name — for example, Anti-Fraud Program Development

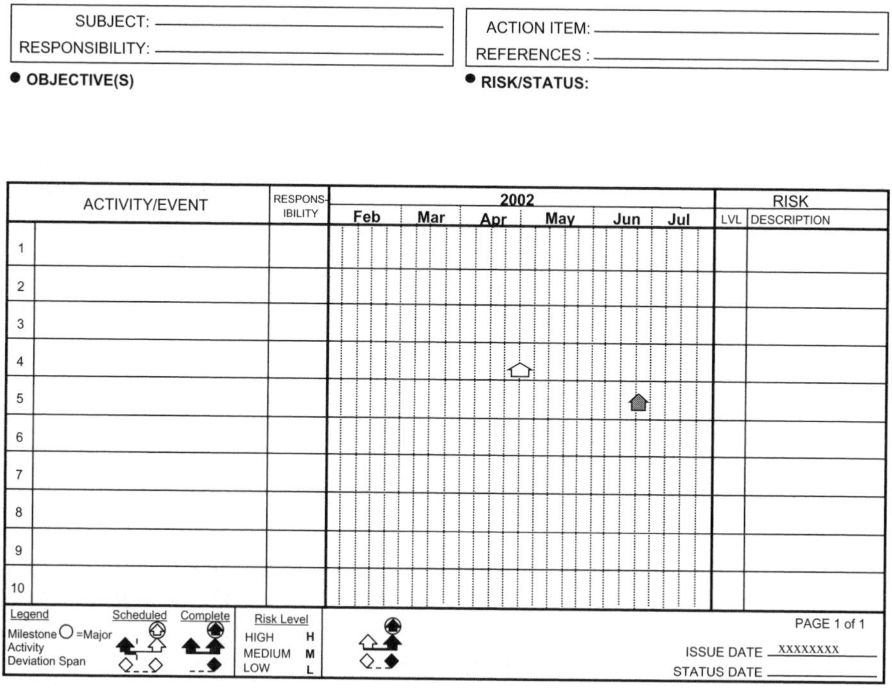

Figure 9-2. Basic project management chart that can be used to track the anti-fraud development program tasks.

RESPONSIBILITY: The name of the project leader — John Doe, security specialist

ACTION ITEM: What is to be accomplished? — for example, A baseline IWC anti-fraud program is to be developed and integrated into the IWC assets protection program with processes in place to periodically update it.

REFERENCES: What caused this project to be initiated? For example: "See CSO memo, dated June 2, 2007."

OBJECTIVE(S): State the objective of the project: Develop an anti-fraud program that will effectively and efficiently protect IWC assets from fraud-threat agents and their schemes.

RISK/STATUS: State the risk of not meeting the objective(s) of this project: Due to limited staffing and multiple customer projects being supported, this project may experience delays as higher priority LOE and other projects take precedence.

ACTIVITY/EVENT: State the tasks to be performed — for example, meet weekly with project team members, review IWC policies.

<u>RESPONSIBILITY</u>: Identify the person responsible for each task. In this case, each team member's tasks would be identified.

<u>CALENDAR</u>: The calendar could be a year long, monthly, quarterly, or a six-month calendar with vertical lines identifying individual weeks. Using the six-month calendar, the Project Lead and assigned project team members would decide what tasks had to be accomplished to meet the objective and, using the "arrows" and "diamonds" identified in the legend, mark the beginning and ending dates of each task. The arrows are filled in when the task is started and when the task is completed, and the diamonds are used to show deviations from the original dates.

<u>RISK — LVL</u>: In this space, each task is associated with the potential risk that it may be delayed or cost more than allocated in the budget for the task. Using "High," "Medium," or "Low" or "H," "M," or "L," the Project Lead, in concert with the person responsible for the task, assigns a level of risk.

<u>RISK — DESCRIPTION</u>: A short description of the risk is stated in this block. If it requires a detailed explanation, that explanation is attached to the project plan. In this block the Project Lead, who is also responsible for ensuring that the project plan is updated weekly, states "See Attachment 1."

<u>ISSUE DATE</u>: The date the project began and the chart was initiated goes in this block.

<u>STATUS DATE</u>: The most current project chart date is placed here. This detail is important because anyone looking at the project chart will know how current it is and can compare it with the ISSUE DATE to determine how long the project has been in existence.

Other types of charts can also be developed to show project costs in terms of labor, materials, and the like. A good, automated project plan software program is well worth the costs for managing projects. As the CSO, you should check within IWC to see if an approved project management software product is available. If so, use it as it will meet IWC standards.

In the case of project charts, the CSO also uses them to brief management as part of the briefing to management relative to the ongoing work of the security organization. The CSO receives weekly updates on Friday mornings in meetings with all the CSO's project leaders where each project leader is given five minutes to explain the status of the projects. Basically, all the CSO requires is that the project leaders state the status of their projects. For example, "The Project is still on schedule" or "Task #2 will be delayed because the person assigned the task is out sick for a week; however, it is expected that the project completion date will not be delayed because of it."

The CSO holds an expanded staff meeting the last Friday of each month. (The CSO should be sure to have coffee and donuts available.) All assigned security personnel attend these meetings, which last two to three hours. At these meetings, one hour is taken for all project and security functional leads to brief the status of their LOE and projects to the entire staff. The CSO does this so that everyone in the organization knows what is going on — a vital communications tool. Also during this time, other matters are briefed and discussed, matters such as the latest risk management techniques, conferences, and training courses available.

ANTI-FRAUD PROGRAM PROJECT TEAM

The next step in developing an anti-fraud program is for the project leader to identify:

- Security staff members who should be on the project team
- Every major action that is to be taken, documented as individual tasks
- Individuals responsible for each task
- When each task will begin and end
- Any budgetary needs

The project leaders must get the CSO's approval prior to beginning the projects. The CSO requires this okay to ensure that all tasks are identified and that the CSO and security managers concur in the use of labor hours and other resources needed for the projects.

ANTI-FRAUD DRIVERS — THE FIRST MAJOR TASK IN ANTI-FRAUD PROGRAM DEVELOPMENT

An anti-fraud program, whether as part of an assets protection program or as a standalone program, is needed because of many factors or security drivers (see Figure 9-1). Security drivers are those factors that cause certain levels of assets protection, anti-fraud defensive measures, to be put in place at certain times. One of the major security drivers is, of course, threats to assets that try to "take advantage" of a security weakness or vulnerability to perpetrate a fraud, other crime, or IWC policy infraction.

The chance that an attack by a fraud-threat agent can take advantage of a security weakness or vulnerability is called a risk. The amount of anti-fraud defenses and related protective measures to be applied to specific corporate assets is determined. If it is determined correctly, it will be based on the amount of money, people, time, and other factors it would take to adequately protect the assets from these fraud miscreants, based on the assets' values.

Other security drivers include various laws, regulations, policies, frauds, fraud schemes, and the like that mandate that anti-fraud assets protection mechanisms be instituted. In other words, these factors are the primary reasons that an anti-fraud program is being developed.

So, a major task is to identify, in detail, all the drivers that cause the need for an anti-fraud program. Each driver should be linked to each anti-fraud defensive measure. This task should be performed graphically and also with supporting text as part of the anti-fraud program document or documents, to be included as part of any fraud awareness briefings and training. Such linkages make it easier for executive management and all employees to see the need for certain anti-fraud defensive measures. It also helps if the CSO is trying to justify additional budget that can be linked to required, specific defensive measures (e.g. Mandated by law or SEC regulation).

IWC ANTI-FRAUD PROGRAM REQUIREMENTS — POLICIES

In developing an anti-fraud program, one must first look at drivers and identify requirements that drive the formation of policies that lead to procedures, which turn into processes to be followed by all those having authorized access to the IWC assets.

> Remember that requirements are derived from "drivers," that is, those laws, regulations, common business practices, ethics, and the like on which the anti-fraud policies are based.

Anti-fraud policies are based not only on drivers but also on IWC policies, which is another type of anti-fraud requirements' driver. The policies are needed to comply with the requirements. The procedures are required to implement the policy, and the processes are steps that are followed to make up the procedures.

RISK ASSESSMENT — THE SECOND MAJOR TASK IN DEVELOPING AN ANTI-FRAUD PROGRAM

After the anti-fraud assets protection drivers and requirements are identified, and an overall anti-fraud IWC policy document is implemented, the next step is to answer the following questions:

- Are the assets being protected from fraud-threat agents as required by one or more drivers (e.g., laws and regulations)?

- How much risk is being incurred, for example, risk is low, high, moderate, or may a statistical measurement be used based on the anti-fraud defenses?
- How much does each of the anti-fraud defensive measures cost to implement and maintain?
- Are the protective measures adequate, more than adequate, or nonexistent?
- What project tasks are needed to provide adequate anti-fraud defenses?

These questions can be answered through the implementation of risk assessment tasks.

As is true for all assets protection needs, a risk assessment should be taken periodically to determine the specific requirements for protecting corporate assets from fraud-threat agents, to measure how well the assets are being protected, and to decide what must be done if they are not adequately protected. This step should be taken in order to provide the most objective look at the threats, vulnerabilities, and risks to corporate assets, as well as to depict the anti-fraud defenses (e.g., protection of these assets) as they relate to their value, cost of protection, and required anti-fraud protection specifications.

The approach that the anti-fraud program project team will use is to develop a risk assessment process to determine the threats, vulnerabilities, and risks to IWC assets posed by fraud-threat agents. Does this make sense? Actually, it may or may not.

We discussed the importance of the two project team leaders, assets protection plan update the assets protection program project, and the anti-fraud program project to communicate on a regular basis and share information. For example, the anti-fraud program project team may be spending valuable time (and time is money in the business world) developing and then conducting an anti-fraud program-related risk assessment. However, as part of the IWC assets protection program, that had already been done. The risk assessment methodology, processes, and so on have been standardized throughout the security department. Therefore, in the case of IWC, there is no need to waste valuable time and other resources by reinventing the "risk assessment wheel."

BASICS OF IWC'S RISK ASSESSMENT PROCESS

Remember that you as the IWC CSO and your security staff are responsible for leading an anti-fraud/assets protective effort, that is, protecting things and people that need protecting according to the requirements set forth by the government agencies and owners of the assets who are willing to pay for that protection. That is, of course, delegated by the owners to management, who in turn delegate the work to the CSO. However, responsibility cannot be delegated away from management. They have final responsibility for safeguarding corporate assets, something that the CSOs often do not make management aware of, or at least not often enough.

---

as·set [á sèt] noun (plural as·sets)

1. somebody or something useful: somebody or something that is useful and contributes to the success of something
2. valuable thing: a property to which a value can be assigned

plural noun as·sets

1. owned items: the property that is owned by a particular person or organization
2. LAW seizable property: the property of a person that can be taken by law for the settlement of debts or that forms part of a dead person's estate
3. FINANCE balance sheet items: the items on a balance sheet that constitute the total value of an organization [mid-sixteenth century. Via Anglo-Norman assetz "sufficient goods" (to settle an estate) from, ultimately, Latin ad satis, literally "to sufficiency."]]¹

The policies, procedures, and processes used to defend IWC assets against fraud threat agents are based on the amount of risk the owner or corporate management, having been delegated that responsibility, is willing to assume, which itself is usually based on the value the owner or management assigns to the assets and the adverse impact to the business if they were not available.

Fraud Threats + Vulnerabilities = Risk

To understand the fraud threats to corporate assets, it is important to view these threats as they relate to the entire process of risk management. Risk management is a much-maligned process that has been improperly used, not used at all, or, in some cases, the wrong methodology or input has been used under the wrong circumstances.

The CSO must understand the basic concepts related to fraud threats, for example, as discussed in Section I of this book, and their associated

---

¹ *Encarta® World English Dictionary* © & (P) 1999 Microsoft Corporation. All rights reserved. Developed for Microsoft by Bloomsbury Publishing Plc.

assets protection risks based on the weaknesses in the current protection systems or processes. The first thing the CSO must understand (relative to assets protection from fraud-threat agents[2]) is the specific threats against the assets of the corporation. Some threats may lead to fraud-threat agent attacks, and others to other forms of attacks. The threats in general will vary for a number of reasons, notably:

- *Corporate environment*: A corporate office in an urban setting in a run-down part of town inhabited by drug dealers, addicts, and prostitutes will be prone to experience more crime that may spill over to the corporate grounds. A corporation may want a "campus" setting and thus will have less physical security than is required.
- *Corporate culture*: The corporate culture may be one that considers every employee trustworthy and loyal, so no need is seen for "excessive" controls that smack of a "police state." This attitude, though admirable, is not realistic in most of today's societies. In this atmosphere there is little control on corporate assets.
- *Products*: Threats against corporations that cut down trees would be more at risk from environmentalists than a corporation that produces baby clothes.
- *Global visibility*: A corporation that is a major force in a nation-state and/or foreign nation-states tends to be the target of attack if the corporation's home nation-state is having political difficulties with the nation-state where the corporation has offices. For example, U.S. corporations in Indonesia may be at risk because of the United States' "war on terrorism," which Muslims in Indonesia may consider as anti-Islam.
- *Vulnerability of assets*: If the assets are perceived to be vulnerable or in fact are vulnerable, there may be more attacks against them. Whereas, if the assets are perceived to be very well protected, and in fact are very well protected, there will be fewer attacks, at least over time. Therefore, the risks to these assets posed by fraud-threat agent attacks may be reduced.

THREATS

As we discussed in Section I, fraud threats can take many forms, and the type of fraud-threat agents' attacks that occur is limited only by the attacker's imagination. The two basic types of threats that the CSO deals with can be categorized as either natural or man-made.

---

[2] This of course applies to all types of threats to corporate assets; however, for our purposes, we are focusing on the fraud-related aspects of assets protection.

> One ought never to turn one's back on a threatened danger and try to run away from it. If you do that, you will double the danger. But if you meet it promptly and without flinching, you will reduce the danger by half. — *Sir Winston Churchill*

NATURAL THREATS

Natural threats are those threats that are not man-made. They are called acts of God, acts of nature, and the like and include:

- Fires, such as those caused by lightning
- Floods, such as those caused by excessive rain
- Earthquakes, caused by movements of earth's plates
- Winds, as when they are caused by typhoons/hurricanes

Natural threats apply to assets protection in general. However, when it comes to frauds, they do not apply, for only humans can perpetrate frauds; nature cannot. One must also be aware, however, that in some instances a fraud is "supported" by nature; for example, as when one falsifies damage caused by a hurricane when filing an insurance claim. If the natural act (hurricane) did not occur, the opportunity to perpetrate this fraud does not exist.

> An act of nature can provide the environment that allows fraud-threat agents to take advantage of a disaster. For instance, consider the allegations of fraud after Hurricane Katrina in the United States.

MAN-MADE THREATS

Man-made threats are defined as all threats that were not caused by nature — therefore, by humans. Historical data and changes in the working environment may assist in foretelling future threat events. Crime, specifically fraud statistics from local law enforcement for the area where the corporation is located, may assist in determining the potential fraud threats to the corporate assets in that area.

The many Web sites on the Internet can also provide useful fraud-threat agent information, fraud schemes, and fraud cases. Remember that due to technology fraud has gone global as never before, and a fraud-threat agent has the ability to attack your corporation at any place where there are corporate assets and from anywhere.

Frauds, like other crimes, can be accomplished either internally or externally. When the corporation is preparing to "downsize" the workforce, there is a better chance that disgruntled employees may want to "get even" with the corporation and therefore perpetrate frauds. These frauds can take many forms, as noted in our discussion of fraud schemes and fraud cases.

> Man-made threats are only limited by the imagination of the fraud threat agent (attacker).

As with most applications of assets protection, in developing your anti-fraud program, start with a common-sense approach and get more sophisticated after the basic anti-fraud defensive policies, procedures, plans, and processes have been installed, maintained in a current state of readiness, and periodically tested.

> **threat [thret] noun (plural threats)**
>
> 1. declaration of intent to cause harm: the expression of a deliberate intention to cause harm or pain
> 2. indication of something bad: a sign or danger that something undesirable is going to happen
>   • a threat of severe thunderstorms
> 3. somebody or something likely to cause harm: a person, animal, or thing likely to cause harm or pain
>   • The dog is no threat.
>
> [Old English þrēat "crowd, menace." Ultimately from an Indo-European word meaning "to press in," which is also the ancestor of English thrust and protrude.][3]

VULNERABILITIES

Remember that for purposes of our discussion, vulnerabilities are weaknesses in the anti-fraud policies, procedures, plans, or program that allow

---

[3] Ibid.

a fraud-threat agent to successfully perpetrate a fraud that adversely impacts the corporate assets.

> vulnerable [vúlnərəbʹl] adjective
> 1. without adequate protection: open to emotional or physical danger or harm
> 2. MILITARY open to attack: exposed to an attack or possible damage
> 3. extremely susceptible: easily persuadable or liable to give in to temptation
> 4. physically or psychologically weak: unable to resist illness, debility, or failure
> 5. BRIDGE liable to increased stakes: liable to higher penalties as well as bonuses, having won one game of a rubber -[Early seventeenth century. From late Latin vulnerabilis, from vulnerare "to wound," from vulnus "wound, injury."][4]

One thing is certain, though: there will always — always — be vulnerabilities that allow a fraud agent to be successful. Although your goal is to eliminate all of them, your only hope is to mitigate the risks they pose.

There are no exceptions to this principle. If you believe otherwise, for example, that you have a fool-proof anti-fraud program in place, we have a nice palace in Iraq with a water view we would like to sell you.

RISKS

Risk management is a key part of both management's and CSO's responsibilities. Since there is no such thing as a perfect anti-fraud program, the CSO must look at assets protection, which incorporate anti-fraud defense mechanisms that provide filters and "security rings" around corporate assets. These filters and rings make it increasingly difficult for a fraud-threat agent to successfully use any fraud scheme to penetrate the anti-fraud defenses and successfully realize the fraud-threat agent's goals. The less sophisticated the fraud-threat agent is, the sooner the defrauder will be defeated by one of the anti-fraud defensive filters or rings.

ASSETS PROTECTION RISK ASSESSMENTS

The process of identifying risks to corporate assets, determining their magnitude, and identifying areas needing safeguards at IWC is called Assets

---

[4] *Encarta® World English Dictionary* © & (P) 1999 Microsoft Corporation. All rights reserved. Developed for Microsoft by Bloomsbury Publishing Plc.

Protection Risk Assessment (APRA). In other words, you are assessing the risk to a particular asset or group of assets, which can also be called the "target" since fraud-threat agents may consider them targets.

---

risk [risk] noun (plural risks)

1. chance of something going wrong: the danger that injury, damage, or loss will occur
2. somebody or something hazardous: somebody or something likely to cause injury, damage, or loss
3. INSURANCE chance of loss to insurer: the probability, amount, or type of possible loss incurred and covered by an insurer
4. FINANCE possibility of investment loss: the possibility of loss in an investment or speculation
5. statistical odds of danger: the statistical chance of danger from something, especially from the failure of an engineered system

transitive verb (past risked, past participle risked, present participle risk·ing, 3rd person present singular risks): (1) put something in danger: to place something valued in a position or situation where it could be damaged or lost, or exposed to damage or loss; (2) do something despite danger: to incur the chance of harm or loss by taking an action — [mid-seventeenth century. Via French risque from Italian rischo, from rischiare "to run into danger," of uncertain origin.][5]

APRA is a formal IWC security department process that evaluates the threats and vulnerabilities to determine the level of risk to corporate assets due to attacks by fraud-threat agents. Assessments are usually done through a qualitative or quantitative analysis, or a combination of the two. It is the measurement of risks.

- *Qualitative* analyses usually use the three categories of risk as high, medium, and low. It is an "educated best guess" based primarily on opinions of knowledgeable others gathered through interviews, review of historical records, conducting of tests, and the experiences of the people doing the assessment.
- *Quantitative* analyses usually use statistical sampling based on mathematical computations determining the probability of an adverse occurrence based primarily on historical data. It is still an "educated best guess" but is based primarily on statistical results.

---

[5] Ibid.

ASSETS PROTECTION RISK ANALYSES

Analyses of the risks, the countermeasures to mitigate those risks, and the cost-benefits associated with those risks make up the risk analyses process. Basically, it is risk assessment with the costs and benefits factors added.

> Vulnerabilities must be eliminated or mitigated or the risk of their exploitation must be knowingly accepted by management. The risks may be mitigated by application of additional protection measures, or management may choose to accept a risk for a limited duration or for a limited population of assets if there is some compelling reason.

DEVELOPING ANTI-FRAUD DEFENSES

Once the drivers and requirements are identified, anti-fraud policies are in place, and the appropriate levels of risk assessments are conducted, you can add to your "to do" list the task of developing the anti-fraud defenses.

The approach is often called "Defense-in-Depth" and is required for the adequate protection of corporate assets. The most common misconception is that protective devices and countermeasures once installed do not require additional steps to adequately protect the assets from fraud-threat agent attacks.

Any protective measures require constant maintenance and testing and are just a component of an effective anti-fraud defensive model. Additional components or layers should be considered as additions to provide an effective protection model within your corporation.

Using multiple layers in an anti-fraud defensive model or system is the most effective method of deterring attackers (fraud-threat agents). Every layer provides some protection, and the defeat of one layer may not lead to the compromise of your entire corporation's assets to fraud-threat agents. Each layer has some interdependence with other layers.

Can you identify cost-effective, anti-fraud mitigating factors relating to the various fraud schemes and threats? This identification is critical since the cost of protecting assets might be more than the value of the assets. Remember that the overprotection of corporate assets also adversely impacts the financial "bottom line" — the profits — as does underprotection.

Remember, too, that the corporate security department is usually an overhead cost to the corporation. It can be a "parasite on the profits" of the corporation. Therefore, it behooves the CSO to keep costs to the minimum

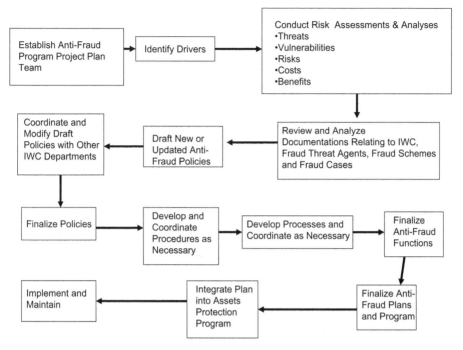

Figure 9-3. One example of the flow of tasks that go into developing an anti-fraud program for IWC.

required to meet the level of risk deemed appropriate by the corporation, thus contributing to the bottom line. If the anti-fraud defenses are properly applied as part of a well-thought-out anti-fraud program, they add value to the corporation because they protect the corporation's valuable assets. Not having some valuable assets available may reduce IWC's competitiveness in the global marketplace.

The anti-fraud or security drivers and requirements are used as part of an anti-fraud risk assessment program, which is then used to mitigate risks. The next step in the process is to use all that information to formulate new or updated anti-fraud policies, then procedures, then processes as part of the overall anti-fraud program for a corporation. (See Figure 9-3.)

THREE KEY INGREDIENTS IN AN ANTI-FRAUD PROGRAM'S DEFENSES

When developing an anti-fraud program, the CSO must remember that attacks against corporate assets by people require that three things must be in place, as often stated by the Association of Certified Fraud Examiners (ACFE) and criminologists. They are:

- **Motive:** If one is not motivated to violate rules, regulations, or laws relative to corporate assets, one would not do so even if the opportunity and rationalization to do so were present.
- **Opportunity:** If one did not have an opportunity, even though motivated and able to easily rationalize defrauding the corporation, one would not be able to perpetrate the crime.
- **Rationalization:** If one were to have the motive (being fired) and the opportunity (lack of verification processes and other controls on travel expense vouchers), one would commit the fraud, if the fraud-threat agent could rationalize it. Rationalization is important. Without rationalization how would one ever commit a crime? For example, we often see those who are loving family members and devoutly religious people perpetrate crimes. They would have been unable to do so without rationalizing it as not being a sin or a violation of their religious beliefs. In other words, one needs an "excuse" to perpetrate the act, such as: "After being loyal for over 20 years I am losing my job so that the corporation can save money, while the CEO gets a $100 million bonus."

Think about it and remember it. When you are developing your anti-fraud program, remember that your defenses (e.g., controls) should take away one, two, or all of the triad's "legs."

Fraud = Motive + Opportunity + Rationalization

IWC'S ANTI-FRAUD POLICIES

When discussing information assets protection policy, we define it as:

A codified set of principles that are directive in nature and that provide the baseline for the protection of corporate assets.

It is always the best policy to speak the truth, unless, of course, you are an exceptionally good liar. — *Jerome K. Jerome*

The corporate anti-fraud policies may be one document or a series of documents, depending on your corporate culture. To keep it simple, at IWC the CSO may want to have only one anti-fraud policy document, and from that all else, such as plans, programs, procedures, and processes, will be driven.

This policy makes up the most important portion of the anti-fraud program as it incorporates the anti-fraud "rules." It is the foundation of the IWC anti-fraud program. It is crucial that it:

- Cover all assets that must be protected from fraud threat agents.
- Cover all aspects of those assets' protection.
- Does not have any loopholes that could contribute to vulnerabilities.
- Be clearly written.
- Be concise.
- Take into account the costs of protection.
- Take into account the benefits of protection.
- Take into account the associated risks to the assets.
- Be coordinated with executive management and others as applicable.
- Be concurred with by executive management and others as applicable.
- Be *actively* supported by executive management and all employees.
- Include a statement relative to the process of maintaining its currency at all times.

One cannot state these requirements too strongly. They are the key to a successful anti-fraud program. If it is not stated in writing, it does not exist. After the assets protection and anti-fraud policy is established and approved in accordance with IWC requirements (executive management approval for all policies that affect the entire corporation), the information contained in the policy must be given to all corporate employees. This will be done through the IWC Security Education Awareness and Training Program (SEATP) and its communications process. (See Figure 9-4.)

A key process that the CSO must establish is one that will maintain all anti-fraud assets protection documents in a current state. Because this is a crucial function, the IWC CSO has assigned one staff member full-time to ensure that the policy and the entire anti-fraud program as documented are current at all times and ensure that when changes are considered, they are properly coordinated and the information is dispensed to all employees as soon as possible. The changes may just be procedural, or they may mitigate a fraud risk to some valuable IWC assets.

The CSO's focal point for the anti-fraud policy is informed of all actions, decisions, and other information that are gathered by the security organization staff and others, such as auditors. That information is analyzed and compared against this and other policies. When conflicts arise between events and the anti-fraud policy, they are analyzed to determine whether the policy must be updated. If so, then a process is implemented to do so.

If an event occurs that does not violate policy but obviously weakens the protection of an asset, a change in policy, procedure, or process is given

Communications Process

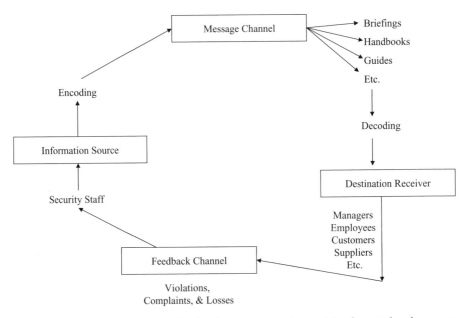

Figure 9-4. IWC SEATP communication loop process to be used for the anti-fraud program SEATP.

priority to eliminate that identified vulnerability based on costs, benefits, and risk. This would of course apply not only to the anti-fraud program but to the assets protection program as well.

An anti-fraud policy letter was issued to the IWC employees to begin setting the stage of the anti-fraud program. The letter, signed by the CSO, was as follows:

To: All IWC Employees

Subject: Protecting IWC's Information Assets from Fraud-Threat Agents and Others in Order to Maintain Our Competitive Edge

We are a leading international corporation in the manufacturing and sales of widgets. Today, we compete around the world in the global marketplace of fierce competition. In order to maintain a leadership position and grow, we depend first and foremost on all of you and provide you the resources to help you do your jobs to the best of your ability. You are vital to our success.

It is the policy of IWC to protect all our vital assets that are the key to our success. You and these other vital IWC assets must be able to operate in a safe environment, and our other resources must be protected from loss, compromise, or other adverse effects that impact our ability to compete in the marketplace.

It is also IWC policy to depend on all of you to do your part to protect these valuable information-related assets in these volatile times.

The protection of our assets can only be accomplished through an effective and efficient assets protection program which incorporates an anti-fraud program. We have begun an aggressive effort to build such programs.

In order for the program to be successful, you must give it your full support. Your support is vital to ensure that IWC continues to grow and maintain its leadership role in the widget industry.

(Signed by the IWC President and CEO)

> It is crucial that the CEO lead the way in the support of the IWC anti-fraud program. To get the above statement published is a major step in that process.

ANTI-FRAUD REQUIREMENTS AND POLICY DIRECTIVE

The IWC anti-fraud policy document will follow the standard format for IWC policies and include the following:

1. Introduction Section, which includes some history as to the need for an anti-fraud program at IWC.
2. Purpose Section, which describes why the document exists.
3. Scope Section, which defines the breadth of the Directive.
4. Responsibilities Section, which defines and identifies the responsibilities at all levels to include executive management, organizational managers, security staff, employees, associates, subcontractors, and suppliers.
5. Requirements Section, which includes the requirements for:
   A. Identification of the assets
   B. Access to the assets
   C. Applicable controls
   D. Audit trails and their review
   E. Reporting of responsibilities and action to be taken in the event of an indication of a possible violation
   F. Minimum anti-fraud defensive/protection requirements

G. Requirements for anti-fraud procedures to be written by all IWC departments based on complying with the anti-fraud policy

ANTI-FRAUD PROCEDURES

Over the years, the CSO has had experience in several corporations. The CSO learned that the best way to provide an updated anti-fraud program is to begin at the highest level and work down. This form of anti-fraud protection evaluation, analysis, and improvements is based on the fact that assets protection is driven and must be supported from the top down. Therefore, the CSO began with the overall IWC asset protection drivers and requirements, followed by the information assets protection policies. Once they were in place and the IWC employees were made aware of them, those related procedures already in place had to be analyzed, and project tasks had to be established to update them and develop new ones where needed.

Each anti-fraud procedure requires that it be written using the IWC standard method that supports the implemented anti-fraud policy, to include its spirit and intent. Some procedures may be written for everyone in IWC to follow, while various departments may write others based on their unique assets environment. Those procedures for everyone should be drafted by the anti-fraud project team and coordinated through the security department and all applicable IWC departments.

Various opinions have been voiced as to the best way to develop procedures because one continues to get to a more detailed level as one goes from drivers, requirements, and policies to procedures. The main issue is this: If the CSO establishes a specific procedure to comply with a specific policy, which in turn assists in meeting the IWC goals as stated in the SBP, TBP and ABP, the procedures may not be practical in one or another of the IWC departments. Thus, the department head may so state and ask for a waiver and state that they can still comply if they have a different procedure that takes into account their unique working environment. More than one department may have similar complaints. So, how does the CSO ensure that people are following proper anti-fraud policy and that the procedures to be written to comply with that policy are adequate?

The CSO has found that the best way to do this at IWC is to require that the individual departments establish, implement, and maintain their own set of anti-fraud and assets protection procedures that comply with the anti-fraud policy. This approach has several benefits:

*   Each department's decision to write its own procedures helps enforce the philosophy that anti-fraud defenses, as well as assets protection, is everyone's responsibility.

- There will be fewer complaints and requests for waivers because one or more of the IWC departments cannot comply with the procedures as written by the CSO's staff. This benefits the CSO as tracking waivers may turn into a nightmare; for example, who has what waivers, why, and for how long?
- The departments can develop procedures that meet their unique conditions, and as a result, the procedures should be more cost-effective.
- The CSO and staff will save time and effort by not having to write and maintain anti-fraud procedures for all IWC departments. To be blunt — it's the department's problem. However, the CSO has offered to make security staff's anti-fraud specialists available to answer questions and to provide advice as to what should be in the procedures' documents. This was done in the spirit of providing service and support to the IWC employees.

The question then arises as to how will the CSO be sure that the procedures written by each department meet the spirit and intent of the anti-fraud policy? Two methods were identified:

- The security staff as part of their risk assessment and analyses processes will conduct limited fraud risk surveys and as part of those surveys, the procedures will be reviewed. The limited risk assessments and subsequent analyses will provide an indication has to how well the procedures in place help protect IWC assets under the control of each department and/or suborganization from fraud-threat agents.
- IWC's audit staff will compare the procedures with the policies during their routine audits. The director of audits agreed to conduct such reviews since they are responsible for auditing for compliance with federal, state, and local laws and regulations and IWC policies and procedures anyway. It also helped that after the CSO's arrival, the CSO and director met and agreed to monthly meetings to share information of mutual concern. The CSO learned long ago that security personnel have very few true supporters in helping them to get the job done, but auditors were one of them.

Procedures, along with their related processes, are the heart of an anti-fraud program because they provide the step-by-step approach showing employees how to do their work and they also ensure the protection of corporate assets from fraud-threat agents. And if it can be done by the departments writing their own anti-fraud and assets protection procedures, it gets them actively involved as valuable team members in the process of protecting IWC's valuable assets.

THE CSO AND SECURITY DEPARTMENT'S ANTI-FRAUD ACCOUNTABILITIES

The CSO and the anti-fraud project team have come up with a set of responsibilities to which the CSO and security department staff will be held accountable vis-à-vis anti-fraud matters. They are as follows:

1. Identify all anti-fraud requirements needed and develop IWC policies and applicable procedures necessary to ensure conformance to those requirements.
2. Evaluate all anti-fraud defensive measures through risk assessments, analyses, and fraud surveys; cause changes to be made when and where applicable.
3. Establish and administer an anti-fraud program to protect IWC assets from fraud-threat agents.
4. Establish, implement, and maintain a process to identify fraud threats and mitigate those threats to IWC assets in a cost-effective manner as part of the anti-fraud program maintenance efforts.
5. Establish and maintain an anti-fraud awareness program, supported by policy, procedures, and processes to ensure that IWC management, employees, and others who have access to IWC assets are aware of the IWC anti-fraud program requirements for the protection of IWC assets, the fraud-threat agents schemes, how to defend the IWC assets against them, and such.

OFF-SITE CORPORATE FACILITIES

The IWC CSO is also the acting manager of the off-site anti-fraud program subordinate organizations. However, the CSO has also determined that it will be necessary to appoint a person as a supervisor to manage the day-to-day operations of the off-site anti-fraud program. At the same time, there were not enough personnel, as stated by HR, to appoint a manager at the off-site locations. However, the supervisor has authority to make decisions related to that activity, with several exceptions. The supervisor cannot counsel the security staff, evaluate their performance (except to provide input to the anti-fraud manager), make new anti-fraud policy, or manage budgets.

RECRUITING ANTI-FRAUD PROFESSIONALS

Once the CSO has gotten the anti-fraud project team started, the CSO adds another task to the project plan, which is to develop criteria for one or more fraud specialists to be subsequently identified and hired as the security department's focal point for all fraud-related matters. The CSO viewed this position as the "in-house fraud consultant" to the security department and IWC in general as part of the CSO's view of the security department as being service and support driven.

The CSO's anti-fraud project team must determine the following:

- How many anti-fraud professionals are needed?
- What functions will they perform?
- How many are needed in each function?
- How many are needed in which pay grades?
- How many should be recruited for the off-site locations?
- Does the off-site locations or main plant have the highest priority?

Once these questions are answered with supporting documentation and approved by the CSO, the CSO should then work with the CSO's boss. If approved by the boss, the CSO should then contact the IWC Human Resources staff to justify the additional staffing and budget and advertise for the hiring to fill that position.

The first choice should be to hire from within IWC, but only if the person meets the requirements. If not, then someone from outside IWC, who of course meets the criteria, would be hired. The advantage of hiring from within is that the employee already knows IWC culture, how things operate, and the like. Furthermore, it may even be a promotion for the applicant, which is always good for morale since other employees can see that they can advance within IWC and have new challenges, expand or change their careers, and so forth.

While all this seems really great, the main problem is that the boss will probably say that the CSO must work within the security department's budget because no additional budget or resources will be made available owing to budget constraints and ongoing layoffs of employees.

What would you as the IWC CSO do under these circumstances?

CASE STUDY

Based on the lack of budget and inability to hire even one additional staff member to be the focal point for anti-fraud matters within IWC's security department, the CSO decided to:

- Compare the fraud specialist criteria developed by the anti-fraud project team as approved by the CSO with the personnel files of each member of the security staff.
- Choose the security staff members who best meet the criteria for the anti-fraud specialist position.

- Contact the candidates' security manager and discuss the candidates' suitability for such a position based on the candidates' individual personality, education, experience, attitude, and such.
- Contact the top potential candidates to determine whether or not they would be interested in such a position.
- If more than one candidate is interested and only one position is available, convene a security managers' board to interview the candidates one at a time, posing a series of fraud-related questions.
- Choose the best candidate for the position.
- If more than one position is available, use the same approach as for one position.
- In coordination with the new anti-fraud specialist and the specialist's manager, the CSO should then develop a training program for the specialist and begin the process of getting the specialist totally qualified as a fraud specialist.
- The new specialist is also added to the anti-fraud project team, or based on the project lead position criteria, is made the anti-fraud program project team leader.

SUMMARY

In today's global marketplace where many corporations conduct business, corporate assets are bombarded by fraud threats to these assets from inside and outside the corporation. The workplace of the modern corporation in today's "what's in it for me" environment has changed over the years, as have the societies in which the corporations operate. With the ever-increasing role and dependency on technology, the threats to corporate assets have never been greater.

The information related to threats, vulnerabilities, and risks as presented in this chapter has been presented in various ways, but a central theme has been used: that all successful anti-fraud programs focus on the drivers, management of risks, policies, procedures, plans, processes, and fraud awareness briefings and training material.

This new era offers increased challenges to the CSO who must develop and manage a cost-effective anti-fraud program. To successfully accomplish that objective, the CSO must understand the threats, vulnerabilities, and risks to the corporate assets presented by fraud schemes, and the CSO must be familiar with fraud cases. These risks must be managed in a cost-effective manner that provides the minimal amount of anti-fraud defenses needed based on the assessed and acceptable risks.

10
Managing an Anti-Fraud Program

INTRODUCTION

No matter what job the CSO has with regard to protecting corporate assets, there are some elements of the CSO position that permeate all aspects of that job, as well as the job of any corporate manager. It is important that the CSO management and leadership aspects be discussed because they are an integral part of the CSO's responsibilities vis-à-vis protecting corporate assets and leading the anti-fraud program efforts.[1]

As the new IWC CSO, you have an identifiable management style. Over the years, hopefully you have honed your skills and CSO "personality" so that you can provide success and professional security leadership and management to IWC and your security staff. Some of the areas that a CSO should concentrate on and continue to learn more about are the following:

- Leadership
- Management
- Customer expectations
- Dealing with executive management
- Dealing with peers
- Dealing with office politics
- Representing IWC in the community
- Managing an effective and efficient security department
- Focusing on an industry model of security duties and responsibilities
- Dealing with the news media

---

[1] Some portions of this chapter were excerpted from the book *The Manager's Handbook for Corporate Security* (Kovacich and Halibozek), published by Butterworth-Heinemann, Elsevier (2003), and used here with permission.

CSO LEADERSHIP

As the CSO, you are the senior security executive within IWC. It is your responsibility to align the security organization to support the corporate objectives, concentrating on those objectives identified in the IWC business plans. In essence, you should create a professional security organization that follows and supports the established corporate objectives while providing protection to the corporate assets (e.g., people, information, equipment, and facilities). One of your goals is to create a vision for the security organization that is congruent with IWC's vision. Remember that the CSO, as the functional leader, also sets the security organization's direction.

> Lead, follow, or get out of the way.[2]

As a service organization, security must find ways to deliver assets protection, that is, anti-fraud services, that least interfere with or impact daily business. Simply stated, one should act as an enabler, work toward achieving company goals and objectives, and find ways to say "yes." This is not always easy to accomplish. Sometimes principles of good security practices will conflict with how people want to conduct business.

Security is sometimes seen as getting in the way of doing business. What executive management expects from a security organization is to integrate its assets protection services into company operations in such a way as to not interfere with operations while providing a sufficient level of assets protection. What executive management does not need or want is a security function that says "no" or "you can't do that."

Always remember that there is always more than one way to accomplish anti-fraud, assets protection functions, with some requiring accepting more risks than others. A successful CSO is one who finds ways to integrate protective measures as seamlessly as possible into the corporation's operation and who can add value to the security department and corporation. Also remember: *where there is a need, there is a waiver.* That is, sometimes there are valid and logical exceptions to the rules.

As the CSO, you must set the tone for the anti-fraud program and your security organization. You lead in part by establishing the nature of the anti-fraud program and the security organization by defining what is important and how they will operate. You are the link between the anti-fraud program and executive management. You must ensure that the anti-fraud functions operate in alignment with corporate norms and values.

---

[2] Author unknown.

MANAGEMENT VERSUS LEADERSHIP

Effective leadership is putting first things first. Effective management is discipline, carrying it out. — *Stephen Covey*

The very essence of leadership is that you have to have a vision. — *Theodore Hesburgh*

Management focuses on getting today's work done today while leaders look to tomorrow. The focus of management is much shorter than the focus of leaders. Having a clear and communicated vision is essential for any leader. If you expect people to follow, you must offer them a sense of direction. Followers need to know where they are going. As a leader, your vision must be clear, easily and regularly communicated, and shared. Leaders with followers sharing their vision stand a much greater chance of success than leaders with followers who do not share their vision.

Getting employees to share your vision will require you to develop their trust. The first task of leadership is to convince followers of your credibility. They must trust you. Developing their trust will require you to do what you say you will do. Be consistent in what you do, and do not stray from your values.

Without followers, no one is a leader. These management and leadership methods must be incorporated into your anti-fraud program if it is to be a success.

As part of a series of executive seminars conducted at Santa Clara University in California by the Tom Peters Group, more than 5,200 senior managers were asked to identify the characteristics they most admire in a leader.[3] These are the qualities they listed:

- Honest
- Competent
- Forward-looking
- Inspiring
- Intelligent
- Fair-minded
- Broad-minded
- Courageous
- Straightforward
- Imaginative

---

[3] Golin, Mark, et al, "Secrets of Executive Success" (Emmaus, PA: Rodale Press), 1991

As important as it is for employees to know and trust their leader, it is just as important for a leader to know and trust their employees. Knowing them and the organization will better enable you as the CSO to develop a connection. Being connected with your employees increases the chance they will share your vision. It also allows you to challenge them to perform beyond their own expectations.

> When developing and implementing the IWC anti-fraud program, it is imperative that some level of employee trust be considered while at the same time balancing that philosophy with incorporating anti-fraud defenses where you actually consider that people within IWC or associated with IWC cannot be trusted.

Why is good leadership important for a security department and the anti-fraud program? As is true of any other function within IWC, to perform well security must have an effective leader. This leader must know and understand the mission, objectives, and values of the company. You as the CSO are that leader, and you must be able to effectively communicate with your security staff the direction and vision for the security organization and the anti-fraud program in such a way as to best support the IWC's mission and objectives. Furthermore, you must lead the effort to develop security organizational goals that incorporate anti-fraud program objectives and that are designed and implemented to support IWC business goals.

MEETING CUSTOMERS' EXPECTATIONS

Security is a service and support organization, as well as a compliance organization. The service and support aspect of security has a set of customers that differ from the compliance customers. Yet, there is some overlap and commonality. Compliance customers expect the security organization to maintain an environment that is compliant with all applicable laws, regulations, contract provisions, and company policy, including those related to the anti-fraud program.

The service and support aspects of security involve those tasks performed in support of other employees and functions but are not required by policy and procedure, code, regulation, and law. Service customers expect the delivery of security services to be timely and efficient. They also expect their needs to be met promptly and to their satisfaction. These customers can be further defined as internal and external.

IWC INTERNAL CUSTOMERS

As the IWC CSO, IWC management is your primary customer for the compliance aspects of an anti-fraud program. Employees are your primary service customers, and they have varying expectations. Management looks to security to ensure that programs and processes are in place that will enable the organization to achieve and maintain compliance with regulation, contracts, laws, and policy. In a way, this is the fiduciary responsibility of security. Furthermore, management expects compliance to be achieved and maintained in a cost-effective manner. Management also expects security to create and sustain a secure environment. The workplace must be an environment where people, physical assets, and information are appropriately protected from fraud-threat agents and other threat agents — a safe and secure place to work.

IWC employees expect security services to be delivered efficiently and seamlessly, causing minimal impact or disruption to their daily work. For example, in the process of accounting, anti-fraud defenses must be in place. However, your customers expect to be able to do their accounting tasks efficiently and effectively with no loss of productivity due to the anti-fraud defenses integrated into their work processes. Delays due to such defenses will be met with resistance and frustration. Furthermore, any time lost as a result of an inefficient anti-fraud process is time not available for other productive activities. Remember the old adage, "time is money."

Other customers may be people who permanently reside on your facility but are representatives of the companies or people who purchase the products and/or services IWC produces and buys, or they may have a long-term business relationship with IWC.

By virtue of their location on IWC property, you should provide some type of anti-fraud service and support for these customers. IWC management must decide how to treat these internal or external customers, and it is up to you to classify them and treat them as IWC looks at them and would like them treated.

IWC EXTERNAL CUSTOMERS

These customers fall into many categories. Although they are not IWC employees, they do have a relationship with, or an interest in, IWC. They may be customers who purchase products and services; they may be suppliers who provide goods and services to IWC; or they may be vendors or contract labor personnel who perform work for IWC but are not IWC employees.

External customers may also be regulatory agencies responsible for ensuring compliance with anti-fraud regulations and laws. An example of a regulatory agency customer is the U.S. Securities and Exchange Commission (SEC).

Depending on their relationship with IWC, the type and degree of customer interests in your anti-fraud program vary. For example, contract labor personnel are interested in working in a safe and secure environment; the SEC is interested in ensuring that IWC is compliant with all applicable federal laws and regulations.

IWC EXECUTIVE MANAGEMENT EXPECTATIONS OF A CSO

Executive management is responsible for assets protection. Like every other aspect of the business, executive management holds the ultimate accountability and responsibility for security. Consequently, they have a vested interest in a successful anti-fraud program — or they should. However, sometimes the CSO must "gently" remind them of that fact. How executive management defines a successful anti-fraud program may differ significantly from how a security professional defines one.

As security professionals, we tend to want to have the best program we can. After all, this is our area of expertise. We want to be compliant in all aspects of our compliance obligations. We also tend to employ as many controls as practical to ensure that the risk to corporate people, physical assets, and information is minimal. In essence, it is important to create an environment that is more risk-averse than risk management. Therefore, as a CSO you may generally be willing to accept fewer security risks than executive management.

Executive management is interested in having a cost-effective anti-fraud program, seeking to achieve an acceptable level of compliance cost-effectively.

Security at IWC, like security at most corporations, is a cost center; it generally is not a revenue-producing organization. That is not to say security does not add value to IWC. Security does add value to IWC. The challenge for you as the IWC CSO is to apply the appropriate levels of anti-fraud defenses and "prove" to executive management and others at IWC that the IWC anti-fraud program does add value to IWC products and services.

A very senior executive in a Fortune 500 company once characterized a successful security program by using a scale of red, yellow, green, and blue (blue being the very best and red being unsatisfactory); the successful program was one that operated in a light green environment. What he meant was that he wanted a program that kept the corporation compliant with laws and regulations; maintained a secure environment for the protection of people, physical assets, and information; and did so at minimal cost. In this executive's opinion, monies spent on obtaining and maintaining a security condition that was green or better was bad for business.

Based on this acceptable level of security risk, any monies spent on security taking the assets protection program beyond that "light green" condition could have been better spent in other areas of the business such as engineering, product development, or marketing. Obtaining and maintaining this condition is a challenge that virtually all security professionals face, and that is the battle for funding.

As the CSO, you must ask and answer many questions relating to anti-fraud programs, including:

- How many anti-fraud defenses are enough?
- When are the physical assets, people, and information of the company effectively protected from fraud-threat agents?
- What are the fraud risks and defensive vulnerabilities for the IWC operating environment?
- How are resources best employed to achieve an acceptable level of risk?
- What tools and processes are needed to ensure an appropriately anti-fraud defensive environment?

Executive management may ask you these and similar questions. You must anticipate their questions and be prepared to offer specific, well-thought-out answers. The more you can respond immediately, not only with answers but also answers from a business application point of view, the more confidence they will instill in you and the more support you will be able to receive from them. In other words, talk their language when addressing their anti-fraud program concerns and always consider business impacts.

Of course, there may be some that you can never convince or win over; however, as long as they are the small minority, you can expect to receive support and understanding from executive management. As you progress in developing the IWC anti-fraud program, you should make it your personal goal to understand those who oppose you and what you are trying to accomplish. Furthermore, instead of avoiding them, thus building up more animosity, you should spend more time with them.

You will find that if they do begin to agree with what you are doing, they will become some of your staunchest supporters. There is nothing more rewarding than winning over an "adversary." As a leader and professional security manager, this offers some of the best personal rewards and demonstrates that you are perfecting your craft. Keep a "win and lost" record and view these efforts as an enjoyable game. If you are "batting" at or less than 50%, it is suggested that you change that record or be sure to keep a resume updated.

> A CSO does not welcome adversity but cannot shy away from it either. Adversity and the challenges that come with it are a major part of what a CSO deals with everyday. If you can't handle it, and in fact don't enjoy the opportunities it brings, change careers.

Remember that, as a CSO, you are responsible for leading and managing the security department and the anti-fraud program. One of your objectives is to achieve and maintain a secure and compliant environment. For this, you are accountable to executive management. It is your responsibility to work with executive management to define an acceptable level of risk, a risk level that you should establish only after fraud threats and vulnerabilities to fraud-threat agent attacks have been identified, validated, and analyzed.

For this process, you must rely on your security staff and other anti-fraud team members such as auditors. (More information on teaming is presented in Chapter 11.) Don't forget that what your staff does reflects directly on you and that they also have occasions to interface with all levels of IWC management. Therefore, you must ensure that they are professionals in their conduct and apply anti-fraud defensive principles consistent with the philosophy of the IWC anti-fraud program. Remember, too, that there are many informal and formal communication channels available to executive management. Thus, what they hear from others about you and your staff has a direct bearing on the support and confidence they have in you.

MANAGING RISK

The *minimum* amount of anti-fraud defensive measures conducive to an *acceptable level of risk* are key terms. The acceptable level of risk is an *executive management decision* and should be based on risk analyses conducted by members of your security department in conjunction with various other IWC staff members who can contribute to the individual analyses.

The executive management's decisions relative to risk will include deciding which of the various options presented, along with the value of the assets and their protection costs versus risks, should be implemented. Thus, the executive management's decisions are a factor in the cost of protection. As their "in-house, anti-fraud consultant," you of course should guide them and make recommendations to help them in their decision-making function.

The CSO should always look at how the job can be done more efficiently. In many corporations, promotions and the amount of salary with benefits that are provided the CSO has to do with the amount of the security staff, the size of the budget, and where in the bureaucracy the CSO reports. The CSO should try to have the minimal amount of budget and staff conducive to getting the job done as stated by executive management, even though you are adding a major anti-fraud program to the integrated assets protection program. Try to get your performance and position grade based on results and impact on IWC rather than on the amount of budget or the number of staff you have.

SECURITY'S VISION, MISSION, AND QUALITY STATEMENTS

As the CSO you are required, as part of the IWC management team, to develop vision, mission, and quality statements that help set the direction for the security department. The statements must support the vision, mission, and quality statements of the Human Resources Department, which in turn support the IWC statements. The CSO, in concert with the security staff, came up with the following statements relative to the anti-fraud program:

* IWC's Security Department Vision Statement: *In partnership with our customers, provide a competitive advantage for the IWC widget business by continuous protection of all IWC's assets from fraud-threat agents and other miscreants without hindering productivity and cost-effectively support increased production of IWC widgets.*
* IWC's Security Department's Mission Statement: *The mission of IWC's Security Department is to provide low-cost, productivity-enhanced assets protection services and support that will assist in defending IWC from fraud-threat agents and other miscreants while helping IWC to maintain its competitive advantage in the global marketplace.*
* IWC's Security Department's Quality Statement: *To provide quality anti-fraud support and services while enhancing the productivity opportunities of the IWC workforce.*

MANAGING THE IWC ANTI-FRAUD PROGRAM

Let's look at the CSO as a manager of the various aspects of the job, including planning, controlling, and budgeting.

PLANNING

Security serves the corporation. An effective IWC security organization that meets the protection, compliance, and service needs of employees, management, and customers cannot be established and maintained independently of the rest of the company. Security is a key component of the IWC business and must be part of the planning process. Beginning with company goals, which are usually identified in multiyear plans or annual business plans, the CSM and security staff must be part of the planning process. The plans and objectives of IWC identify the path that IWC will take to achieve its goals and mission and to satisfy its shareholders and stakeholders. Obviously, IWC's anti-fraud program is incorporated into the planning function.

In the process, the IWE CSO must determine what management intended to achieve when they wanted to be made safe from fraud-threat agents:

- Are there specific fraud issues and concerns?
- What fraud incidents occurred in the past?
- What are the vulnerabilities of, and fraud threats to, IWC?
- What anti-fraud plans, policies, procedures, processes, and projects should be implemented?
- What level of risk is management willing to accept?
- How do you know when you have achieved your anti-fraud goals?

These are just some of the questions that the CSO should ask to be able to effectively plan, and then execute, that plan in support of corporate goals.

Since IWC is in business to make a profit for shareholders, a great amount of planning is focused on directing and growing the IWC widget business. Strategic planning groups conduct market, product, economic, and competitive assessments with the intent of finding opportunities for business growth and understanding customers, competition, and threats. Security needs to be part of this process in order to plan for supporting it.

Establishing and managing an anti-fraud program for IWC is part of those service and support duties and responsibilities. For example: if the strategic planning group identifies a high potential market opportunity for a joint manufacturing venture in a foreign country where fraud runs rampant, are there any issues that should be of concern? Clearly, the answer is yes, and some issues are quite fundamental:

- What is the crime or fraud rate in that country?
- Are there risks due to political instability?
- What fraud-threat agents are unique to that country?
- How much will you be able to rely on that country's law enforcement and security agencies to support IWC's anti-fraud program?

These questions are best addressed during the anti-fraud program planning stage. Waiting until after the operation is up and running may very well be too late.

The cost of correcting a problem is generally more expensive than the cost of preventing one.

SOME ASPECTS TO INCORPORATE INTO AN ANTI-FRAUD PROGRAM PLAN

Establishing an effective and efficient anti-fraud function within the IWC security department will require some analysis. Furthermore, it may require selling the need for a staff to perform that function, as was discussed in the previous chapter.

Even if you have been specifically hired to establish an IWC anti-fraud program, you will still be expected to define to management the size and scope of such a program and its related functions, including its costs and impacts on employee productivity. As part of your analysis, you should consider the following:

- *Define your Statement of Work (SOW).* Determine what needs to be protected from fraud-threat agents, for now in general terms or groupings and later in specific detail. You must also determine the amount of protection needed. To do so, you need to understand executive management's general expectations of the IWC anti-fraud program:
  - What does executive management believe needs to be protected?
  - Does it have special fraud-related requirements or concerns?
- *Determine if your customers have any anti-fraud and related assets protection requirements.*
  - Are you contractually bound to provide specific types of anti-fraud defenses?
  - If so, what is the scope of those requirements?
  - What, if anything, do your internal and external customers expect from you, the anti-fraud program, and your related services and support?

You may also want the opinion of an outside anti-fraud specialist — someone who has no vested interest in IWC so that he or she may make a more independent assessment of your overall anti-fraud program needs.

If you decide you may want to hire an outsider, be very careful. *Select a specialist with proven experience in your particular industry, and use caution as there are many who are good at talking but short on actual experience in what you are asking their opinion and recommendations about.*

> Anyone can read a book and say what needs to be done, but there are few who are *experienced* enough in the anti-fraud program consulting field to actually *know how to do it* and have *done it successfully* before.

If you do think a security consultant would be a good idea:

- Be sure to interview previous clients of the consultant for their nonattribution input.
- Verify the consultant's background.
- Contact several anti-fraud consultant specialists to receive bids on statements of work, but remember that the lowest bidder is not always the best one to select.

In addition, consider this: Executive management may wonder why you need an anti-fraud program consultant's help. If so, why did they hire you? Are you the right person for the job?

A specific type of anti-fraud program-related consultant may be needed in the future; however, as you build the anti-fraud program according to IWC's needs as you see them, you may decide that the use of a consultant is premature. After you establish a list of projects that are to be accomplished, you may find you do not have the experienced staff needed to successfully complete the anti-fraud project. In that case, a consultant may prove useful.

An advantage of hiring an outside anti-fraud program consultant is that with limited staff and/or the staff's fraud experience, a consultant may be able to complete some of the related anti-fraud program tasks or projects faster. You may also have at least one of your staff to assist the consultant, thus providing needed training for at least one member of your security staff. That person may then have the basic knowledge required to be able to conduct future anti-fraud-related projects or functions that you need a consultant to do for you now.

Another disadvantage of hiring a consultant is that it may create a morale issue for your staff, who may believe they can do the task themselves and should be given the opportunity to try, However, you want an experienced person to do it now, and this position does not endear you to your new staff. Nor is it the right thing to do. You should offer them the challenge: you might be surprised by the results.

Three major components of a corporation require some type or degree of anti-fraud defenses that you must assess. This point is again stressed so that you as a CSO do not lose focus on the basics. Often, CSOs are so inundated with crises and day-to-day operations that they forget why they are employed in the first place. You are employed to protect IWC assets:

- *People*: Virtually all companies identify people as their most important resource. This is particularly true in this, the Information Age and in a knowledge environment. It is people who use assets such as information and knowledge to create and deliver products and services. Skilled people are the critical component of wealth creation for a company. The category of people generally refers to employees; however, a company has an interest in protecting many other groups of people as well. While on company premises, security is also concerned with protecting customers, suppliers, and visitors.

  Executive management knows that people are important, but it also knows that more often than not, people are the most expensive assets and the first to go when business is bad. Furthermore, in some environments, especially manufacturing environments like IWC, executive management continues to try to find ways of automating processes and taking people out of the processing loop. Remember: robots can work 24 hours a day without stopping for a rest; they don't get sick, they don't take vacations — and they don't usually make mistakes.

- *Physical Assets*: Although physical assets come in many forms, for the purpose of our discussion, they are considered the physical items of value that the company uses in its production of goods and/or services. Capital assets such as plant and equipment are the most visible and costly physical assets. Buildings, computers, vehicles, and other like items represent a substantial investment for the company and are essential for the operation of the business. Protecting them is critical.

- *Information*: Some argue that all information has value and therefore requires protection. Others maintain that only sensitive information, proprietary or private in nature, requires protection. Working with management and those identified as owners of information, the CSO can determine what types of information require anti-fraud protection and to what degree it must be protected. In our age of information, the ability to share ideas and have a free flow of information is essential to the development of products and services. Being faster to market with products and services impacts the performance and ultimate survivability of a company. Also remember that information is time-sensitive and that as a result its protection will vary over time. Protecting information is the most difficult of all assets to protect and also the most difficult to evaluate.

BUDGETING

Once you have determined your anti-fraud program's statement of work and have identified the needed people, equipment, and facility space, you must develop an anti-fraud budget to incorporate into your overall assets protection and security department budget. Failure to develop a quality budget may inhibit your ability to develop and manage an effective organization and anti-fraud program.

> An ineffective security organization can only lead to an inadequate anti-fraud program.

Let's assume you will be asking for additional budget in order to establish and manage an IWC anti-fraud program. Please do not play the budget "game" and ask for more than you need. If you as the IWC CSO can show specific justification for your needs and what will not happen with no additional budget or worse yet, a budget decrease, you have a better chance of getting what you need. If you end up getting a reputation for inflating your budget requests, the next time around you may get a budget far less than what you may actually need.

> Merriam-Webster defines budget as a plan *for the coordination of resources and expenditures.*[4] It is used to assist in the proper and prudent allocation of resources.

The budgeting processes you will encounter may vary considerably. Different businesses or companies choose to use the budgeting approach that best fits their needs. Even within companies, you may encounter different processes for budgeting. Below is a description of two different approaches you as the IWC CSO may find:

- *Zero-based budget:* This budget process requires the CSO to assess the complete security statement of work (SOW), which includes the anti-fraud program SOW, and to identify the resources needed to fulfill that SOW. A critical component of this process is ensuring that the SOW is valid. With the zero-based budget process, it is necessary to first identify the drivers to that SOW. Drivers are the specific regulation, laws, contractual requirements, company policy, customer expectations, or executive management needs and requirements that cause the IWC security department to take a protective action (e.g., those related to the anti-fraud program).

---

[4] Merriam Webster, Webster's Ninth New Collegiate Dictionary (Springfield, MA: Merriam-Webster Inc.), 1987

Resources cost money and must be planned for, budgeted, and acquired. The resources may be in the form of labor, material, capital assets, or services provided from a supplier. Regardless of their form, they cost money and must be planned for within the budget process.

- *Affordability-based budgets:* This budget process differs significantly from the zero-based budget process. With this budget process the security SOW is shaped by the available budget. Here the CSO works to form the security SOW to fit into the available budget. Generally, this process provides less available budget than what is necessary to maintain a fully compliant and fully serviced SOW. Therefore, the CSO must identify areas of the anti-fraud program in which a risk of noncompliance or borderline compliance will be accepted or a degradation of services will occur. Usually, this means imposing less timely or less efficient processes on your customers — which may in fact increase costs. Simply stated, customers may have to wait longer to receive the services they need in order to offset the lack of available resources needed to deliver them more expediently. This can be dangerous in that the corporation's work may continue but at an unacceptable level of risk because security does not have the time or resources to provide the needed anti-fraud defensive service or support and business cannot wait.

Through this process, all SOW requirements must be identified. Once identified, an assessment of the necessary anti-fraud program resources to perform the anti-fraud SOW must be made. In an ideal world, the necessary resources (budget) would be provided to the security department for the implementation of processes supporting the SOW. In the real world, the SOW is often aligned with "available" resources causing a risk acceptance evaluation.

If enough resources are not available to fulfill the SOW, then some degree of risk must be accepted for the portion of the SOW that will not be fulfilled. Often the choice of what does not get accomplished or is only marginally accomplished is left to you as the CSO. Nevertheless, executive management should be aware of and accept or acknowledge this condition.

Whatever process is employed to establish the anti-fraud budget, the following categories of resources must be addressed:

- *People*: The human resource (security professionals) needed to execute the statement of work.
- *Equipment*: The tools needed by security which do not fit into the capital asset category.
- *Capital Assets*: The fixed or permanent assets, or those employed in conducting business.

- *Training and Development for the security professionals*: In order to maintain a skilled and effective anti-fraud-trained workforce, periodic education and training is necessary. Keeping up with fraud developments in the security or management field is just one example of the type of training an anti-fraud specialist or specialists need.

For the budget process to be successful there must be an identifiable relationship to available resources (expressed in the form of monies budgeted) and the SOW. Questions that must be considered when developing a budget include:

- What must be done?
- For whom must it be done?
- What results are expected?
- What will it take to do it?
- How much will it cost?
- What are the recurring costs?
- What are the one-time costs?
- What is the return on investments?
- What happens if you don't develop a budget?

CONTROLLING

The CSO develops action plans to facilitate achieving the anti-fraud program and its related quality, vision, and mission statements, goals, and objectives. Controlling means that the anti-fraud action plans are implemented in accordance with defined and documented expectations.

Performance of the action plans is monitored, compared to expectations, and adjusted or improved accordingly. Simply put, when you as the CSO implement your anti-fraud action project plan, ask yourself:

- Did you accomplish what you expected to accomplish?
- If you did, how do you know?
- If you did not, how do you know, why not, and how do you improve?
- How much did it cost you?

When establishing an anti-fraud program consider the following:

- *Organization design*: The security organization and security job structures are designed to match the organization's assets protection program that includes the anti-fraud program SOW, that is to say, the anti-fraud program work your organization must perform. Plans are developed to align your resources in part with the requirements of the anti-fraud program SOW. Procedures and processes are written and mapped to define and describe how the work gets done and what expectations will be met.

- *Expectations:* The security organization is expected to deliver an IWC anti-fraud program that operates effectively and efficiently. It may be a called a "security product" incorporating aspects of service or support functions. In any event, targets of performance levels or delivery of specific anti-fraud related products, services, or support must be defined. It is necessary to determine just how fast, how frequent, how many, or how effective are the anti-fraud products and services produced and delivered.

  Boundaries must be set and balanced in accordance with customer expectations and available resources. Boundaries provide a standard to measure against to determine effectiveness of performance and achievement of anti-fraud program goals. Key success factors should also be identified. Anti-fraud success factors are activities, events, or milestones that must occur for you to be successful. Knowing what key success factors are, and monitoring them, will assist in periodic determinations and assessment of progress.

- *Monitoring:* Monitoring the IWC anti-fraud program performances in relationship to alignment with plans will provide you with early and periodic assessments of progress. Measuring results with performance metrics (additional information on metrics is available in Chapter 13) and measuring customer satisfaction with customer surveys should provide sufficient feedback to compare performance with expectations. Perhaps the most important benefit from measurement is that it provides for early feedback on performance.

  Knowing if you are on or off track early in the process allows for performance adjustments and improvement before things get out of control. Periodic measurement is essential for problem identification. By monitoring performance, you develop an understanding of how well you are performing. Through measurement, you may validate performance to determine if it is as expected, or you may identify systemic and individual problems, causing corrective action to be taken.

- *Improvement:* When problems with one or more aspects of the anti-fraud program are identified, corrective actions must be taken. Failure to take corrective action can either cause you to operate at a reduced level of efficiency or allow problems to get out of control. Thus, the fraud-threat agents' attacks may be successful and the protection of assets will suffer.

  When problems are identified, include your security staff in the problem-solving process. Use tools such as process and workflow diagrams to map all steps of a process. This will enable identification of non–value-added steps and even the root causes of any systemic anti-fraud defensive mechanisms and related problems. When beginning the problem-solving process, consider the following steps:

- Clearly identify the problem.
- Involve employees in developing potential solutions.
- Assess cost and impact of changes.
- Rank all potential solutions.
- Develop strategies to implement the best solution.
- Change process, command media, or work instruction.
- Train employees on the new standard.
- Monitor performance of the new standard.

- *Reward:* It is important to offer positive recognition for improvements made by employees. Any time employees correct a problem or improve an anti-fraud program process, a positive response from you and your appropriate manager is in order. When employees use measurement data to identify and solve problems, that behavior should be reinforced.

    Reinforcement will encourage them to continue to make decisions and changes based on data. The amount of recognition or reward should vary depending on the magnitude of the problem solved. In some cases, the mere acknowledgment of their efforts will suffice; in other cases, more significant rewards such as monetary incentives and promotions may be necessary. Examples of rewards include certificates of appreciation and attendance at security conferences.

QUALITY, PROCESS IMPROVEMENT, AND ASSESSMENT OF ORGANIZATION PERFORMANCE

Once you, the IWC CSO, have all anti-fraud related functions up and running, you need to assess how well they are performing:

- Has the goal of "doing it right the first time" been met?
- Can processes be improved and efficiency gains made?
- Are workload, process performance, and costs effectively measured?

The following section provides an overview of these important concepts.

PROCESS MANAGEMENT

To determine the effectiveness of any single anti-fraud process it is necessary to measure that process. What gets measured will depend on how the process works. For example, a transactional process may require measuring the cycle time of each transaction. In some cases, the amount of what is being delivered is most important. In other cases, the frequency of delivery matters most. In any event, determining what gets measured is a product of what the process is intended to do. In other words, the process is designed to do something. Does that something get done? If so, how efficient, effective, frequent, or cost is the process of getting it done?

> A process is a series of steps or actions taken to produce products or services.

To measure an anti-fraud-related process first requires an understanding of the process itself:

- What are the requirements that drive the process? In other words, why do it at all?
- What is the final product or service delivered?
- Who are the customers?
- Are their needs and expectations being met?
- How does the process itself work?
- Are there dependent subprocesses?
- Who are the process owners?

You will need to know the answers to these questions in order to successfully assess the anti-fraud program's processes and their effectiveness.

A tool used by the IWC CSO to assist in developing an understanding of how a process works is the process flow diagram. In this diagram, each step in any process is identified and examined in regards to how that step fits into the whole process. Furthermore, the value of each step itself is assessed. In other words, is it necessary to perform that step and does it bring value to the customer? By placing each step of the process in a flow diagram form, each step can be assessed individually. Unnecessary or non–value-added steps should be eliminated or redesigned into value-added steps.

Once a process is diagrammed and refined, measuring the actual performance of the process against the desired outcome is essential. This will tell just how effective the process is. Comparison of the actual cost and production or process time to the desired cost and production or process time will tell the CSO whether they are effective and efficient.

PERFORMANCE MANAGEMENT

The IWC CSO understands that determining the success of the IWC anti-fraud program can be, and usually is, measured in many ways. Some processes, like those related to compliance with anti-fraud-related laws and regulations, are usually measured through the government or regulatory agency inspection process. Here a government organization with oversight responsibilities will conduct an inspection at a site or facility to assess the level of compliance. Any areas found noncompliant will require corrective action and may lead to the issuance of a citation.

Compliance with IWC anti-fraud program policy and procedures can also be measured through the internal audit process. In addition, IWC's anti-fraud program should include a self-inspection process. Self-inspections should be conducted periodically by the security organization and used as a tool to help understand the organization's level of anti-fraud performance and help prepare for external agency reviews. Furthermore, such tools can be offered to department managers for their own self-inspections.

USING TECHNOLOGY TO DELIVER ANTI-FRAUD PROGRAM SUPPORT AND SERVICES

There are many reasons to deploy technology in the effort to protect assets through an anti-fraud program. However, technology can also be used to improve the efficiency of how anti-fraud processes, services, support, and products are delivered. Some available technologies are quite obvious to the IWC CSO and have been in use for some time; others may even reside within IWC and are just waiting to be tapped into. Many information technology tools and capabilities already exist, which, if deployed properly for the delivery of anti-fraud program support and services, could reduce anti-fraud program costs, perhaps significantly. As a responsible CSO, the IWC CSO is continually looking for ways to achieve more cost-effective delivery of anti-fraud program support and services.

In today's IWC with its tight resource environment, efficiency and timeliness are not the only motivation to seek alternative means of providing services and support. The lack of budget to explore other options or add staff may drive you to seek help from technology. Furthermore, if you cannot get more budget allocations for additional anti-fraud resources that you have determined to be necessary to improve or enhance the anti-fraud program, then the use of technology to free already committed resources may be a possibility. This should allow you to re-deploy those freed resources to other areas — for example, enhance the anti-fraud program personnel resources where they may be needed.

Again, remember that at IWC security is a cost center and not a revenue-producing entity; therefore, it is in competition with other organizations for budget. How that budget is obtained varies and is often dependent on the demonstrated added value of the anti-fraud program and the assets protection program. As an example, if a security risk assessment or fraud survey shows that an anti-fraud program is out of compliance and that this noncompliant condition could adversely impact sales or a contractual obligation, management will divert resources to correct this problem.

The only concern you may have as the CSO is that someone other than you may be the person who receives the additional resources to fix the problem. This of course assumes that the noncompliant condition was a result of something you did or did not do. It is not necessary to be completely dependent on the budgetary discretion of management. The solutions may rest within your own creativity as a CSO and willingness to explore other options. You should take the initiative to do this and not wait for a budget or compliance crisis.

MANAGING QUALITY AND MANAGEMENT OVERSIGHT

It is a mixed blessing that the IWC anti-fraud program is often subject to very close oversight. Although it is good to have an external (outside of the security organization) perspective and assessment, dealing with these activities and entities (SEC) is time consuming and can be difficult. Internal audit programs, government inspections, or customer reviews are some of the various methods employed to determine the effectiveness of an anti-fraud program.

Dealing with audits and inspections takes much time and effort. However, they provide a CSO with periodic feedback on the condition of the anti-fraud program. The other down side is that more often than not the focus is on compliance and not on efficiency. Efficiency needs to be measured, and the good news is that the CSO can take care of this task.

Perhaps the most important method for measuring the efficiency and effectiveness of an anti-fraud program is to have solid metrics in place measuring all key processes for delivering products and services and to conduct self-assessments (or self inspections).

Conducting self-inspections helps a security organization understand where it stands in relationship to all anti-fraud compliance obligations (i.e., policy, procedures, regulations, and contractual obligations). Self-inspections also allow the IWC CSO to tailor the inspection or assessment process to focus on issues of efficiency. During a self-inspection or self-assessment, special emphasis can be placed on assessing the efficiency or effectiveness of processes and the delivery of anti-fraud program support, products, and services.

WHAT IS RISK MANAGEMENT AS IT RELATES TO IWC'S ANTI-FRAUD PROGRAM?

The risk assessment and risk analysis topics were discussed in the last chapter. Here, we will discuss the management of risks as part of an IWC anti-fraud program. The reason for doing so is to separate the actual "technical" aspects of risk assessment and related methodologies from the management of risks.

In order to understand the anti-fraud risk management methodology, one must first understand what risk management means. Risk management is defined as the *total process of identifying, controlling, and eliminating or minimizing uncertain fraud attacks or events that may affect the protection of the corporate assets.*

Risk management incorporates some aspects of risk assessments; risk analyses (to include cost-benefit analyses); target selection; implementation and tests; security evaluations of safeguards; fraud surveys; and overall reviews.

Many corporations also have risk management staff to deal with various aspects of business risks (e.g., insurance coverage as part of a risk mitigation strategy). CSOs should contact these specialists and coordinate activities related to the management of risks to corporate assets caused by fraud-threat agents. You may be surprised to learn how much they may be able to help you with techniques, data, and the like.

The goal of the assets protection risk management process is to allow the CSO, in coordination with executive management, to be able to manage the risks posed by fraud-threat agents to IWC assets. Risk management emphasis should be placed on management decision-making processes incorporated into the IWC anti-fraud program.

Although the ideal goal is to eliminate all risks, it is not a goal that can usually be achieved. The CSO and IWC managers deal with the uncertainty that arises in the course of daily activities associated with the threats posed by fraud-threat agents.

MANAGING AND REDUCING RISKS TO CORPORATE ASSETS

The starting point in managing and reducing risks to enterprise assets is assumed to be a basic anti-fraud program that uses integrated protection measures. An ongoing monitoring and surveillance program augments this baseline program and addresses both internal aspects, coupled with attention to external factors that could drive the threat. The risk of a fraud attack is not static; it is a dynamic variable that will fluctuate in part based on business cycle elements and in part on the ripeness of new products and new technologies for exploitation. Varying the degree of watchfulness, in effect adopting a process of heightened alert for periods of increased risk to fraud attacks and of basic vigilance at other times based on the inputs received from the monitoring and surveillance systems, helps protect assets at lower costs.

The response element should include a combination of internal and external assets capable of determining the facts in a legal and expeditious manner. Whereas investigations in the physical world may precede at a deliberate pace (hours, days, weeks, or longer), today we increasingly do business and work in cyberspace where the response to asset fraud attacks and subsequent inquiries must move at Internet speed, which means nanoseconds, minutes, hours, and days at most. Such speed is necessary because some key information may well be perishable.

The best possible resolution of a fraud incident or of known or suspected fraud attacks against corporate assets is the arrest and conviction of the perpetrator(s). In some circumstances, however, it may be preferable to turn the matter over to a counterintelligence operation. An attempt that is detected early enough may misdirect or mislead in a way that will feed the opponent inaccurate, incomplete, or misleading information (misinformation) to confound their analysts. After all, if the intrusion is detected quickly and is done properly, then the intruders might believe that they had avoided detection by the anti-fraud defenses of the target. Playing to this belief, the fraud attackers may be subtly deflected.

As global competition increases and the global power of a nation-state is measured in terms of economic power, such attacks are expected to continue to increase, and to increase exponentially, as the global marketplace competition becomes more of a global economic battleground where one cannot be neutral. You are either a player or a victim.

Regardless of the outcome, it is vital that every case of known or suspected fraud attacks against the corporate assets be carefully analyzed and that weaknesses in anti-fraud defenses, operations, and procedures that facilitated the breach should be addressed. This leads once again to the beginning of the cycle where enhanced anti-fraud defenses are implemented and await the next onslaught of attacks.

PROGRAM FOR MANAGING ANTI-FRAUD DEFENSIVE RISKS

The following points should be considered in building a framework for managing risks arising from fraud-threat agents: in many ways the operational and procedural anti-fraud defensive measures are as important as or more important than purely technical measures. This is true because some of your automated anti-fraud defensive systems, such as those related to computer and network systems, are vulnerable to compromise and breakdown. Therefore, there should always be a backup plan that includes a human in the loop.

Anti-fraud defenses must be managed with a combination of technical, procedural, and operational safeguards.

> Risk management: analysis of possible loss: the profession or technique of determining, minimizing, and preventing accidental loss in a business, for example, by taking safety measures and buying insurance.[5]

Remember: preventing, detecting, and responding to fraud threats is a dynamic process that will grow and change as rapidly as new technologies and processes are developed. Keeping up with the rapid pace of these changes is essential if the CSO is to defend key corporate assets against pernicious fraud threats.

> Risk-benefit: studying risks and benefits: studying or testing whether the benefits of a procedure, process, or treatment outweigh the risks involved.[6]

Remember that the most fundamental and essential step is to provide management leadership, direction, and support in conducting an anti-fraud risk assessment that considers all logical types of fraud-threat agents' attacks and vulnerabilities to those attacks.

The purpose of such an assessment is threefold:

1. To identify the full range of the corporation's important assets, including property, personnel, and sensitive proprietary information, especially assets that are unique to the corporation. Determine where they are physically located and how they are protected.

2. To create a value matrix of the assets and determine their relative contribution to the corporation's business. Stratify them to identify the top tier, the assets of greatest significance. We generally refer to the most important ones by the term *the crown jewels*. Although there is no precise formula for determining when a specific asset qualifies for such status, most senior managers and executives of a corporation can reach a rough consensus as to the items they can all agree are "crown jewels." Subsequent steps in the anti-fraud risk assessment should focus on managing and reducing the risks to these, the most significant assets.

3. Review the existing framework for safeguarding the corporation's most valuable assets using an interdisciplinary team that can evaluate

---

[5] Ibid.
[6] Ibid.

technical, operational, procedural, and legal protective measures. Consider how well the existing array of anti-fraud defensive measures will defend the most critical resources against the multiple technologies and techniques that will be used by fraud-threat agents if they are assigned the task of obtaining them.

The primary objective of the review called for in (3) is to ensure that the corporation has invested sufficiently in the integrated technical and operational anti-fraud defensive measures as well as a complete legal and procedural foundation to prevent, detect, deter, and respond to known or suspected incidents of fraud attacks.

In those corporations, such as IWC, which have had known or suspected incidents where fraud attacks have resulted in loss of assets, a two-pronged response is necessary.

- First, management must ensure that it makes a serious effort to determine all the discernible facts concerning the incident. Too often the tendency is to either write off an incident as an isolated event or as simple "bad luck." Although both may be true, the opportunity also exists to gain valuable insights regarding the strengths and weaknesses of the existing assets protection program. The insights gleaned from such a detailed analysis may help prevent future, and perhaps even more serious, incidents.
- Second, management will be better prepared to make informed decisions concerning steps to actively enforce the corporation's rights through litigation or prosecution, if it is armed with a complete report of the incident. Of course such an analytical process presupposes that the corporation has anti-fraud mechanisms to identify and report known and suspected fraud incidents in a timely manner such that an investigative response is possible.

Management must also consider that in order to get assistance from law enforcement to investigate an incident of known or suspected fraud attacks (where applicable), several key hurdles must be overcome.

- How does the corporation know a fraud incident (crime) has happened?
- Was the asset protected consistent with its status (did the corporation take reasonable steps commensurate with the value of the asset)?
- Have they calculated the value of the asset and any associated losses?

Although an ability to answer these questions is not a prerequisite for contacting the local or federal law enforcement agency, the investigators will likely ask for these and other details early in any official discussion concerning a fraud incident.

RESPONDING TO FRAUD INCIDENTS

The topic of how to respond to incidents, including proper investigation protocol in detail, goes well beyond the focus of this book. Suffice to say at this point that, although the corporation has many options when it knows or suspects an incident, one should not expect any public agency to come in and act as the internal security team for the corporation. The corporation must be prepared to conduct its own inquiries and should only approach law enforcement when management believes there is a reasonable basis for suspicion that an incident requiring law enforcement support has actually occurred. This can be done through an inquiry or perhaps through an inquiry in conjunction with a limited risk assessment or fraud survey.

The anti-fraud risk assessment is limited to the specific objective in determining the risks of a successful fraud-threat agent attack against a specific asset and the costs of mitigating that risk — for example, the cost of anti-fraud policies, procedures, processes, and the like, including the cost of compliance by all IWC employees, and/or the rationale for the requirement.

The assessment is also limited in time. For each of these issues where different assets and departments were involved, such as manufacturing or marketing, a separate, limited risk assessment will be conducted.

The approach can also be used for anti-fraud assessments and includes developing baseline anti-fraud policies, procedures, and processes while at the same time identifying specific anti-fraud requirements for each different work environment of the IWC, the Human Resources Department, the Manufacturing Department, and the like.

The results of the limited risk assessments will then be provided as part of a formal briefing by the CSO to the vice president of that particular department. A copy of the report to the vice president of Human Resources, the CSO's boss, will be given just to ensure that the boss was in the communications loop and because a copy will be available for use when briefing the CEO and the executive management team on the new anti-fraud program. The limited assessment would be part of the backup documentation for the briefing. The CSO could reason that a copy to the CEO would not be a good idea at that time because then the CSO would have to explain what it was and why the CEO had it.

The limited risk assessment will state the risks, mitigation factors, and estimated costs of the increased anti-fraud protection of that particular asset or set of assets. If the vice president of that department, who is also the person immediately responsible for the protection of that asset or assets, does not concur in the anti-fraud protection requirements, then the vice president must formally accept the risks in writing on the last page of the report and send it back to the CSO.

The acceptance of risk statement reads as follows: *I have reviewed the findings of the limited risk assessment conducted by members of the IWC anti-fraud program project team. I understand the potential loss of, or damage to, IWC assets under my care that may occur if additional protective processes are not put in place. I accept that risk.*

Another approach may be that management is not authorized to accept such risks because these risks are not acceptable to the welfare of IWC. This decision must be coordinated by the CSO with the CSO's boss and executive management. Their decision on how to proceed on this vital issue should be required because management has overall responsibility for the protection of IWC assets and the CSO is the "in-house" consultant and assets protection specialist. The overall assets protection responsibility lies with the CEO and executive management.

Most people will be unwilling to sign such a document or will try to delay signing, hoping that the issue will be forgotten. The CSO can never let that happen. To resolve that issue, a reply of concurrence or nonconcurrence will be set forth in the document with a suspense date. If no reply is forthcoming by that date, the report states that additional safeguards will be put into effect no later than a specific date because of the action person's failure to sign the document. A nonreply is taken as concurrence.

Often the executive will try to find a way out of the dilemma, and "negotiations" will take place during which various options will be examined, other than those already stated in the report. The CSO cannot turn down such a request, for to do so would give the executive the ammunition needed to conclude that the CSO was not being cooperative, was not a team player, or had a "take it or leave it" attitude. At the same time, negotiations cannot go on indefinitely. If a roadblock is reached, then the executive and the CSO should agree that the matter will be discussed at a meeting with the CSO's boss or possibly even the CEO.

MANAGING FRAUD THREATS

It is extremely important to understand as many fraud threats against corporate assets as possible. Remember that if it were not for threats, there would be no need for an anti-fraud program. That should be understood as obvious, but it is stated here because sometimes a CSO loses sight of the objective of an anti-fraud program, which is designed to achieve the following:

- Protect corporate assets from fraud in a cost-effective manner from all applicable attacks by fraud-threat agents, and since there is no such thing as perfect, impenetrable security, the CSO must also have an anti-fraud program that:
  - Minimizes the probability of a successful fraud attack by a fraud miscreant.

- Minimizes the damage if an attack by a fraud-threat agent occurs.
- Provides a method to quickly recover in the event of a successful attack.
- Provides a process to quickly mitigate the fraud threats and eliminate or reduce the vulnerabilities that allowed the fraud attack to succeed.
- Provides for a rapid inquiry or investigative response, the collection of evidence, the conducting of interviews as documented in the event IWC wants to pursue legal action against the identified fraud-threat agents.

CASE STUDY

As IWC's CSO, you must find some efficiency gains in order to properly establish and manage an IWC anti-fraud program. You are technology literate and believe that the use of technology to support efficiency gains is worth studying.

As the IWC CSO, how would you proceed?

Some thoughts on that question are as follows:

When looking for ways to use information technology to enhance the delivery of anti-fraud program support and services you may want to focus on those services only. However, the best way is to look at all security functions and to ascertain where any gains realized efficiently in the security department can be allocated to the anti-fraud program functions.

First the CSO may want to start with examining transactional services. It is the transactional services and not the consultative or oversight services where information technology can be deployed most cost effectively. At IWC, the CSO first examined the security education and awareness training program process, which also includes anti-fraud aspects, and determined it to be an ideal candidate for the use of information technology as a means of delivering this service.

It was determined that in many ways, security education is a transactional process. At IWC, security education is accomplished by a department that has responsibility for the implementation of a training and awareness program for the "rank and file." How they manage to accomplish their task is through a labor-intensive process, yet much of the work is reccurring and repetitive (transactional process), covering subjects such as the following:

- Workplace violence prevention training
- Protection of company information
- Automated information systems user security training
- New employee indoctrination
- International/foreign travel security and safety briefings

- Protection of classified information for IWC's government customers
- Anti-fraud defenses and what employees must know and do

Traditionally, these products were delivered through standard briefing packages designed for all company employees. Each addressed the areas where particular employee awareness is needed or even mandated (company policy or government regulation). On some sort of a scheduled basis, employees are identified as requiring awareness training and are notified to attend a formal presentation. These presentations are delivered to a group of employees who attend together. In this case the following steps take place:

1. The requirement(s) is/are identified.
2. The briefing is designed and developed.
3. A target audience is identified and scheduled.
4. An IWC security professional conducts a formal presentation (to a group or to an individual).
5. Each employee security/personnel record is annotated to indicate requirement fulfilled.

Steps 1 and 2 are one-time events. First, a requirement is identified. It may be in the form of a government regulation or a company policy or, it may be a management desire to have employee awareness increased in a particular area of concern. Once the requirement is established, training materials are developed. They may be delivered as a briefing or presentation, brochure, pamphlet, videotape, or computer program. This process, excluding revisions and updates, is a one-time creative process and is the process most dependent on the expertise of the security professional. Steps 3, 4, and 5 are reoccurring transactional steps and could be more efficiently executed with the help of information technology.

Using technologies such as computer-based training, one can build a Web-based security education and awareness program into the IWC intranet. Feeding from, and connected to, the human resources employee database, a security information system can be established where the criterion is developed by security and compared against the HR database. Those employees who require a particular type of awareness training could receive an electronic notification directing them to a Web site to complete their mandated training. At their leisure, and in lieu of taking scheduled time to attend a group presentation, the identified employee can visit the specified Web site and complete the training course. This process usually takes significantly less time to complete than the process of attending briefings. Upon completion of training, the computer system can generate a notification updating the personnel/security record for that employee. A security professional can create custom reports allowing for the review of this process to ensure that it works as designed. Overall, this process would save time for the employee (someone else's costs) and for the security professional (your costs) preparing and conducting these briefings.

SUMMARY

The CSO in IWC has a dual role of being the *leader* of the anti-fraud program and corporate security efforts and a *manager* of the security department. The CSO should treat those who are provided assets protection and security service and support as the customers of the CSO and security staff. They can be grouped as internal and external customers.

The CSO expects certain things from executive management and vice versa. The CSO expects support for the anti-fraud program and the security staff functions. The executive management expects the CSO to develop and maintain a cost-effective anti-fraud program.

Establishing and managing the IWC anti-fraud program requires the development of a statement of work and an understanding of the internal and external customers' assets protection requirements that are additional to the basic assets protection requirements of any publicly owned corporation. The anti-fraud defensive requirements are based on people, information, and physical assets. When you as the new IWC CSO come to work, you should come to work with a plan and then work the plan.

CSO responsibilities include the normal management responsibilities of planning, budgeting, controlling, staffing, and counseling. It also requires working in a team-emphasized environment where the CSO encourages everyone to work in a cooperative manner, as well as to communicate extensively throughout the security department and IWC.

Because IWC is an international corporation, it has offices in the United States, Europe, and Asia. Consequently, the CSO must establish and manage an anti-fraud program and security department that includes the foreign locations.

11

Winning Through Teaming

INTRODUCTION

In today's business world, the use of teaming techniques is almost mandatory. Sometimes, a strong leader who can quickly get things done is preferred; however, it seems that today's managers do not want to take chances, jeopardizing their careers and bonuses, so they use teaming as a way of building a consensus so that if anything goes wrong, they are not personally to blame.

Finagle's Eighth Rule: Teamwork is essential. It allows you to blame someone else. — *Proverb*

ANTI-FRAUD PROGRAM TEAM BUILDING

Teams work toward common goals that are understood and accepted by all team members: to achieve long-term goals and objectives. Team members must work openly and honestly with each other toward developing and maintaining a successful anti-fraud program. They must collaborate with each other, and the various anti-fraud teams are no exception. Some disagreement is expected. Both listening to others and offering ideas are essential skills.

To build an effective anti-fraud team, the CSO must operate in a collaborative way. Working with team members, the CSO working with the security managers must first identify the purpose of the teams and their objectives. The teams themselves, such as the anti-fraud program development project team, should identify issues and problems and work together to develop and implement short-term and long-term strategies. Effective teams will improve the performance of your organization — at least these are the formalized methods and goals. Sometimes they work and sometimes they don't work so well.

Teaming has its advantages. In today's budget-conscious corporate environment, teaming allows the CSO to be able to call on other resources to assist in meeting the security department's goals such as establishing and managing an anti-fraud program. In addition, teaming with other IWC departments allows the CSO to rely on the anti-fraud related expertise of others such as auditors, legal staff, ethics staff, and such.

As part of teaming, there are expectations on many fronts. These expectations positively or negatively impact teaming in order to successfully meet the CSO's goals such as an effective and efficient anti-fraud program.

EXECUTIVE MANAGEMENT AS TEAM MEMBERS

The most important thing vis-à-vis an anti-fraud program that IWC executive management can provide to a CSO is overt support for the anti-fraud program. By providing that support, executive management is actually part of the team responsible for the success of the anti-fraud program.

> Executive support for the anti-fraud program is essential to its success.

The chairman of the board, CEO/president, and all others in executive management must make it known throughout IWC that they are supporters of the anti-fraud program. Of course, executive management providing an increased budget does not hurt either.

Those in executive management should recognize the criticality of a successful anti-fraud program and their relationship as team members to that goal. They must communicate their support for consistent applicability of anti-fraud defenses to all employees, from other senior executives through management to the rank-and-file employees. Without executive support and commitment to a sound anti-fraud program, it will fail. Without senior executive support, managers and employees will find reasons, usually cost driven, to circumvent and even avoid anti-fraud policies and procedures. This condition leads down one path, and that is a failed anti-fraud program and damage to IWC through successful fraud attacks targeting IWC's valuable assets.

As part of that teaming, the CSO should have access to IWC's executive management. Although access is generally not required on a regular basis, when a CSO needs access to the most senior executive managers, it is usually for issues that can directly affect the IWC's welfare, that is, the anti-fraud program. Sometimes this is a difficult matter with the CSO reporting to the vice president of Human Resources who reports to the CEO. The vice president, as your boss, will more than likely have some serious concerns about any one-on-one meetings with the CEO and other members of IWC's executive management team.

As the CSO, you must establish a criterion with your boss for direct contact to the executives. Furthermore, you must ensure that you truly require any requested meeting. Based on the established criterion, you should expect that the CEO or others whom you want to contact are receptive to such meetings and not have them delegated to a lower level of management. Of course, most issues can be handled, and should be handled, at the lowest level of management deemed appropriate where effective decisions can be made. However, as the CSO, you should make it known, diplomatically of course, that you require this type of support. So, when you ask for a meeting, executive management knows that it is important enough for them not to put it off or delegate down to a lower level of management.

> The CSO must ensure that executive management knows that they are an integral part of the anti-fraud program and are valuable team members.

TEAMING WITH IWC EXECUTIVE MANAGEMENT THROUGH A BUSINESS APPROACH

Members of executive management in any business generally speak the same language, the language of business, that is, profits, losses, cost-benefits, return on investments. Establishing and selling an anti-fraud program to IWC's executive management will not require the CSO to justify such a program. After all, that is one of the reasons they hired the new CSO. What will be required is for you as the IWC CSO to take a business approach if you are to convince them that the methods, processes, approach, and philosophy you want to use in developing an anti-fraud program makes good business sense.

It is imperative that you remember that executive management is accustomed to approaching business decisions in the context of requirements, resources, cost, return on investment, and associated risks. For example, when working to convince an executive to support the requirements and budget of an anti-fraud program, that executive will expect you to present a business case. The executive may look for answers to the following:

- Why is a formal anti-fraud program even needed?
- What will it cost?
- Will the anti-fraud program really eliminate or reduce successful fraud attacks?
- How long before one can expect a return on the initial investment?
- What is the risk of establishing a formal anti-fraud program versus not establishing one?
- What makes this program different from the assets protection program?
- Isn't this program the same as the assets protection program and, therefore, wasting resources?
- What are similar companies doing to defend their assets against fraud-threat agents?
- More specifically, have you benchmarked with similar corporations? In other words, have you compared your anti-fraud program concepts and proposal with a security organization and corporation of similar sizes and within a similar industry?

Understanding the business perspectives of executives is a must if you are to be successful in developing an anti-fraud program and getting them to be active team members. Different executives take different approaches and have different priorities. When working with IWC's chief financial officer (CFO), you can reasonably expect the CFO to place a high priority on cost, risks, and return on investment.

When working with the vice president of Human Resources, your boss, you can expect employee welfare and workplace environment issues to have a high priority. This is not to say that either perspective is, or should be, more important or weighed with greater value. It is to say that understanding each will enable you as the CSO to better support your anti-fraud program business case or gain their support in this or other related matters.

TEAMING WITH CORPORATE PEERS

Understanding the culture of an international company like IWC and the various subcultures, as well as cultures in foreign countries, of different business units, and functional organizations, is critical to your success as a CSO. Working with heads of different departments, you will encounter cultural similarities and cultural differences. Some organizations will have a risk-taking approach, whereas others will not; some will be more creative, whereas others will be less creative. Remember that you are dealing with people and not nonlife forms. They have needs, feelings, problems, goals, and individual personalities. That is why it is so very important that as a CSO you are a "people person" and genuinely enjoy interaction with your peers and others at IWC.

Understanding their needs, desires, and agendas is absolutely necessary if you want their support. Remember President John F. Kennedy's now famous phrase spoken at his inaugural: "Ask not what your country can do for you but ask what you can do for your country"? Well, that same approach, modified of course, is a good attitude for you to take in dealing with management, in fact with anyone at IWC. Keep in mind that you lead a *service and support department.*

> Ask not what you need from others but what you can do to help others succeed.

It is important for you to understand how and perhaps even why corporate peers are different and how you should interact with them and gain their support to meet the anti-fraud program objectives. In dealing with your peers and others, your goal should also be to help them succeed while building an anti-fraud program. If you can do that, the IWC anti-fraud program will meet the needs of everyone at IWC with the least impact on productivity and costs, and you will have a better chance that management and employees will support it.

When dealing with creative and more open organizations, you can probably be very straightforward in sharing your views and seeking theirs. The managers and staff of these organizations encourage open and frank communications. They generally treat everyone with respect and encourage exploration of new ways to do things.

When working with risk-averse or more closed and traditional IWC departments, you may have to be circumspect in your approach and more conscious of their signals and indicators. They may not always say what they are thinking. The personnel of these organizations tend to be more conservative in their approach in conducting business. "Rocking the boat," expressing disagreement, or not sharing information is usually inappropriate behavior, and you will probably encounter resistance in getting support for the anti-fraud program.

You should understand the duties, responsibilities, overall processes, and limitations of each IWC department. Generally, we humans like to talk about our work and ourselves. As the CSO, use this opportunity to listen to what everyone is saying. Be sincere in your interest in their activities as there is no doubt what you do will impact them in one way or another. Also remember the old saying, "You were born with one mouth but two ears for a reason."

Since security in general and the anti-fraud program are generally compliance-related functions, you may find common ground with other compliance organizations. Audits, Environmental Health and Safety, Ethics specialists, and the Legal Department all deal with compliance-related issues. Each works to ensure that the policies, procedures, and processes developed and implemented facilitate compliance with contractual requirements, regulations, and laws. As such, their approach to conducting business may provide insight into how you should proceed.

> Take the time to learn how other functional organizations interact with each other and how they conduct daily business, for that will give you insight into your efforts to effectively deal with them and build a successful anti-fraud program.

The CSO must be able to work with peers and others in order to get the job done. If the CSO can get an understanding of the needs of the IWC managers and employees and help meet those needs, it will also help the CSO in meeting the anti-fraud program goals and gain their support for that effort.

TEAMING AND DEALING WITH OFFICE POLITICS

Office politics is a fact of life in today's business world. It is imperative that the CSO understand that and ensure that office politics does not adversely impact the CSO's objective of establishing and managing an efficient and effective anti-fraud program for IWC.

Much of what you as a CSO do to achieve success in any company, and IWC is no exception, depends on your skills and willingness to work hard — in other words, how well you perform your duties. However, some of what you do to be successful depends on your understanding of and participation in what is called office politics; IWC politics cannot be ignored. Individual success and departmental success require that you become engaged in some manner in office politics.

You cannot isolate yourself from office politics without limiting your ability to succeed. If you do isolate yourself, you cut off a valuable means of understanding IWC and facilitating success for you and your department. Furthermore, your opportunity to form successful anti-fraud teammates will be significantly reduced.

Not all information within IWC flows through formal channels. Much important information is distributed and shared informally. Having access to that information, in essence being part of the informal information flow process, will contribute to your understanding of the corporation and your overall success.

Understanding who has power and influence is also important. Aligning yourself with decision makers and with those who influence and serve the decision makers will offer you an advantage. If it is too difficult to align yourself with the decision makers, then focus on alliances with those who influence decision makers. Influencing them will ultimately have an impact on the decision makers. If you find this distasteful, get over it.

Alliances are a part of organizational behavior. Without them your influence will be limited, as will your success. That being said, remember that this does no mean compromising your personal values, honesty, or integrity. In other words, it does not mean having to "kiss butt" or "bend over and take one for the good of the corporation." However, life is full of compromises, and as long as your personal and corporate values are intact, then proceed.

Look at it this way: as nasty and distasteful as it is to admit it, we humans use others to get what we want. Isn't that what management is all about? That is a fact of life whether one likes it or not. It is how one goes about doing it that makes the difference. For example, as mentioned earlier, if you can help others succeed and by doing so help the anti-fraud program succeed, what is wrong with that? That is what is called a "win-win" situation. In this case, you are using people to meet your objective, but they may also be using you in return.

One may even want to plan on how to get others to support the anti-fraud program based on their individual needs and personalities. You, as the CSO, may want to target them and exploit their personality strengths and weaknesses. This approach may sound "cold and impersonal," but in fact if done right and for the right reasons, why not use this tactic as part of your toolbox of methods for dealing with people?

As a CSO, you must get things accomplished through others, and it is much more effective and efficient if you can work with them instead of pulling or pushing them into supporting an IWC anti-fraud program, such as by threats of disciplinary action. It takes less energy, and it almost always proves to be more successful.

Understanding your own political tendencies, behavior, and personality will help you in the political environment and further your goals to establish a teaming environment relative to gaining support for the anti-fraud program. Be observant and listen. Knowing how people react to you allows you to focus on your positive characteristics and to control or change your negative characteristics. Although it is difficult, you must try to be objective if you are to succeed in this endeavor.

Controlling your behavior will help you in relationship building, which is essential in developing alliances. In any event, never lose focus on your primary role and responsibilities. It is important to be aware of and to understand office politics. It is also important to participate. Company politics can be a nightmare, or it can be a vehicle that helps you accomplish your objectives. Recognize that and learn to manage within the political environment without it getting in the way of fulfilling your obligations.

The CSO works in a world of office politics where security is often given a bad name. These positive office politics tactics help show that you the CSO and the corporate security department staff are "team players" and are doing their part to support the IWC goals.

You may be thinking, "Why do I have to do all this work? Why can't they just cooperate in the interest of the corporation?" The answer is simple: that's life! No one said it was perfect. If you want to have a successful anti-fraud program, then you must do whatever it takes (legally of course) to accomplish that goal. Yes, it is hard work, but as a CSO and security professional, it is your responsibility to strive to create a successful anti-fraud program, and using teaming techniques helps you accomplish that goal.

TEAMING WITH YOUR SECURITY MANAGERS

As the CSO of IWC, you have other managers working for you. Your management team will be the primary vehicle for you to use to get things accomplished. Setting your expectations for them early on can help ensure good performance. Work with your management team to establish the boundaries within which you expect them to operate, vis-à-vis the anti-fraud program and other duties and responsibilities.

Consider the following:

- What do you expect from them?
- What constitutes a job well done?
- What is their level of authority?
- What are their responsibilities?
- Define the limitations of their role.
- Make sure they understand organizational goals and objectives.
- Provide them with regular performance feedback.

A common problem for new or inexperienced security managers is to rely on the skills that got them the job in the first place. In other words, they need to do the work themselves instead of managing others to get the work done. Management requires a different set of skills than those of the non-managerial security professional. Often, when faced with problems or difficult situations, new CSOs will try to do the work themselves, thus avoiding what they should be doing: managing others to get the job done.

A major role for you as the IWC CSO when working with your managers is to be their coach. Spend time with them, ensuring that they understand how to get things done through their employees and not by doing the work themselves. Your managerial approach to your managers is a key factor in how they will treat their employees. It is also a key to establishing and managing a successful anti-fraud program.

TEAMING WITH YOUR SECURITY STAFF

> The essential skill of management is the ability to develop and work with people.[1]

As the CSO for IWC, you and your security management team will depend heavily on your employees to perform their duties to the best of their abilities as professionals, thus helping to make the security functions and anti-fraud program effective and efficient. Good performance does not happen by accident. It is your responsibility as the leader and manager of the security department and anti-fraud program to create an environment in which your employees can be successful.

Without successful employees, the IWC anti-fraud program and your security services and support will fail. Creating this environment requires work. A conscious effort to get the most from employees is needed, so you must plan to develop the behavior of your security staff. When you embark on this effort, consider the following issues:

- *Collaborating:* The effectiveness of a security organization and its anti-fraud program is totally dependent on the performance of its people. For the organization to benefit the most, all employees must participate. A participatory environment is one in which all employees are part of the decision process. This environment is best accomplished when they work together cooperatively within small groups to solve problems. In this way, each member has a say in the process and a stake in the outcome. The CSO's directed initiation of an anti-fraud program project team is a good way to begin to facilitate or improve this collaboration.
- *Communicating:* Communication can be accomplished in many ways: letters, memos, e-mail, voice mail, messages, telephone calls, and face-to-face meetings. Although all these methods have value, face-to-face communication is the most effective because it allows for speaking, listening, observing, and feedback all at once. It is a very interpersonal process. When people engage in open and honest face-to-face communications, not much is hidden. Face-to-face communication allows each person to react to what is communicated at the moment it is said. Moreover, during face-to-face communications you have the advantage of reading body language, which can be very

---

[1] Lane, Byron, "Managing People, A Practical Guide" (Grants Pass, OR: The Oasis Press), 1990.

telling. Regular communications with your employees is a must. Communications must flow both ways — from you to them and from them to you.

Everyone in the security department must feel they are free to speak openly and honestly. Open and honest communications facilitate trust between people. Being direct and candid in all your communications will reduce the possibility of misunderstandings and also encourage people to be direct and candid. Honest communications includes being able to say, "I don't know — what do you think?" Employees hearing this said would realize you are being honest and open with them, and so you will expect them to communicate in kind. Half of the art of communicating involves listening. Being an effective listener enables you to better understand the communication, and it also demonstrates to the person speaking that you are interested in what they have to say. Listening effectively to someone will encourage him or her to be more open and candid with you. These techniques are crucial in the development of an anti-fraud program.

> Some managers say they have an "open door policy," but often they don't really mean it.

- *Motivating:* Many theories have been offered on how to motivate employees. Since everyone is different, it is difficult to determine what most motivates each individual. Perhaps the best you can do as the CSO for IWC is to focus on creating an environment in which people are inspired to motivate themselves. According to Dr. Byron Lane of Pepperdine University, a critical component of motivation is giving people a stake in the organization. This will apply to the anti-fraud program development and management. When people are involved in the process of goal setting, decision making, and implementation, they will hopefully develop their own motivation. Making employees part of the process, challenging them to be involved in the organization of an anti-fraud program, and encouraging them to perform to high expectations can all generate quite a bit of positive energy and a teambuilding environment.

> When you get the security staff involved, they not only feel part of the process but the message they receive from you is *they are trusted*. Participation, involvement, and trust can be a powerful means to motivate people.

- *Delegating:* The act of delegating responsibility to others can be difficult and problematic for managers. It requires giving up some control and placing your full trust in someone else. For managers who are used to getting the work done themselves, it can be difficult to rely on others. Watch for this tendency in your managers, and be careful you don't do it yourself. As the CSO for IWC, you will have many responsibilities, obligations, and, more than likely, a large workload. In effect, you cannot do it all. To be successful you must be able to delegate work effectively. This means assigning meaningful tasks and participating in the anti-fraud program, as well as giving managers and employees the authority to determine how to get the job done and the responsibility for successful completion of the effort.

> Caution: Don't usurp the management authority of your security managers when dealing with their security staff.

Not everyone works the same way or has the same set of skills. Some employees to whom you delegate work require only that you clearly advise them of your expectations and then stay out of their way. Let them get the job done. They tend to be self-motivated and work well with little or no supervision. Others may require more consultations or coaching from you. They need you to be involved with them to some extent by providing guidance and support. In any case, understanding the capabilities of your employees and demonstrating your trust in them are critical components of delegating successfully. As a CSO, your delegation of authority will generally be to one or more of your managers. It is up to them to delegate to their employees.

> Delegation never relieves the CSO from the ultimate responsibility of what has been delegated. If something goes wrong in the security department, it is always the CSO's responsibility. You may counsel your staff when they fail; however, to anyone outside the security department, you take full responsibility for your staff's failures, and they are given full credit and acknowledgment for their successes.

- *Goal Setting:* Establishing goals must be a process of participation. As the CSO, you will be responsible for setting department and individual goals and for aligning these goals with company goals. Setting individual goals allows you as the CSO to define what you expect your employees to do. It also tells the employees what the company expects from them. Setting department goals helps bring the organization together working toward the same outcome. Goals should be clearly and concisely stated: they need to be specific, realistic, measurable, and mutually understood.

All involved personnel ideally should agree to the goals. Individual and department performance to goals should be monitored. If performance to the goal is not adequate, corrective action should be taken, or alternative plans should be made to get performance to goal on track. To be meaningful, goals should be valuable to the organization and the company. Goal setting is crucial to the success of the anti-fraud program project and its subsequent maintenance.

- *Evaluating:* If done properly, assessing an employee's performance does not have to be a difficult chore. Providing performance feedback to employees is essential for their development. Without honest feedback, employees don't really know how management views their performance. The performance appraisal process is best used as a development tool. It is a vehicle to facilitate open and honest discussion of issues between you and your managers or between one of your security managers and employees. Performance evaluations should not be an annual event. It should be a process that occurs all year long. This is not to say that evaluations take place every day. Periodic and timely review sessions, both formal and informal, should occur throughout the year.

Reviews can be as casual as a brief discussion of what went well and not so well with the completion of a project. Sessions might also be scheduled for specific discussion of performance issues. Most companies have a standard process requiring an annual performance assessment along with a comparison ranking system. This is not enough. Providing performance feedback (e.g., on anti-fraud program project progress and the employee's role on that project team) should not be saved up for an annual occurrence. Moreover, the documentation should not be a checklist. A narrative describing both positive and negative aspects of the employee's performance is best. This approach will lead to very specific discussions of performance issues promoting the process of communication between employees and managers. However, as much as possible, performance measurement should be as objective as possible. Giving employees measurable goals will assist in the endeavor. The employee may not like you and/or you may not like the employee; however, it is their performance to goals, and not their personalities, that should be objectively measured.

TEAMING AND DEALING WITH SATELLITE OFFICES IN IWC HEADQUARTERS IN THE UNITED STATES

As the IWC CSO, your primary focus will be on the corporate office and its main business units, not the satellite offices. It is in these main business units that most of the people, revenue, activity, and problems are found. Satellite offices, usually sales and marketing offices, generally do not require as much of your attention. They are geographically distant from the main business units and have fewer people, and thus, hopefully, fewer anti-fraud needs and problems. The IWC satellite office staffs operate independently, usually interfacing with customer representatives and other marketing and salespeople. The business environment and even the culture are different from those of the rest of IWC. You may have security managers or supervisors assigned to each satellite office to act as your representatives.

The off-site security managers' or supervisors' anti-fraud related job is to provide input to the anti-fraud program project team and especially to explain any unique differences in their working environment from that of the main office. Once the anti-fraud program is implemented, their primary relative job is to ensure compliance and offer advice to the satellite office staff as part of their overall services and support function.

TEAMING AND DEALING WITH SATELLITE OFFICES IN FOREIGN LANDS

Not surprisingly, the biggest problem with satellite offices located in foreign countries is their great geographic separation from the main business units. Other issues that impact a CSO's ability to provide overall effective and efficient anti-fraud program and CSO management oversight to those offices are that these offices:

- Have different cultures
- Speak different native languages
- Obey different government laws
- Employ mostly citizens of the foreign state, who may thus see things differently
- Use local management employing foreign methods to manage most of the functions
- Operate in different time zones

These all contribute to creating an environment that is more difficult to manage and also perhaps less safe from fraud-threat agents. As in the case of IWC, the employees in these offices operate independently with little or no supervision. Since they include sales and marketing functions, much like satellite offices in the United States, but also manufacturing facilities, they share some of the same fraud-threat agents and vulnerability issues of those of the U.S. manufacturing plants and offices. Satellite offices must operate within the legal structure of the country they are in. This does not mean that the laws of the nation-state where the corporation is headquartered (e.g., in the United States for IWC) are not applicable to these offices; however, the laws of the country they operate within are paramount.

As the IWC CSO, you have the responsibility to work with satellite offices and the company's international lawyers to assess potential vulnerabilities and problems. As with domestic satellite offices, perhaps the best anti-fraud defense you can provide is to help them develop and incorporate an anti-fraud briefing into a security awareness program. This should increase employee consciousness of fraud in general and make them aware of potential fraud-threat attacks, vulnerabilities, and problems. However, three other functions are also very important for successfully protecting IWC assets at these foreign locations:

- Close liaison with the local law enforcement and security agencies
- Fraud-related risk assessments relative to the assets at those facilities
- An IWC anti-fraud program subset for each IWC foreign facility, which takes into consideration their unique environment. (*Note*: the basic IWC anti-fraud program should only be changed to meet the unique needs of the foreign office and should not detract from the IWC's overall anti-fraud posture.)

Based on the location of IWC's foreign offices and manufacturing plants in Asia and Europe, the CSO, with the approval of IWC executive management, has hired a U.S. citizen with security, anti-fraud, and management experience to head up each security offices abroad. Those managers were recruited away from firms already operating in those continents; therefore, travel/moving costs were minimized. In addition, they were already familiar with the local cultures.

CASE STUDY

The success of using teaming concepts will adversely be impacted by conflicts and by how you as the IWC CSO deal with the conflicts.

Assume that you as the IWC CSO have just been informed of some conflicts between members of your anti-fraud project team. How would you deal this problem?

The following information is offered as one approach to consider:

Managing conflict and dealing with difficult people is part of a CSO's job. Failure to properly deal with conflicts as they may arise on the anti-fraud program project has a direct bearing on the overall success of the program. It is not the fun part, but it is a necessary part. Failing to deal with conflict or difficult people is a recipe for disaster.

When you do not confront conflict or difficult people, you reinforce their negative behavior. Conflict will not go away on its own. You must deal with conflict when it occurs and deal with these people early on. Before confronting those in conflict, try to determine what may be causing their improper behavior. Think about why they are acting in such a negative way:

- Is it something you or one of your managers directed the team to do that is the basis for the conflict?
- Are their differences in interpretation in management direction as to the best way to proceed?
- Have personality problems arisen on the project?
- If so, who are the ones in conflict?
- Do they have personal problems that are affecting their work?
- Are they having disagreements with other employees that continue to fester?

You and/or your security manager may need to consult with others, such as Human Relations specialists, to help you understand what is going on. Think about the consequences of conflict and what you must do to eliminate it. After you have thought through the situation, you must decide to ask the employee manager to confront the person or persons involved; you may want to sit in on the meeting; or you may want to handle it yourself — depending on the circumstances and personalities involved.

One word of caution: remember that if the employee does not work directly for you the CSO but for one of your managers, that manager is the one who must take the action with your support. Since people are not mind readers, you should discuss the matter with the manager of the employee:

- Tell the manager what you know about the conflict.
- Be brief and to the point.
- State the facts and your observations, but don't dwell on them.
- Approach the situation in a positive way but be firm.
- Do not argue if the person becomes angry.
- Try to establish a positive tone.
- Listen to what everyone has to say.
- Share your perspective and concerns without being condescending.
- Never, never embarrass or humiliate the people involved.
- Treat them with dignity and respect.
- Be firm and committed in expressing your concerns and expectations.
- Ensure that the conflict and issues are resolved and that everyone concerned agreed to the actions taken.

SUMMARY

Teaming is necessary in today's corporate environment. It has both advantages and disadvantages. It allows for the sharing of resources from other departments in order to successfully provide IWC with an anti-fraud program. It also has disadvantages, including often gaining a consensus rather than leading an aggressive effort without others trying to tell you how they think it should be done. One advantage of others' input is that they may have good ideas; a negative consequence is that they may be wrong and conflicts between team members may arise.

To be successful, the CSO must use teaming techniques to gain the support of all IWC managers and employees, including executive management, other managers, employees, associates, suppliers, and subcontractors.

12

Anti-Fraud Functions

INTRODUCTION

As part of IWC's anti-fraud program, certain anti-fraud functions must be performed. In order to get the best use of the available resources, the IWC CSO will direct that the anti-fraud program project team identify those functions that should be performed in order to establish and maintain an efficient and effective IWC anti-fraud program.

ANTI-FRAUD PROJECT TEAM FUNCTIONAL TASKS

One thing the CSO has recently learned and explained to the anti-fraud project team is that executive management has decided that no additional budget is to be allocated to the anti-fraud program. Therefore, it is incumbent upon the CSO to ensure that the project team understands that and focuses on allocation and reallocation of resources instead of proposing that more resources be added to the security department.

Since the IWC anti-fraud program will be a subset of the IWC assets protection program, some of the assets protection program functions can be expanded to incorporate the anti-fraud defensive measures.

Furthermore, the CSO directed that the anti-fraud program project team look at other departments within IWC to determine which ones (e.g., auditors, legal staff, ethics specialists) could provide additional or supplemental support to meet the objectives of the anti-fraud program.

The project team was also directed to:

- Identify all anti-fraud functions that would be unique.
- Develop a job description for each of those functions.
- Identify the reallocation of security department resources that would allow the implementation of the function, including:

- Logic for that reallocation
- The benefits of the reallocation
- The costs of the reallocation in terms of budget and adverse impacts to the security department's other duties and responsibilities
- Providing the CSO with any other information to assist the CSO in making that reallocation decision

The anti-fraud project team, through research, determined how other corporations handled their anti-fraud duties and responsibilities, including unique and general assets protection functions. They found that very few had established an anti-fraud program and those who did just expanded their assets protection functions to place greater emphasis on fraud-related matters.

The question then arose: Is a separate, albeit subset of the assets protection program actually needed at IWC? The CSO advised the project team that the idea of an anti-fraud program was based on the history of fraud-threat agent attacks against IWC and executive management's decision to place greater emphasis on anti-fraud defenses. They did not care how it was accomplished as that was the CSO's problem.

The CSO decided that the anti-fraud program as a subset but high-lighted would emphasize IWC's anti-fraud philosophy and get IWC employees and others to view it as an important program for protecting IWC assets. Furthermore, after several serious past frauds against IWC, the government agencies that were concerned about IWC management protecting the stockholders' (owners') corporation would see that IWC management was placing a great deal of emphasis on fighting fraud and protecting the stockholders' value.

ANTI-FRAUD FUNCTIONS

The anti-fraud project team identified the following primary asset protection functions that were now being performed by IWC's security department:

- Administrative Security: assets protection plans, policies, processes, programs
- Physical Security: physical access control
- Personnel Security: preemployment background checks and workplace violence program
- Security Education and Awareness Training Program: assets protection briefings and related training programs
- Fire Protection: fire prevention, protection, and response
- Contingency Planning: business continuity, emergency response, crisis management, and contingency planning

- Investigations: investigations or inquiries into violations of IWC directives
- Government Security: assets protection and other support to IWC's government contracts
- Information Security: assets protection related to automated information, computer hardware, software, and related telecommunications systems
- Executive Protection: physical protection of specified members of executive management
- Event Security: assets protection projects related to IWC's sponsored events such as the annual stockholders meeting

The anti-fraud project team also found that each of these functions was authorized to conducted risk assessments and analyses related to areas under their function.

The project team found that the following security functions duties and responsibilities should be expanded to incorporate anti-fraud program functions:

- Administrative Security: Provide administrative oversight for the anti-fraud program by having the anti-fraud project team develop the program under this security organization, and once the program was implemented, to ensure it was maintained current at all times.
- Personnel Security: Ensure that all preemployment checks incorporated, in addition to normal law enforcement check inquiries, the applicant's credit, indications of bankruptcy and interviews of individuals who could vouch for the integrity and ethical conduct of the applicant.
- Security Education and Awareness Training Program (SEATP): Incorporate anti-fraud briefings, pamphlets, and training into the overall SEATP.
- Contingency Planning: Incorporate responses to fraud-threat agent attacks into the contingency planning function, including responsibilities for coordinating with the Administrative Security staff to have a fraud attack response team and processes in place to be initiated in the event of an attack.
- Investigations: Handle responsibility for conducting preliminary investigations into allegations of employee violation of government laws and regulations; inquiries to prove or disprove allegations of employee violation of anti-fraud program policy, procedures, and processes; coordination of investigations and inquiries with the IWC ethics director and IWC legal staff, and local law enforcement, when outside coordination is approved by executive management after legal staff consultations.

- Government Security: Serve as the focal point for all fraud-related matters concerning government contracts.
- Information Security: Incorporate anti-fraud defenses into the IWC computers and related networks.

The anti-fraud project team recommended that an anti-fraud specialist be assigned to provide oversight for the CSO relative to the anti-fraud program and all its aspects since so much of the anti-fraud functions were spread over almost the entire IWC security department. That person would report to the manager of the administrative security organization and be responsible for maintaining the anti-fraud program, related plans, and the like.

The CSO decided that each security manager or security organizational supervisor would be the focal point for the anti-fraud day-to-day level of efforts (LOE) within their security function. The CSO concurred with the project team recommendation and established a position within the Administrative Security organization to be the overall focal point within the IWC security department, who reported to the manager of that organization. This change was accomplished through reallocation of available resources within the security department.

ANTI-FRAUD PROGRAM'S NON-SECURITY TEAM FUNCTIONS AND MEMBERS

The anti-fraud project team identified other IWC departments that should be integral team members by function and support to the IWC anti-fraud program, as follows:

- Auditors: The CSO would coordinate the security department's anti-fraud matters with the manager of audits, who would identify the audits to be performed and incorporate anti-fraud indicators checks in all audits. The CSO and manager of audits would meet periodically to discuss anti-fraud areas of mutual concern.
- Ethics Director: The ethics directors would have the CSO as a member of the IWC Ethics Committee, and the CSO's investigations organization would conduct all fraud-related inquiries and investigations requested by the ethics director, except those minor allegations whose inquiry could easily be conducted by the applicable IWC manager.
- Legal Staff: The IWC legal staff would provide legal advice concerning fraud-related matters brought to them by the members of the investigations organization, security anti-fraud specialist, and the CSO.
- Human Relations Specialist: The Human Relations Department specialist would act as a focal point on employee matters in which some fraud-related matters were identified.

The anti-fraud program project team also recommended that the CSO head an IWC anti-fraud committee to coordinate and discuss fraud matters of mutual interest. The CSO agreed in principle to such a committee but decided against forming a separate IWC committee. Instead, in coordination and with the agreement of the ethics director, the ethics director's monthly ethics committee meeting, which includes the CSO, audit department manager, legal staff representative, and Human Resources representative, would be used as the forum for discussing fraud-related matters.

The CSO reasoned that such matters would fit well into the committee's charter of duties and responsibilities, as fraud allegations were often received via the Ethics Hotline, and all fraud-related allegations were also allegations of unethical conduct.

CASE STUDY

As the IWC CSO and member of the IWC ethics director's Ethics Committee, how would you respond to a request to conduct an inquiry into a series of anonymous Hotline calls concerning allegations of falsification of time-cards by various personnel within an IWC department? These calls appeared to be coming from one person and started when that department announced a series of employee layoffs within that department.

Would you decline to conduct an inquiry or conduct an inquiry?

As the CSO, you could decline the inquiry because it seems that someone is trying to make other employees look bad and hope that such accusations would put those employees at the head of the layoff list, thus (in the eyes of the caller) protecting the job of the anonymous caller.

On the other hand, these may be valid calls and not previously reported as the person making the calls did not want to get involved — until the latest layoff announcement was given to IWC employees.

What if the ethics director did not agree and requested that the CSO's staff conduct the inquiry? If you declined, the ethics director might take the matter to your boss, or at least your relationship with the ethics director would suffer. In that event, the ethics director might decline to refer a potential fraudulent matter to you because you declined the request for inquiry in the past.

Would you recommend that the manager of the department wherein the allegations were made be told of the matter, and would you request to conduct an internal inquiry? The upside is that this matter would no longer be one for the CSO. The downside would be that such an inquiry would be conducted by inexperienced people, might cause undue animosity in that department, and might also make the Ethics Hotline process appear to be indicative of a "witch-hunt."

In this case, the IWC CSO agreed to have the security department's investigations organization to, as covertly as possible, conduct an inquiry to prove or disprove the allegations and provide a report of findings to the ethics director and the department's manager.

SUMMARY

Anti-fraud program functions can be viewed as independent functions, or they can be integrated into the normal security department functions. The CSO's decision in that regard is often based not only on what executive management wants but also on the available budget allocated to the security department.

The most cost-effective approach, assuming limited budget — and security budgets are almost always limited — is to integrate the anti-fraud functions into the applicable security department functions and also into other IWC department functions, when logical to do so and upon agreement with the managers of the other departments.

13

Are We Winning the Battle? How Do We Know? Measure It!

INTRODUCTION[1]

Thus far we have discussed how to develop and manage an anti-fraud program. When the program is implemented and basically goes into maintenance mode, how do you know that the anti-fraud program is meeting the goals and needs of IWC? In other words, how do you know that it is successful? We touched on some ways to measure in the previous chapters. Now, we will focus on an anti-fraud metrics management system.

Another thing that the IWC and probably executive management would like to know besides whether the IWC anti-fraud program is successful is how much it is costing. Is there a cost benefit to the anti-fraud program? Is IWC getting a return on its investments?

As the CSO, are you in a position to answer such questions? If not, then you are not doing your job as a CSO and a member of the IWC management team. You may in fact be wasting resources and impeding productivity by requiring certain policies, procedures, plans, and processes be in place and followed, which in fact do not provide a cost benefit vis-à-vis protection of IWC assets from fraud attacks.

In order to not waste valuable IWC resources or abuse them, the IWC CSO must develop some measurement processes to help answer the above questions.

[1] Portions of the information provided in this chapter was excerpted with permissions from: *Security Metrics Management: How to Measure the Costs and Benefits of Security*: December 2005, co-authored by Dr. Gerald L. Kovacich and Edward P. Halibozek; published by Butterworth-Heinemann.

MEASURING AN ANTI-FRAUD PROGRAM'S COSTS, BENEFITS, SUCCESSES, AND FAILURES

When we talk about metrics, we are talking about a system of measuring the costs, benefits, successes, and failures of the IWC anti-fraud program. As previously stated, there are two basic categories of anti-fraud program actions: (1) the level of effort (LOE), in other words the day-to-day operations such as conducting fraud inquiries. Although each inquiry has a beginning and an ending, the function itself is an ongoing function.

(2) There are also projects that have a stated objective with beginning and ending dates. These projects are not ongoing and are used as a formal management tool to make changes in some part of the anti-fraud program, for example, a change in a process. So, pretty much by definition, projects are measurable in that they include a list of tasks to be performed, the time it takes to perform them, and the cost of performing the tasks.

In addition, projects can be easier to measure as one can use project management software to keep track of incurred costs in materials, labor, and the like. This type of measurement is rather straightforward. Where many CSOs have difficulty is in measuring the LOE costs.

The LOE costs, benefits, successes, and failures must also be measurable. If not, then how do you know they are worth performing or whether they are working out as planned?

So, when we talk about a security and anti-fraud program's metrics management approach, we are talking about those related primarily to LOEs as projects already have built-in measurement processes. What the CSO needs is a similar built-in measurement for, as a minimum, each of the LOE anti-fraud program functions.

As you will recall, the security department's primary anti-fraud functions have been identified as:

- Administrative Security
- Personnel Security
- Security Education and Awareness Training Program (SEATP)
- Contingency Planning
- Investigations
- Government Security
- Information Security

In addition, the other IWC departments employ the following personnel to perform anti-fraud program support functions:

- Auditors
- Ethics director
- Legal staff
- Human Relations specialist

As it relates to the other IWC department's anti-fraud program support functions, the CSO does not want to impose measurement standards on these departments but can use their support to measure the LOE that flows from their support. Furthermore, other IWC departments can provide an estimate of how much time they use to support the anti-fraud program so that a total IWC cost estimate of the anti-fraud program can be made, excluding the costs by employees.

A word of caution here: be careful that the other departments don't try to charge or make a case for charging their anti-fraud tasks to your budget. Managers are always looking for ways to decrease their budget or obtain additional budget. So, don't put it past any of them to try this approach. After all, they are part of one or more aspects of the anti-fraud program processes and support the CSO in the CSO's anti-fraud program responsibilities.

COMMON LOE MEASUREMENT TECHNIQUES FOR EACH FUNCTION

Certain common measurement techniques can be used across the CSO's anti-fraud program functions. Remember that each LOE function should be measured to determine whether it is operating efficiently and effectively as determined by measuring its processing times, costs, benefits, successes, and failures.

How does the CSO establish the common measurement system for each function? The first thing the CSO should do since no measurement system is currently in place is to facilitate tracking processing time, costs, benefits, and so on, and initiate a project plan with the goal of developing a common measurement system across all anti-fraud program-related functions.

As part of that project plan, the following tasks, as a minimum, have been identified for action:

1. Determine the anti-fraud policy drivers and requirements for each function: if there is no driver or requirement for a specific anti-fraud LOE, then why do it?
2. Determine the policies that are used by the functions: policies should come from the drivers and requirements.
3. Determine the procedures that are used by the functions: they should be the most effective and efficient way to do the anti-fraud work.
4. Determine the processes that are used by the functions: processes should be continually evaluated to be sure they are as effective and efficient as possible.
5. Determine the costs to perform the functions in terms of equipment, people, and other support material using a process improvement methodology.

6. Determine the objective of each function: each objective should be linked to the drivers, requirements, and so on.
7. Determine whether each function is meeting its objective.

These tasks are then mapped using a flowchart process for each function so that the CSO can see the "big picture" for each function and also obtain the related costs and ascertain whether process improvements are required.

The IWC CSO decided to evaluate and measure the security department's anti-fraud program functions separate from the entire function (e.g., SEATP), which as you recall includes other aspects of assets protection functions. The CSO decided that the focus was on the anti-fraud program first as it is new compared to the assets protection program and provides a smaller piece of the CSO's management oversight duties and responsibilities.

The CSO will subsequently use the same approach for evaluating the entire LOE functions within the security department as a separate project. This approach will later be used in a separate project to analyze the cost benefits of the support departments to the CSO and the anti-fraud program — from the CSO viewpoint. Any changes that the CSO seeks from a support department will be requested using the results of the project plan for that support department's analyses.

EXAMPLES OF METRICS BY FUNCTION

Investigations and Noncompliance Inquiries

Anti-fraud investigations and noncompliance inquiries (NCI) are both anti-fraud program LOE functions, which, at some corporations, may be candidates for outsourcing. At this time, both are internal functions at IWC. At IWC, these two functions are very similar. However, the primary differences are scope and magnitude. That is, the term *NCI* is used to describe an investigation that is conducted due to a violation of corporate policy or procedures where a law has not been violated. At IWC an investigation is generally a much more complex process associated with a more serious situation and would involve a violation of the law or a regulation external to the corporation.

One primary reason for the differentiation is for public relations purposes. When one hears that an investigation is being conducted, it sounds more serious than if one hears a NCI is being conducted. In addition, an NCI may be used as a preliminary inquiry to assess if something is wrong and requires a full investigation. An NCI may be conducted by nearly any security professional or member of management. An investigation requires someone skilled in the techniques and processes of investigations, which will need to have a working relationship with different governmental investigative organizations (local, state, and federal).

INVESTIGATIONS AND NCIS METRIC CHARTS

The Investigations and NCI function's primary drivers are identified and graphically depicted. In this case, the complaints and allegations from various sources are considered the security drivers. (See Figures 13-1 and 13-2.)

Beginning with this overview diagram, the CSO's security manager and staff can begin to analyze the function in more detail, identify each step in the process, and determine:

- The time it takes to do each step in the process
- The number of people involved in each step
- The number of times one LOE is performed each month (e.g., one NCI)
- The pay of each person involved in each step broken down into an hourly wage
- The cost of the equipment and supplies that support the function

Using this information for each fraud investigation and fraud NCI, one can begin to determine the costs of this function in total and also broken down by labor, equipment, supplies, and such.

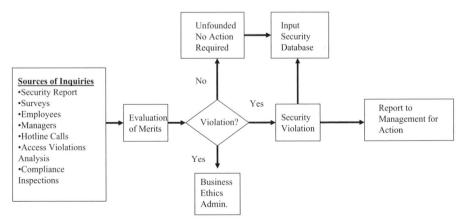

Figure 13-1.   Overall flowchart of the drivers of investigations and noncompliance inquiries (NCI).

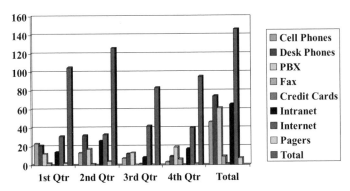

Figure 13-2. Number of technology fraud-related NCIs by calendar quarters and by type.

One can also add the square feet of office space, use of utilities, and the like if micro-detail is needed. In doing so, however, one must look at such costs across all investigations and inquiries and then take the total number that makes up the fraud investigations and NCIs and prorate the costs accordingly for fraud investigations and NCIs.

This approach can be used for all anti-fraud functions.

Remember: one important driver for the Investigations and NCI process is the total number of IWC employees: The more employees, statistically the larger number of employees who will violate IWC's anti-fraud program policy, procedures, or government laws.

Another driver is the number of fraud-related requests for support from other organizations (such as the legal and ethics staffs and their need to have investigators support their processes). Remember that the Investigations and NCI organization is also a service and support organization and as such must provide professional support to other IWC organizations when that service and support is requested and determined to be warranted.

EXAMPLES OF ANTI-FRAUD INVESTIGATIONS METRICS

A CSO can use many different anti-fraud metrics to help understand, assess, and manage the fraud investigations and fraud NCI processes. A problem that may face the CSO, as with all other security metrics, is determining the most useful metrics. When in doubt as to the most valuable metrics, the CSO can start by identifying as many as possible and then sort through them to determine which offer the most utility.

Don't forget that once the CSO or project team appointed by the CSO develops a process flow diagram depicting the macro process and then develops flow diagrams for the investigative subprocesses or micro processes, the CSO can begin to develop points for different processes measurements.

An example of such a data collection list for fraud investigations may look like the following (a list for the NCI function would be almost identical):

- Number of investigations opened per month
- Number of investigations closed per month
- Number of investigations pending per month
- Average time used to conduct an investigation
- Average cost in terms of investigator's time, IWC employees' time, administrative time, and cost of resources used
- Same information as above broken down by type of fraud investigation
- Same information as above broken down by quarters, year, and multiple years
- Identification of the IWC departments where the incident took place
- Identification of the IWC departments where the subject (employee) of the investigation was assigned
- Number of allegations proven correct
- Number of allegations proven wrong
- Subject of investigations employees' position and job code
- Type of investigations broken down by departments
- Department information broken down monthly, quarterly, annually, and multiple years
- Association of a cost chart with each of the above charts, where applicable

By using this approach, one can begin to get a sense of the type of information that offers potential for developing useful metrics. Furthermore, the CSO can relate the potential data points to what he or she needs to know. For example, if the CSO is attempting to determine the average time to conduct a fraud investigation, tracking the time taken to complete all steps from the opening of an investigation to the closing of an investigation will provide that data. The CSO can further analyze that information by sorting investigations by type. An investigation into the fraudulent timecards, on average, may require less time than an investigation into fraudulent use of information systems.

Remember also that once the time elements are known they can be costed-out by using the salary rate on an hourly basis for the investigator, those interviewed, time conducting records' checks, surveillance, report writing, and the like.

Metrics developed and used in the fraud investigations and fraud NCI processes may provide value beyond the investigative processes itself. Trend data may be developed and used to drive changes in other routine anti-fraud policies, procedures, and processes. For example, if investigative trend data or fraud survey results reveal the potential for travel voucher fraud by a group within one department, additional controls may be implemented for that department or throughout IWC to deter the submission of fraudulent expense claims; for example, a travel briefing can be given to the employees before they go on a business trip and in that briefing (preferably provided online for convenience and to save money) it can be explained that controls are in place to identify fraudulent travel claims and that such claims once submitted by the employee and proven false would be grounds for employment termination.

The information gathered may be used proactively to reduce the number of incidents requiring fraud investigations, thus reducing the overall workload for security investigators. Learning from security incidents helps prevent their occurrence in the future.

The following figures (13-3 through 13-9) are just a few examples of graphically depicted security metrics charts that a CSO may find useful in the effort to assess the effectiveness of the Investigations and NCI process and better manage the organization.

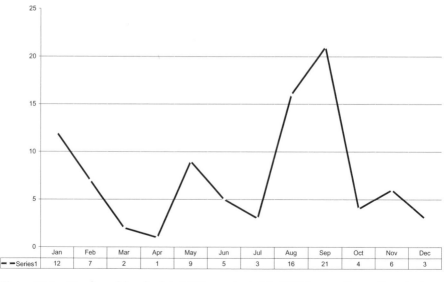

	Jan	Feb	Mar	Apr	May	Jun	Jul	Aug	Sep	Oct	Nov	Dec
▬ ▬Series1	12	7	2	1	9	5	3	16	21	4	6	3

Figure 13-3. Number of fraud-related NCIs conducted in 2006 by month as a line chart.

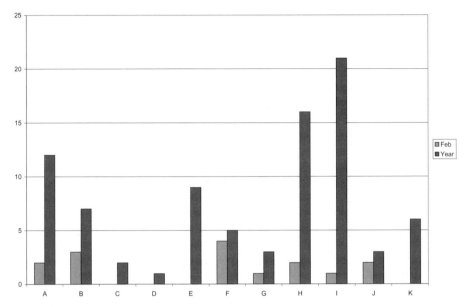

Figure 13-4.   Number of fraud-related NCIs conducted in 2006, by department.

- The number of IWC employees has increased based on IWC's need to rapidly build up the workforce to handle the new contract work.
- The number of fraud-related noncompliance inquiries has increased during that same time period.
- The number of fraud-related investigations has increased during that same period of time.
- This increased workload has caused some delays in completing the inquiries and investigations in the 30-day period that was set as the goal.
- The ratio of incidents compared to the total number of employees indicates:
  - Personnel may not be getting sufficient information during their new-hire briefings.
  - Personnel being hired may not be thoroughly screened prior to hiring.

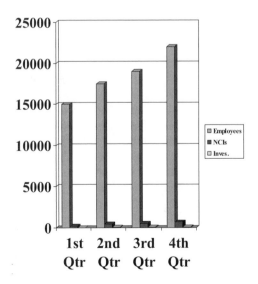

Figure 13-5.   Number of fraud-related investigations and NCIs in 2006 based on IWC population.

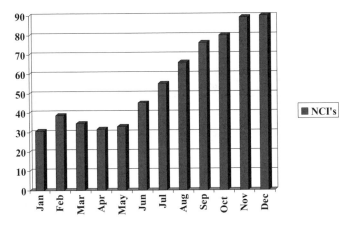

Figure 13-6. Number of new fraud-related NCIs per month — all locations — 2006.

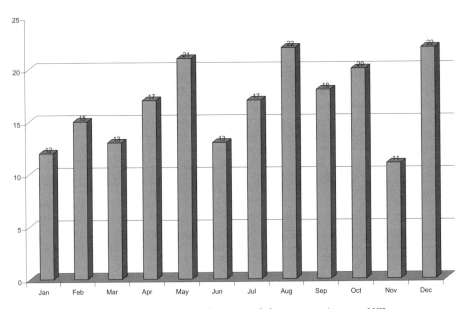

Figure 13-7. Number of NCIs conducted per month by average time per NCI.

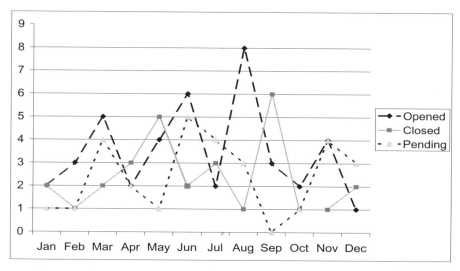

Figure 13-8. NCIs opened, pending, and closed per month.

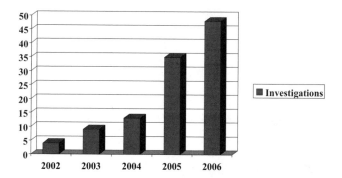

Figure 13-9. Total number of fraud-related investigations over a five-year period.

PROCESS MEASUREMENTS

Process measurements can tell you a lot about a process. The type of measures used should correlate to what the CSO wants or needs to track and understand. For example, if it is important to the CSO to know what percentage of cases are closed each month, then that information should be tracked, quantified, and a cost associated with each, total and average.

The ultimate goal for the CSO should be to understand what it is that drives the need for fraud-related NCIs and investigations. Can those drivers be changed to such a degree as to eliminate or reduce the need for fraud-related NCIs or investigations? Maybe employees are not aware of some anti-fraud controls in place and thus violated them out of a lack of knowledge. Or perhaps more emphasis in the anti-fraud portions of the SEATP and a special online bulletin to each employee would make them all aware of the controls and how to follow the proper procedures. Measuring will also tell the CSO if the changes made had any effect on the process. Of course, cost issues must always be considered

> Quality in a product or service is not what the supplier puts in. It is what the customer gets out and is willing to pay for. A product is not quality because it is hard to make and costs a lot of money, as manufacturers typically believe. — *Peter Drucker*[2]

So, by linking drivers and requirements to policies to procedures to processes and so on, one can begin the analyses of each fraud-related function to determine their costs, whether or not such function should be performed in the manner prescribed — in other words, determine the most cost-effective approach to complying with the anti-fraud program, making changes to the anti-fraud program and minimizing violations of the anti-fraud program defensive measures (e.g., controls).

CASE STUDY

As a CSO, you decided that it would be a good idea to use the anti-fraud program driver's metrics, which tracks the number of employees, the number of anti-fraud inquiries, and investigations conducted over time. You have gone through the analytical process to make that decision based on answering the following how, what, why, when, who, and where questions:

- *Why* should this data be collected? To determine the ratio of employees to the workload, manpower requirements could therefore be forecasted over time.
- *What* specific data will be collected?
  - Total number of IWC employees
  - Total number of anti-fraud noncompliance inquiries
  - Total number of anti-fraud investigations
- *How* will these data be collected?
  - Total Employees: The collection will be accomplished by taking the total number of paid employees from the Human Resources Department's master personnel database file.

---

[2] http://www.quoteland.com/search.asp.

- Total Number of Fraud-Related NCIs: This information will be gathered by the unit coordinator from the unit's NCI database file.
- Total Number of Fraud-Related Investigations: The unit coordinator will also gather this information from the unit's investigations database file.
- *When* will these data be collected? The data from each of the previous months will be compiled on the first business day of each of the following months and incorporated into the crime investigations drivers' graph, maintained on the Investigations and NCI's administrative information system.
- *Who* will collect these data? The data will be collected, input, and maintained by the unit's coordinator.
- *Where* (at what point in the function's process) will these data be collected? The collection of data will be based on the information available and on file in the Investigations and NCI's database at close of business on the last business day of the month.

The CSO organizational manager and security staff can analyze the NCI data, for example, to determine:

- The reason for each employee's noncompliance
- The position and organization of the employee
- The employees' seniority dates
- Identification of the patterns
- Main offenses

That information would then be provided to the project team assigned to the goal of decreasing the need for fraud-related NCIs and Investigations. Based on that information, the briefings would be updated and more emphasis placed on those areas causing the majority of problems. In addition, the departments with the highest number of fraud-related NCIs and investigations may be targeted for special briefings and meetings with the department managers to discuss ways of improving their anti-fraud program support.

Remember that numerous types of graphic depictions of data can be a great tool for management. They include bar charts, pie charts, and line charts and can be monthly, quarterly, weekly, or annually. The timeliness of the charts should be dependent on the manager's need for the information.

The key to the data collection and their related graphic depictions is to give more attention to trends than to monthly numbers. The goal is to continue to maintain and improve on positive trends. Negative trends should be analyzed for systemic causes, and project plans should be implemented to reverse the negative trends. The metrics could then be used to monitor the process and to determine whether process changes actually cause the reversal of the negative trends. If not, then new analyses and a rethinking of the problem are needed.

The organizational manager in coordination with the CSO began this process by, of course, identifying the drivers requiring the functions to be performed. Subsequently, the processes were flowcharted, and a process analysis summary was developed to help provide a high-level view of the process. That process summary included the following information:

- Security Department: Investigations and NCIs
- Process Definition: Professional fraud-related investigative services in support of IWC and its customers
- Subprocesses
  - Conduct fraud-related investigations
  - Conduct fraud-related NCIs
  - Conduct fraud prevention surveys
  - Conduct fraud prevention special briefings
- Requirements and Directives that Govern the Process
  - IWC's Assets Protection Program (IWC APP)
  - Contractual security requirements
  - Position descriptions
  - Corporate policies
- Suppliers
  - IWC employees
  - Customers
    - IWC management
    - IWC customers
- Input
  - Complaints
  - Allegations
  - Requests for assistance
  - Security requirements
- Output
  - Investigative reports
  - NCI reports
  - Inspection reports
  - Fraud risk assessment reports
  - Fraud survey reports
  - Briefings
  - Testimony
- Key Metrics
  - Subprocess 1: Case totals year-to-date and five-year trends, case aging charts
  - Subprocess 2: Fraud Prevention Surveys completed; Results; and Cost-Benefits charts

- Subprocess 3: Number of fraud-related NCIs completed each year; costs; and IWC departments where conducted
- Subprocess 4: Number of fraud-related investigations completed each year; costs; and IWC departments where conducted
- Customers and Expectations
  - IWC management (Internal customers): Timely and complete investigative and NCI reports
  - IWC customers: Timely and complete investigative and NCI reports as applicable to external customers
  - All: Most effective and efficient anti-fraud program possible.

Using the preceding identification process, the IWC CSO can not only view a summary of investigative and NCI organizational fraud-related metrics and processes but establish a form or format for such summaries and require their use throughout the security department.

SUMMARY

Metrics is an excellent managerial tool that can be used to determine the costs, benefits, successes, and failures of the IWC anti-fraud program. Project plans are a formal management tool used to establish measurement projects and subsequent processes. The LOEs are the anti-fraud program functions that can also be measured and subsequently analyzed to ensure the most cost-effective and efficient anti-fraud program possible.

THE FRAUDULENT FUTURE

Section III, the final section of this book, summarizes the author's views on future corporations and frauds, on where high technology is headed, and on what that means to you and fraud-threat agents.

The final chapter provides a summary of the main points of this book, as well as some final thoughts about fraud. The four chapters of Section III are:

Upon completion of this last section of the book, you should:

* Have a basic understanding of the twenty-first-century corporate environment, fraud-threat agents, and their modus operandi.
* Know how to establish and manage a basic anti-fraud program for a corporation or other business entity.
* Be able to begin to defend corporate assets against defrauders and potential defrauders.
* Gain some insights into who should lead an anti-fraud program so that you can decide for yourself where such a position should be located within the bureaucracy of a corporation.

14

What Will the Fraudulent Future Hold for Corporations?

INTRODUCTION

Two of today's best interpreters of trends and projecting them into the future are Alvin and Heidi Toffler. Over the years they have talked about viewing our history and the future in terms of "Three Waves." Use of the Tofflers' model of evolution provides a useful framework for discussing the future of corporations and fraud.

The *First Wave* is the agricultural revolution, which took thousands of years to develop, mature, and in some countries, has begun to fade. According to the Tofflers, this period — at least in the United States — started with the beginning of the human race and ended in about 1745. Obviously, agriculture is necessary for us humans to survive, but in modern societies, it does not have the force it once had. During this period, people lived in small and sometimes migratory groups, feeding themselves through fishing, foraging, hunting, and herding.

During this First Wave, information was passed by word of mouth or in written correspondence, usually sent by a courier. People were dispersed, and transportation was primitive. This meant that there was less contact among people. During this period, relatively few people could read or write.

Today very few nation-states remain in this First Wave of existence as technology has allowed the once less-advanced nation-states to begin to catch up to the rest of the world. For example, the use of cell phones has permitted developing nation-states to minimize their land lines for telecommunications and for the most part to go directly to wireless, which is a tremendous cost savings and permits faster communications development. They have also been able to take advantage of satellites provided by more modern nation-states.

The problem of fraud in the First Wave societies is as one would expect: it is mostly a one-on-one, person-to-person type of fraud. After all, defrauders take advantage of what they can, and defrauding a poor farmer offers little opportunities to be successful or profitable.

Although there were always defrauders around in the First Wave period, their schemes were generally not very sophisticated compared to today's fraud schemes because they lacked sophisticated technology to support their schemes. Furthermore, they were more localized owing to the lack of modern transportation systems.

The Second Wave, or what the Tofflers call the "rise of industrialized civilization", took less than three hundred years to develop and mature, at least in the United States. This was the age of steel mills, oil refineries, textile plants, mass assembly lines, and the like. People migrated to centralized locations to work in these industries. This period lasted until just a few years after World War II. In the United States, its decline, according to the Tofflers, is believed to have started about 1956, when for the first time, white-collar workers outnumbered blue-collar workers.

The Second Wave period saw the building of great cities and the era of great inventions like the telegraph, telephone, air transportation, automobiles, and computers. This period also witnessed expansions in education, mass transportation, and exponential growth in communications — the sharing of information.

The sharing of information became easier following the development of communications systems and the increased consolidation of people into large cities. This change also made it easier to educate the people, giving them the skills needed to work in the more modern factories and offices of the period.

The sharing of information through various communication channels brought new challenges. For communication protection, cryptography came into its own during this period. Cryptography was used primarily by the government as a high-technology anti-espionage tool. During the post–World War II years, the U.S. federal government owned most of the computers. Although businesses were beginning to look at the use of computers, most were cost-prohibitive; these systems were primarily operated in standalone mode. In other words, the computers did not talk to other computers.

As societies and corporations began massing into cities and using some of the advanced technologies that were coming into their own, the defrauders also migrated to the cities. However, since technology was limited, so was the defrauders' use of it. It is believed that they were able to take advantage of "modern" transportation systems to ply their fraud schemes throughout larger regions than in the past.

The *Third Wave*, the age of technology and information, is sweeping across the globe and will have done so in decades, not centuries.

> Mass production, the defining characteristics of the Second Wave economy, becomes increasingly obsolete as firms install information-intensive, often robotized manufacturing systems capable of endless cheap variation, even customization. The revolutionary result is, in effect, the demassification of mass production.[1]

We are now in the Third Wave, with some saying we are moving into the Knowledge Age; during this period, we have witnessed more advances than during the First and Second Wave periods combined. We have experienced the rapid growth of high technology, which is playing a major role in our rapidly changing world.

Remember the old business saying, "Time is money"? Well, in our world of international, global competition, that saying is truer now than ever before. Managers and security professionals must also understand this better than ever before. Fraud concerns cannot be a roadblock to business; however, the issue must be addressed.

Since this is "our age," it is easier to see the development of fraud in this period. Through today's technology and the advantage of technologies' vulnerabilities criminals have had more opportunities to successfully perpetrate frauds.

As suggested earlier, today's frauds are more sophisticated and more global, and their numbers have grown. It is expected that unless corporations take some significant actions, notably implementing aggressive antifraud programs supported by government agencies and a realignment of criminal justice priorities, the current trend of increasing frauds is expected to continue.

> Globalization is the term used to describe the changes in societies and the world economy that result from dramatically increased international trade and cultural exchange. It describes the increase of trade and investing due to the falling of barriers and the interdependence of countries. In specifically economic contexts, the term refers almost exclusively to the effects of trade, particularly trade liberalization or "free trade.... More broadly, the term refers to the overall integration, and resulting increase in interdependence, among global actors (be they political, economic, or otherwise).[2]

---

[1] Quoted from *Creating a New Civilization* by Alvin and Heidi Toffler, and published by Turner Publishing Inc., Atlanta 1995.

[2] http://en.wikipedia.org/wiki/Globalization

As the war on terrorism and violent crimes continue, it is expected that fraud will be given low priority by all concerned. However, even terrorists are using fraud schemes to gain access to funds for their attacks as governments continue to try to stop all illegal financial funding of terrorism around the world.

GLOBALIZATION OF BUSINESS TO CONTINUE

Corporations will continue to expand their markets, facilities, and areas of operation around the world, many of which are supported by the host nation-states that also benefit from such trades from:

- Increased employment of its citizens
- A rise in the nation-states' standard of living
- More tax revenue to the nation-states
- The ability of citizens to purchase cheaper goods

Many oppose globalization, believing that it contributes to the exploitation of the poor. Arguments can be made on both sides of this issue, but suffice it to say that globalization will not stop. Along with that expansion, increased risks due to today's and tomorrow's defrauders and their attack methodologies may be encountered for the foreseeable future.

All businesses evolve over time and take advantage of new markets, new technologies, and new processes as they become available. Today's business environment has become increasingly more global and more competitive with more corporations, foreign and domestic, competing with like products for the same customers.

Corporations have always sought ways to cut costs and increase profits. However, in view of today's rapidly changing business environment with increased competition from all over the world, this is no longer something to consider but something that must be immediately implemented as new ways are discovered to replace employees with robotics, streamline processes such as inventory, and the like.

For example, one day we may see robots reporting the news as news anchors. After all, those reporting the news from the newsroom desks basically just read the teleprompter. Since they are computerized, they can also provide updated news broadcasting through news media feeds from around the world.

EMPLOYEES OF THE FUTURE

Employees will continue to be the first to go in the effort to become more competitive. With modern corporations not only paying wages but also providing very expensive benefits such as medical costs for employees, when employees are laid off, more than an employee's salary is being saved. Also being saved are the once paid-out benefits and even office space and office supplies. Although the saving of office space and supplies may seem trivial, just think about the cost of maintaining and leasing office space, and if a corporation were to reduce its employee base by say 1,000, an immense savings would be accomplished.

Corporations' executive management also consider the benefits of encouraging employees to leave after some period of time so that they can also save money in the following areas:

- Higher wages paid long-term employees
- Medical costs associated with employees; as employees stay on and get older, they are more susceptible to medical problems, which may increase over time and thus cost the corporations more money
- Retirement pay
- Corporations' agreement to match or provide some funds for an employee's long-term savings accounts

Corporations are for the most part no longer interested in employees who are loyal to the corporation over their working lifetime until retirement. They only want employees to be loyal to the corporation for the short period of time they will be employed and then move on.

In tomorrow's corporations, it will be very unusual for someone to work for the same corporation for 40 or so years, until they are ready to retire. It is also unlikely that these corporations will also hire their sons or daughters, who during the Second Wave would also work there until retirement.

Employees of the future will be of two basic types: generalists and specialists. Both will be needed, and each will be their own "company" and be hired for specific jobs for a specific period of time. Corporations will pay them a fee with no additional benefits.

There will be a demand (it is already starting in the United States) that these contracted employees have a "mobile" benefits plan for such benefits as medical and dental insurance. When not on contract, they will draw unemployment as they do today. They will also be able to build up retirement funds as they do today with some government support.

THE FUTURE GLOBAL CORPORATION

What will the future global corporation look like? It will continue to be dependent on and be process-driven by high technology. This situation will increase their process efficiencies and allow them to expand into new markets and in fact create markets where none exist today. This dependency on high technology coupled with the products and locations will also make them more and more vulnerable to fraud-threat agents.

> The ability to learn faster than your competition may be the only sustainable competitive advantage — *Arie de Geus*[3]

Future global corporations will be more automated and take greater advantage of high technology, using robotics and employing fewer people all over the world but working together electronically. So, employees, as is the case for some today, will be working out of the local kiosks or their homes. Having such globally dispersed environments may make it more difficult for defrauders to do serious harm to globally operating corporations except through computer networks.

It would not be surprising that the competition increases to such an extent that competitors may under the guise of a fraud-threat agent attack its competitors. In the past, criminal tactics have been used to steal information and proprietary processes and devices from their competitors, so why not use fraud tactics to delay and stop their competitors' progress in gaining a competitive edge; for example, use a front corporation to supply them with counterfeit products such as drugs and aircraft parts (as is already occurring)? How would one know the difference? That of course would be another challenge to add to the assets protection and anti-fraud burden of the security professional, corporate procurement, and supply managers.

> An analysis of the history of technology shows that technological change is exponential, contrary to the common-sense "intuitive linear" view. So we won't experience 100 years of progress in the 21st century — it will be more like 20,000 years of progress (at today's rate). The "returns," such as chip speed and cost-effectiveness, also increase exponentially. There's even exponential growth in the rate of exponential growth. Within a few decades, machine intelligence will surpass human intelligence, leading to The Singularity — technological change so rapid and profound it represents a rupture in the fabric of human history. The implications include the merger of biological and nonbiological intelligence, immortal software-based humans, and ultra-high levels of intelligence that expand outward in the universe at the speed of light."[4]

---

[3] Toffler, *Creating a New Civilization*, page 257.
[4] http://en.wikipedia.org/wiki/Law_of_Accelerating_Returns

FUTURE OF FRAUD ATTACKS ON CORPORATIONS

It is expected that the current trends of global fraud attacks, whereby advantage is taken of technology and technology vulnerabilities, will continue. Gradually, some nation-states will see the negative aspects of these fraud attacks on their economies and will pressure corporations in their nation-states to stop using fraudulent tactics when doing business and also increase their anti-fraud defenses because it hurts both the nation-state's economy and the world-view of that nation-state.

As pressure is brought to bear on these businesses from competing nation-states and their corporations through such global organizations as the World Trade Organization (WTO), fraud will be fought more aggressively in some nation-states than in others. Nonetheless, other developing nation-states and their corporations will seek to use fraud to their advantage to help their economy.

Based on the current management philosophy of corporate management as noted earlier, there is less and less chance of employees being loyal to the corporation. Therefore, there are fewer employee concerns about protecting corporate assets from any types of attacks, including fraud attacks.

> America is where the future usually happens first. If we are suffering from the crash of our old institutions, we are also pioneering a new civilization. That means living with high uncertainty. It means expecting disequilibria and upset. And it means no one has the full and final truth about where we are going — or even where we should go.[5]

With less concern for the protection of corporate assets, it then follows that the corporate employee are more likely to take advantage of assets protection vulnerabilities and perpetrate a fraud or other types of crimes that will be to their advantage and easily justified. For example, employees may get a layoff notice at the same time that the corporation announces record profits and the issuance of large bonuses to management. The employees may resent the corporation to such an extent that they will perpetrate a fraud to get their share of the profits. After all, one must take care of oneself and family first.

Other potential defrauders would be those employees contracted for a specific period of time. They may have access to corporate assets to complete their contracts. In the event of a contract dispute, the contracted employee may very well rationalize that fraud against the company.

---

[5] Ibid.

FUTURE ANTI-FRAUD PROTECTION NEEDS OF CORPORATIONS

Today's security professionals have been rather complacent as to their responsibilities vis-à-vis anti-fraud programs. To date, they have more often than not opted to let auditors and others take the lead in this endeavor, to include conducting initial inquiries to prove or disprove allegations of fraud. In the future, this trend is expected to continue unless assets protection security professionals take on this aspect of their assets protection duties.

> [I]nformation is now the same thing as a physical object. If you view an organism as so dangerous as to require P4 containment — the highest level complete with airlocks, moon suits, double door autoclaves and liquid waste sterilizers — then keep information about that organism under the same kinds of wraps.[6]

How will financial customers feel when they can no longer trust the financial institutions' calculations or ATMs due to attacks from fraud-threat agents?

Corporations responsible for these and other infrastructures have a serious duty to make them impervious to attacks from fraudsters. All corporations have the responsibility to protect their employees and to safeguard the corporate assets of their owners from such attacks:

- As a security professional, do you think this safeguarding is adequately being accomplished today?
- If not, why not?
- What responsibilities do you have to ensure that your corporation's assets are protected from fraud attacks?
- If you are not leading this defensive effort, as a security professional responsible for assets protection, don't you think you should?
- If so, what are you doing about it?

All corporations should have sound plans to defend their assets against all types of attacks from threat agents — and fraud-threat agents' attacks are no exception. Security professionals should incorporate those anti-fraud plans into their assets protection and business plans, maintain those plans, and periodically test the anti-fraud defenses.

---

[6] See *Radical Evolution: The Promise and Peril of Enhancing Our Minds, Our Bodies- and What it Means to be Human,* by Joel Garreau, page 165. Doubleday and Company, NY. 2005.

A combination of proactive offensive and defensive methodologies should be used, and high-technology and sophisticated processes should be integrated into your anti-fraud plans, policies, procedures, processes, and projects. You must also help to ensure that such philosophies are integrated into all aspects of your corporation's business.

CASE STUDY

As the CSO for an international corporation, you are asked to provide a briefing to executive management on the global state of fraud and its potential impact on corporate facilities worldwide.

How would you go about gathering information and presenting that information?

One approach would be to:

- Identify the information you will need to provide in that briefing and meet the expectations of the executive management.
- Use an Internet search engine to search for that information.
- Collect the information.
- Analyze the information.
- Determine the location of all corporate facilities.
- Determine the threats, vulnerabilities, and risks to the corporation associated with the fraud-threat agents.
- Determine the location, number, type of fraud-threat agent attacks against the corporation over the last five years, and produce trend-line charts for each location and a summary chart.
- Develop not more than ten briefing charts:
  - Number of charts depending on the time allotted for the briefing
  - Half the allotted time left for discussion and questions
  - One chart to be a list of recommendations with backup charts of justification and cost benefits that can be used to support the recommendations
  - One chart for each facility location showing the results of your previously conducting fraud risk assessment and a summary chart

Remember that executive management does not have time for lengthy and complicated briefings.

SUMMARY

Corporate globalization will continue into the foreseeable future. Defrauders will also continue to go global and reach into corporations from around the world. Defrauders will continue to take advantage of technology vulnerabilities and the lack of aggressive anti-fraud defenses to stop them.

As nation-states mature and become a part of the global economy, some will continue to look the other way while defrauders ply their skills, which by side-benefit help the nation-state become more economically competitive through attacks by fraud-threat agents on foreign corporations, providing fraudulent products and services.

15

The Impact of High Technology on Fraud

INTRODUCTION

Since today's and tomorrow's fraud schemes so often use high technology (technology based on the microprocessor), it is important to discuss its use to perpetrate frauds and to defend against frauds.

HIGH-TECHNOLOGY FRAUDS

The number of frauds related to high technology has increased as the number of individuals, networks, corporate intranets, the Internet, National Information Infrastructures (NIIs), and Global Information Infrastructure (GII) accesses have grown. More networks therefore means that more people have access to more information. Some of those who have this access, both legal and illegal, will be defrauders.

The price and power of cellular phones, computers, and many other high-technology devices have made them more accessible to an increasing number of people on a global basis. This has occurred as the communications infrastructure has expanded and as nations have entered the Information Age, to the point where the technologies in many regions are now almost ubiquitous, with children as young as six having cellular phones and computers.

Some of these "children" are computer hackers because the protection of these valuable assets is often not what it should be and the vulnerabilities of the high-technology devices and equipment make it rather easy to break into the computers.

> As with any industry, technology, or other assets that have a real or perceived value, there are those who want to take what others have; however, they neither want to pay for them nor work for them. This has been the case since the beginning of the human race with no end in sight.

High-technology frauds are therefore expected to continue to increase in terms of both number and impact. The level of sophistication is also expected to increase, as the high-technology itself becomes more sophisticated. Because the global accessibility of networks, computers, and information provides mass communications, those fraud miscreants and juvenile delinquents who use these devices for illegal acts also share their techniques with others around the world. This gives those "hacker wannabes" and others the ability to download attack tools and execute them with little knowledge of how they operate and what systems they are attacking.

Current communications and computers are such that these miscreants no longer have to physically meet to exchange knowledge and tools. In the past, they would only pass their knowledge on to people they knew and trusted. Now, with the need to meet removed, the information spreads much more rapidly. These types of attackers have and will continue to increase in the foreseeable future because very little technical knowledge is required.

> The more sophisticated attackers will also continue to grow in number.

Although the Internet originated in the West, the countries that are now joining the Internet are some of the most densely populated regions of the world. As the people in countries such as China, India, and Pakistan gain access to the Internet, the result will inevitably be a huge cultural shift.

According to an online source, Global Reach,[1] the online users' language by population had reached over 801.4 million as of September 2004. The languages involved were as follows:

- Dutch 1.7%
- Portuguese 3.1%
- Italian 3.8%
- Korean 3.9%

---

[1] See http://globalreach.biz/globstats/index.php3 — last revised March 2004.

- French 4.2%
- German 6.9%
- Japanese 8.4%
- Spanish 9%
- Chinese 13.7%
- English 35.2%

The West will suddenly find itself in the minority, and the values it subscribes to will not necessarily be those understood by most users of the Internet. Furthermore, the fraud miscreants in these countries may use sophisticated fraud attack programs that have been developed in their regions and that have not been found on the Internet before. These and others will continue to find an increasingly more profitable job market. They will be the new "hired defrauders" of the global organized crime rings, drug cartels, terrorists, and governments. They will be hired to infiltrate systems and to perpetrate frauds.

With the increased dependencies of businesses and government agencies on the Internet, NII, and GII, these miscreants will select more and more lucrative targets. This high-technology global increase in crime will be fueled by the exponentially increasing electronic commerce and electronic, online banking. Crime always follows the money, and the penalties for online crimes are much lower than those for the equivalent physical crime.

Justifiable concerns have long been raised regarding the possibility that the highly skilled workforce of the former USSR, encountering difficulties finding work, might be recruited to work for other nations and organized crime. The next area of concern must be countries such as China and India, both of which have large numbers of highly skilled but very poorly paid workers.

Do you recall the discussion earlier in the book about motive, opportunity, and rationalization? When you are out of work, have a family, and are hungry, it may not take much convincing for you to turn to crime. The rationale is that after all, you're going after foreign corporations and governments, which during your whole life have constantly been labeled the "evil enemy." With such a backdrop, it is easy to convince yourself (rationalize) that attacking and defrauding them are of little consequence.

The future will continue to see major increases in fraud-threat agent attacks related to high technology as more and more global businesses and government agencies become more reliant on the Internet.

As noted in earlier chapters, many cases have been documented showing the use of networks to defraud corporations and perpetrate other criminal acts.

HIGH-TECHNOLOGY ANTI-FRAUD DEFENSES

Information systems security (InfoSec) is the main tool for preventing high-technology frauds through the Internet, GII, NII, and corporate networks. In the future, the gap between the sophisticated attacks on systems, PBXs, cellular phones, and other devices, and defenses will close, but the reality is that improvements in security will never catch up.

Although new fraud-threat agent attacks will still hold the edge, the future will find quicker recoveries, countermeasures, counterattacks, and new defenses all working together to provide an anti-fraud "layered defense" approach.

The increase in InfoSec will occur because corporations and nation-states, which are already almost totally dependent on access to the GII, Internet, and NII, will start to understand the importance of this resource to their effective functioning and anti-fraud defenses. As greater dependence on the networks is acknowledged, fraud-threat agent attacks will be detected, but it will be absolutely crucial to immediately address any attacks and to learn and share lessons with others in the profession.

The information systems security profession will become one of the most important and dominant professions in the twenty-first century, gaining executive management recognition, support, and authority. This will be coupled with more aggressive defense and high-technology fraud prevention programs that will include tracing the sources of the attacks and possibly even counterattacking. This aggressive approach by businesses and government agencies will be due to the continuing inability of law enforcement agencies to identify, apprehend, and prosecute these miscreants.

As microprocessors and new uses for them in support of anti-fraud defenses begin to emerge, hopefully corporations will begin to make more concerted efforts to integrate them into their anti-fraud processes.

Effective and efficient use of high technology will result in the delivery of more timely anti-fraud defenses and, in so doing, may even drive down the amount of fraud. This is because some frauds are thought to be committed out of the defrauder's belief that the corporation's defenses are vulnerable to attack.

In the future, secure local, national, and global links will be established to track convicted fraud miscreants regardless of their location. High technology will also assist in the investigation of frauds related to high technology, but once the defrauder is apprehended, anywhere in the world, the production and delivery of evidence and the prosecution and incarceration will be done on a global scale using means such as teleconferencing as the medium.

Therefore, because of the global dependence on the Internet, NII, and the GII, the United Nations and organizations such as the European Union will support international global high-technology anti-fraud laws that will lead to the investigation, apprehension, and prosecution of these offenders. All or most of the information-dependent nations will support such processes because they will all be the main victims of these global attackers.

The fraud investigator should look at both current and future high technologies and study ways that they could be put to good use in supporting the corporation's anti-fraud defensive processes and investigations.

The CSO responsible for the corporate anti-fraud program must be computer literate and work closely with the information technology (IT) department to ensure that the security is in place and will also support the anti-fraud defensive efforts. More often than not, the InfoSec specialist or manager will report to the corporation's chief information officer (CIO) or IT manager, and not to the CSO as should be the case. However, that is another matter and beyond the scope of this book. Nevertheless, since many of today's fraud trends indicate that the GII, Internet, and corporate networks are used as the vehicles to perpetrate fraud attacks, a successful corporate anti-fraud program must take into account the vulnerabilities of these high-technology networks, equipment, and devices to successful fraud-threat agent attacks and coordinate the needed anti-fraud defenses with the InfoSec specialists.

CASE STUDY

As a CSO concerned with the vulnerability of the corporation's networks to successful fraud-threat agent attacks, what would you do to ensure that adequate anti-fraud measures were in place and current?

One approach would be to meet with those responsible for the networks' protection, determine what protective measures are in place; and then match those to the fraud schemes associated with high technology and related cases to determine the extent of vulnerabilities to fraud-threat agents.

One could coordinate with the InfoSec specialist and management and jointly conduct as risk assessment of the networks specific to the fraud threat indicators. Defensive measures would be increased if the identified risks were unacceptable.

SUMMARY

The future, based on today's trends, continues to indicate that we will be getting more of the same — more frauds, security lagging behind the fraud miscreants, and their techniques used to successfully attack computer networks around the globe.

High technology will be used as part of the corporation's anti-fraud defenses or to support the anti-fraud defenses. The criminal justice systems of nation-states will continue to be slow but will adopt and adapt high technology to provide for more effective and efficient investigations of frauds and better prosecution of the defrauders.

16

What the Security and Other Anti-Fraud Professionals Must Do Now to Personally Prepare to Combat Tomorrow's Frauds

INTRODUCTION

Whatever aspects of security — assets protection — one talks about, there are insufficient defenses in place to protect the corporate assets. This insufficiency is caused in part by:

- Security professionals not establishing a proactive, or an aggressive, anti-fraud program.
- Defensive policies, procedures, processes, plans, and programs not keeping pace with the fraud threats.
- Supporting devices or equipment (e.g, high-technology devices) not available or not installed to meet the new fraud threats.
- Lack of sufficient budget to install proper anti-fraud defensive measures (but this is also used as an excuse as security professionals and others do not properly allocate resources based on the associated risk to the assets as the primary priority).
- Failure of security professionals and others responsible for some aspect of the assets protection and anti-fraud programs to meet the challenges.

In this book we have focused on those aspects of the assets protection efforts and a program as they relate to defending corporate assets against fraud-threat agents through policies, procedures, processes, plans, and programs.

It is now time to discuss what the security (assets protection and anti-fraud) professionals must do so that they will be at least as knowledgeable of fraud schemes, techniques, and related attack methodologies as the defrauders who attack the corporate assets.

BECOMING AND STAYING PROACTIVE AND AGGRESSIVE IN FIGHTING FRAUD

In order to be successful in protecting corporate assets from attacks by fraud-threat agents, one must know at least as much as the attackers. Sadly, this does not seem to be the case inasmuch as fraud after fraud is being committed against corporations while the corporation's chief security officer (CSO) may often be surprised; as are the others on the fraud fighting team responsible for protecting corporate assets.

The response of most, if not all, CSOs is that they are very busy, doing the best they can, and as the old song goes, "and the beat goes on." Such comments may have some truth, but that does not help protect these assets from successful fraud attacks. The CSO and the others responsible for protecting corporate assets from successful fraud attacks must do better.

> For these fraud fighters to consider themselves professionals, they absolutely must do better or not call themselves professionals.

It is a sad commentary on the state of anti-fraud efforts throughout corporations that the defrauders and associated other miscreants continue to outsmart the assets' defenders. Often these defrauders do so with very little challenge from the assets' defenders. What is more, these defrauders often operate with very little education or even business experience.

GETTING A FRAUD EDUCATION

So, what can an anti-fraud program leader, for example, the CSO, do personally to help gain the edge on these defrauders?

The CSO, security staff, and others on the anti-fraud team must begin by educating themselves on the:

- Profiles of fraud-threat agents
- Specific motivations of fraud-threat agents
- Fraud schemes

- Fraud cases
- Anti-fraud defenses that have worked
- Anti-fraud defenses that have not worked

This education can be done formally through fraud-related courses at universities, technical institutes, and colleges. This "education" can also be gained by attending conferences that offer fraud-related topics as part of their lecture series. You may even be able to find online anti-fraud-related courses that will make it more convenient to gain this knowledge.

The informal education process must also include the CSO and others who set up communication channels with government agency representatives, peers, consultants, and others who can share fraud and anti-fraud related information with you.

In addition, you should identify a set of Web sites that you should check anywhere from daily to weekly in order to stay up to date on fraud-related matters. Some websites may even offer notification of fraud-related updates and e-mail services, sending you the latest information on fraud-related matters.

Yes, it takes time and you have other things to do. I guess my response to any complaints would be "Too bad!" It is part of your assets professional job. Take a time management course and move on!

GAINING FRAUD-RELATED CERTIFICATIONS

As an assets protection and/or fraud fighter, related certification programs are available that would be to your advantage to obtain. You will not only learn more about fraud-related matters but also obtain certification, which may help you get that next job.

What is meant by certification? For our purposes, certification means that, based on your experience, education, and successful passing of a test, generally given by a related association, you are certified as having the basic knowledge and ability certifying you as a professional or an expert in a particular field.

Using the word "expert" may not be the right thing to do because in the security and anti-fraud business, everything seems to be changing so rapidly that it is impossible for anyone to be an expert. Let's then say that by being certified, you are considered to have the *expertise* in the particular field.

Several certifications are directly or indirectly related to the position of a CSO and fraud fighters. A professional CSO should have the basic knowledge in some, if not all, of these anti-fraud and CSO-related certifications' areas of study.

Several associations certify professionals in various security-related professions. Some certifications are widely acknowledged throughout industry whereas others are not. Its sponsor may have developed some as part of a "get-rich" scheme. These certifications may look good on paper but are meaningless in the field.

No certification is worth anything without being accepted by the professionals responsible for assets protection and anti-fraud defenses, by related professions, and, most importantly, by executive management. The Certified Public Accountant (CPA), for example, is widely recognized throughout industry.

ASSOCIATIONS

As a security professional, it is more than likely that you will be involved with professional security associations. These associations differ in specific focus, but all have one common purpose: to enhance and improve the profession of security. Be they private, corporate, institutional, commercial, industrial, governmental, or any other type of security organization, these associations seek to advance the cause of the profession.

Members are asked to support the associations' efforts to seek a higher degree of professionalism and recognition of the security discipline. Some of these associations will work with local colleges and universities in an effort to build curricula consistent with contemporary issues in security. Together, they assist in the preparation and development of future security professionals, experts who are capable of dealing with new and more complicated security issues.

Association membership may be a general membership, as is the case with the American Society for Industrial Security (ASIS), the largest professional security association in the world. Membership may also be very specific to a type of industry such as the security committee within the Aerospace Industries Association (AIA). Within AIA, security professionals from aerospace companies work together for the benefit of the entire industry. Common challenges, issues, practices, and objectives are addressed by the memberships, who are usually senior security managers of member companies.

At least six security and anti-fraud-related associations have been around for many years and are also considered to be very professional organizations:

- American Society for Industrial Security (ASIS), which offers a Certified Protection Professional (CPP)
- Association of Certified Fraud Examiners (ACFE), which offers a Certified Fraud Examiner (CFE)

- Information Systems Security Association (ISSA), in association with another organization, which sponsors a certification as a Certified Information Systems Security Professional (CISSP)
- High Technology Crime Investigation Association (HTCIA)
- Information Systems Audit & Control Association (ISACA), which offers certifications as Certified Information Systems Auditor (CISA) and Certified Information Security Manager (CISM).
- Communications Fraud Control Association (CFCA), members of whom consider themselves "the Premier International Association for revenue assurance, loss prevention and fraud control through education and information."

These associations sponsor conferences and lectures through which you can gain additional knowledge on matters related to fighting fraud.

Although not an association, the MIS Training Institute (MISTI) offers excellent fraud-related courses. They consider themselves the "International Leader in Audit and Information Security Training." Whether or not you agree with that statement, you will find that overall their conferences and courses are very informative.

GAINING ANTI-FRAUD EXPERIENCE

Let's assume you agree and establish a personal fraud awareness program for yourself as part of your own career development program and maybe those of your security staff, assuming you are the CSO or one of the security managers for a corporation. How will you gain the experience to help you establish, maintain, and manage a corporate anti-fraud program?

The best experiences may be unwanted and come from being involved in attempted or successful fraud attacks against your corporation's assets. Yes, this is good experience but surely an unwanted one.

Another way to gain experience is through fraud survey or risk assessment processes. As you gain new information about defrauder profiles, schemes, and actual fraud cases, you can attempt — under controlled conditions — to determine whether such attacks would be successful against one or more of your corporation's assets.

Such tests can often be conducted in a teaming effort with members of the audit staff and based on the corporate cultures, coordinating the matter with the legal staff and ethics director.

For example, you may know of cases where defrauders successfully set up bogus employees and had the corporation issue them weekly paychecks, paid them an excessive amount of money, and/or paid them for overtime that was never worked. You would be checking for anti-fraud defenses (controls) in place so that would not happen. This can be checked by getting on a computer used by one of the payroll employees and establishing a bogus employee and see what happens.

If the defenses prevent an employee from adding a "ghost" employee, such as maintaining adequate separation of functions so that a bogus employee cannot be inputted, then controls may be adequate. But further testing may be needed to be sure. Be certain to operate under adequate safeguards.

As a test, you may want to establish a bogus employee with a certain profile for overtime, pay, and such. Once that ghost employee is in the database, an attempt should be made to provide that employee with more pay than is authorized based on the employee's profile.

Another test would be to compare the payroll of checks issued against the employees in the corporation and determine whether checks are issued to employees not in the employee database. Also test to see whether more than one check was issued to an employee, contractor, supplier, and so on.

These are just some simple examples of what can be done to gain experience as you take on the role of the defrauders and use the schemes you have learned through your education process; as well as learn about the actual cases of frauds that are being perpetrated on a regular basis.

The examples cited are based on actual fraud investigations of schemes that have been used much too often against both government agencies and corporations. Controls should be in place to prevent these very basic frauds; however, you may be surprised to learn how often they are successful even today.

This controlled test method allows you to gain a type of "real-world" experience while at the same time determining whether your corporation has adequate anti-fraud defenses.

Many of these types of tests in some corporations are continually being conducted by auditors who are aggressive and get into a more proactive anti-fraud mode. If you determine that your corporation's audit department has such a test program, you should discuss the program with the audit manager and establish a process for conducting these with the assistance of the security department's fraud specialist.

Beware of office politics: the auditors may believe you are trying to take over what they consider one of their primary functions. Building up rapport with the audit manager over time may help you in mitigating that potential problem.

In addition, as the CSO, you may be able to get into the anti-fraud communications loop that the auditor has access to, or you may at least be in a position to receive the latest information about fraud from the audit manager's point of view.

Once your relationship as the CSO is established with the corporate audit manager, you can also provide that manager with the information you received about fraud-related matters. You can also share information about fraud inquiries, risk assessments, and fraud surveys that your staff have conducted or are scheduled to conduct as the audit manager shares the audit schedule with you. So, it is a win-win situation.

> If the audit department has an aggressive anti-fraud audit process in place, be careful and remember teaming methods as well as office politics issues. You don't want to alienate your best anti-fraud friend, the audit manager.

TO CONDUCT OR NOT TO CONDUCT FRAUD LECTURES AND WRITE FRAUD ARTICLES

Once you become a "fraud expert," you may want to share your information with your peers and others. You can do so by volunteering to teach a course on fraud at the local college or university or at a conference. You may also consider writing some fraud-related articles for a newspapers or magazine.

This is an admirable goal that you should strive for if you want to consider yourself a true security or anti-fraud professional, giving something back to the profession. However, a word of caution is needed here. By placing yourself, and thus your corporation, in the public spotlight, you may also be spotlighted by the defrauders of the world. So caution is needed, and one should discuss the matter with the ethics director and legal representative, and of course your boss.

Such a spotlight may make the corporation appear to be doing a great job in protecting the assets of the corporate owners, or stockholders. However, some may take it as a negative by implying that the corporation is so rife with fraud that it needs a special program in order to defend itself against frauds. The corporation's public relations manager should also be contacted and discuss the pros and cons of such public visibility.

In addition, global defrauders, having heard about your lectures, witnessed them, or read your articles, may consider it a challenge and attack your corporation in order to successfully perpetrate a fraud and also make a point as they think of you as throwing down the gauntlet to challenge them.

CASE STUDY

A CSO decided to get "up to speed" on fraud-related matters. If you were that CSO, how would you begin?

If you say you would take the approach cited above, well, yes, eventually that would work. However, first you may want to consider the following steps:

- Identify your current and specific fraud-related education.
- Identify your current and specific fraud-related experiences.
- Identify what you would consider the perfect, more knowledgeable fraud-related expert's profile.
- Using a matrix approach, identify the areas where you are lacking in your fraud education and experiences.
- Set up a project plan to obtain the necessary education and gain the necessary experiences.
- Once completed, establish a maintenance process to keep current.
- Consider obtaining various fraud-related certifications. (These may also help when seeking that next career development position.)

SUMMARY

In order to call oneself a true security or assets protection professional, one must maintain currency in fraud-related matters. As a professional, you should bring yourself up to date by obtaining continued education and experiences in fraud-related matters.

Establishing a formal career development program related to anti-fraud matters will provide a focused approach to gaining the required fraud-related knowledge.

17

Summary and Final Thoughts

INTRODUCTION

This final chapter, as the title implies, summarizes some main points scattered throughout this book and provides some concluding thoughts on fraud and on who should lead an anti-fraud program.

This book was written with the objective of trying to convince the security "professionals" that today's current approach to fighting fraud does not seem to be working inasmuch as frauds continue to increase and therefore, some professional should take the leadership role and devise a formal program to fight fraud. That role should be assumed by the corporate CSO, the assets protection and security professional, who is already responsible for the overall protection of corporate assets.

Fraud is a multibillon dollar industry and is growing. This situation must be stopped, for all frauds hurt not only the corporations and employees who are the victims of frauds but also the nation-states where the corporations do business. It is a drain on the economy and on the nation-state's income from tax revenues; it also adversely affects the global economy.

> Modern nation-states are battling for economic power, and fraud attacks against nation-states and their corporations that adversely impact their ability to successfully compete in the global marketplace.

Methods tried in the past have not worked as well as they should. A new, aggressive, and formal approach must be taken, led by the security professional such as the CSO. At the same time, this approach must be cost-effective, for, as with all overhead functions (and this is considered an overhead function), it is a "parasite" on the profits of a corporation.[1]

SUMMARY

We live, work and play in a fast-paced, global environment where, thanks to technology, we can communicate and do business around the world in nanoseconds. Technology has changed not only the way we communicate but also the way corporations operate.

Today technology is driving the world where the only constant seems to be change itself. These changes seem to be occurring faster and faster. No position, no job, no process, no corporation, no product, no way of doing business is safe from change. Some welcome it, others hate it, while still others take advantage of it for their own selfish reasons. These include the global miscreants perpetrating frauds from within and outside corporations.

Fraud victims are ordinary people, stockholders and any other being or entity that will provide the greedy miscreants their rewards without having to legally earn them. In this book, the focus was on establishing and managing an anti-fraud program for a corporation with the premise that the corporate CSO must lead that effort.

As part of that effort, a formal corporate anti-fraud program must be established and managed as a standalone program or as a subset of the corporation's assets protection program. This includes identifying the assets protection and anti-fraud drivers and requirements and subsequently establishing anti-fraud policies, procedures, processes, plans, projects, and related operations.

[P]ractitioners aren't saints, they're human beings, and they do what human beings do — lie, cheat, steal from one another, sue, hide data, fake data, overstate their own importance, and denigrate opposing views unfairly. That's human nature. It isn't going to change.[2]

---

[1] Remember that the term "corporation" is being used as a "catch-all" term for corporations, charities, government agencies, and any other entity that can be considered a fraud target.

[2] Quoted from Michael Crichton's book *NEXT*, published by Harper Collins Publishers, New York, 2006.

FINAL THOUGHTS

The premise put forth in this book is:

A chief security officer (CSO), having the overall leadership responsibility for protecting the business's or government agencies' assets from threat agents, should therefore lead the anti-fraud program to protect those assets from fraud threat agents.

As discussed, that is a team effort, but there must be a leader for that program, and that leader is the one responsible for the overall protection of assets. If the person responsible for leading the protection of assets for the corporation is a person other than a CSO, then whoever that person is should lead the anti-fraud program efforts.

An anti-fraud program is more necessary than ever today when increasing amounts of frauds are being perpetrated throughout corporations. Depending on the corporate culture and assuming that the anti-fraud program is necessary, should it be a standalone program or a subset of the corporation's overall assets protection program?

I believe it should be a subset of the overall corporate assets protection program. Why? Because there would be many resource allocation issues and potential for redundancies if it were not. Redundancies are not an affordable option in today's tight budget environments, especially in the budget of the security department, which never seems to be large enough.

Now that you have completed all but this final chapter of *Fighting Fraud*, you should have some opinions on how you would proceed to establish and manage an anti-fraud program for a business or government agency, whether it be for a corporation, charity, government agency, or any other entity.

Your experience, coupled with your formal education and training, may tend to favor one profession or another in leading an anti-fraud program.

WHAT OTHERS THINK ABOUT THE ANTI-FRAUD LEADERSHIP POSITION IN A CORPORATION

• **Roscoe Hinton, special agent (Retired), U.S. Air Force Office of Special Investigations and former fraud investigative specialist and supervisory agent, who has conducted and overseen many investigations into corporate fraud and government-related frauds,** says: *It should be someone who had authority to change procedures,* *correct systemic weaknesses and dole out punishment as deemed fit.*

That's why central system fraud dropped off the map. No one could ever prosecute the person(s) at the top so settlements became the norm. Pretty soon AUSA (Assistant U.S. Attorney)'s saw no benefit in prosecuting the lowly employee who was simply following procedures without being able to hold the "procedure" person liable. . . . this was given in testimony.

Corporations, top audit firms and even small businesses adopted the stance "I will get as much as I can from the government and if he is not smart enough to catch me then what's the harm since the government is omnipotent." That mentality was and still is pervasive, look at the Gulf contractors, the contractor hiring practices in D.C. to include involvement from high ranking government officials.

WE HAVE REVERTED BACK TO THE POLICY OF "NO HARM NO FOUL.". I am speaking for US government contract fraud. . . . Until the government prosecutors take fraud seriously, the criminal punishment will be light, therefore not a deterrent.

- **Joseph T. Wells, CFE, CPA, chairman of the Board of Directors, Association of Certified Fraud Examiners**, says: *Frankly, I think that your . . . premises are totally off the mark.*
- **Motomu Akashi, former security manager for an international corporation**, says: *Fraud examiners and investigators could be included in the security organization, but, on the other hand, it could be part of an audit organization or finance office or any other organization depending upon the desire of the CEO. Many times, specialized examiners and investigators are placed outside of the main organization structure to allow them independence and free, unobstructed access to all organization within the corporation.*

  The CSO, in many cases, is not positioned high enough in the corp. ladder to effectively conduct independent fraud examinations over the entire corporate structure without interference of other senior executives.

  So, I feel that you could make your premises, but I wonder if it will hold water in all cases.
- **Ed Halibozek, Vice President of Security, Northrop Grumman Corporation,** says: *How we do it is really a joint effort with Corporate audit (lead), security and legal.*
- **Charles A. "Chuck" Sennewald, CPP, CSC, CPO, security management consultant and author, says:** *Of course the premise is valid! In my view to have no program and/or no fixed responsibility for such a protective strategy would be a form of corporate negligence.*
- **Andy Jones, head of Security Technology Research at the Security Research Centre for British Telecom, United Kingdom**, says: *I believe that the leadership for a corporation's anti-fraud program should be*

with the Chief Security Officer (CSO) as this is the rational place for it to sit. The CSO is responsible for the security of all of the company assets, whether they are physical, electronic or personnel and they must be able to address fraud as he/she would address any other threat to the organization.

- **Bill Boni, Corporate Vice President (of a security sector for an international corporation)** says: *In my opinion the emerging role of CSO's at major organizations is to manage holistically all operational risk management processes to keep impacts within acceptable range. Since every company has fraud and since the volume of losses can be significant, perhaps even rise to level of material losses the overall fraud prevention and response program role should be under direction of the CSO.*

This allows the CSO to make decisions with full appreciation as to the extent of resource/effort required in each operational risk area; to manage operational risks as a "portfolio," not as an independent silo of controls!

Thus the CSO's role and principal value to the organization is to balance off investments and results in fraud prevention controls against other areas such as info security controls, disaster and business continuity control, etc. — to reach the overall lowest level of adverse/acceptable losses.

The CSO should be focused on optimizing controls across the risk portfolio so as to leverage investments in policy, process, technical and other operational controls with expected impact of reducing fraud through innovative application of prevention, detection and response mechanisms.

Some examples probably include the investigative processes, digital forensic tools which are commonly used for a variety of activities not strictly limited to fraud. In our age of blended threats involving cyber, human, and financial dimensions the prevention, detection and response mechanisms all bring greater value to the organization if they are operated with understanding of the value they bring to cover multiple threats.

A CFE should help ensure the CSO's overall program is managed with the best practices experience offered by this certification and associated references/research/resources;

The CSO may be the CFE or if they are not, a CSO would probably be very well served by having on staff or on retainer senior and skilled personnel possessing the CFE capabilities, just as the CSO may well need a CISM/CISSP, certified info security officer (CISO); a CPP certified expert in physical/corporate security or other credential and experienced "experts" for those elements of the operational risk mgt framework of greatest significance to the specific organization's mission.

Saying "only" a CFE can lead fraud prevention programs is self evidently not true, absent a governmentally mandated regulatory licensing scheme (like CPA's), which I believe is very unlikely to happen.

Saying the expertise such as a practitioner will obtain via CFE certification and programs of study/training will significantly enhance the effectiveness and impact of a fraud prevention program, especially if operating synergistically across the portfolio of risks, makes a lot of sense to me.

The above is my opinion and does not represent the official position of the management or shareholders of my employer, nor of any professional organization in which I am member or on the Board of Directors.

TOBY J. F. BISHOP, CFE, CPA, FCA, PRESIDENT AND CHIEF EXECUTIVE OFFICER, ASSOCIATION OF CERTIFIED FRAUD EXAMINERS WORLD HEADQUARTERS

The following are some of Bishop's comments taken from e-mail discussions with the author:

> *There are a few points. . . . The rationale section states* (That of the author's book prospectus): *"Fraud examiners specialize in fraud-related matters; however, few come from outside the audit or investigative profession. Furthermore, within a corporation they are usually investigators (react to fraud allegations) or auditors (look for compliance). They are all in a reactive role. They are not in a leadership position responsible for the protection of corporate assets — defending the assets against frauds — a proactive but defensive posture is needed."*

> *The ACFE's membership statistics do not match up with the statement that few fraud examiners come from outside the audit or investigative profession. It is also not accurate to state that all fraud examiners are in a reactive role and that they are not in a leadership position responsible for the protection of corporate assets.*

> *That might perhaps have been true fifteen years ago but certainly not in recent years or today, as I know from my own experience in practice over the past twenty years. I meet an increasing number of fraud examiners in major corporations who are senior members of management with proactive anti-fraud responsibilities. Also, there is a massive shift in emphasis taking place right now that is shifting corporate resources from mainly a reactive role to mainly a proactive role, as many fraud examiners (including me) have been recommending for over a decade.*

*. . . It would definitely be a good thing to have corporate security profes-
sionals who are trained in fraud prevention, deterrence, detection and
investigation participating at all levels in the anti-fraud efforts for companies. I share your enthusiasm for having trained and experienced
anti-fraud professionals involved. I have a somewhat different perspective of the outlook if security professionals choose not to participate in
this activity. If they don't others will fill that role. Either way, the job
will get done.*

*We should strongly encourage fraud examiners, auditors, investigators
and corporate security professionals to share a common body of anti-
fraud knowledge and work together to fight fraud effectively.*

*Having rival factions would not only be counter to the ACFE's philoso-
phy of spanning all professions and industries but it would also likely
impair outcomes. . . .*

*. . . I'm happy to agree to disagree on some points. The world would be
a dull place if we all agreed on everything. I am very sensitive to the
points about the role of CFEs, since that is what the ACFE is all about
and it's my duty to act in the best interests of our members.*

IN CONCLUSION — MY THOUGHTS

In the past, security professionals have been very lax in meeting their
responsibilities in protecting corporate assets. Many are retired government law enforcement officers hired by executive management based on
their past titles because corporate management seldom thinks of security
as anything other than a guard and the group that controls security alarms
and badge systems.

Many of these retired law enforcement persons (local, state, and
national) are more than happy to sit around and be "retired in place"
because they do not want to take on more than they have to. After all, they
will get good pay and good benefits, so why work harder than management
demands? Not all think that way of course, but one may be surprised as to
how many do.

Such thinking still permeates many of the corporate security offices
and staff. That may be at least one reason why stockholders/owners continue to be victims of crime.

If we look back, we see that with the advent of the computer and
automated information systems and networks, the task of protecting the
systems and the information that they stored, processed, transmitted, and
displayed fell to the information technology department within a corporation. This occurred because, as with fighting fraud, the security specialists
failed to provide the leadership needed to protect valuable corporate

assets — information systems and the information that they processed, stored, transmitted, and displayed.

History has shown the results: information stolen, fraudulently manipulated, and destroyed, and systems compromised, even by children! Even to this day, it seems that most security professionals are very happy to leave the protection of these very vital corporate assets to the "computer folks."

One wonders what would have happened if at the very beginning of this age of information and computers, the security professionals had led the protection efforts of these vital assets. Would we still have the same assets protection issues that continue to plague us? I guess we will never know.

One would think that when it came to fighting fraud that the security professionals would have stood up and led the anti-fraud program efforts, but for the most part they have not. They have left it to the accountants and auditors with obvious results — fraud continues to increase on a global scale.

> Today's frauds are becoming more technology driven, more sophisticated, more numerous, and more global.

What has been the response of some corporations in fighting fraud? They appear to:

- Do only the minimum necessary to stay out of trouble with government agencies.
- Want to "hide" frauds when they can so that stockholders don't find out how corporate managers are failing to properly safeguard the corporate assets.
- Try to hide them so that they don't have "public relations problems."

What has been the response of criminal justice agencies regarding fighting fraud?

- Legislators pass new and more complicated laws.
- Regulators pass new and more complicated rules and regulations.
- Law enforcement at all levels tends to give secondary importance to frauds with priorities and budgets going to fight pornography, drugs, and violent crimes.[3]

---

[3] This is not to say that these are the correct priorities and the priorities voiced by the public, but rather to point out some possible reasons that fraud matters are given a lower priority.

- Courts in general give only "slap-on-the-wrist" punishments, often with immediate probation and community service in lieu of incarceration.
- The judges, when they do give the fraud miscreants "jail time,"send them to a confinement facility which some do not consider to be much of a prison at all since they offer tennis courts and allow the inmate to do pretty much whatever he or she wants except leave the facility — sort of a little home away from home.

> Does crime pay — often yes! Does fraud pay? More often than not these days it appears so!

The problem is compounded by those miscreants who operate in a global environment and are out of reach of their victims' legal retaliations and the law enforcement agencies where the victims are located.

Sometimes the major fraud miscreants are the "neighbor next door," the little ole granny, or CEOs and CFOs who are respectable members of the community, give to charities, help the community, and are church-goers.

The juries are made up of like people who may find that the defrauders' rationale has some validity, and they feel sorry for them as these poor defrauders cry:

- "I didn't know it was wrong!"
- "I am sorry and have prayed every night for God's forgiveness."
- "No one really got hurt."
- The big corporation, government agency, or insurance company was the only one affected, and we all know how they operate!"

So, in the absence of some drastic changes, which are doubtful, frauds will continue to pay.

SOME REFERENCES

In writing this book, some thought was given to supplying the reader with an attachment full of Web sites, books, and other references relating to fraud as discussed here. That approach was abandoned because one should be in a position to keep current with fraud-related matters. In order to do so, when it comes to obtaining more information and the most current information on any and all aspects of frauds, what better place to look these days than the Internet?

Therefore, it did not seem logical to provide information that in many cases would be outdated before this book was published — another example of the fast pace of things driven by or supported by technology.

Another reason we decided to forego references was that you the reader may have unique needs and require more specific and more narrowly focused information on fraud matters. So, what may seem to be a good list of references may in fact not meet your needs at all.

Using one of the more popular search engines, by typing in the word:

- *Fraud*, the systems found 138,000,000 hits
- *Fraud Prevention*, 8,800,000 hits
- *Fraud Defenses*, 6,000,000 hits
- *Fraud Crimes*, 2,150,000 hits
- *Fraud Laws*, 8,860,000 hits
- *Fraud Regulations*, 5,870,000 hits
- *Fraud Rules*, 17,500,000 hits

Keep in mind that the "hits" probably include some sites that are not relative to our discussion or your needs. So the problem also revolved around which ones to list.

With that observation, I close and hope that neither you and yours nor your employer or the corporation in which you hold your savings in the form of stock ever fall victims to fraud. However, the chances these days that you will go unscathed are not very good, nor are the chances good that you will recover your losses or that the defrauders will be identified and incarcerated for as long as you think they should be. Such is life in the fraud-ridden twenty-first century.

For those in the security profession who are responsible for assets protection but who do not consider fighting fraud to be part of the duties and responsibilities, I say, "Shame on you! You cannot consider yourselves security professionals!"

For those those who are the professional fraud fighters of the twenty-first century — Good Luck and Good Hunting!

END OF LINE[4]

---

[4] Phrase borrowed from that classic Sci-Fi movie, *Tron*.

About the Author

Dr. Gerald Kovacich has over 40 years of anti-fraud, security, information warfare, counterintelligence/counterespionage, criminal and civil investigations, and information systems security experience in the US government as a special agent, as a manager for global corporations, and as an international consultant.

He has worked for numerous technology-based, international corporations as an information systems security manager, corporate information warfare technologist, investigations manager, security audit manager, and anti-fraud program manager, as well as an international lecturer and consultant on these topics.

More specifically as it relates to anti-fraud matters, Dr. Kovacich specialized in anti-fraud programs in the public and private sector. As a special agent with the U.S. Air Force Office of Special Investigations (AFOSI), he conducted numerous operations to include numerous fraud surveys, overt and covert fraud operations, and fraud investigations and provided consultation on how to mitigate frauds for U.S. Government agencies as well as international corporations.

Prior to retirement, Dr. Kovacich was the Deputy Fraud Chief of a major regional AFOSI office that had responsibility for U.S. Air Force and related U.S. government fraud investigations, surveys and risk assessments. In that position, he also provided management oversight to approximately 25 special agents conducting fraud inquires, risk assessments, surveys, operations, and investigations.

During the period 1980–1982, Dr. Kovacich developed and was supervisory agent for the first five U.S. Air Force computer fraud surveys and risk assessment operations. This included handpicking the team members, writing the operational plans, leading the team's operations, and writing the final reports based on a unique format that he developed.

Dr. Kovacich was formally trained in combating fraud at the U.S. Air Force Office of Special Investigations Academy; on computer fraud investigations by the FBI; and as a contracting officer, logistics officer and supply officer by the U.S. Air Force. This has given him unique insight on how such processes worked and their vulnerabilities to frauds.

As a consultant, Dr. Kovacich worked to establish proactive anti-fraud programs for international corporations as a consultant to their management teams. He has also conducted numerous international and national lectures on the topic of fighting fraud.

Prior to his retirement, as a security professional he was certified as a Certified Fraud Examiner by the Association of Certified Fraud Examiners (ACFE). He was also the ACFE project lead for ACFE's chapters' development in Southeast Asia and was the project lead for developing ACFE's computer fraud manual. He has also presented numerous lectures for ACFE.

He was also a Certified Protection Professional (CPP) and also a Certified Information Systems Security Professional (CISSP).

Dr. Kovacich is currently living on an island in Washington State where he continues to write and conduct research relative to these topics and other security-related topics.

Index

Creating a Focused and Confi

CONTROL
Unleashed

Leslie McDevitt, MLA, CDBC, CPDT

CONTROL UNLEASHED
CREATING A FOCUSED AND CONFIDENT DOG

For information contact:
Clean Run Productions LLC
17 Industrial Dr.
South Hadley, MA 01075-2621
800-311-6503
Website: www.cleanrun.com

Edited by Nini Bloch, Monica Percival, and Rosemarie Stein

Book design and typesetting by Marianne Harris

Cover photos: Action photo by Barry Rosen and still photos by Clean Run

Cover design by Alex Preiss. Agility Action photo on cover by Barry Rosen, Ain't Mutts Behavin' and still photos by Clean Run.

All photographs unless otherwise noted are by Kienan Brown and Bryan Hahn, Kibrion Photography.

First edition
First printing 2007
ISBN 978-1-892694-17-1

DEDICATION

For Snap, little heart dog

Table of Contents

LIST OF EXERCISES (IN ORDER OF APPEARANCE)

Every agility instructor should read this book. With so many dog training clubs launching agility classes, instructors need clear, detailed, and creative steps for keeping classes safe while making sure that problematic dogs are not left out of the fun. *Control Unleashed* addresses helping those dogs that need the outlet and benefits of agility the most but who so often, unfortunately, are the least suited for group classes.

While the book is a bible for agility clubs, its value extends well beyond the agility arena. It serves as a practical guide for owners of excitable, hypervigilant, or unfocused dogs. *Control Unleashed* provides a gold mine of training and behavior modification advice for any trainer or behavior counselor who works with dogs that exhibit focus and arousal problems.

In clear and readable language McDevitt presents the science of desensitization and operant conditioning in an accessible and pertinent way and thoroughly outlines training steps. Her methods are fluid and dynamic, sensible and sensitive to the needs of each particular dog. It's a pleasure to read a book that provides such a sound knowledge of learning theory but at the same time never fails to adjust techniques for individual dogs' temperaments and personalities. Anecdotes throughout the book make visual the practical applications for McDevitt's program and help the reader envision how, when, and for what types of dogs to use the exercises. McDevitt's experience and keen knowledge of dog behavior are evident throughout and ensure that even the most reactive dog can benefit from the Control Unleashed program.

Sue Sternberg
Rondout Valley Animals for Adoption
Accord, New York

Preface

Several years ago, when I was the Obedience Director of Y2K9s Dog Sports Club in Wyndmoor, Pennsylvania, the agility instructors at the club were faced with a frustrating situation. Some of their students had dogs that were highly distractible or reactive, lost focus, or ran away during class. Some of these dogs even got away from their owners and aggressively went after other dogs. The agility instructors' job was to teach agility. They could not address these other issues as well as follow their curriculum. Moreover, they were competitors skilled in agility, not behavior counselors, and some of the dogs needed help they could not provide.

At a board meeting the agility instructors asked for some kind of periodic workshop for students whose dogs were considered "problem dogs" in class. The instructors particularly wanted a class for students who came to us for agility and didn't take kindly to their instructors telling them to first go through our obedience program.

As a professional behavior counselor and the obedience director of our club, I could make sure dogs that went through our obedience program had the beginnings of a working relationship with their handlers, and the control needed before graduating into agility. But there also were dogs entering our agility program from other training programs. For a brief but happy time these problem dogs were a source of income and a challenge for me. The owners came to me for privates because our agility teachers told them to work with me before returning to class.

Although I helped some wayward dogs and confused handlers get what they needed in order to return to class, once they were there, they found themselves in the same situation that had caused their dogs to be reactive, distracted, or to shut down in the first place. Both the owners and teachers got frustrated again. There were two reasons for this chain of events. First, the typical agility class environment is not set up to train dogs with special needs. This is why I spend so much time helping handlers become aware of their environment and of what they can do to optimize their dog's ability to deal with it. Second, almost all the students just wanted a quick fix so that they could hurry back to class. They thought one or two lessons with me should be enough. But these were problems that weren't amenable to quick fixes, so a student who returned too early to agility class soon found that her dog was up to his old tricks again.

I decided occasional workshops weren't enough. We needed an entire course to deal with the types of issues that make agility instructors tear their hair out. I volunteered to create the course, which was immediately dubbed "Control Unleashed" by our then agility-training director, Julie Norman. In designing the Control Unleashed (CU) program I drew heavily on my experience as a behavior counselor for thousands of pet dogs that

- Could not think or control their impulses when they were excited.

- Needed to learn both to relax and to focus in the presence of their triggers without becoming reactive.

- Needed to learn to work off leash in stimulating situations without getting distracted.

As an initiate into agility culture, I saw the same behavioral issues I had spent years helping dogs work through in the new, would-be performance dogs taking classes at the club. These dogs needed some kind of foundation program before they were ready to be thrown into the highly stimulating and challenging environment of agility classes—not to mention trials. This was where I could help. I had had my ups and downs as an agility handler and competitor with my own dogs and had extensive experience with helping dogs that have issues with lack of self-control, arousal, reactivity, and anxiety. My years of observing the behavior of dogs in agility classes and at trials from my dual perspective as a behavior consultant and an agility student put me in a unique position to create the CU program.

Each class is an experiment, and I change the course every time I teach it depending on the mix of people and dogs and the dynamics and needs of each class. Although the form of CU remains fluid, it quickly became the most asked-for class at the club. I was shocked at the huge response to what I thought was going to be a small, informal experiment. Suddenly I was turning away distraught people and making waiting lists! Both instructors and students from other clubs began taking the class. After I wrote my first CU-inspired article for *Clean Run* magazine, "When It's Not Your Turn..." (April 2005), people started asking me for a CU seminar. At this point I've given foundation- and advanced-level seminars, am teaching the original course and an advanced level course at my home, and may possibly create a camp.

My CU students are particularly excited about my new advanced-level course, which I am team-teaching with an agility instructor. It is an agility class within a CU format, where the agility instructor coaches the handlers and dogs through sequencing exercises, while I work behind the scenes to help handlers prepare their dogs to work. They learn to manage their environment, be aware of their dogs' body language, and use the CU principles to make each class a positive experience. I designed the CU advanced class as a bridge to help my students make the transition from the structure of CU to the different structure of an agility class, and to help them generalize what they've learned in CU and apply it in an agility class context.

When I first offered CU I wasn't sure where I was going with it, and I certainly never dreamed that it would gain the enthusiastic following that it has. One of the CU program's greatest assets is its versatility. You can use the CU philosophy, foundation training, and all the exercises for dogs in training to compete in different venues—especially, but not limited to agility. It works as well for dogs in training to be pets that can relax, focus, and behave reliably in challenging situations. After I started writing articles, I got some "buzz" on dog training lists and received many appreciative emails from people describing diverse applications of CU principles and exercises. The variety of applications that readers mentioned reinforced for me the versatility of the CU program. One of my favorite emails came from a woman who teaches students to clicker-train their own service dogs. She was very excited about integrating various CU concepts for teaching dogs self-control and focus into her organization's service-dog training program.

At the same time that I was creating the CU program, I adopted Snap, a two-year-old "Shborderjack" (his mom is a Sheltie/Border Collie and his dad is a Jack Russell Terrier). Nicknamed "Spaz Attack" by his previous owner, Snap had serious impulse-control issues. When I got him he was quite reactive to other dogs at times, but he also shut down easily out of stress and overstimulation; he needed my class just as much as any of the students' dogs. I thought up many of the exercises with him in mind. I joked with the first several groups of CU students that I was using this course as an excuse to train my new dog, and nobody minded. At some point, Snap became the ultimate CU dog. He exceeded my expectations with his focus, attention span, and happiness to work. He loves teaching with me. It is an incredible facet of our relationship. I can't imagine teaching CU without him at my side. This is Snap's book, as much as mine.

Thank you, Snap.

ACKNOWLEDGMENTS

Thank you to Clean Run Productions, in particular to Monica Percival and my high-drive, awesome book editor Nini Bloch. Thank you to my good friends at Y2K9s Dog Sports Club, especially Deb Norman, for giving me a place to grow and always being there for me. Thank you to my Control Unleashed students for your infectious enthusiasm and dedication and to my irreplaceable Control Unleashed assistant, Kienan Brown. Deep heart thanks to Dawn Prentiss, CPDT, and Alexa Karaoulis, for your feedback, patience, relentless moral support, and faith in me. Thank you to Dr. Karen Overall, for your guidance, encouragement, and trust. Thank you to my agility coaches, Snap's "Aunts," Paulena Hope and Barb DeMascio. Thank you to Quicksilver Border Collies for giving me an injection of joy in the shape of a little blue dog. There are no words to express my thanks to my husband Bill—you make everything possible.

Thank you to the dogs who walk with me and light my way: Gordie and Snap, Master Teachers; Maggie, my anchor; Rumor, my comfort; Easy Coyote Boy, my smile.

Leslie McDevitt, MLA, CDBC, CPDT, is a Certified Dog Behavior Consultant through the International Association of Animal Behavior Consultants and a Certified Pet Dog Trainer through the Certification Council for Pet Dog Trainers. She holds a Master of Liberal Arts Degree from the University of Pennsylvania, where she combined studies in Creative Writing, Folklore, and Cultural Anthropology. Before becoming a dog trainer, Leslie worked with children as a museum educator, environmental educator, and humane educator, and played Celtic harp professionally. Working with at-risk kids and playing music in a couple of Irish bands helped develop Leslie's senses of teamwork, timing, and rhythm, which have been great assets in her work with dogs.

Nine years ago, she rescued an American Pit Bull Terrier/German Shepherd Dog, Gordie, and, in trying desperately to help him through his crushing anxieties and fears, met her inspiration and mentor—world-renowned veterinary behaviorist Dr. Karen Overall. Through Gordie, Leslie found her calling, and devoted herself to becoming a dog trainer and later a behavior consultant. Leslie was volunteering at shelters and studying behavior and clicker training when she caught the dog sports bug and started flyball and agility training with her terrier mix Maggie. Her work with anxious and reactive dogs gave her a unique perspective on dog sports classes. Leslie served in many capacities (including president and obedience training director) at Y2K9s Dog Sports Club. Her background in behavior modification and her experience working with dog sport clients led her to create her popular course, Control Unleashed. Leslie's behavior-based articles have been published in *Clean Run* and *Dog Fancy.* She is an evaluator for Sweet Border Collie Rescue and is the training advisor for the Pennsylvania-based Animal Welfare Project. Leslie lives in a suburb of Philadelphia with her very understanding husband Bill, four dogs, and two cats.

Chapter 1

NUTS & BOLTS

- Is CU for you?
- For instructors
- Which dogs are appropriate for CU?
- For agility students: Stand up for yourself and your dog

Is CU for you?

I've written this book aimed primarily at two audiences:

1. Students of dog sports or the companion dog owner whose dog has difficulty concentrating or working off lead near other dogs or in exciting situations.

2. The experienced agility or obedience instructor who reads dogs well and wants to get a handle on dealing with the disruptive dogs in class.

Although many CU students have dogs that are reactive, easily aroused, or easily distracted, you don't have to have a dog with "issues" to benefit from this book. For example, you can use this book as part of a foundation program for puppies or young dogs that will be doing performance events where they will be expected to work loose around strange dogs in highly arousing environments.

The exercises in CU build on each other. In every class we repeat the warm-up exercises (passive and active attention and box work), raising criteria for each dog as appropriate. In each chapter you will see sections for that night's "Concepts" and "New Exercises." It is more important to make sure you're continuing to raise criteria for the basic exercises before trying the more complicated ones. Always keep in mind that there are *no limits* to raising criteria, especially for box work! The ultimate goal of box work is a dog that is totally focused around any type of distraction or former stressor, and can work with his handler off-leash and without any gates or barriers— in other words, *working with self-control, unleashed.*

For each exercise or game, I include its goal and purpose, a description of the rules, and sample modifications. The modifications are not necessarily more advanced; some modifications can make the exercise easier for the dog that is having difficulty.

At left, CU assistant Kienan Brown keeps her teenage Doberman Jynx engaged as they work near his favorite playmates, Blitz the Border Collie and Dillinger the American Pit Bull Terrier. Jynx (middle image) remains engaged with Brown as she raises criteria by releasing Blitz and Dillinger from their down-stays and letting them know they are free to move about. At right, Jynx manages to remain engaged in his work even while Blitz gives him the Border Collie crouch-and-stare.

The modifications are merely examples of how to adapt the exercises to the needs of an individual dog at any given point. Most of the modifications offer suggestions for raising criteria for each game so that you challenge your dog as he becomes more proficient at playing it. For many of the games I have included a case study so that you can see how I applied the principles of the game to a real dog and how he progressed through various phases. In some cases, I have included examples of typical dog candidates that might benefit from a specific modification of an exercise.

I individualize the exercises as much as possible. I recognize that each dog/handler team has its own reasons for participating in CU. I also recognize that the same solution might not work for two different dogs that are displaying the same behavior. For example, one dog might wander off to sniff on course because he just doesn't know his job yet. Another might wander off to sniff because he isn't connected with his handler and finds the smells on the floor more intriguing and motivating. A third dog might wander off to sniff simply because he is stressed. The owners might not realize the cause of their dogs' distractibility, so a major goal of the course is just to make each student more aware of her dog and his individual needs as a companion or a potential performance animal.

I've come to see many behavioral issues in terms of a dog's level of stimulation. To make a generalization based on experience, many overstimulated dogs are reactive, environmentally vigilant, or unable to think. Conversely many understimulated dogs tend to disengage, wander off, and sniff. Finding the right balance for each dog has become a key concept in the class. I talk later about the exercises I have developed to find that balance point between over- and-understimulation. My major goals in the class are as follows:

- To teach each student how to find the right balance of stimulation for her particular dog.

- To teach each student how to break behaviors down into small steps to ensure that her dog truly understands what is required of him so that he can deliver a confident, happy performance.

- To put the handler and dog team on the road to forging a deep connection, which I believe is the goal of all training.

- To teach each student how to apply the lessons of CU to real life.

I try to make the course seem like a private lesson for everyone while maintaining the dynamics of a group class, but it's not easy! Each student goes at her own pace. I tailor the exercises to each handler/dog team (or create new ones just for them) and continue to raise criteria. I work at each dog's pace and micromanage the environment. I always try to avoid putting a dog in a situation where he will be unsuccessful.

I like to have six dog-and-handler teams per class, seven maximum. Initially the classes at my club lasted an hour a week for a seven-week session. My CU classes were never finished by the end of the allotted hour, and students always wanted to stay and keep going. Usually, if there wasn't a class scheduled right after ours, we did. I think that an hour and a half for each class would work better if you wanted to fit CU training into a seven-week session. When I started teaching the class at home, the first thing I did was change the length of the session to 10 weeks. Because I was in the final stages of writing the book, the classes remained organized as a seven-week program. Keep in mind that organizing the various exercises into a certain number of weeks is *arbitrary*. If you are interested in teaching a course, use the concepts in the book and concentrate on raising criteria for each exercise when each team is ready. Don't feel you must fit everything into the seven-week structure. Instead, view it just as a general outline.

Because the CU course I teach is tailored not only to the individuals in each class but also to that particular group, it is difficult to present a curriculum set in stone. Despite requests I've been resistant to write a curriculum for others to follow because of the highly individualized nature of the course. Being able to gauge an individual dog's state of mind and adjust the training structure to help that dog succeed is the core of the CU program. Keep in mind when reading about the exercises and their modifications that I never teach these things by rote. The exercises are general structures, built on the principles of learning theory, that I play with in order to help each dog and handler team succeed.

FOR INSTRUCTORS

Be extremely careful about which dogs you accept into your class. Don't advertise it as a "problem dog" class unless you are a problem dog person. Instead, accept friendly dogs whose owners want a sports foundation class or want to work on focus around other dogs. If you are comfortable working with easily aroused or reactive dogs, try to balance your class so that you don't have a roomful of just reactive dogs. Screen each team carefully before accepting them into class.

When I was at Y2K9s, I tried to screen my students to make sure they were appropriate for a group situation. Sometimes people fell through the cracks and registered without first communicating with me. The following is a good example of a dog that was not ready for CU.

One that Got Under the Radar Screen

A woman emailed me about CU class for her highly reactive Sheltie that barked the entire hour of his agility class. I told her she would need to work with me privately before I could let her take CU. Instead of setting up an appointment with me, she went to our registrar and signed up for my class. On observing the dog that first night I realized I was correct in my guess that he would need private help before being ready for a class environment. I asked the student to come back only after she had worked privately with me. The dog was anxious but ironically his breed's reputation had hidden his problem. Shelties have a reputation for being barkers, so when this dog barked through his agility class at other dogs, everybody thought, "Oh, it's just a Sheltie." Meanwhile, the dog was having an hour-long panic attack and his handler was not getting any advice that could help him. The handler's former instructors had approached the problem from the perspective of "Correct what you don't like." In fact, the dog needed a behavior modification program aimed at relieving his anxiety and teaching him to relax.

Which dogs are appropriate for CU?

This book is for anybody who wants to teach her dog to focus in difficult situations. It's also especially for people whose dogs are easily distracted, stressed, or reactive. (See page 25 for a discussion of what I mean by "stressed" or "reactive.") For these dogs there is a spectrum of what is acceptable in a group situation. If they don't fall within the spectrum of what is acceptable in CU, they certainly shouldn't be in an agility class! Dogs at the high end of the stimulation spectrum should not be in any class. After working with an experienced behavior consultant, many of these "high-end" dogs will be able to take a CU-type course and maybe later learn agility. Some just shouldn't be put into potentially explosive situations, period. We are not trying to fry a dog's nervous system. We are trying to help him feel better! Recognize that not every dog is appropriate for a highly arousing sport, even if that's what his owner would really like.

The appropriate types of dogs for learning this program in a group situation are at the low end of the stimulation continuum. Dogs at the higher end need private behavioral training. Once successful there, they can be re-assessed for a group environment.

Typical low-end behaviors (appropriate for a CU class)

- Dog gets sniffy (very often, but not always, a stress-displacement activity).

- Dog wanders away on course.

- Dog is environmentally oriented out of mild concern or normal interest (knowing which is which, is important).

- Dog's mind drifts off easily.

- Dog listens to his handler but his body language continually shows that he feels stress (for example, the dog yawns, licks his lips, scratches as a displacement behavior not because he's itchy, "shakes it off," or doesn't want to look directly at his handler).

- Dog barks and/or pulls and lunges at dogs and objects he is uncertain about but can be interrupted before having a reactive response, or he recovers quickly from a response and continues working.

- Dog is mildly responsive to sudden environmental changes (such as a falling chair or a person entering the far end of the room) but recovers quickly.

Is this dog sniffing the ground because he doesn't understand what's expected of him, is stressed by the other dogs nearby, or is simply distracted by an enticing odor? Learning to read your dog in context will help you understand why your dog is sniffing so that you can address the cause and regain his focus.

Typical high-end behaviors (inappropriate for a CU class)

- Dog is hypervigilant (can't stop scanning and worrying about everything in his environment) and extremely responsive to sudden environmental changes.

- Dog has low arousal threshold (as in a "hair-trigger dog" that is always ready to go off).

- Dog cannot easily or quickly recover from a stressful event (for example, the Sheltie that screamed in agility class for an hour without being able to calm down).

- Dog barks almost nonstop and pulls/lunges so forcefully at dogs or unfamiliar objects that his handler is in danger of dropping his leash, being pulled off her feet, or being injured.

How can you distinguish distracted sniffing from stress sniffing?

Observe the dog in context. Does he look happy and interested in what he is sniffing? Or is he sniffing the floor because his handler just told him to do something he doesn't want to do or doesn't understand? Is he sniffing because he just heard a frightening noise, or because a strange dog passed close by? Is he engaging in other displacement behaviors in conjunction with sniffing, such as scratching himself and yawning?

Is all stress bad?

For the purpose of this book, when I describe a dog as "stressed" I mean he is in a state of distress that needs to be alleviated through the various tools I offer. It should be recognized, however, that stress is a normal part of learning and living, and that not all stress is the bad type of stress we call distress. There is also a good type of stress, called eustress. This type of stress is what my sister-in-law, who is a serious runner, feels when running a marathon. I imagine that dogs that live for agility experience the good type of stress running a course. Dogs also experience stress when learning something new, and it is up to us to teach them in a manner that leaves no room for *distress*.

What is reactivity?

Reactivity comes from anxiety, which comes from feeling uncertain about something. Reactivity is an information-seeking strategy. A reactive dog will rush toward something or someone that he is uncertain about, barking, lunging, growling, and making a big display. People sometimes perceive reactive behavior as aggression, but a reactive dog is not rushing in to do damage; he is attempting to assess the threat level of a given situation. His assessment strategy is intensified because he is panicking as the adrenaline flows through his body. If a reactive dog learns to feel confident about something, he is less worried about that thing and therefore reacts less to it. People also sometimes perceive reactive behavior as "dominance" because they view a dog that flies at his triggers as a dog that wants to take charge. This is absolutely not the case. Reactive dogs are anxious, and their response is intense because they are freaking out.

That is why clear rule structures are necessary for anxious dogs. They need to know what is happening next, and they need to know they are safe. If left untreated (or if treated inappropriately with physical punishment), reactivity can escalate into aggression. Much, but not all, aggression is anxiety-related. Reactivity and anxiety-related aggression are simply different levels of response to a stressful situation. Anxiety-related aggression will occur when the dog is put in a situation that pushes him beyond what he can manage with a measured response. In these cases the dog's anxiety takes him to the next level of response.

Which dogs are reactive and which are merely excited?

The best gauge is to observe the dog's behavior. How intense is the behavior? Is the dog shrieking his head off in a panic or is he just barking? And, how long does it take him to recover from reacting to a trigger?

Above all, when accepting dogs into class, use your instinct. If you see a dog that looks like a furry hurricane, with every hair on end and his tail arched high over his back, staring at the other dogs in class as if they were squirrels, *don't let him into your class.*

Bear in mind that some handlers may not realize there are serious underlying reasons, behavioral and/or physical, for their dog's problems in agility class or at trials. It is the *instructor's responsibility* to know when a dog is not appropriate for class and to know where to send that dog for help. To force a dog to engage in a sport when it is clearly inappropriate for that dog is inhumane. Conversely, agility can be used as a therapeutic tool to boost a troubled dog's confidence, increase his ability to focus, and build a sense of partnership with his person. A dog's response to agility depends on the individual dog and on the way in which agility training is presented.

FOR AGILITY STUDENTS: STAND UP FOR YOURSELF AND YOUR DOG

Some dogs are not suited to the sport their handlers chose for them, and their handlers need to take a step back to assess what's happening. Some dogs are well suited to a given sport but have special needs that require an instructor who reads dogs well and knows how to adjust her training program to set these dogs up for success. I have seen a few dogs in group agility classes who have potential to both enjoy and excel at the sport, but they have certain fears and anxieties that don't get addressed, and their handlers and instructors unwittingly push these dogs until they burn out. When you have a dog with issues, agility can bring out the best in him, or the worst. Choose your instructor carefully, always giving your dog's needs top priority. I have seen students allow themselves to be intimidated by instructors, either because those instructors have put impressive titles on their own dogs, or because they have a very strong personality, or both. If you go against your gut feelings about your own dog because an instructor wants to fit a square peg into a round hole, you can set your training program months back, or worse. The right instructor is out there for the CU dog, though he or she may be harder to find than an instructor who has had a lot of success with dogs whose personalities are closer to "bombproof."

If an instructor asks you to do something that you think is wrong for your dog, however, don't be so impressed by performance titles that you blindly accept the suggestion. With few exceptions, agility instructors are not behaviorists and don't always understand the principles of behavior modification: it's not their job to. Many are good at teaching obstacle performance and handling skills to dogs with no issues but don't know how to read stress signals and other dog body language correctly. There are also plenty of instructors who read body language well and can be very helpful to you and your dog. Sometimes teachers are quick to blame the handler for all a dog's issues when that isn't necessarily the case. (In fact, sometimes it is the teacher who exacerbates an issue!) Because of this attitude among some agility instructors, I have had a lot of clients who felt badly that they were to blame for all sorts of problems such as noise phobia, motion sensitivity, extreme fear, which they absolutely did not cause. Let us never forget that biology and behavior are bedfellows. You can't be solely to blame if your dog's neurons are misfiring. But I've met some agility instructors who will convince you that you are!

I tried out a new instructor for Snap because I greatly admire her handling style and her way of teaching it, but I let my desire to please her override my responsibility to protect Snap. I wanted to work on Snap's weave pole performance in our lesson. Snap had been doing 6 straight weaves and 12 channel weaves, and maybe he had done 12 straight a couple of times in the backyard, but we were only just getting started with it. The instructor wanted to try Snap on 12 straight poles; already I thought that we should start with 6 since we were in a different environment, but I was open to giving this a try. She set up a couple of jumps before the weaves, and she wanted Snap to take the jumps and go into the weave poles. Now Snap was being asked for two new criteria that he wasn't really ready for: 12 straight poles in a new place, and jumping before taking the poles. Snap is so fast that I needed to address as a separate training component teaching him to enter and perform the weave poles at the speed he would gather from jumping and running. He needed to learn this skill incrementally, perhaps at first with one jump into six channel weaves.

I knew the instructor was asking a lot of Snap, but I didn't want to question her and I thought maybe he could do it. Snap had trouble controlling his speed from jumping in order to get the correct weave entry and had trouble striding correctly through all 12 poles. I am always careful to introduce one new criterion at a time, and make any adjustments Snap needs so that he can succeed. Snap was stressed from this exercise and I saw his eyes start to glaze over. At that point I should have taken him for a walk outside the facility, taken him to a different part of the facility to do some easy exercises that he enjoys, or just played with him. I shouldn't have let him get to the point in training new and important obstacle criteria that his eyes glazed over. Next would be the total Snap checkout. I pointed Snap's state out to the new instructor and she saw that he was getting ready for the checkout. Nevertheless, she insisted that he continue trying the exercise until he did it correctly because he had to learn to "get over" his stress and work through it.

Knowing Snap, I realized that was not going to work for him. But I didn't want to argue with the instructor, and I continued asking Snap to do the exercise over and over just to make her happy. Inwardly I was dismayed and wishing I could just take Snap home. The instructor's plan of making Snap repeat the exercise until he got it right didn't work. Snap got more upset each time he tried it, and she finally gave up after 15 minutes of repeated drilling, realizing he wasn't going to do the exercise right. She then said, to end the lesson on a "happy note," I should run a course with Snap. I ran a course with Snap, and he looked like a zombie. There wasn't anything behind his eyes. He did what I asked him to do—a testament to his tremendous improvement and his ability to bounce back, at least partially, from a stressful situation. Before all our hard work together, he never would have been able to do a course with me after such an experience; he would have run far, far away and sniffed and become mentally unreachable. I couldn't see how the instructor thought this was ending on a good note, since Snap looked miserable, but it looked like a good note to her, because he did what I asked of him.

It took three months to get Snap weaving again. Every time I brought him near the weave poles in my backyard, his eyes would glaze over and he'd totally shut down. So I started over training him from scratch, as if he'd never seen a pole before, with the assistance of my current primary agility coach, ex-World Team member Paulena Hope. Eventually Snap got his confidence back, and I taught him in the yard and then in the training facility to weave 12 straight poles, and then to take other obstacles and run into the weaves at speed. I got him loving the weaves to the point that he squeaks happily while plowing through them at the speed of light, but we went through a few months there where both of us were very frustrated and the weave poles had become a big problem.

The instructor that had wanted Snap to "get over it" had the best of intentions, but Snap is not a get-over-it dog. He should not be forced to work when he is shutting down. He shouldn't be brought to the point of shutting down in a lesson to begin with. Agility is supposed to be fun for the dog! There was a lot of fallout from that experience for him. Plus, I felt very badly that I had put Snap through that experience just because I was too intimidated to just say "No" to a teacher. At the time, I didn't know how to talk to her about it and explain that while I truly appreciated her instruction in handling skills and knew she had plenty to teach me on that front, I needed to take care of the behavioral health of my dog and not put him in a situation that I knew wouldn't work for him.

The bottom line is:

- Don't let anybody push you into something you feel is wrong for your dog.
- If you have a CU dog, be picky about whom you train with. Some agility instructors are wonderful at handling our dogs with issues. You can find one.

Chapter 2

BASIC CONCEPTS

- A behavioral program
- The principal principles
  - o Conditioning a relaxed response
  - o Reading your dog
  - o Working with thresholds
  - o The Goldilocks Rule
  - o Using the Premack Principle to teach focus
  - o Reframing the picture
- If it's not working

A BEHAVIORAL PROGRAM

CU is *not* an agility class though it can help with agility-related behavior problems. CU is also *not* an obedience program though it incorporates aspects of operant conditioning, which is the method I use in training obedience skills. *CU is a behavioral program.* Many of the core exercises are based on the principles of desensitization and counterconditioning, which are principles used in behavior-modification programs, not in obedience classes.

Briefly, here is the learning theory operating behind CU:

The dog learns that his own behavior causes a reward to happen. An event marker such as a clicker speeds this process. This is called "operant conditioning."

Note: If you are not using a clicker, you can do every exercise in this book, but be sure to let your dog know the nanosecond he's done something right with some kind of marker. Many people like the short and sweet word, *Yes!* If you are not using a clicker, then whenever I refer to clicking in this book, substitute *Yes!* or whatever marker you have chosen.

A fundamental aspect of operant conditioning is shaping, marking (usually with a clicker), and rewarding any behavior that puts the dog on the right path to figuring out the big picture behavior that is desired. This process helps the dog learn to solve problems and to stay in thinking mode as he experiments with various behaviors. It also boosts a dog's confidence as he learns that his behavior can make a click happen. When shaping, there is no behavior too small to mark and reward. For example, if you wanted to shape your dog to back up, you would start by clicking any movement of a hind foot to give the dog the idea to try stuff with his hind feet. Shaping teaches the handler to be acutely aware of her dog's behavior and to capture all his successes. The dog is never wrong in this discovery process and there is no force involved. Done with the necessary timing and precision, shaping is a dance that fosters a sense of awareness and connection between dog and handler as both team members solve the puzzle together.

"Desensitization" means what it sounds like: a process by which the dog becomes less sensitive to something that triggers a "yucky" response in him. The less sensitive he is to the triggering stimulus (known hereafter as the "trigger"), the more comfortable, focused, and ready to learn and work he will be. Desensitization involves gradually increasing levels of exposure to the trigger while the dog is kept subthreshold, so that he can get used to the trigger a little at a time. Desensitization is the opposite of the get-over-it school of dog training. I am amazed at what some instructors think a dog should get over just because we say he should! If you have ever had a panic attack, you can imagine that being told to get over it and stop that nonsense wouldn't do much for you in that situation. Yet I see dogs panicking in classes, trials, and life that are met with the same attitude.

"Counterconditioning" aims to change a dog's associations or predictions regarding a certain event or trigger (such as a loose dog running up into his face while he's doing agility) so that he no longer panics or attacks when he encounters that trigger.

CU is also about handlers and their dogs finding that space where they connect with each other as a true team. It is about awareness, respect, and honoring individual differences. To me, a real connection with animals is a spiritual thing, not quantifiable by science. This type of connection can only be achieved when a person sheds all her beliefs and perceptions and just lets her dog show her who he is. Then she must take in that awareness of her dog, with acceptance and love. My Belgian Tervuren, Rumor, taught me a lot about the difference between having a working relationship with a dog and connecting on a deeper level, the heart level.

HEART CONNECTIONS

When you were a kid, did you have a dog that followed you everywhere, listened to your secrets, and slept in bed with you at night? This was most likely a pet dog that had little or no training—at least, mine were. I always had a feeling of deep connection with my dogs growing up. I had the same connection with the two I adopted as an adult before I got bitten by the sports bug. With these dogs, I had no expectations. They weren't supposed to do anything in particular but just be themselves, and I loved them for it. My feeling of connection evolved from just being with and enjoying my dogs, personality quirks and all. It evolved from a feeling of wonder that, for better or worse, this amazing species chose to throw in its lot with ours and because of that choice, we could feel the high of that deep, magical connection with another species.

After I got involved in agility and flyball with my terrier mix Maggie, I left the rescued pet world and entered the dog sport world. Suddenly I wanted a dog with a certain structure, a certain temperament, and an aptitude for specific activities. I developed detailed plans for how I was going to raise and train this dog. After a couple years of research I got a new dog for obedience, freestyle, and agility competition—my Tervuren Rumor—and raised him with high expectations. He was the first dog I had bought from a breeder, my first purebred dog, and the first dog I got after becoming a professional trainer. He was supposed to be *the* dog. I wrote down what I did with him daily. He grew up with a "program."

I was heartbroken when I found out one and a half years later that Rumor has an incurable spinal condition that prohibits him from jumping. I was heartbroken because he wasn't going to be able to compete. I also felt bad about his chronic pain. His back legs buckled under him and he couldn't run or play for long periods without getting sore. But I think the majority of my tears were for all the time spent preparing him for his career gone out the window, and my sudden "sport-dog gap" since my terrier mix Maggie had retired after a shoulder injury. Some of my new sport friends saw Rumor as broken and useless because he couldn't do sports and urged me to return him.

I did not return Rumor. I had not wanted another pet, yet he still was part of the family. But I stopped doing the things with him that he loved, like our shaping games. He loved learning the foundation behaviors that I had been teaching him for sports, but I didn't feel like doing anything with him anymore. I felt it was a waste of time. Why teach him a behavior unless it was going to help us compete?

I never had felt as connected to Rumor as I had with my other dogs, even though I had spent most of the time since I brought him home working with him on building a "performance relationship." I believe you can have a good performance relationship with a dog if you define that by how many titles and placements you achieve, without feeling that deep sense of connection, which is what brought me to dogs in the first place.

Looking back on this period, I cannot believe how much my attitude toward dogs had changed in a few years. I had spent a lifetime loving and enjoying my dogs for being themselves. Now I was resenting my dog for being who he is. He is one of the sweetest, kindest, funniest dog spirits that has graced my life. He always had a lot to teach me, but I wasn't listening.

After his diagnosis, I turned to Rally Obedience, which Rumor could do without hurting himself, and he finished his Novice title with a flashy performance that won him the blue ribbon. When we got outside after being congratulated by everybody, I really looked at my dog, perhaps for the first time. He wasn't having fun, he just wanted to go home and curl up on the couch with a bone. Trial environments stressed him out, and even though he worked well for me, he did it because I told him to, without the pure joy with which Maggie pursued every sport we tried. (After training in obedience, agility, flyball, musical free-style, and Frisbee, at the age of nine, she was attacking Rally-O with a ven-geance). I looked at Rumor and felt that if he could have talked, he would have told me that he would do anything I asked that he was physically capable of doing, but that he really would rather stay home.

So Ru became "just a pet." Many of my friends thought this decision was weird. We had just won. Why wouldn't I continue and get his Rally-O champion-ship? "Because he doesn't feel like it," I'd say. Since taking that pressure off Rumor and returning to my old way of living with dogs—getting to know and enjoy him for who he is, doing things with him that he likes to do—our connec-tion has flourished. I became aware of the powerful lessons I could learn from Ru. I learned what kind of person I am, how I approach relationships, what I value, and what my responsibility is toward the dogs I work with. I had always loved Rumor, but my plans, expectations, and dreams for him had gotten in the way of really getting to know him. That afternoon after the Rally-O trial a door opened that allowed me to honor him for being himself, and suddenly I saw him with different eyes.

I feel that Ru came into my life to remind me about who I am and why I work with dogs. I was straying from my path, and it was going to affect the dogs that are brought to me for help.

I know some people don't believe that dogs have choices. They choose a hobby for their dogs, tell them what to do, when to do it, and for how long. I believe that dogs have choices. I believe that achieving true awareness of these amazing beings that have entered our lives is more important than titles and placements. Whatever your beliefs, you can benefit from the information in this book.

THE PRINCIPAL PRINCIPLES

Rather than just looking at the exercises in the CU program, it helps to consider the underlying principles. These principles will bring depth and color to the program and help you understand the larger picture of what affects dog behavior.

The principles are:

- Conditioning a relaxed response

- Reading your dog

- Working with thresholds

- The Goldilocks Rule

- Using the Premack Principle to teach focus

- Reframing the picture

Conditioning a relaxed response

My behavioral mentor, Dr. Karen Overall, wrote in her book, *Manual of Clinical Behavioral Medicine for Dogs and Cats,* that teaching relaxation is the foundation for all behavior modification programs. If your dog is overly aroused or upset, he is just not going to learn as well. Most CU dogs come in either overly aroused or upset. Their handlers have learned how to get their dogs revved up but have no clue about how to calm them down. Dogs that are reactive, that worry, or that just are unable to return to their individual baseline after becoming overstimulated do not need more motivational games to perform well in agility. *They need to learn how to relax in the face of their triggers.* Once they learn, then they will be able to concentrate better, focus on the handler better, and stress will no longer get in the way of their achieving their potential. Criteria such as speed and enthusiasm can come into the picture later. Once these dogs are able to cope with their environment and able to give all of their attention to their handlers, they can stop worrying about the proximity of dogs or other events, beings, or objects around them.

What is biofeedback for dogs?

Every time your dog is in a physiologically relaxed state, his behavior reflects that state. If you mark and reward that calm behavior, you are both reinforcing the relaxed state and sending your dog's nervous system a powerful message that eventually can cue relaxation. For example, when dogs are about to fall asleep, their eyelids get heavier. You can reward a dog for "sleepy eyes." I usually start biofeedback training by rewarding blinking, which softens the eyes, and in turn the entire facial expression. When a dog catches on, he blinks at me to earn a reward, but because the soft eyes are linked to a calm state, eventually the dog actually will learn to feel calm on cue. I also teach dogs to catch their breath and exhale (see page 67 for an explanation). Never underestimate the power of the body/mind connection when training a dog.

THE PROTOCOL FOR RELAXATION

My favorite tool to decrease anxiety is the Protocol for Relaxation, a canine biofeedback program designed by Dr. Karen Overall that conditions a relaxed response in dogs to increasingly stressful activities occurring around them. Detailed in Dr. Overall's book, *Manual of Clinical Behavioral Medicine for Dogs and Cats,* the protocol consists of a series of exercises that you can do while your dog is sitting or lying down. After each exercise, the dog gets a small food reward. The exercises range in level of difficulty from your simply standing still for five seconds, to running in circles around the dog while clapping or singing, to leaving the house, ringing the doorbell, counting to 20 and returning. Once you've finished with the basic protocol, you can add your own customized exercises.

The dog learns that as long as he remains in a relaxed position no matter what weirdness is happening around him, he will get rewarded. This protocol is not a *Stay* exercise. The dog is free to change his position, and any body language that tells you the dog is feeling calm (watch his eyes, ears, tail, rate of breathing, and position of hind legs if he is lying down) should be marked and rewarded. Also, you can use your own body language to encourage your dog to relax. Try moving slowly and fluidly, taking deep breaths, and looking at your dog with heavy-lidded, soft-focus eyes.

Reading your dog

Essential to the whole CU endeavor is understanding your dog's physical signals that tell you what he's feeling. How can you tell if your dog is feeling calm or relaxed (defined here as a much deeper version of calm), or tense, or stressed?

Have you ever glanced at a friend or coworker who just walked into the room and immediately asked, "What's wrong?" What was different about that person that let you know something had happened? Was her jaw tense? Was the expression in her eyes different from usual? Was she doing something that looked stressed out, like wringing her hands, breathing harder than normal, touching her hair, glancing around the room nervously, or avoiding eye contact when she greeted you? Did she move differently? Did she walk faster or slower?

I think most people that live with dogs instinctively know when a dog is having a bad day. As agility students become more indoctrinated into the competitive culture of dog sports, however, they become more focused on what the dog should or should not be (the dog *should* be in drive, the dog *should not* care about the environment, and so on). Somehow it becomes less natural for students to just look at their dog and wonder, "What's wrong?"

Here are some signals to look for in your dog, to give you more information about his frame of mind in different situations.

Muscle tension: Is your dog's jaw tight? Is the base of his tail tight? Where is he holding his weight—on his front feet, or on his back feet? If he's lying down, does he look as if he's about to pop up or is he relaxing into the down? Is he grinding his teeth? If his mouth is open, is he panting in an anxious manner, or is his mouth

relaxed and just hanging open, giving him a smiley look? Is his mouth shut tight? Does he look as if he could use a good massage? Many dogs rear on their hind legs before they start barking reactively. Often I have shown people how to stop a reaction before it starts by noticing tension or weight shifts in the dog's back legs. The handler then can redirect the dog before he rears up, interrupting the behavioral sequence that would lead to barking, lunging, or more before it gets started.

McDevitt's young Border Collie Easy looks "floppy" as he enjoys his massage with eyes closed and a smiley face, which indicates a relaxed jaw.

Movement: Observe your dog when he's playing with his friends, when he's running naturally, and when he's relaxing. When dogs are relaxed they have a nice "floppy" look about them. How does your dog move when he's enjoying what he's doing? Look for freezing in the body or just the head, or dogs moving in slow motion very deliberately since these are warning signs in an upset, potentially aggressive dog. One exception is my Border Collie Easy. He is the floppiest, most seemingly "boneless" dog I know. He usually has a big relaxed smile on his face. But when he sees toys or bodies of water he goes into a fixed motor pattern of giving eye, crouching, and moving very slowly. *Moral: You have to know your dog and to look at his behavior in context.*

Eyes: Are his eyes hard or soft? Is your dog displaying "whale eye;" that is, showing a lot of the white of his eye? That type of eye indicates the dog is in a very troubled state. What's your dog's normal blink rate when he's doing an activity, versus when he's hanging out? A dog that doesn't blink is way too tense or aroused and needs to settle down. Bear in mind some breeds such as Border Collies like to stare. That doesn't mean they should never blink or that you can't tell in your own Border Collie if his eyes are in normal stare mode, or if they're in about-to-cross-threshold mode, or if his eyes are softer or harder than usual.

Tail: We already mentioned the base of the tail, which is good indicator of the state of tension in the low back. What else is going on with the tail? Is it held high? Is it wagging fast, signaling overarousal, or is it wagging slowly with the base down, signaling in many dogs a "kinder, gentler" state of arousal? Is it between the dog's legs? We all know that a tail between the legs indicates a worried dog, yet in class all the time I see people leading dogs to the start line whose tails are tucked between their legs. When asked to sit at the start line, the worried dog often looks away from his handler or sniffs the ground, indicating that he feels stressed in that situation. Then he gets corrected for not paying attention.

Breath: Is your dog breathing shallowly, deeply, fast, or slow? Is he holding his breath? What's his breathing like at home compared to at the vet or at a trial?

Vocalizing: What types of noises does your dog make when he's frustrated? What types of noises does he make when he's excited, or anxious, or happy? What type of noise does he make when he's uncertain about a situation?

Ears: Are your dog's ears constantly whizzing in all directions to pick up every bit of information from the environment? If your dog doesn't have completely pricked ears, are the bases of the ears relaxed, giving the ears a floppier look, or are they totally erect?

Even though Labrador Retriever Ranger has a friendly expression, she got a little too close and personal for Snap's comfort. When McDevitt first adopted Snap, this encounter would have triggered a loud reaction. Snap looks alarmed. His ears, which are always erect, look like exclamation points! But his eye remains soft and he is comfortable enough to remain in a sit, cued before the Lab's "hello." Snap handled this situation by turning back to McDevitt for a treat.

Stress-displacement behavior: Does your dog circle the ground and sniff? Context is important here. He could be circling and sniffing because there's an interesting scent, but he could be doing it because he is trying to diffuse a situation with you where he feels tension. Is he looking away from you, yawning a lot, licking his muzzle, scratching or licking himself right after you have asked him to do something, shaking as if he's wet when he's dry? Turid Rugaas's short book, *On Talking Terms with Dogs: Calming Signals,* provides a good list of related behaviors.

All of American Pit Bull Terrier Dillinger's focus is on CU assistant Brown. Doberman Jynx remains in his down-stay and watches Border Collie Blitz break and sniff the ground as a stress-displacement behavior.

There are a lot of other great resources if you want to learn more about stress signals and dog body language. My purpose here is to raise your awareness of the importance of learning how to read your own dog, especially if he is prone to getting overly stressed or being reactive.

A lot of people assume their dogs are just being disobedient when they disengage. Instead the handler should look at both the dog and the training structure. Is the dog stressed or simply done and needs a break? Does the training structure simply not work for that dog so he seeks out better things to do with his time? Whatever is going on, the handler needs to do a lot of adjusting to help the dog succeed. If you look at the big picture, telling a dog "No, it's not acceptable that you disengaged; you must work" is not going to be enough to meet your long-term goals for that dog. You have to know your dog and what works for him. Misinterpreting your dog's behavior can be not only counterproductive but also unfair to the dog, as the following two case studies illustrate.

THE BALLISTIC BORDER COLLIE AND THE INQUISITIVE PORTUGUESE WATER DOG

A Portuguese Water Dog (PWD) and a Border Collie (BC), both already being shown at the Novice level in competitive obedience and agility, were brought to me separately for private behavior counseling. Each dog was having similar serious problems. Both were reactive to other dogs and unable to focus on their handlers because they were hypervigilant to their surroundings. The BC had been thrown out of an agility trial for running out of the ring and "going after" another dog. The PWD had been labeled aggressive for her reactive response to dogs coming near her, especially from behind. She whipped around and screamed bloody murder at them. Both handlers had been told by their competitive and successful obedience instructors that they needed to knock their dogs down a peg and correct them on prong collars for these behaviors. The hypervigilant BC had been reacting to environmental stimuli that he felt uncertain about, such as people jogging in the park where they trained. His handler had been told that his dog reacts because the BC's prey drive makes him want to chase everything. This analysis was an oversimplification that did not present a picture of the whole dog. The answer was to correct bad behavior on the prong and then maintain the dog's interest by tugging, tugging, tugging, because you should always tug with your BC. The PWD was also uncertain and hypervigilant to environmental stimuli including people jogging in the park where they trained. Her handler had been told that all PWDs are "inquisitive by nature" and therefore she should receive physical corrections because she needed to learn she should focus only on her handler rather than be curious about the environment.

These dogs lived in different states, trained with different people, and are different breeds, but they had been raised similarly and behaved in eerily similar ways. Neither dog had much experience greeting and interacting with strange dogs because the handlers' instructors had told them that their dogs should grow up learning to pay attention only to them and to curb their desire to interact with other dogs. When both the BC and the PWD met other dogs, they displayed their anxiety about not knowing how to greet properly by showing teeth, vocalizing, and lunging. These are normal responses for a dog that is trying to say that he feels uncertain and doesn't know what to do. This reactivity thus was not true aggression. Both handlers were told to physically correct their dogs for this behavior because it was "unacceptable."

Each of these dogs suffered from generalized anxiety, which triggered both the reactivity to other dogs and the hypervigilance to their surroundings. When each dog was focusing on his owner in class, at matches, and at trials, each also had the same type of anxious reaction to dogs that came up unseen from behind. Both dogs were easily startled and uncomfortable with a dog invading the space in which they interacted with their handler. Neither of their instructors had made a connection between the interdog reactivity and the environmental hypervigilance/ startling at sudden environmental changes. In fact, both handlers regularly brought their dogs to busy parks specifically to work on training attention. The handlers corrected their dogs for noticing joggers, other dogs, people on bikes, and so on, and physically forced them to watch their handlers. The handlers were told that the BC wanted to scan the environment because of prey drive; the PWD, because of curiosity. Actually, both dogs wanted to scan the environment because they were uncertain and thought something might sneak up behind them, which often was the case. When that happened, each dog had a loud reactive response (read panic attack) and got popped because he or she wasn't paying attention.

Because the BC was a BC, his handler was exhorted to keep tugging with him, so when he wasn't correcting him, he was tugging, which for this particular dog was causing his nervous system to reach the point of explosion. When the tugging stopped, the dog was even more adrenalized and therefore set up to have a reactive response to the next trigger that appeared. If a dog is relaxed and happy about play and can learn to deal with certain anxiety-producing situations because his handler is skilled enough to elicit a playful mood in him—great. For a dog that is highly aroused by play and also happens to be reactive, the mix is a recipe for trouble.

Both the BC and PWD quickly improved when I showed their owners how to reduce their anxiety by

- Giving them positive feedback instead of corrections.

- Using the conditioned relaxation exercises I will mention later.

- Doing bodywork (TTouch or massage).

- Counterconditioning the dogs to events that worried them ("A dog is sniffing your butt"—click!).

- Introducing them to totally nonreactive, "bombproof" dogs that would show them the right greeting signals.

- And, most important, *letting the dog watch the environment.*

The concept of clicking the dog for looking at other dogs and "stuff" was the total opposite of everything these two handlers had ever been told. Since they were invested in their dogs and they realized the other solutions they'd tried were not working, they dove in and started clicking their dogs for looking at other dogs. It helped right away. Soon both dogs were able to offer looking at other dogs, kids on skateboards, and so on as a clicker trick and confidently turn back to their handlers as if to say, "Did you see that I looked at that?" We will talk more about this concept later since it plays an crucial role in the CU program. Both handlers started hearing the same comments from people who knew their dogs: "I have never seen your dog look so calm!" Both handlers had to deal with skepticism from people who thought it was insane to give a BC treats instead of playing with him, or insane to give a PWD treats when other dogs came near her instead of correcting her for getting distracted. Both handlers got results quickly and began to understand their dogs a lot better, thereby becoming much better working teams. Both dogs have successfully returned to the trial environment.

The PWD and the BC used a reactive strategy to deal with their stress. At the other end of the spectrum is the "shutdown dog"—one that withdraws and disengages under stress, using displacement behaviors to handle anxiety. Some resort to our old stand-by—sniffing the ground—or just glaze over, stare into space, and cannot concentrate. These shutdown dogs are equally at risk for being misinterpreted or punished for their nervous system's particular style of coping with stress. Take the case of the floor-sniffing terrier.

THE FLOOR-SNIFFING TERRIER

I once observed a handler attempting to train her little terrier (known for being a great floor-sniffer) to pay attention to her on course. The handler was fairly new to the sport and was not signaling clearly to her dog which obstacle to take next. When the terrier took the wrong obstacle, the handler spoke sharply to her and told her she was wrong. Each time she rebuked the dog, the terrier's response was to turn away from her handler and sniff the floor. This was a normal, healthy canine response to a perceived threat. Every time the terrier responded in this normal way, her handler literally picked her up off the floor by the scruff of the neck and shook her in an attempt to teach her that sniffing the floor was unacceptable.

The handler did not realize that she was the reason her dog was sniffing the floor in the first place. The terrier was sniffing in an attempt to diffuse what she perceived to be a volatile situation, but it kept backfiring because her handler's behavior escalated every time she sniffed. Not knowing how else to communicate, the terrier sniffed even more as she became increasingly stressed at being picked up and shaken. The handler had every good intention of teaching her dog to pay attention, but she was setting her dog up to fail by being unclear. Then she was misreading her dog's attempts to pacify her as something unacceptable, disobedient, perhaps even self-rewarding. The response on this handler's part is what is known as "crazy-making behavior." The dog was trying to communicate but was not being heard and was not given any feedback that would help her formulate a different strategy. The floor sniffing was not going to stop until the handler learned to take stock of her dog, recognize the miscommunication between them, and set up a situation to help the dog succeed.

Working with thresholds

Learning to gauge your dog's threshold and work under it, or help him settle after he crosses it, is vital to the CU program.

So what's a threshold?

You've had a very bad day today. Your kids had a fight this morning, which you quickly and skillfully managed. They lost their homework, which you found. They missed the bus, so you drove them in horrible traffic with a smile on your face. You were late for work. On the way home you got into a fender-bender. Even though the accident wasn't your fault, you remained polite and accommodating to the jerk that hit you. As you're giving the report to the police officer, he makes a comment about your inspection sticker being one day out of date, and you scream in his face. You just crossed your "threshold."

All of us have a threshold. Beyond it, depending on our personalities, we might have a totally reactive response, or we might shut down and sit rocking in the corner sucking our thumbs. Each of our dogs has his own threshold, too, and his own response once he's crossed it. Once a dog has crossed his threshold, he is too pumped, scared, or stressed to learn.

I deal with thresholds all the time since most of my work as a behavior consultant is helping dogs that keep crossing them. These dogs may posture by screaming, lunging, snapping, and generally making a huge display of their anxiety and arousal. We call these dogs reactive. They may actually bite and cause damage or they may shut down and withdraw. A dog may be so on edge that the slightest sound or tiniest change in the environment causes him to panic.

These are not the dogs that I see in my CU classes (they need a quieter environment and one-on-one help), although the principles in this book drive the programs I individualize for these dogs. In CU we deal with thresholds all the time. The core exercises and all their little modifications are designed to keep a dog under his point of having an undesirable response—of crossing his threshold. If your dog has an extremely low-arousal threshold and a paper bag rustles in the breeze, he might have a panic attack and even displace aggression onto an unlucky bystander. If he has an extremely high-arousal threshold, a piano could drop on his head and he would barely notice. With time and effort, we can raise our dogs' thresholds to help them cope with more "stuff" (or triggering events) before they have a negative response. So when I talk about "subthreshold" or "over threshold" I am referring to whether or not the dog has crossed the line that triggers an undesirable reaction. The CU program will only be successful if the dogs are kept subthreshold so they can learn. If a dog barks every time other dogs move and he sits through the entire CU course barking while other dogs are moving, his handler has wasted her time. When I teach CU, the dogs are quiet. There will be many suggestions in this book for what to do to keep dogs subthreshold.

False Reassurance

When I say in this book that I talked to Snap and told him something was safe, I am not referring to the type of false reassurance that nervous owners attempt to give fearful or reactive dogs by telling them everything's okay while their own tone and body language tell a different story.

There is a big distinction between talking to your dog to help him move away from a reactive state and offering false reassurance when your dog is being fearful or reactive. When a handler tries to reassure her dog in such a situation, her own mannerisms typically betray her worry. Often she speaks faster and at a higher pitch than normal and communicates tension through her body language. This combination of signals can escalate the problem, or at the least, does nothing to help it. I actually have seen dogs take their owner's worried "It's okay!" as a cue to react because the owner's tone and those specific words, always repeated just before the dog has the reaction, have become paired through classical conditioning with the behavior itself.

There are various tools offered in this book to help you teach your dog to take cues from you that will enable him to relax, interpret things in context correctly, and develop coping skills when confronted with a trigger. These tools, especially when used along with Dr. Overall's Protocol for Relaxation, will give you a foundation that eventually will allow you to communicate with a neutral, calm voice and body language that says everything is cool. The cues include touching your dog as well as talking to him. There is a difference between trying to "pet away" your dog's upset, and using what I call "clinical touch" to calm him. A clinical touch could be anything from a simple ear massage to a series of particular Tellington Touches designed to soothe the nervous system. The dog's handler should remain neutral, breathe deeply, and model calm behavior for her dog.

I am at a point with Snap where just talking to him quietly can stop a reactive response dead in its tracks. But I laid a lot of foundation before I reached that point. You will notice that I did not communicate in the same way with the dogs in the case studies because I was still teaching them and their owners the foundation skills to develop that deep relationship. So when you read in this book that I talked to Snap, acknowledged he was worried about something, told him it was not a threat, and so on, recognize that this is a type of communication that you earn after you have taught your dog to relax and trust you as an interpreter or guide in a situation he feels uncertain about.

The bite-threshold model

After I wrote "But He Only Plays At Home!" about Snap in *Clean Run* magazine (July 2005), one reader emailed me perplexed about her Sheltie. The dog usually seemed bright and happy running in trials, but occasionally and inexplicably balked at the weave poles. He did the weaves fine at home and at 9 out of 10 trials in various locations. Why was he sometimes unable to do them?

This is the type of behavior that drives people crazy, but I actually have an answer. My theory in this particular case is that the Sheltie was acting according to The bite-threshold model (BTM), which refers to a dog having an undesirable response because he's crossed his threshold.

Simply, this model states that it takes a certain number of variables (or triggering events) to make a dog pass his threshold. For a dog with a biting problem, when the requisite triggers are present, he crosses his threshold and predictably will bite. We can apply the same logic to the Sheltie with a weaving problem. If the right triggers are present, he can't weave. The trick is figuring out what the triggers are. I asked the Sheltie's owner to think back and remember every similarity and difference she could about each trial they'd attended. Using the structure of the BTM, she could process information from a different perspective. She realized her Sheltie didn't perform as well when he was hot or when he was at an indoor trial. She also thought there was the possibility that certain models of weave poles were more difficult for the Sheltie; variations in weave pole construction became another variable for him. I suggested that when variables A, B, C, and D come together at a trial, the dog crosses into undesirable response territory and whichever obstacle he is weakest in performing will go first.

To work through the combination of variables that made life hard on him, this Sheltie needed to be conditioned to perform obstacles automatically without having to think about them. As it turned out, he was conditioned for automatic performances—on everything except the weaves. In addition, he also needed to do some foundation work that would help him relax, think in exciting or distracting situations, and better accept environmental changes. You can't always change, control, or even notice all the variables that affect your dog's performance, but you can give your dog the coping skills he needs to be less affected by those variables.

I suggested that his handler completely start over with the weaves. She needed to use a different method that didn't resemble the original one he learned, put a different cue on the weaves when ready, work on building criteria, and generalize to a variety of locations. In addition, she needed to gather more information on potential triggers to look for at trials that might conspire to affect her Sheltie's performance as well as ways to better manage him, whatever the variables. I also suggested exercises to teach relaxation and impulse control, which were two other areas in which her Sheltie needed work. Again, the only problem with the BTM model is that our dogs notice so many more things than we do. We usually cannot figure out exactly which variables came together in a certain situation and caused the dog to lose it. But we can still try!

Postscript: About six months later the Sheltie's owner called to let me know he was back to trialing and had not had any problems. She had been working diligently on the program we came up with over the phone and reported that people at the trials were very impressed with her Sheltie's change in overall behavior, not just with his trial performance.

The Goldilocks Rule

Just as important for the student as learning her dog's threshold points is learning to pinpoint when her dog is at his optimum stimulation level, a critical CU concept that I call the Goldilocks Rule.

Each dog has his own level of stimulation within which he can achieve his maximum performance. If he is either overstimulated or understimulated, you won't get the best from him. Whether or not a dog is going to be over- or understimulated, or "just right" depends on various factors: his mood, your mood, and the environment. You should be aware of which state your dog is in and whether you need to work with him to help him get higher or lower. Don't peg your dog as an understimulated dog and work constantly on tugging. Don't peg him as overstimulated and work constantly on controlled focus. *Stimulation levels are fluid and depend on context.* Of course, some dogs are more apt to be one than the other, but avoid becoming complacent and expecting your dog always to behave in a certain manner. Even if your dog is highly reliable in his tendencies, you should still remain flexible and leave room for possibilities. Always read the dog, be aware of his needs, and be ready to adjust. When making a plan to get your dog to his just-right point, look at his blink rate, his breathing, feel his heartbeat, and check how keyed in he is to environmental stimuli.

Arousal vs. Drive

Arousal is not drive. Drive is a primal force at work, such as prey drive or sex drive. Dogs given a job that channels their drive are satisfied and eager to work. Do not mistake the intense eagerness of a dog in drive for arousal. Arousal is a behaviorist's word for excitement. When I say "overaroused," I mean overexcited. As the Goldilocks Rule states, dogs that are overexcited—in other words, past their arousal threshold—cannot think as clearly and will not perform as well as those that are under threshold. Some handlers think they can shape the extreme excitement of arousal into agility drive. Actually they cannot get a clear-headed performance from an aroused dog until they teach him to relax and help him learn to think through his excitement.

Dogs that get "the zoomies" on course are showing one form of arousal behavior. Getting the zoomies is not about drive. This is not a behavior to channel although I have encountered people that misread it as such. Instead, getting the zoomies is a great indication that the dog has passed threshold and is too excited to think clearly. In times of great excitement or stress, dogs that were bred for a certain purpose revert to behaviors related to that purpose. Instinct switches on. Although any dog can get the zoomies, I see it often in herding breeds. It's no big surprise that when herding dogs cross their threshold, they would run in circles. They are not trying to herd per se; their brain is just reverting to "basic code" under pressure.

I adopted Snap around the time I was creating CU. Many of the strategies I tried to help him find that space where he could learn and succeed, be excited to work but not so excited he couldn't think clearly, and be calm but not bored, made their way into the course. Most people are lucky. Their dogs tend to be the easily aroused type or the easily turned-off type, but Snap reminds us that dogs are complicated, and that training needs to be adjusted to honor each dog.

Snap: Stress at Both Ends of the Stimulation Continuum

Snap was an exceedingly complicated dog to train because he so quickly switched from being overstimulated to being understimulated. Within the same brief training session he could go from hyperarousal—jumping all over me about a toy or food, or offering the tricks he'd learned in his original home at a frenzied speed—to completely shutting off and showing no interest in working just because of an unexpected sound or because he'd felt too much pressure from social interaction.

Consequently it took months to help him find that zone where he was in balance, where he could truly start learning. It took awhile to find a rhythm of interaction that would work for Snap. In the beginning, the sight of any kind of reinforcement brought out a panicked, over-the-top response. For at least the first six months Snap earned every piece of kibble from every meal for lying down and making eye contact with me. At first it was hard for him to relax and focus even at this level. I didn't want to reward the tricks he'd learned in his former home because these tricks weren't under "stimulus control" (meaning that the dog only performs them on cue). Once Snap started offering these tricks, he went into a total frenzy and stopped thinking. I had to let his tricks extinguish and only reward him for being still. I felt bad watching this little dog repeatedly whack himself in the nose with his paw (one of his tricks) and offer swimmers turns (what dogs are trained to do at the flyball box) off my walls and doors and his metal crate. He offered a variety of other behaviors before he learned that I would only interact with him when he was calm. "Calm" was not in his behavioral vocabulary. Snap was like a wind-up toy, but I couldn't just focus on his impulse-control problems. He also had a strong tendency to stress out, shut down, and just let his mind drift off to a galaxy far, far away. Unlike any dog I'd seen before, he could switch between these two extremes so quickly that there seemed nothing in between. That was what made him so complex and challenging.

When Snap left me to sniff, he did so because he got overwhelmed trying to process too much information at once. Just being inside our training facility was too much for him at first. Depending on his mood and other variables, he responded to being overwhelmed either by shutting down or by having an ADD (attention deficit dog) attack. Both of these cycles started in the same fashion, with Snap disengaging from me and wanting to wander and sniff. To know which way our training session needed to go, I needed to learn to read him.

I needed to know if he was on his way to shutting down or if he was on his way to having an ADD attack and acting as if he was anchorless and adrift in an overstimulating sea. That distinction was fairly simple—if he was having an ADD attack, he disengaged, sniffed, then zoomed around our training facility. He appeared happy in his frantic way, bouncing off agility equipment and unable to harness his runaway mind, He was the perfect picture of an overstimulated dog. If he was heading for a shutdown, he disengaged, sniffed, and just kept on sniffing. During an ADD attack, I could recall him, but he was too frantic to give me the focus I needed. During a stress attack, there was no point in trying to re-engage him because he simply was fried. It was my job as his trainer to keep him from experiencing either of these extremes. I not only had to teach him that there was a middle ground, I also had to train proactively, instituting rule structures to prevent him from going to either extreme in a variety of contexts.

One of the major goals of the CU program is to create awareness of complex responses to stimulation and to help each handler think through how she can adjust for her dog in different situations.

Using the Premack Principle to teach focus

You are going to see this concept pop up time and again in this book. The Premack Principle is simple and powerful and plays a critical role in my training methods. It states that what *the dog* wants to do (called a "high-probability behavior") can be used to reinforce what *you* want the dog to do (called a "low-probability behavior"). In other words, you can reward the dog (or person, or whale) by giving him access to do what he wants after he does something that you want. This is the you-scratch-my-back-I'll-scratch-yours school of dog training.

That sounds obvious. What makes this principle so interesting is that it takes the conflict out of training your dog. If your dog is dying to sniff a spot of grass, and you say, "No, you are not supposed to self-reward; you must pay attention only to me. Never think about grass. Now watch me!" you are not making the grass any less interesting. But if your dog really wants to sniff that patch of grass, and you ask the dog to do something else for you—make eye contact for a moment, perhaps—and then send him to sniff the grass, you have reinforced him for paying attention and taken the conflict out of the situation by letting him do what he wanted.

A student that doesn't allow her dog to sniff often feels she's caught in a constant battle between winning the dog's focus versus losing the dog to the environment. Using the Premack Principle and letting the dog do what he wanted to in the first place allows you to become the gateway to the environment. The dog learns that being attentive to you is not in conflict with doing other activities; being attentive to you is the way your dog gets access to the other activities. In this way, your dog becomes patterned to pay attention to you even in very distracting situations.

At a seminar I gave recently, I was handed an Aussie mix that was wild. The dog ran around the ring, sniffing the floor, and staring at other dogs. She had no concept that "We're here to work." Although she was not a clicker-trained dog, I just started clicking and treating any bit of orientation the dog gave me (like slight turns in my direction). Once she ate, immediately I pointed her in the direction of whatever she had been doing, simultaneously giving a verbal release. In about five minutes I couldn't get that dog to look away from me. People were shocked. Some protested that the dog was paying attention only because she liked my treats so much. They said if I had lesser value treats she would still be running off and sniffing.

Not true. Using the Premack Principle allows you to pattern a behavior chain in the dog where returning to you and paying attention is connected to going away from you and sniffing. I told the people at this seminar that I teach Go Away at the same time that I teach Come. I teach these two behaviors as a pair. It doesn't matter what kind of treat you have (and I changed treats to prove my point). The reason this technique works is that you are patterning the dog, teaching her that going away is connected to coming back to pay attention.

But wait... there's more. There is a strong reverse psychology component operating in this principle as well. The more you tell the dog to do what he wants, the less he wants to do it! Therefore, not only have you patterned the dog to pay attention to you as part of his going away and sniffing, but sniffing is no longer the big deal that it once was because there's no conflict. Nobody is telling the dog it's not allowed. In fact, I keep telling the dog to go away from me, and the more I do it, the more he starts wanting to re-engage with me. "But wait, I wasn't done staring at you yet!"

I played the same game with the other dogs in this seminar, most of which were brought to me because they were considered the problem dogs at their agility club. By the end of the seminar, everybody present was totally sold on the Premack Principle. They called it "come-and-go training." As an unintentional side effect, they also were so totally sold on clicker training they wanted to integrate it into their classes. Come-and-go training worked particularly well with a dog that was so reactive and hypervigilant outdoors that he could not think or focus on his owner.

THE REACTIVE GERMAN SHEPHERD MIX

A woman who had adopted a German Shepherd mix from a shelter brought the dog to me because he was reactive to other dogs and went after them on leash walks. He was also so hypervigilant (meaning, too aware of everything in his environment to be able to pay attention to his owner) and so aroused just by being outside that he could not settle down. I needed to get him to a point where he could feel calm outside before adding other dogs into the mix.

I had ring gates in my backyard and I made them into a little box. I sat on a lawn chair inside the box, clicked every time he moved toward me, and put a soft treat in his mouth. While he was swallowing, I told him to go sniff the grass and off he went. He started orienting more and more frequently, and suddenly, his face changed. He looked as if he had just awakened from a deep sleep. He had not been able to think when he was outside, but this pattern had gotten into his brain. Suddenly he was cognizant of the game and offered to come to me for a click and a treat. At that point, I removed the ring gates and started walking around my backyard. I let his leash drag. He followed me. I clicked and treated and sent him away. He went away a few times, thought twice about it, and returned to me. The whole process took about 20 minutes. At the end of it he was heeling off lead around the yard with me while I kept insisting he go away and sniff grass.

His owner was bewildered, but she knew some big connection was being made inside her dog's brain. She had had the dog for a couple of years already and had never gotten him to pay attention outside.

It's not magic; it's just the Premack Principle! My favorite example involves my little Snap and some squirrels that disrupted our backyard agility training, which I discuss later (page 176).

THE MOST INTERESTING THING

As the guest speaker at an awards banquet for the local West Highland White Terrier Club, I decided to go ahead and say something out loud that I had been mulling over for a long time and see what kind of response I'd get.

I told my audience, "I know that most or all of you have been told by your instructors that to train your performance dog you must be the center of his universe, the most interesting thing in his life." Having heard this a thousand times before, the Westie people nodded and expected me to reinforce the point. I went on, "I understand, however, that you are not always able to be the most interesting thing in the world. I understand that sometimes your Westie might think a running rodent is more interesting than you. And that's okay! You can train your dog anyway."

I don't remember how I ended this part of my speech. What I do remember is thinking that people were going to leap from their chairs and smother me in hugs. Everybody had the same look on her face: grateful, and shocked.

Since that experiment, I have repeated this thought to my CU students and gotten the same response. People don't like being told they have to be the center of the universe at all times; it's a lot of pressure. They especially don't like being told that if a dog goes off to do anything self-rewarding (in other words, anything a normal dog might feel like doing that he wasn't given permission to do) that it was because his handler wasn't being interesting enough and therefore she was a failure.

Fast forward almost a year to a CU seminar I was giving to a group of agility instructors who wanted more tools for handling difficult dogs in their classes. When I brought up this subject, they all said, yes, they do tell their students they have to be the most interesting thing to their dogs all the time. I said, "But what you don't realize is that afterward some of your students go home and cry, because they feel as if they'll never be able to do that!" They all laughed, thinking I was exaggerating, but the group of students who were also present all nodded vigorously. I had given them the opportunity to communicate something they would never have dared say to an instructor on their own. For their teachers, it was a big eye-opener.

Of course I'm not saying you shouldn't be interesting or rewarding to your dog. But I am relieving you of the burden of having to be the best thing in the galaxy at all times. The concept is well-intentioned: it should be very rewarding for your dog to work with you, and I hope it always is. If it isn't, you need to thoroughly examine your training structure and methodology. But you don't have to take this concept to the extreme to train your dog to do well in agility, and you don't have to feel like a total failure if your dog occasionally wants to act like a dog, either.

Using the Premack Principle and other tools explained in this book, you can get the attention you want from your dog without constantly feeling as if you are battling the environment. Remember, one of the reasons I love the Premack Principle is because it can take away that conflict for you: the conflict of you vs. everything else.

After I demonstrated various exercises with the dogs brought to me for help in the CU seminar, the instructor that was the first to say she always told her students they had to be the most interesting thing at all times said, "Okay, I'll never tell them that again!" After seeing the students' reactions when I brought up that point—the eye-rolling and looks of hopelessness—and then watching the "difficult dogs" they brought me as demos for the seminar quickly start paying attention using some of the CU exercises, the instructors at this club gained these insights:

- The "most interesting thing" mantra makes some students feel as if they'll never be able to train their dog.

- To create a good performance dog there are alternatives to the view that you must always be the center of your dog's universe. Conversely, you do not have to prevent your dog from enjoying anything else in the universe besides you.

I will never forget the time I made a client cry by telling her I thought it was okay to let her Border Collie play with other dogs in the park. She had brought her Border Collie to me because the dog was reactive in several specific contexts that needed to be addressed: She was way too easily aroused and often went over her threshold with no way of calming herself down. As a result she was not focusing in agility or flyball class. The instructor had told my client that her dog should never be allowed to go to the park again *because she enjoyed it.* The instructor felt that the dog would never learn to focus and would never become a sport dog unless her owner became the only thing the dog enjoyed. It was the dog's significantly low arousal-threshold that was causing the trouble. She needed to learn coping skills to raise her threshold. Her problem had nothing to do with socializing with other dogs or going to the park. My client had followed the advice but secretly had been feeling sad because she really missed taking her dog to the park.

This client ended up being one of my first CU group class students. I showed her how her dog could learn to focus and also how to teach her dog to feel calm in situations that aroused her. I showed her how counterconditioning would decrease the reactivity. I told her to take her dog back to the park. Ironically, the same instructor that outlawed the park brought her own reactive dog to CU class about a year later and ended up becoming one of CU's most enthusiastic students and supporters.

Reframing the picture

Tied into the technique of using counterconditioning to offer a shift in perspective to a worried dog is the concept that psychologists call "reframing." I have modified this theory to make it relevant to dogs. For a situation that evokes an undesirable response, reframing means using cues and familiar rule structures to make the situation look different. That altered dynamic transforms the situation into one in which the dog can more easily learn a better response. In other words, the dog says, "A dog is running toward me. I hate that. WOOF! WOOF!" We say, "A dog is running toward you. That must mean we are playing the Dog in Your Face game! Hooray! Here's your favorite treat! I *love* this game!" With the groundwork laid, the dog is able to respond, "Oh, right, we're playing that game! Cool!" Reframing allows us to give a new spin to an old, stressful situation.

There are lots of examples of reframing in this book. I often use mats from the Go to Place exercise at the start line for dogs that stress about start-line stays. "It's not a start-line stay anymore. Now it's a Go to Place exercise, and you *love* that exercise! And it happens to be at a start line!" There's a Dog in Your Face! and Look at That! are both games designed to take a situation that might make a dog feel uncomfortable and reframe it for him as an enjoyable game. Think about how you might change the picture in any situation that elicits an undesirable response from your dog.

REFRAMING FLYBALL CUES FOR HAPPY CONTACTS

A CU student had a terrier that was stressing after stopping on his contacts. She gave him his two-on/two-off cue, and he performed the behavior correctly with a concerned expression. When she gave him his *O.K.* release, he slowly crept off the contact, sniffing the ground and disconnecting from her before she sent him to the next obstacle. My student wanted her dog to run quickly off the contact once released and enthusiastically take the next obstacle.

I saw that she was giving agility cues in her formal obedience voice and standing rigidly. Her dog, who generally worried when asked to sit or lie down with the obedience voice, was responding to this sudden change in her tone and body language at the contacts.

What this dog loved most of all was playing flyball. I knew he already had a strong conditioned emotional response (CER) to his flyball cues and felt that using these cues would solve the contact dilemma. I asked the student what her release word was in flyball. It was *Get It!* I placed myself behind the little terrier on a dogwalk contact and held him back in a flyball-style restrained recall, whispering, "Reaaaaady...?" to him. He immediately assumed his happy, excited flyball posture, straining against my hands but staying solidly on his contact. I asked his handler to stand near a tunnel, release him with *Get It!* instead of *O.K.,* and then immediately give the tunnel cue. Instead of the usual creeping off the contact and sniffing around, he flew off and dashed into the tunnel so fast he hopped up in the air as he entered it, which was adorable.

My friend Jacky Judd pointed out that not only had the dog's attitude changed on hearing the flyball cues in the new context, but also my student's demeanor had drastically changed when she was giving the cues. When she used her flyball voice her posture relaxed. She did not feel tense in flyball, though she sometimes felt tense when training in agility or obedience. Flyball to her was a relaxing, fun sport, and her body therefore gave the message to her dog that she was relaxed and having fun, and her dog responded in kind.

That was a quick but powerful fix, and a nice example of reframing.

Another CU student's dog offers a different example. This retriever was so anxious about meeting new people that she barked reactively at them. The dog excelled at search and rescue and enjoyed the game of finding people to earn her tennis ball. So I had her owner give her the *Find* cue when greeting a person, and the dog's behavior immediately improved. This simple reframe enabled her to feel new confidence about finding people to say hello to, rather than bracing herself to be approached by strangers she felt uncertain about.

IF IT'S NOT WORKING

If you tried something in this book and it didn't work, look at the following.

Thresholds

Was your dog over threshold? You and your dog should be doing the CU exercises when he is *under* threshold. If your dog went over threshold at any point during an exercise, take note of it. Then take about 10 steps back and start over again. For example, if your dog barked during the There's a Dog in Your Face! game, how close did the other dog get to him before he had a reaction? Was it 10'? Your dog is letting you know that, for that particular exercise, he crosses his threshold when the other dog is 10' away. So, do the exercise from 20' away. There's no race here. Take the time you need to make your dog comfortable or you won't get the results you want.

Rate of reinforcement

Was your dog too distracted during an exercise? Chances are he either was stressed or your rate of reinforcement wasn't high enough. If your dog was stressed, you'd treat it as a threshold issue, take some steps back, and start over. Find the point at which your dog got sniffy as a reaction to stress and then work well under that point. If your dog was just plain distracted because your rate of reinforcement was too low, notice at which points your dog disengages from you. Notice if faster movement on your part or your tone of voice affect him. In the beginning, keep the rate of reinforcement very high (ratio 1:1, one treat per one behavior) and click or otherwise mark everything that you can.

Criteria

Were your criteria too high? Maybe your dog simply wasn't ready for what you asked him to do. Again, take some steps back and start over. Make sure your rate of reinforcement is high enough, that you are not asking for too much, and that your dog is under threshold. You then will get the results you want from the exercises in this book. If you are a green trainer, it's a good idea to attend a clicker course or seminar to learn more about rate of reinforcement, timing, and operant and counterconditioning. For students in North America wanting to get the greatest amount of learning in the shortest amount of time, I recommend taking one of marine scientist and dog trainer Kathy Sdao's three-day clicker seminars. Or you can purchase the DVDs of her seminars. I also recommend attending a Karen Pryor ClickerExpo if it comes to your region.

Chapter 3

NIGHT ONE

CONCEPTS
- Connecting with your dog requires understanding his state of mind
- Twilight times
- To leash or not to leash
- The Great De-bait
- The ballet of teamwork

NEW EXERCISES
- Passive attention
- Leash exercises
  - Default behaviors
  - Release cues
  - Reorienting points
  - Sacred space
  - "I'm gonna get you!"
  - "We don't need no stinkin' leashes!"
  - "But he runs off the second I unclip the leash…"
  - Leash comes off, toy comes out
- Management
- Teamwork exercise in the box
- Beginning of box work

BEFORE THE FIRST CLASS

I have started each CU course slightly differently. I try to get a handle on who is attending and what each student's issues are before the first night so I have some idea of what to expect. I also screen people and dogs to make sure they are appropriate for the course. If they're not, I will work with them privately. For tips on screening dogs, see "Which dogs are appropriate for CU?" on page 23.

I tell each prospective student that she must bring to class each night a crate and a mat or bed that the dog loves. Conditioning dogs to relax on a specific, portable, comfortable mat is an essential element of the CU program.

On the first night, I look around the room before class begins, just taking in the feel of that particular group of handlers and dogs. I watch how the people interact with their dogs and what the dogs are doing. The energy of each group is different. While I might really emphasize one concept for one group, the next session I might barely cover that same concept. It amazes me how this works. Sometimes I'll have a group where all the dogs are young and just starting out, with handlers that signed them up for foundation work. The progress these young dogs make astounds me. I am constantly pressed to make up new exercises for them during class. Other classes are made up of dogs that have already been through many agility classes or are actually trialing. Some of these dogs might have a long history of running away on course, getting highly distracted, or being reactive. In these types of classes we could spend the entire seven weeks going over the same three exercises! Sometimes, I get mixed classes where some dogs need remedial work and others fly through the exercises.

Whatever the mix of the group, there usually is an underlying theme explaining why these particular dogs are here and why the group has come together. And, of course, the dogs help each other. Usually the mix of dogs offers appropriate pairs for all my "buddy exercises." This way the hair-trigger dog has the chance to work next to a mellower dog (at least in the beginning), rather than putting dogs together that wouldn't complement each other.

Although I screen dogs for entry into every CU class to make sure they are appropriate, the first night may take some extra management since, for some dogs, just being in a new place with strange dogs and people is stressful or distracting. Students with reactive dogs especially need coaching to train how to keep their dog subthreshold. I am grateful to have had my wonderful assistant Kienan Brown to guide those students and help them get settled in while I am taking in the bigger picture of the rest of the class. I have huge barriers constructed of tarps and PVC frames for dogs that need to have their visual stimulation reduced. I also have lots of space for each dog's working station, surrounded by ring gates if that type of barrier helps them feel more comfortable. The major ground rule that everybody hears right away in CU is: Unless Leslie purposely has set up a situation where interaction is part of the training, dogs *do not interact* with each other in class. *Period.*

Since I am familiar with the dogs' issues before class, I can tell if there is a particular dog that has special needs and inform the other students if they need to be aware of his issues. Usually if I do accept a special-needs dog into class, I ask his person to arrive early to let the dog check out the environment, and set up his station before the others come in. Then his handler can feed him through his crate as the others arrive.

Connecting with Your Dog Requires Understanding His State of Mind

Sometimes on that first night, if I see students looking lost and disconnected from their dogs (waiting for direction rather than taking the opportunity to interact with their dogs), I ask them to show me how they warm up their dogs before working with them. Typically the students try to rev up their dogs with a lot of cheerleading, fast circle work, and tugging. Some of the dogs aren't motivated by these activities and appear totally disconnected. Some are turned on and then have no channel for all that adrenaline when the activity stops. Revving up your dog and suddenly disconnecting from him to talk to a fellow student or to listen to the instructor leaves a high-drive dog feeling "all dressed up with nowhere to go." That is when these dogs start scanning the environment for something else that will stimulate them; they have been taught to be stimulation junkies.

Revving up an easily aroused dog like Belgian Malinois Rosie (at left) without giving her any structure or impulse-control training leaves her feeling "all dressed up with nowhere to go." At right, Belgian Sheepdog Trixie's high tail carriage indicates arousal. Trixie was getting too excited watching other dogs moving in the distance.

Many a dog sports student has been told a million times to tug with your dog. But most of the people I have worked with have not been told how to switch a dog into or out of a state of high arousal, or when it's appropriate to tug versus when it's more appropriate to do a different activity (such as massage or self-control games). Massage or self-control games will help a dog focus and connect without overstimulating him. After I watch the warm-ups, I ask the students to look at their dogs and see if those warm-ups achieved the goal they sought. Did they even have a specific goal when they started, or were they just going through the motions of what they thought I expected from them?

I tell students that this is a class about engaging and connecting with your dog. The exercises are just tools to help foster that connection, so even if a student and her dog do not perform an exercise perfectly, as long as the dog is looking happy and engaged with his handler, I count that as a win.

Each CU class is about engaging and connecting with your dog.

Sometimes I start class right off the bat with massage, showing students how to connect with their dog through touch. I used to turn the lights off, and once I lit a candle, but the agility instructors started teasing me. I remind the students with dogs that are easily adrenalized that their dogs have been crated or left at home all day while they've been at work. Even though the human half of the team often perceives agility as a fun way to unwind after work while giving the dog much-needed exercise, the canine half of the team may become overexcited or distracted after a long, boring day because the dog wants to bark, explore, visit, and *move*.

This state leads to much frustration on both ends of the leash because there is a culture clash between tired handlers and wired dogs that needs to be put in balance. If you expect total attention from your dog, you must give total attention to him in return. Connecting is a team effort. I find it odd how many people want their dogs to focus on them when they are not at all focused on their dogs.

BEING PRESENT

In preparing to train your dog (especially if he has a behavioral problem that upsets you), or preparing to compete in a performance event, take a moment to connect with your dog on a deeper level by simply "being present" with him.

Being present with your dog is a bit like meditating with him. First, you must become aware of yourself. With eyes closed, sit upright in a chair, feel your spine against the back of the chair, and your feet on the ground. Breathe. Let any thoughts you have just pass by you; stay connected with your breathing. When you are ready, open your eyes, keeping them soft and unfocused, and look at your dog, staying with your self-awareness as you sit quietly with him. It doesn't matter what he is doing, just keep him in your awareness and let everything else go.

Let any competition worries, training concerns, or errant thoughts pass by. Share this moment with your dog unaffected by the outside world. In time everything around you will fade away as you focus only on the connection between you and your dog. It is much easier to train your dog when you feel fully present in the moment with him. If your mind is in several places at once and your energy is scattered, you will not have the same quality of connection.

The great competitors and trainers are very good at being absolutely present with their dogs, even if they don't think of it in this way. Dogs know and appreciate when you connect with them, and they will respond by being more attentive and more open to working with you.

~~~~~~

Starting class off with some bodywork and breathing enables handlers and dogs to begin feeling a connection and an awareness of each other without the pressure to concentrate or focus. As a result, their scattered energy can settle, and both team members will be able to think more clearly and focus better. Whether I start off that first night with warm-ups or with massage, my observations of what happens between my students and their dogs gives me the opportunity to explain a central concept of the CU class, what I call "twilight times."

TWILIGHT TIMES

These are the times before class starts, or during class, or at an agility trial well before it's your turn. During these times it's easy for your dog (and you) to get distracted from the work at hand. I believe that a dog is working as long as he's in class, or *getting ready for* class. For the dog the concept of "class" should start in the car in the parking lot. Class is not something that suddenly sneaks up on your dog when he finds himself in the ring after dragging you from your car into the building, greeting other dogs, sniffing around, and looking for stuff to do. If you don't remain engaged with your dog in some way during these times, chances are he won't remain engaged with you unless you happen to be lucky enough to have a dog like my terrier mix Maggie. She lives and dies for a tennis ball, and always watches me (as the source of all tennis balls) in case I might have one.

Three options for staying connected

During the first night, I offer my CU students three options for connecting with their dogs during twilight times. For the rest of the course and without reminders from me, I expect each student to explore these options and see which combination works best for her dog. I call the options passive attention, active attention, and management. Because of time constraints, I usually discuss active attention on the second night; the first night I concentrate on the concept of passive attention and briefly cover management.

Passive attention

These connection exercises are designed to help the dog and handler feel relaxed and able to focus on each other in a stimulating environment, and hence help prepare them for more active work. You can use breathing, massage, Tellington Touch, awareness walks, or any other activity that your dog enjoys and that puts relatively little social pressure on him. By social pressure I mean any pressure in a social context—whether between dogs or between the handler and her dog. Many handlers put too much pressure on their dogs.

Active attention

These exercises emphasize handler focus or impulse control, switching your dog to a more active level of interaction and preparing him to work. The level of excitement and the amount of social pressure that active attention games generate depend on a particular dog's response. For example, hair-trigger dogs that can't think when they're too high will do best with some targeting and impulse-control games such as Leave It. You can also change to toy play in the context of an Off-switch game (as described on page 154). We are aiming for active engagement here. An actively engaged dog is a dog that's happy and focused on you; his arousal level is just right; his whole body ready for your next move.

Management

If a handler can't be either passively or actively connected to her dog in class, then it's a good time to give the dog a break from the stimulation and the handler an opportunity to talk with friends, watch other people run the course, or listen to her instructor. The most obvious solution is crating; however, a dog that has learned to relax on a mat or bed can just lie next to her handler's chair.

Handlers waiting their turn in agility class engage in management (crating dog, left), passive attention exercises (massaging dog, middle), and active attention exercises (playing tug, right).

Passive Attention

On that first night, regardless of whether I ask students to show me how they warm up their dogs or start them off with massage, the first exercises I introduce are passive-attention exercises. My students learn that every subsequent class will start with the dogs on mats and the students doing bodywork before we move on to other things.

I talk a little about Tellington Touch and encourage everybody to get a book or video to learn more. I recommend Linda Tellington-Jones's book, *Getting in TTouch with Your Dog: A Gentle Approach to Influencing Behavior, Health, and Performance,* and the video, *Unleash Your Dog's Potential* (both available from www.ttouch.com). The therapeutic touch work stimulates the dog's nervous system, and prepares him to learn. It also helps him focus when he is overly excited, or relaxes him when he is stressed. This work is a great way to begin any training activity. An alternative is massage. I recommend Maria Duthie's DVD, *How to Massage Your Dog* (see www.cleanrun.com for more information).

McDevitt does TTouch circles on Easy's ears (left). The dog's ears contain acupressure points for his whole body. Note the soft, happy expression. At right, McDevitt moves on to applying light compressions on the masseter muscles of Easy's jaw, a technique she learned from animal massage expert Maria Duthie.

After each student has gotten her dog on the mat or bed she brought to class, I have everybody start touching their dogs' ears because dogs' ears contain acupressure points that affect their entire bodies. There is no magic way to do this. Students can gently fold the ears, rub them in between the palms of their hands, or do tiny clockwise circular motions at the base of the ear and around the ear. If the dogs' ears are cropped, the students should work on them as if the entire ear were still present, motioning in the air.

After working on the ears we move to the jaws. This is a helpful exercise because dogs carry so much tension in their jaws. Students do gentle compressions on each side of the jaw or small circular motions around the jaw and even on the gums themselves. If a dog is particularly vocal in class, jaw work is the place to concentrate. Then I ask students to do long gentle pulls, or circular touches, down the dogs' back toward the tail, ending with the tail. Since flexibility of the tail can indicate tightness or looseness in the low back, I have students gently pull the tail from side to side, and up and down. If the tail is docked, they should work as if it were still there. By this point most of the dogs are lying on their sides or backs, and the energy of the room has markedly changed. For people whose dogs are especially fidgety, I suggest holding the dog's collar while starting the bodywork, feeding the dog when he offers relaxed positions, and/or bringing a stuffed Kong to class and letting him lick it while the student works on him. Usually by the second or third night all the dogs get it and sit in their handler's lap or lie down without fidgeting.

When the dogs look comfortable and relaxed, I review with the handlers the signs of a calm dog. Beyond the typically prone position, the dog's eyes may be closed or his lids heavy and the bases of his ears relaxed. For a more extensive and detailed list of signs of relaxation, refer to "Reading your dog" on page 37.

Then I ask each student to take five deep breaths and put a hand on her diaphragm so she can really feel her breaths (the other hand should remain on the dog). When all the students look ready, I tell each of them to put both hands back on the dog, and feel his breathing. Don't worry about where the dog is looking or what he is doing. Just feel his breathing. Is it fast and shallow or slow and deep? Is it similar to her own breathing? After becoming aware of their dogs' breathing, the students realize that their own breathing has synchronized with their dogs'.

Sometimes you can also get your dog to hold his breath for a second and exhale by quickly inhaling while he watches your face. Many dogs hold their breath in response to your holding yours, then exhale when you do. Mark and reward your dog for the behavior of catching and holding his breath. If your dog is panting, you can more easily see him catch and hold his breath because he will close his mouth and his cheeks will puff out. In some dogs I'll reward even a slight nostril flare—anything that suggests he caught his breath a little. This technique comes from my invaluable friend and mentor, Dr. Karen Overall.

While doing any type of calming work with your dog, you can always sing, hum, breathe deeply, or make any other soft sound that becomes paired with the work. That way, if your dog starts to get overstimulated, you can cue him to settle down by making that sound.

When the dogs and handlers look ready, I ask each student to close her eyes and, while keeping her hands on her dog, remember the first time she saw her dog. I give her a minute to take in that memory. Then I ask her to think of something her dog does that makes her laugh. Lastly, I ask her to think of something her dog has done that made her proud. I love to watch my students, beaming and chuckling and petting their dogs as they're doing this exercise.

Another passive activity that we don't usually use in class is an "awareness walk." This is not formal heeling, nor circle work, nor is it haphazardly allowing your dog to pull you around and sniff the floor. The walk requires that both team members are aware they are performing a quiet, pleasurable, pressure-free activity together. This is a nice exercise you can do at home before training your dog as well as in a class environment when appropriate (such as CU class in my backyard, which offers plenty of space to walk with your dog among trees, far from the other students). You can also do an awareness walk any time you start to feel frustrated during a training session and need a break. Start by following the instructions on how to be present with your dog. When you feel you are in the zone, leash your dog (if you are in a situation where the leash is necessary) and walk with him. Stay present, stay with your breathing, and just experience moving with him without any agenda or expectation. Let him sniff around as long as he is not pulling you, and keep your focus on him. If he does pull or otherwise disengage, take a breath and stop moving, refocus yourself and notice when he reengages with you. Then restart the walk in that moment when you are both back together. Notice thoughts or environmental stimuli and then let them pass by. I have had some pretty cool walks in the deep woods with my dogs while I am in a trance-like state of feeling connected to them.

To LEASH OR NOT TO LEASH

A square of ring gates plays a huge role in CU. One at a time, I ask each student to enter "the box" and, without any cues or interaction, to simply unclip her dog's leash. Most students want to cheat by subtly cueing the dog to pay attention or sit, thinking I won't notice. I notice. I want to see each dog's immediate response to being let loose without being told what to do. Unfortunately the students who follow my instructions correctly are often disappointed by the result: The dog gets an "I'm free" expression and wanders around the box, sniffing.

After this exercise, I tell my students one of the key concepts behind CU:

Your dog should differentiate between working and not working based on your interaction with him, not based on whether or not he is on leash.

A leash should be a moot point. It should not affect dogs one way or the other. Students need to have clear cues for work time and break time, independent of the leash. They can also use the removal of the leash itself as a cue to work or to play.

In a class environment there are two types of dogs that always go off to explore once unleashed.

- The first type is easy to spot because he's already thinking about it while he's still on leash. He's scoping out his options (just watch his ears and eyes). He may be scanning because he is worrying, or he may be scanning because he's disengaged from his handler and he's looking for stuff to do. The handler is set up to fail but usually is not aware of impending disaster; the connection with her dog simply is not there. This type of handler tends to be exercise oriented and views class as a place to take her dog through his paces. She may view her dog's correct performance of an exercise as evidence of a good relationship. To me, a good relationship means the person and dog deeply understand each other, are highly aware they are working *as a team,* and honor each other's needs as best they can. For the exercise-oriented handler, I focus on just making her more aware of and connected to her dog and his needs. I would rather have such a handler sit and cuddle her dog for seven weeks than do any of the exercises. That might be what it takes to raise her level of awareness to the point where she really "lets her dog in" rather than pushing her dog through his paces.

COOKIE CUTTER DOGS

Unfortunately, I often seen instructors with exercise-oriented tunnel vision insist that each dog and handler team do every exercise the same way as everyone else. It's as if they were in a dog training factory and just looked at the end result as good or bad, rather than looking at the team, assessing what the team member's needs and abilities are, and coming up with a plan that will allow that team to succeed at a particular exercise. So many dogs fall through the cracks in these classes. Some dogs in my classes are so nervous they're not even ready to do an exercise. I just have their handlers massage and feed them and spend some quality time while allowing them to watch the other dogs working. It usually doesn't take long before the nervous dogs are choosing to participate more actively. But each dog needs to proceed at his own pace.

- The second type of dog that reacts strongly to being unleashed is trickier to spot. This is a dog that has good focus on leash but accidentally has been conditioned to believe that being off-leash means he is free to stop working. Typically the dogs that react this way have been trained by older methods that use leashes as training rather than as management tools. When I clicker train dogs, I almost always have them off-leash, so being loose is much less of an issue. My own dogs are so addicted to being trained that I have to give them clear release cues to go away from me and play when I take them to an outdoor space. If I don't, they just hang around hoping, assuming I have work for them to do and food for them to eat or toys for them to play with!

A Big Event

I don't want unclipping your dog's leash to be a big deal to him. Years ago at the park I wanted my dog to earn the privilege of playing based on her behavior. When we got there, I told her to sit and stay, unclipped the leash, and then released her to go play. She exploded into the park and had a great time. I realized years later that this ritual is a misdirected kind of obedience; it conditions dogs to get excited and enjoy running away from you when they are free. In fact it creates (or at least reinforces) the concept of "free" and thus makes unclipping the leash a big event.

Changing perceptions

There are two alternatives that will change the picture for dogs that perceive being loose as a ticket to environmental Disneyland. These alternatives are especially easy to teach puppies because they don't yet have any emotions associated with being leashed or free.

- Teach your dog that being taken off-leash is a nonevent that means absolutely nothing.

- Teach your dog that being taken off-leash is a cue that you are going to do something fabulous with him.

These alternatives are not mutually exclusive. If your dog is aware of your moods and body language, he will know whether to expect a big game or a quiet walk. Or he'll know you released him to go do his own thing. Here are some of the games to play to convert the habitual off-leash runaway into a training addict you can't get rid of.

LEASH EXERCISES

For McDevitt's dogs Snap and Maggie, eye contact has become a default behavior.

Default behaviors

Teach your dog some "default," or automatic, behaviors (my primary ones are eye contact, sit, and down). Whatever behaviors you reward the most will become the defaults. I always wait for my dogs to give a default behavior before I give them dinner, let them out of a crate, or do anything else they are going to enjoy. Default behaviors are not cued; the dogs offer these behaviors because they have a strong reward history for doing so. These are behaviors that the dog automatically gives you when he wants something from you or doesn't know what to do and is asking you for information. The stronger these automatic behaviors are, the more self-control your dog will show. Teaching default behaviors will give your dog some behaviors to immediately offer—and get rewarded for—when he is let off-leash.

Teaching a Default Behavior

Truly conditioned default, or automatic, behaviors can override instinctive behaviors. A default behavior is one that the dog can fall back on when he is upset, frustrated, excited, or just plain wants something he's not getting. A default down is a nice behavior for a dog that has a tendency to leap up and nip. Other default behaviors I like to condition are a sit and eye contact.

1. To condition a default behavior, I reward the dog every time he does the chosen behavior. I reward even when I haven't asked him for it and he's just giving it to see what will happen.

2. Once the dog is regularly offering the behavior, I make access to his primary resources (food dish, going outside, getting to do his favorite activity, such as playing with dogs in the park) dependent on performing the behavior. I don't ask for the behavior. This is critical, because to me the point of conditioning a default behavior is to help the dog start learning the concept of self-control. I want him to be able to think for himself and offer the right behavior for the right context rather than being told what to do. So, to earn primary resources, I wait for the dog to give me the default behavior.

Release cues

Teach your dog a release cue. Don't fall into the trap of making the release seem fun. So many people go for the "Your training session is over—*Woo-hoo!! Hooray!*" Why would you want the end of the session to be more fun for the dog than the session itself? A release should be given in a neutral tone, and be disappointing to the dog. It should have the energy of, "The wonderfulness is over for now. Sorry, honey." My release is an *Okay* with my hands making the universal "All done" sign. My dogs will take either the verbal or the hand cue. Teaching a release cue is important so that you can let your loose dog know when it's okay to go away and do doggie things.

Reorienting points

Your class or trial experience does not begin and end inside the ring. Your dog's behavior getting out of your car in the parking lot, entering the training building or trial grounds, and coming out of a crate are all part of the experience. At each of these "reorienting points" the dogs should focus on you, not on what's out there. It's part of the engagement you need during those twilight times.

First, your dog should learn that when he is at a physical threshold (like a doorway) with something exciting happening on the other side, he needs to wait until you cue him to go through. If your dog rushes toward a door as you open it, calmly shut it. If he doesn't rush at the door, click and treat him. Open the door just a little bit and let him figure out that rushing and disconnecting from you causes the door to shut. He'll soon learn that waiting and orienting to you causes a click, a food reward, and a cue to go out the door. When I teach this form of self-control, I don't cue the dog to sit, stay, look at me, or do anything else. I let the dog figure out what's going to work and what's not. The open door itself becomes the cue to orient to you and give you a behavior. You shouldn't have to keep asking your dog to stay at these reorienting points.

After going through the gate, Easy automatically reorients to McDevitt.

Once your dog has learned this threshold game, you can go on to step two: teaching your dog to orient to you once he has gone through the door or out of the crate. I taught my dogs this behavior by giving them the cue to cross a threshold while I simply stood still. Because they were aware that I had stopped, my dogs turned around to see why I wasn't coming along with them. I clicked and rewarded them for turning around. Now it's become habit. When my dogs go through a door or out of a crate, they turn back toward me. I did not use a leash when I taught this behavior, but for the headstrong bolter, you can put the leash on and just stand there holding it after he has crossed the threshold you're working on. After awhile he will wonder why he isn't going anywhere and turn back to you for information. Click the instant he turns back. Then you can raise your criteria by hiding on the side or behind the crate, so when your dog exits, his job is to find you.

Sacred space

I tell my students that the ring is a sacred space that you and your dog enter as a team. Do not walk your dog into the ring, in practice or at a trial, until both of you feel totally connected, grounded, and ready to read each other's minds as a good team should. Massage, visualization, breath work, circle work, self-control games, structured toy play, and other warm-up activities will help you and your dog prepare to step into the sacred space together.

"I'm gonna get you!"

This rescued American Pit Bull Terrier puppy is learning that a collar touch is associated with yummy treats.

Since some instructors like to hold on to a dog's collar for restrained recalls, and since people in the real world sometimes grab for a dog's collar, for your dog's own peace of mind, he should feel comfortable with being handled by his collar. Teach a collar grab game. Grab your dog's collar and click and treat him. Build a prediction that when you grab your dog's collar it means something nice will happen. Attach a silly cue to it, like *I'm gonna get you!* Make it a running game, using changes of pace and turns and a tug toy or treats. Hold the dog's collar as you start the game, then after a few steps let go but continue the game, then grab it again—it shouldn't matter to the dog if you're holding on or not. What should matter is that you are playing an exciting and reinforcing running game. When your dog is enjoying the game, take the collar off, treat him and keep running, put the collar back on. Some performance venues do not allow dogs to wear collars in the ring. If a dog has issues with getting overaroused (being unable to think and disconnecting when his leash comes off), chances are he will have the same response when his collar comes off as well.

"We don't need no stinkin' leashes!"

I saw this slogan on a t-shirt once. To teach the "We don't need no stinkin' leashes!" game, start by walking or running with your dog on leash. Click and treat him for whatever you want—heel position, turning nicely with you, and so on. When he is engaged in a rewardable activity, drop the leash, but act as if nothing has happened. Just continue the game. You may need to raise your rate of reinforcement when you drop the leash if you have a dog that has an issue with being free. Pick up the leash again, drop it again—it just shouldn't matter. Take it off and continue the game; again, you may have to raise your rate of reinforcement at this juncture. If you play this game at a park and then give a disappointing release ("Sorry, the fabulous game is over so why don't you go sniff that other dog's rear end now") that will make freedom seem like much less of a big event than the old *Sit! Stay!* and exuberant "Okay, I've taken your leash off, so go run away from me and have a blast!"

"But he runs off the second I unclip the leash..."

For dogs that are leash-wise and are going to take off at the speed of light the second you unclip the leash, teach them that unsnapping the leash is paired with a click. Unhook the leash and, as you're doing so, click and scatter food on the ground. You want the dog to orient to the ground rather than looking out at the world. While your dog is eating, start walking away from him. That way, as soon as he finishes and looks up, the first thing he'll see is you walking away. So far, every dog I have tried this experiment with has run to catch up with his handler. When he does, he gets clicked and treated, or a game of chase and tug incorporated into a collar grab game, or the We don't need no stinkin' leashes! game, and then the release. Every time you unclip the leash, remember to click and throw food on the ground, and walk confidently away. Then expect a good game to come out of it. I play these games within barriers in my CU class with an assistant and me standing ready to handle would-be escape artists. We micromanage the environment and set up the dogs for success.

Hoping for a clicker game (left), Cayenne focuses on her handler as he unclips the leash. Once unleashed (right), Cayenne scans the ground for treats. When she looks up, she will see her handler walking away and hurry to catch up with him.

Leash comes off, toy comes out

Many people teach their dogs this pattern without even realizing it by taking out a Frisbee or ball as soon as they let the dog loose. For dogs that have tons of play drive, that is all you need to do. When the leash comes off, the toy comes out. For dogs more motivated by food, you can teach them that when the leash comes off, it is an opportunity for them to earn a food reward. You can reward any offered behaviors that you like or give cues for behaviors the dog enjoys such as barking or jumping up, or play the collar or leash game. The dog should be enjoying the activity and receiving a high rate of reinforcement until you give that disappointing, boring release cue. And, of course, whenever the dog checks in with you, he gets rewarded generously until you give the disappointing release cue again. *Always* release the dog *before* he wants to leave.

Ticker knows that when the leash comes off, the Frisbee comes out.

If you incorporate some of these games into your daily routines, pretty soon you will have created a training addict that doesn't lose his mind the second he loses his leash.

MANAGEMENT

When students want to take a break from working, to watch a friend's run, or to listen to their instructor, management is a good option. A dog that knows the Go to Place behavior (discussed on page 98) can lie on his mat quietly next to your chair. For dogs that aren't ready for this step, crating is a great option. I caution each student to make sure her dog has cooled down if he has been running or working hard before being crated, to avoid cramps. The dog should also have a stuffed Kong or bone or interactive toy so he has something to occupy himself, if he chooses. Crating works best as a management tool when your dog knows the rules.

Calm behavior opens the crate door

Dogs should understand that barking, scratching, and any other excited behaviors will not buy them freedom from their crate. This should be the rule at home, in the training building, or at a trial. Only quiet, calm behavior will work. I show the students that when I open Snap's crate, he remains inside—no matter what I am doing—until verbally released. There are always several crates in the classroom so people can practice. I tell students to simply start opening the crate a crack, and if the dog tries to rush out, to shut the door without any fanfare. When the dog gives any alternative behavior or any hesitation, he gets clicked and treated. Soon the dogs are remaining in the crate with the door open. Then I show the second piece of crate management: what your dog should do when he exits the crate.

Reorienting to your handler is the ticket to going anywhere

I don't like to see any student let her dog out of a crate without a release cue and then stand there at the end of a tight leash while her dog (totally unaware of his handler) takes in the show. When I release Snap from his crate, he flies out, spins around in midair, and lands in a sit in front of me. His style is never to have four feet on the ground at once if he can help it. But for my students, any version of the dog's turning back toward his handler, rather than scanning the environment, is fine. This critical step is easy to teach. I have each student leash her dog while still in the crate. Then, as she calls him out, she just stands there and does nothing. The dog may come out and look around, and when he finally thinks to turn around and say, "Why aren't we moving, mom?" he gets clicked and treated for reorienting to his handler. Only then does he get to rejoin the class. Dogs learn this reorienting behavior quickly and easily. I don't care if they sit. I am clicking them for turning back to their handlers.

Management for the hypervigilant dog

On being released from his crate, Snap automatically spins around and orients to McDevitt.

For super-reactive dogs that get frantic coming out of a crate, I do things differently, since waiting for a hypervigilant dog to turn around could take all day and his nervous system doesn't need all that time to fuel up. But these dogs are not dogs I would accept into CU class without a lot of previous private work. With the super-reactive dog, I do steps from the Protocol for Relaxation while he is crated, until he learns to feel relaxed in his crate. I incorporate the behaviors of waiting with the crate door open and reorienting upon leaving the crate into the protocol. Once the dog is out of the crate, I do some of the bodywork and mat work that we will cover later. Then I set up a situation (possibly using ring gates or other barriers) where he can come out of his crate while still under threshold and create a reliable ritual. For instance, "Every time you leave a crate, I will toss a handful of food on the ground for you. Then you go to your relaxation mat and I will toss another handful of food on the mat while you get a massage. Then you get clicked for looking at other dogs so you can see who's around you in a very structured way."

THE GREAT DE-BAIT

I have noticed that the majority of CU students show up for class with bait bags displayed prominently on their belts. I do not see this many bait bags in any of our agility classes, and I don't think this is a coincidence. Some of the dogs have already learned that when the bait bag is out, it's time to work; and when it's not, it's time to disengage. The presence or absence of bait bags accidentally can become environmental cues just as leashes and collars can. Dogs are experts at differentiating. That's why a dog can behave completely differently depending on who is handling him, or appear friendly to a hatless person until she puts on a hat, and then all hell breaks loose. Dogs that are used to seeing bait bags all the time and relying on those bags as their reward source are much less likely to want to work when they don't see the bags. The bag is like a constant lure, and any clicker trainer will tell you that if you're using a lure to get a behavior you want, you'd better fade it fast before the dog only performs the behavior when the lure is present.

Some people who are working on increasing a dog's play/prey drive use the bait bag as a tug toy before delivering the food reward. That is a great use of a bait bag, but it doesn't mean the bag has to be on your belt all the time.

So it's not bait bags per se, but how they are used, that elicits a rant from me. If you are using a bait bag as a constant lure—*put it away!* If you say to yourself, "But my dog won't perform without it," then I've proved my point! Put your treats in your pocket. Tease a behavior out of your dog, and give him the reward from your pocket. When he's comfortable with that step, put the bag on a chair—separated by a baby gate or ring gate if you're at a training building—or a high shelf. Get some behaviors out of your dog and then take him to the chair, or shelf, or whatever, and reward.

If your dog can't perform a behavior because he is ignoring you and trying to get to the bait bag, do not despair. I'll address this problem when I talk about teaching Leave It. If your dog is working well with the reward in the room but not on your person, then it's time to really hide it. Your dog should trust that something good will happen as a result of his behavior, without having to know where that something good is. Environmental rewards are useful here too—behaviors earn freedom from crates. Behaviors earn access to playmates, or access to the backyard. The more variable the rewards, the less the dog can predict what he is getting and where it's coming from. He should just trust that you're going to provide, and leave the rest to you. Also, the more you intersperse play rewards or environmental rewards with food rewards, the less of an issue a bait bag becomes.

Usually I prefer that a student reward a dog in the position she wanted, such as on a contact, but if the dog needs to learn to work without having food or a bag visible, then teaching him that the reward is somewhere out there (and he'll get it afterwards) is a good idea. You don't want your dog turning off in the ring because you're not wearing his bait bag!

THE BALLET OF TEAMWORK

I want my students to get a feeling of what it's like to move completely in sync with their dogs so they develop that sense of the teamwork that should rule when they enter the sacred space of the ring. This exercise ends up looking more like interpretive dance than ballet—sometimes it looks more like performance art! Many students let their dogs move ahead of them and sniff the floor as they walk into my little box of ring gates. That is not a good way to start an exercise. When it's their turn in class, I want my students to keep that feeling of being in sync in mind. If they're not feeling it, they're not going to get the optimum performance out of their dog. If they're not feeling it, they need to take a minute to reconnect. (On the first night, if a dog is so distracted he can't pay attention at all, I often play the Give Me a Break game I describe in Night Four, page 148, and guide his handler through the steps to gain his focus.)

TEAMWORK EXERCISE IN THE BOX

To play this game I double-leash the dogs. The handler has the regular leash, and I put a slip lead over the dog's head so I have a second leash. The dog should be exactly in between the handler and me as we walk around the inside edge of the square. Sometimes I have my assistant do the walking so that I can stand outside the ring and click when I see two humans and one canine moving in perfect synchrony. I am not clicking just the dog here, I am clicking the team. Since both humans are moving along the path of a square, they have to figure out who is going to take the

Scorch, CU assistant Brown's American Pit Bull Terrier, is double-leashed for the teamwork exercise. He shows good attention to his handler as she and McDevitt guide him into a right turn.

initiative to turn. To keep the dog in the middle, one person will have to turn in toward the dog and other handler while the dog and other handler will have to move back a few paces. The name of the game is moving together effortlessly while keeping the dog in the middle on a loose leash.

Sometimes the dog gets excited and pulls. When this happens, I have the people stop and wait for the dog to turn back to them. When the dog reorients to them, the leash slackens, and the people can start moving again. One person is in charge of clicking (unless I am clicking the team on the outside) and one is in charge of treating. If a dog gets confused at being in between people, he may need to be treated just for sitting or standing in the middle before you start moving. He may need to work on moving in a straight line rather than turning.

Having a strange human standing next to the sweet but shy Weimaraner Arial frightened her, so I just asked my assistant to stand near Arial while her handler treated her until she was more comfortable. Then my assistant and the handler took turns feeding her. Eventually she perked up a little, understanding that she was playing a game where people on both sides of her took turns giving her treats, and that no demands were being placed on her other than just being there. That's all we did with her for that exercise.

When both humans and the dog get this exercise right, it is lovely to watch. The instructor can keep raising criteria, directing faster or tighter turns, pace changes, figure eights, and so on. On the flip side, invariably somebody will end up all flustered and tangled up in a leash, and that's okay. We laugh a lot during CU.

BEGINNING OF BOX WORK

Box work is usually the last exercise I do on the first night. Everybody gets a turn to move about with her dog on leash within the little box of ring gates. As the weeks go on, I refine this "moving about" into circle work and turns, with the dog on either

At left, a handler does box work with her Weimaraner Arial on leash and with the box of ring gates closed. Arial is comfortable with her job in the ring and is ready for the modification of dogs lying on their mats near the gates. The Sheltie Boing! relaxes and watches her handler, but the Labrador Ranger feels fidgety and wants to get off her mat. Ranger needs more distance from the box. At right, as a further modification, McDevitt has removed the ring gates that served as a barrier between Arial and the dogs lying on their mats. Because this modification makes it more difficult for Arial to stay focused, her handler feeds Arial close to where Boing! and her handler are lying. Ranger has settled back on her mat.

side of the handler. In later weeks, I start adding distractions such as a person walking outside the box or dogs lying on mats outside the ring (see "Box Work Modifications," page 82).

Box work provides a major opportunity for students to sharpen their timing and dog-reading skills. The two major criteria (for the handler, not the dog) are rate of reinforcement and click for orienting.

Rate of reinforcement

Most everybody that has taken this course has really needed to work on her rate of reinforcement. Many students don't realize how critical the rate of reinforcement is in changing a dog's behavior. I have seen many a dog transformed from a distracted floor-sniffer to an avid, heads-up heeler within a couple minutes just because his handler understood the power of rate of reinforcement. *Click often, and click everything you can.* Many students wait for what they consider to be perfect behavior before they click. In the process they miss dozens of opportunities to give feedback and help the dog understand the intended direction of his behavior. Being stingy and slow to give feedback will not motivate a dog that prefers sniffing the floor to interacting with his handler. To reinforce well, you must really watch your dog so you can catch every possible second of rewardable behavior. Learning how to *watch your dog* is one of the hallmarks of this class. In turn, your dog will be *learning to watch you* as he becomes engaged in this game of behavior and feedback. Often I walk outside the box, clicking whenever I see fit. I click about a hundred more times than the average student because I notice tiny things that many handlers miss. They are looking for heel position; I am looking for any kind of orienting to handler, which brings us to criterion number two.

Click for orienting

Any desirable behavior (read: anything that's not outright naughty) is clickable within the box, and the more you click and reward, the more attention and enthusiasm you're going to get from your partner. But there is one particular thing I want my students to be on the lookout for: orienting to the handler. This means that every time your dog even vaguely notices you, you are going to click him. If the dog starts getting distracted, notices something in the environment, you are going to wait. The second your dog reorients to you, that's what you'll click. I want each student to become adept at noticing when her dog is even slightly tuned in (even if the dog wasn't directly looking at her handler, but her handler made a soft sound and his ears responded); even ear movement can be clicked. Perhaps the dog's handler changed directions or stopped moving and the dog's pattern also changed even if he wasn't staring at his handler. That behavior, too, is the dog showing awareness and should be marked.

When the handler has achieved these two major criteria of box work, she may start letting the leash drag. If the dog is still meeting both criteria as the leash is dragging, the handler may take the leash off. Sometimes a dog is not ready to move within the box right away. I ask the student to reward her dog for the same exercises as the others while remaining in one place. She then does the leash work with the dog stationary before graduating to starting over again with the dog moving.

Box Work Modifications

The following modifications can be used throughout the course depending on each team's progress.

1) Decreasing the rate of reinforcement

As the dog becomes comfortable with the box work, his handler can decrease the rate of reinforcement. Every time I raise criteria, however, such as adding another dog or taking away a gate, the rate of reinforcement should increase.

2) Adding distractions outside/inside the box

I may walk or run along the outside of the box, either alone or with another dog. I may ask a student to heel her dog around the outside of the box, gradually working up to running him around the outside. I may actually go into the box and leave a treat (or toy) on the ground, which I can easily step on if a dog misses his Leave It cue. I may go in and take the dog from his handler, get him revved up and leave. This gives his handler an opportunity to work on a heightened arousal level in a controlled context. (What can the handler do? Go back to passive or active attention exercises, send the dog to his mat, or reward soft eyes and blinking.)

3) Removing ring gates

Once the dog and handler have the basics down, I make a space between two gates so there is an escape route. If the dog has no problem with this step, I start removing ring gates, once at a time. As the team progresses I continue removing gates until the dog is working loose, doing circle work throughout the classroom.

4) Using other dogs

I put a dog that can lie calmly on his mat on the other side of a gate from a dog that is working. Some dogs will ignore the other dog; others will be distracted. For the distracted dogs, handlers can play a Look at That! game (page 122) or merely raise their rate of reinforcement and lower their criteria so their dog can succeed in front of that gate. When the dog is working within his box and has no interest in the dog on the mat, I start removing gates, working toward removing the gate between the dogs. Alternatively, instead of removing gates, I can start adding more dogs on mats. Ultimately what I want from this exercise is for the dog to move with and attend to his handler loose, while doing circle work around a room populated with dogs lying on mats. The series of photos on page 20 shows Brown and her teenage Doberman Jynx performing an increasingly challenging form of box work—without the box and with the distraction of two other dogs.

Chapter 4

NIGHT TWO

CONCEPTS

- Playing with stimulation levels
- Active attention: Transitioning from passive to active work
- Recognizing when to drop the leash
- Balancing environmental challenges and performance criteria

NEW EXERCISES

- Active attention exercises:
  - o Doggie Zen
  - o Leave It (stationary and moving)
  - o Targeting (stationary and moving; building up to remote object targeting)
  - o Go to Place
- Starting start-line stays

Reminder: Continue working on passive attention and box work at the beginning of each class, raising criteria as appropriate for each dog.

My students take me seriously during Night One when I tell them I expect them to do the passive attention work by themselves without being reminded for the remainder of the course. On the second night, I walk into my classroom happily since the students each have found their spot and are massaging their dogs that for the most part are lying quietly on their mats or beds.

PLAYING WITH STIMULATION LEVELS

Once the students and dogs have gone through some passive attention work and are looking calm, I raise criteria by telling the students to move their dogs closer to each other. I don't want handlers to get their dogs feeling calm and then suddenly pop up without warning and move the dogs closer to each other. That would set up any dog in class that is sensitive to sudden changes in the environment to have a reaction. So I ask each student to make a plan about how she is going to get up and move without changing the energy in the room too much. Then the students start to get up slowly while continuing to massage their dogs, inviting their dogs to get up with them, then feeding their dogs for paying attention (for some dogs, feeding continuously to prevent them from flying off the handle or starting to bark is enough!), and move closer to each other. I orchestrate the move, choosing which dogs should be closer or farther away from others. Students take their mats with them and put them down in the new spot. I then ask the students to get back on the floor and do some more passive attention work while the dogs get used to being in this new situation, closer to other dogs. The goal is to get the dogs calm again after this brief spike in stimulation.

WHEN REAL LIFE RUDELY INTRUDES

The typical CU dog has a response to sudden changes in the environment. This response can manifest as anything from noticing the change and being concerned for a second to wild barking and lunging. We practice counterconditioning our dogs' responses within the class structure, but without foundation work, they are not ready to handle a sudden environmental change (SEC) "cold." After a lot of controlled, subthreshold exposure the CU class should give these dogs and their handlers a foundation to deal with these sorts of situations in the future. For example, I occasionally have a decoy enter the room and walk around so people can practice calmly communicating, "Yes, there is a sudden environmental change. No big deal. Have a cookie." The dogs should come to equate unexpected events that might startle them with something of high value from their handlers. Once an association has been made, the handlers can use either the Look at That! rule structure (page 122) or just click sustained direct focus, depending on the dog and on the context.

Every time a dog comes out of a crate in class, he provides a sudden environmental change for the other dogs. Some will worry but quickly recover on their own, some will habituate quickly, and others will continually need their handlers to be vigilant and always ready to pair the SEC with something of high value. I can control the types of SEC we have in class. I warn the handlers that things are about to change, and remind them to prepare their dog before the dog has a chance to even think about reacting. My students get a lot of practice dealing with SEC. Of course, real life happens, even in CU, but students with reactive dogs need to learn how to recondition their dogs' responses, or at the very least manage their dogs, so that SEC becomes a predictor that the dog goes into his crate and gets something nice there.

Later in the course (or even on the second night, depending on the group of dogs) we can play the Pop-up game. In this game the students purposely get their dogs up quickly and disruptively from the mats and then settle back down for body-work, then suddenly pop up again. The Pop-up game is a version of what I call an "off-switch game" that we discuss in detail on page 154. These games allow the dog to reach a certain level of arousal and then get rewarded for calming down before resuming activity. Periods of calm interspersed with arousing play will help your dog

At the start of each class (at left), students massage their dogs as a warm-up to active attention exercises, gradually moving closer to each other as the dogs get more comfortable. When the dogs are comfortable, McDevitt can sit Snap in the middle of the class (middle image) and eventually run an unleashed Snap right through the class (at right). A dog like Snap that worries about being near strange dogs had to work up to the challenge of running unleashed through a group of dogs on mats. In fact, this challenge is a form of advanced box work—moving off-leash and without ring-gate barriers among other dogs.

learn to focus through his excitement and will make it easier for him to settle down after stimulating activity. When the dogs are all cool with their new proximity to the next dog, often I raise criteria again by walking Snap among them. Then I ask my students to move a little farther away from each other so I can start them on the active attention exercises. Since for most dogs the active work is more stimulating than the passive work, I want the dogs to have more space when initially learning the active exercises. As with the passive work, I gradually move the dogs closer and closer until at some point during the course they are all doing the active work on top of each other, most of them off-leash.

ACTIVE ATTENTION: TRANSITIONING FROM PASSIVE TO ACTIVE WORK

These exercises are mostly about targeting. Their purpose is to help with focus and impulse control, warming the dog up for the more intense attention he will need to give his handler when it's his turn to work, in an agility environment or other classes. These exercises are meant

- To key the dog into his handler's body (eye contact, hand targeting, getting into heel position on both sides, moving with the handler).

- To give something for the dog to focus on while he is working off-leash at a distance (Go to Place).

- To remind the dog about the need to control his impulses (Leave It).

Most of the targeting exercises give the dog a body part (eyes, sides, hands) to target. Thus, as the handler moves his dog around the other dogs, interaction with the handler's body keeps the dog focused. If the dog is focused on a body part, you don't need a leash to keep him near you. Targeting exercises also give a dog something to think about that helps diminish his attention to the distractions around him. This works for humans as well.

TARGETS FOR THE OVERSTIMULATED DRIVER

I get overstimulated driving on busy highways. It is an unpleasant and sometimes scary experience for me. Once I accompanied my friend Deb to an elementary school to do an agility and Frisbee demo as a reward for the children, who had won an academic award and were promised a big surprise. I usually get to be a passenger in these types of situations, but this day we had enough equipment and dogs to fill Deb's huge van and my station wagon, so I, too, had to drive. I was worried but told myself, "This is going to be a target-training exercise. I am going to focus on Deb's huge bright red van in front of me, all the way to this school." It wasn't fun, but I did it.

~~~~~~

Think about it: A lot of agility is also about targeting. Each obstacle is a target that the dog needs to interact with in a specific way. Each weave pole is a target that the dog needs to pass with his head on one side or the other. Contacts are target behaviors. Tugging is a target behavior as is "going to your station" or the Look at That! game described in Night Three (page 121). So much of life is targeting. Targeting gives our dogs and us a structure for the rules of engagement with the environment and other beings.

There are many more options for active attention, such as tricks or heeling. Some tricks have the side benefit of a physical warm-up, such as standing on the hind legs, taking a bow, weaving in and out of handler's legs, and spinning in both directions. You can use any trick your dog enjoys performing on cue as an active attention exercise. You also can use the Look at That! game as an active attention exercise. All of the active attention exercises are good transitions into more arousing work such as Off-switch games involving intense toy play.

If I feel it's necessary, I start the active exercises while students remain seated with their dogs on mats and slowly switch into some standing exercises. If the dogs are calm enough as a group that everybody can just get up and start working, we go straight to stand-up exercises.

When I started teaching CU, all the students had taken at least one obedience class with Y2K9s. Thus the dogs already knew some of the behaviors we use in CU because I teach these behaviors in our puppy and beginner obedience courses. Those behaviors are Doggie Zen, Leave It, Go to Place, and Targeting. Now that so many students come from elsewhere to take the course, I sometimes have to take time out to teach these behaviors. All of the behaviors I just mentioned can be used as active attention exercises. A key CU behavior and active attention exercise that is not taught in our obedience courses is the Look at That! game described in Chapter 5. Another is getting into heel position on the handler's left and right sides.

ACTIVE ATTENTION EXERCISES

Doggie Zen

I see this popular training game as a two-for-the-price-of-one exercise. Its purpose is to start teaching the dog the concept of self-control while simultaneously teaching eye contact. I think it's a nice focus warm-up for any activity. If your dog has a serious arousal problem, you can incorporate biofeedback into Doggie Zen, rewarding soft, sleepy eye contact.

Teaching Doggie Zen

I start with the Doggie Zen game to get the dogs focused. Most people know some form of this game. I do not put a cue on eye contact; I expect it to be a default behavior. I expect dogs to watch their handlers in class unless they are

- Cued to do otherwise.

- Enjoying a passive attention activity.

- Crated

- Officially released to do what they want.

At this point in the course I use food for dogs that are not ready for the excitement of a toy and that are still just getting used to being close to each other. I ask each student to hold a treat away from her face and wait for the dog to look away from the treat, toward her face. If the dog jumps up or in any way moves toward the treat, the student is to put the treat behind her back. For dogs that are new to this game, I reward any flicker of an eye away from the treat. You can continue raising criteria until the dog will make prolonged eye contact the second he sees a treat or anything else he wants. I often tell students to think of themselves as a gateway to resources. The dog goes through the handler to get something he wants. The dog's behavior is like a key that opens the gateway and causes you to give access. Dogs are starting to learn this concept with the Doggie Zen exercise. It is also a foundation concept for teaching self-control.

Leave It

Teaching a rock-solid Leave It behavior is essential for any self-control program. This behavior helps dogs learn to control their impulses both on and off the agility field and in a million real-life situations (leave that dead squirrel carcass at the park, leave those other dogs, leave the pies on the picnic blanket, leave the kid who is afraid of dogs, leave the jogger/biker/cat/rodeo clown).

I just love teaching Leave It. I especially love teaching it to dogs whose handlers loudly insist it can't be done. They say, "You can't teach that to a terrier/scent hound/insert dog breed here." I like to pick the dog whose handler is the most adamant that the dog can't be taught and show her how fast her dog *can* learn it. Here's how I like to teach it.

Teaching Leave It

1. Make sure your dog has at least one strong default behavior, so he has something to offer you when his instinctive behaviors (such as digging under your shoe for the treat) aren't working.

This is the first time Savvy, a 10-week-old Whippet, has encountered a treat under a shoe and initially she tries to get it out from under the shoe. She will learn that when she offers any behavior that is not about trying to get the treat, she will get a reward.

2. Also make sure your dog knows the Doggie Zen game where he looks away from a treat and makes eye contact with you, since this is the foundation for Leave It.

3. Put a treat under your shoe without asking the dog to do anything, and let the dog try to get it. Click and treat any tiny piece of behavior that isn't about trying to get under your shoe. Eventually the dog understands that he is in a bizarre world where everything is the opposite of his expectations: He gets food by leaving it alone, not by trying to take it. The dog either starts giving you his primary default behavior or whatever behavior you have ended up shaping by rewarding those little pieces of behavior where he hesitated, looked away from your foot, or took a step back.

4. Put the treat next to your shoe and quickly start feeding the dog while he remains in default mode. You want him to get used to seeing a treat on the floor (that you can cover with your foot if he makes a move toward it) while being fed from another source (you).

5. When your dog is okay with that step, crouch down and, from 6" off the floor, start slowly dropping the treat next to your foot. Continue to click and treat any "legal" behavior from the dog. Gradually build to dropping the treat from a greater height,

then start throwing it farther away from your foot. The sequence should be:

- Place the treat on the floor.

- Drop the treat from increasing heights.

- Throw the treat, increasing the distance.

Note: I never release the dog to take the treat from the floor. I either give him something of equal or greater value from my pocket, or I pick up the treat from the floor and give it to him.

6. If the dog at this point decides to go for it, be ready to move fast. It will end up looking like a game of Twister. Once you are able to throw the food a distance from your foot while the dog offers a sit or a down and is just watching you waiting for his treat, add the cue. Start saying *Leave It* as you throw the treat.

7. Start putting the treat closer and closer to the dog.

8. Start dropping multiple treats (talk about having to be ready to play Twister!).

9. When the dog's ready, start moving Leave Its, which I also call the "Level 2 Leave It." Walk around with the dog, give the cue, and place the treat right by your shoe. Since this is such a different picture from what you have been doing, don't expect the dog to generalize (occasionally a dog will). You can continue raising criteria with moving Leave Its until you're running around, getting the dog excited, and throwing a handful of food right in his face. I like demonstrating this step with Snap—I have literally thrown handfuls of meat right in his face, and he just stands there as if nothing has happened. This was a dog that, when I first adopted him, leapt up on all the counters like a cat and ate anything he could find. Once I caught him standing with all four paws in the kitchen sink, eating a sponge.

10. You can also practice Leave It by placing the food on top of a crate, a coffee table, any place within reach where a real life resource might be left that you don't want your dog to take for himself.

11. The Level 3 Leave It is closer to approximating real life. Leave food on the floor while the dog is in a different room or crated where he can't see what you are doing. Bring in the dog. I don't use a leash to teach any of this (just my foot to cover the food when necessary) so by the time I raise criteria this high, I really trust that the dog will be able to succeed. If he's tempted, it will be a race between him and the shoe.

In the early stages of Leave It training, Easy has learned to ignore the single hotdog on the floor (left) to get a treat from McDevitt's hand (middle). Easy is learning that just because the food is on the ground doesn't mean he should take it and that the available food comes from McDevitt. She remains close by. Snap (right) can maintain focus, even when surrounded by hotdogs, with McDevitt a good distance away.

Of course you are not limited to food when teaching Leave It. For tug or ball fiends, Leave It is a wonderful way to teach impulse control. And it's another great application of the Premack Principle; dogs leave the toy alone on cue so you give it back (or send them to get it)!

Leave It is a critical component in my teaching of a solid recall, as is something I call the "Whiplash Turn." This behavior is the first thing I teach my own puppies since it builds a recall foundation and teaches them to orient to their name all at once.

Lightbulb Moment: A Kinder, Gentler Leave It

For many years I taught Leave It as a collar-correction exercise. It was a holdover from my years of traditional training, and even after I went over to clicker training, I relied on pure force of will to take the dog away from a desired object. Leslie introduced a new approach to Leave It in our obedience program at Y2K9s.

I watched her teach it to classes and decided to teach it to my BC pup, Shiner. She learned it in five minutes and was leaving her Frisbee in flight to turn back to me. I started using a system of leaving toys around the agility field and releasing her to get them as her rewards. I use it in teaching high-drive behaviors, where she wants the toy and races toward it but performs an agility behavior correctly before being allowed to get it. I love this system and feel it is one of the pillars of my training.

—Deb

The Whiplash Turn

The Whiplash Turn is a foundation behavior in any obedience course I teach. It is a great behavior to have in CU as well. The Whiplash Turn, combined with use of the Premack Principle and a rock solid Leave It are key elements of my recall training. When asking a dog to attend to you if he is doing something else:

- First, he needs to be able to disengage from what he was doing (Leave It).

- Second, he needs to reorient to you (Whiplash Turn).

- Third, he needs to return to you quickly.

This is where you use chase-me games, high-value reinforcers, and, of course, the Premack Principle (come away from X and I will send you right back to X, see page 51). I see a recall as a chain of behaviors to perfect separately. It's not just getting the dog to run back to you. Many of the exercises in CU strengthen the various recall behaviors.

1. *Getting the head turn.* The Whiplash Turn is so named because I want to condition a dog to whip around toward his handler at the speed of light upon hearing his name or any other cue to orient. For a dog that has gotten the chance to practice ignoring his name a million times, I give him a nickname that his handler should use only as a cue for the Whiplash Turn. I stand right behind the dog's ear as he is occupied with something and looking away from me and say the name while staring at his neck. The nanosecond I see that neck start to swivel the head in my direction, I click. The timing of the click, or whatever mark you are using, is critical here because it is the behavior of turning the neck that I am focusing on.

At the sound of his name, Easy immediately disengages from play with Rosie the Malinois, whips his head around, and barrels back to McDevitt.

2. *Adding distance and distractions.* Once the dog is whipping around at the sound of his name, you can call him from farther away. You still mark the turn, but you can then start running so he has to catch up to you for his reward—and at that time you can incorporate a chase game into the picture. The Whiplash Turn is good for recalls at a

distance as well as asking your dog to orient to you away from something that's captured his attention while you are standing right behind him (for instance, when you're out on a walk or in class).

If you want your dog to attend to you during the ring-gate box exercise or any other exercise, you can *wait for* him to reorient and reward that with a continuation of the training game; or you can *ask* him to reorient. If you ask, be sure you mark that Whiplash Turn behavior!

Targeting

Targeting is so easy to teach and has so many excellent applications. It helps a dog learn to focus on a specific object and block out distractions. It teaches distance work and reinforces attention at the same time. As the dog gains confidence working farther and farther away he is still engaged in a feedback loop with his handler. It enables a stressed dog to move through crowds or across a classroom because he can focus on something safe. If you think of the obstacles as targets for the dog to be sent to and interact with, targeting also becomes a foundation agility behavior.

Having a dog that will target your hand from a distance not only gives the distracted or reactive dog something to focus on when in motion among other dogs; but also is a primary tool for moving the dog around an agility course. Here, McDevitt takes advantage of Easy's hand target training to teach him the position she wants him to find after exiting the tunnel.

Teaching your dog to target your hand

1. Hold your hand (or thumb, or a couple of fingers) near your dog's face and wait for him to sniff or touch it. The second he does, click and give him a treat from your other hand. (Do not keep a treat in the hand your dog is targeting; he needs to learn to touch an empty hand.) Decide exactly what your criteria are going to be: A gentle nose touch or a muzzle touch? How much force do

you want your dog to use? Do you care if he gives an open-mouth vs. a closed-mouth touch?

Hint: For a dog with arousal issues that uses his mouth a lot, teaching a gentle nose touch is preferable. Otherwise, if you ask for a hand target when he is feeling fired up, you're going to get what I call the "shark touch."

2. Repeat presenting your hand and clicking and treating when your dog touches it. Gradually move your hand slightly so that he has to turn his head one way or the other to reach it.

3. When he's solid on one hand, switch hands and repeat.

4. Once your dog is moving his head right, left, up, or down to touch your hand, you can add a verbal *Touch* cue—although the hand itself being offered in the target position is an obvious cue.

5. Then start moving away from your dog, with your target hand clearly inviting the dog to touch. Build to the point where you can yell *Touch* and run with your target hand out and your dog will enthusiastically race to you and target your hand (showing impulse control by lightly tapping you with his nose).

Note: Some people teach a hand cue for stay that resembles the hand cue I use for touch. Make sure your touch hand cue looks totally different from your stay hand cue. Instead of showing the dog a flat palm as I do, you can teach a finger touch, a fist touch, a peace sign touch, and so on.

I use a hand touch to teach dogs the heel position on the right and left and for the Get In exercise during the active attention phase. This is totally straightforward. Once the dog understands hand targeting, start with him in front of you and show him where you want him to go by making a loop with your hand for him to follow until his head ends up in heel position on the appropriate side. Loop your right hand clockwise and your left hand counterclockwise.

At a later point in the course I teach dogs to go to remote targets. Using remote targets such as the Go to Place mat and jump standards for Get Outs helps the dog stay focused on a task while working away from his handler. Later, with the Out 'n Mats game, I make a maze of mats and standards and send the dogs zigzagging around each other focused on their targets, much as I focused on Deb's van. The first step in teaching your dog to work away from you is to teach him to touch a target on the floor.

Teaching the floor target

Once your dog is well versed in the Touch game, put a neutral object in your hand. Go through the steps above to train him to touch the neutral object. Then put it on the floor right under your dog's nose. Wait for the dog to lower his head toward it, click, and reward. Your dog will soon be touching the object on the floor. Then start increasing distance. Once you are sure that your dog will move toward the object, start putting it farther away a couple of feet at a time. While your dog is returning to you for his reward, take some steps back as you feed him so that the next time he has to run a little bit farther to reach the target. Add the verbal cue when you feel your dog is ready. Alternatively, use different verbal cues for touching your hand and touching an object. Some people feel this distinction is important; others don't. My own dogs haven't gotten confused when I've used a single cue for both.

Another option is to reinforce the dog at the target rather than feeding him when he returns to you. It depends on what your ultimate goal is; both ways work fine. The goal for using target objects in CU is two-fold:

1. A target gives the dog something to focus on while he is loose.

2. A target keeps him in a feedback loop when he is moving away from, but still interacting with, his owner off-leash.

You can teach your dog to target your hand or to touch an object like this target stick.

TARGETING TO BUILD CONFIDENCE IN THE SHY DOG

I often use targeting with dogs that are uncertain about meeting people. If you give a shy dog a rule structure that he feels comfortable with, he feels empowered to choose to approach and interact with a stranger. You can train a shy dog to focus on just a body part rather than the whole person, or on an object the person is holding that the dog already has a reinforcement history with. For instance, if you have rewarded your dog a hundred times for touching Mr. Teddy Bear or an upside-down jar of peanut butter (that can be flipped over so the dog can take a lick after hitting his target), you can probably send him to touch Mr. Teddy Bear or a peanut butter jar that is near or being held by a stranger.

McDevitt's Belgian Tervuren Rumor demonstrates targeting a peanut butter jar. A shy dog gains confidence in approaching scary people if the person holds an object the dog has been trained to target.

Rather than having a person walk up to the dog, which puts too much pressure on the dog, the dog can now choose to go up to the person to touch the body part or object and return to his owner for a treat. This way, his interaction with the person is brief and always predicts a good thing. Often I have worked with dogs that snap (or worse) when rude strangers approach them on the street or in the park and stick a hand out toward the dog. My Maggie used to shriek and snap at children until she learned to view them as target objects that she could interact with in some way (sit in front of them, put her nose on their shoe, and so on) to earn a treat. Ultimately she was able to tolerate being petted by strange kids at pet expos and trials. One of the things I do to help dogs cope with strangers who insist on waving hands near them is to teach them the hand target behavior. Then as a person's hand reaches toward such a dog, his owner can give the *Touch* cue to remind the dog of that fun game he gets to play when he sees hands near his face. The more comfortable the dog becomes with the rule structure and doing the Touch behavior with anyone, the better chance he has of generalizing it to rude strangers who offer an outstretched hand. Dogs that are upset by hands reaching toward them can benefit greatly from this sneaky little reframing.

Go to Place

The Go to Place exercise teaches your dog to go to a specific location on cue and remain there in a sit or down until verbally released. The Go to Place behavior is also a targeting behavior, but the dog is using his entire body to interact with the target object (mat) rather than just his nose or muzzle.

McDevitt's dogs (Rumor, Snap, and Maggie) and cat (Harley Quinn) wait on their Go to Place mats until released.

Training Go to Place

1. Get a mat, blanket, dog bed, or towel—one that your dog has not seen before—and examine it as if it were the most interesting thing in the world. Then, without saying anything to your dog, put it on the floor near you. The second that your dog shows any interest (by looking at it, sniffing it, putting a paw on it), click or verbally mark the behavior, and put a treat on the mat.

2. As long as your dog continues to interact with the mat, keep on marking behaviors and putting treats on the mat. A dog that has been shaped before will quickly start offering various behaviors to see what gets rewarded. Any behavior offered on the mat is worthy. My preference is a down, but I also want to reward sits or any other behaviors the dog is offering on the mat. So I use at least two kinds of treats when I train Go to Place. The highest value treat is for downs, the lesser value is for anything else. That way a dog does not learn that any behavior on the mat is wrong or unrewardable but that a down gets the better reward. It took my last puppy about three minutes to figure out that downs on a mat got cheese-flavored popcorn while sits on a mat got kibble; it was downs from then on.

Hint: If the dog gives you downs, reward the position multiple times in place as you would if you were teaching a two-on/two-off contact position.

Baby Whippet Savvy experiments with a Go to Place mat to see what will cause a click to happen (left image). She gets rewarded for putting her front paws on the mat (middle image), and she learns that lying down on the mat pays off (right image).

3. Once the dog is offering the desired behavior on the mat, reward him in position, then give your release cue, and encourage him off the mat. You have various options here. You could call him, you could throw food a distance from the mat and tell him to get it, or (if he has become glued to the mat) you could walk him off with a leash. It is my preference to reward dogs on the mat, but some trainers instead like to throw the reward off the mat to get the dog up so that he has to return to the mat to continue earning reinforcement. Throwing the reward off the mat is an alternative to releasing the dog from the mat yourself.

4. The second the dog leaves the mat, all clicking, praising, and treating ends. Stand quietly and wait. Most dogs at this point will go back to the mat in an effort to restart the game. When they do, throw treats on the mat. Continue to reward everything, giving the highest value treat for a down. Remember that at this point in the game, you are rewarding the dog for thinking about the mat and returning to it. Don't wait for a down or any other particular behavior. Make sure he understands that it's the behavior of returning to the mat that is getting rewarded. Each time he returns to the mat, mark it, and treat him on the mat. Each time you release him from the mat, step back a bit farther so he has to take another step or two to get back to the mat to restart the game.

5. When the dog is committed to being on the mat, you can start increasing the time between rewards. If he leaves the mat before you give a release cue, pick up the mat for a minute and ignore him, then give him another chance. If he is confidently remaining on the mat until your release cue, you can start taking little steps around him. If you have an excitable dog, start by just bending your knees as if you are about to take a step. After each little movement you make, return and reward the dog if he has remained on the mat. It should not take long for the dog to figure out that no matter what you are doing, he will continue receiving rewards if he stays on the mat until you release him.

Eventually three things will happen:

1. Your dog will figure out that downs are the most rewarded behavior on mats.

2. He will be able to move a reasonable distance away from you to the mat.

3. He will be confident remaining on the mat until you release him.

When you reach this point, you can add your cue—*Place* or whatever you want to call it. The cue *Place* should mean to go to a mat and lie there until released, so you don't want to start using it until all those behaviors are happening reliably.

You may decide you want your dog to race to and slam down on a mat with great enthusiasm. To shape this behavior, reward your dog multiple times on the mat, give your release cue, pick up the mat and sit in a chair, holding it and ignoring your dog for 30 to 60 seconds. During this time, if your dog is like mine, he will try to get the mat back. He may target it with a nose or paw, offer downs on your feet, or stare at the mat. One of my student's dogs grabbed the mat while his owner was sitting on a chair holding it and tried to drag it away. It was rude, but he was definitely demonstrating drive to get on his mat! My All-American girl Maggie, who used to compete in Disc Dog events, once shocked my students and me with an amazing demonstration. I was showing my students how you can rev up your dog and throw the mat so that the dog runs to it, another way to build enthusiasm for this behavior. I threw Maggie's mat into the air. She leapt into the air and literally lay down on the mat in midair before it hit the ground. My students' jaws were on the floor. I just casually said, "She likes going to her mat."

If your dog doesn't show interest in the mat while you are on "break time," it means that next time you work on Go to Place you should raise your rate of reinforcement and work on it for a shorter period of time. The sequence should be:

- Dog gets on mat.

- Reward-reward-reward.

- Release dog from mat.

- Dog wants back on mat.

After the break, put the mat back on the floor and generously reward your dog for getting on it. If your dog is a tugging fiend, you can start tugging with him on the mat rather than putting food on it. Intersperse three or four brief sessions of rewarding on the mat with break times.

We use mats frequently in the CU class to help reactive dogs feel calm about other dogs being loose and working near them. Sometimes I set up a jump and have one team work on start-line stays while two other teams are sitting on the floor doing relaxing mat work on either side of the jump. Sometimes I have a team doing off-

Go to Place quickly becomes a main-stay in CU classes, where every station has a mat. The Go to Place exercise helps distracted dogs focus and helps reactive dogs stay calm.

leash circle work within ring gates while other teams are sitting on the floor doing mat work next to the gates. When a team is ready, I take the gates down one at a time so dog and handler can do circle work around other dogs that are calmly lying on mats.

The potential applications are endless

You can take a mat anywhere. You can use a mat to help generalize or transfer behaviors. You can send your dog to his mat when you let your guests in the door, or send your dog to a mat while you are eating dinner. You can use a mat to practice distance work in your living room or anywhere else, or make a pattern of mats and send your dog to them while practicing crosses on the flat. You can use a mat to teach fast downs and then transfer that behavior to the pause table. If your dog has the zoomies or other impulse-control issues such as grabbing your pant legs or biting you while running, you can place mats on course and send your dog to them after brief sequences, as my friend, agility instructor Deb Norman, would say, "to get a grip."

One of the all-time most useful applications of Go to Place is as a management tool when students want to take a break from working, watch a friend's run, or listen to their instructor. Dogs that have the Go to Place behavior down to a science can lie on their mats quietly next to your chair.

I also use mats in a game I designed for dogs that get distracted when other dogs are running near them. Once the dogs are committed to the behavior of running to their mats, I set up two lanes separated by ring gates and start sending the dogs to their mats from an increasing distance. Perhaps their handlers will have to stay close by them at first, but eventually the handlers can send their dogs from one end of the room to the other while the dogs are running parallel to each other but focused on their targets. At that point, I can remove the gates. By taking it slowly and raising criteria when the dogs are ready, you can easily teach dogs to run parallel and loose, and ignore each other. You can also set up the gates so that the dogs are facing each other and teach them to pass on their way to their targets, a more difficult exercise because the dogs will be head on.

Mat work can also ground an excitable dog that has trouble staying at the start line and allow him to think. Sonic was my test case for this solution to antsy start-line behavior.

THE EXUBERANT DOBERMAN

Sonic the Doberman was a bright, gorgeous, exuberant boy who got overexcited and tended to zoom around the course. I started helping his owner deal with the issue and he improved, but his nemesis remained the start-line stay. The excitement of waiting to start a course was too much for him. Fortunately, I had taught Sonic Go to Place and, for the first time, I applied that behavior to start-line stays.

Sonic had an excellent stay on the table. So I put his Go to Place mat on the table and set up a short, easy sequence that began with the table. He did not break his start-line stay while he was on the table, even if his owner ran, waved her arms, or showed him his toy. I asked his owner to walk him through the sequence (since running would be too exciting) a couple of times and then let them run it. He stayed connected with her and they were both having a good time. I then moved the table but kept the mat on the floor in front of a jump. Again I had him lie down on the mat while his owner went through the same ritual, gradually moving faster, and waving her arms. She rewarded him after each potentially exciting behavior as he lay on his mat. Then she released him. They walked the course again; and then they ran it.

Sonic had never been so successful at holding his start-line stay. Part of the reason was that we changed the picture of what was happening by asking for a slightly different behavior (first, Table, then Go to Place). That different behavior was not emotionally charged as was his traditional start-line stay. Our next step was to ask for a sit on the mat instead of a down, a behavior that is harder, in my experience, for many dogs to maintain when in a state of anticipation. He sat on his mat as his owner went through the whole rigmarole again, then they ran the course.

It was time to take a risk and ask for a down without the mat. Sonic lay down, stayed successfully, and ran his course. Then we asked for a sit. This time he was able to remain seated until released to run. Following the experiment with Sonic, I have successfully helped other dogs relearn start-line stays by using a mat.

~~~~~~

In a similar fashion, mat work can help a scared dog feel more confident, in agility class and at the start line.

~~~~~~

THE SOFT WEIMARANER

Arial the Weimaraner was a sweet, doe-eyed, little girl who was one of the softest dogs I have ever had in a CU class. Arial's owner had told me that Arial had become increasingly worried about performing cued behaviors at home. It had gotten so bad that if her owner asked her to sit and stay, Arial ran and hid behind the couch. This fearfulness stumped her owner. Although I had not seen what was happening at home, I decided that Arial needed a break from all things that seemed like obedience. I told her owner to stop asking her to perform behaviors at home for several weeks, but to praise and reward her if she happened to sit, lie down, and so on, on her own. This temporary vacation was soothing for Arial's relationship with her owner. For the first couple weeks, Arial was too worried to do many of the exercises in class, so I asked her owner simply to massage and feed her and let her watch the others until she gained confidence and chose to join in.

Arial was so sensitive to pressure that if she thought you wanted her to do something, she easily shut down. She had been clicker trained since puppyhood, however, and could be easily shaped to learn a behavior. Since the procedure for shaping allows a dog to figure out for himself what behaviors are being rewarded, it took a lot of pressure off Arial and helped her gain confidence to try new things for a click without worrying that she might be wrong, or that her mom might say the dreaded "Uh-uh!"

The Go to Place game, which Arial picked up quickly, boosted her confidence greatly, and she happily performed it. Since we weren't asking for *Sit, Down,* or *Stay,* but a brand new cue, *Go to Your Mat,* Arial didn't realize she was performing the same behaviors that caused her to panic at home.

Once a dog has learned that the mat is where rewards happen, he'll run to it. Here, Weimaraner Arial flies confidently to her mat.

When it came time to work on start-line stays, Arial's owner and I had concerns. Arial had gained the confidence to actively join the class and no longer needed to be massaged and fed on the sidelines; she was becoming happier every week and just blossoming before us. We didn't want to give her the same cues we were avoiding. Remembering Sonic, I told Arial's owner to send Arial to a mat in front of the jump I had set up and then do the rest of the exercise the same as everybody else. Arial as usual flew happily to her mat and slammed down on it. She ended up with the best start-line stay in her class.

My all time favorite application for mats is using them as part of a biofeedback program that my mentor Dr. Karen Overall created, called the Protocol for Relaxation. The protocol, which originally was published in Overall's book, *Manual of Clinical Behavioral Medicine for Dogs and Cats*, conditions a relaxed response to potentially overstimulating or stressful events. Once you have gone through the basic protocol, you can go back and customize it for your dog. Doing the relaxation work on a mat conditions the dog to associate that feeling of being relaxed with the mat itself. Then you can take that mat with you to class, to a trial, to anywhere your dog gets stressed, to remind him about feeling relaxed. The case of the Sheltie with angst over the photocopy machine offers a fine example of how a dog may associate the cue *Place* with feeling calm, even in an environment that normally would trigger a reactive response.

THE HIGH-STRUNG SHELTIE

A friend rescued a Sheltie that was reactive to any unexpected environmental stimulus. He had agility potential but his reactivity posed a big stumbling block. Doing the relaxation protocol on a mat in various locations helped him greatly. The Sheltie was fearful of a photocopy machine that my friend had in her home. After doing the necessary foundation work, they did mat work in the room with the machine while it was copying, and he ended up loving being trained next to the machine.

A breakthrough moment happened when my friend brought her Sheltie to an agility trial to see how he would cope in that environment. He was doing well until a plane flew overhead. My friend noticed the plane at the same time as her Sheltie and knew he was preparing himself for an extreme reaction in a matter of seconds. She had forgotten to bring the mat, but she found herself giving the cue for going to the mat anyway. Her Sheltie immediately lay down on the ground and did not react to the plane. The cue itself, because of all the work they had done, had become not simply a cue to perform a behavior, but a cue to relax.

If you want your dog to associate feeling calm with being on his mat (without going through the protocol) there is a shortcut for dogs whose troubles don't warrant a clinical work-up. My shortcut is to mark and reward any behaviors from the dog that are associated with physiologically calm responses. My favorite behavior to use for this is blinking. Once a dog figures out that you're rewarding blinking, he offers it readily and his lids get heavier and heavier until he looks as if he might fall asleep. The dog begins this exercise by giving you a behavior, such as blinking, for the reward, not because he is actually feeling calm. Since the behaviors you're rewarding are associated with the physical feeling of being calm, however, eventually the dog actually starts feeling calm. Other behaviors you can shape or elicit from your dog for this purpose include yawning, lying on his side or with his back feet out to the side rather than tucked under, or resting his head on his paws. Another way to help your dog associate feeling calm with being on his mat is to massage him or do Tellington Touch as he lies on his mat.

I seem to be forever making up new applications for the Go to Place behavior. I'm sure if you try it, you will think up some new uses for it too, like this one.

Using a Mat to Unstick the Stuck

Right after my article, "Confessions of a Mat Freak," was published in *Clean Run* magazine (October 2006), I came up with yet another application for the Go to Place behavior.

My baby Border Collie Easy was having a hard time lying down in the presence of a toy. We'd worked hard teaching Easy to stay thoughtful around toys. Toys, especially tug toys, held a magical power over him that caused him to get stuck in herding mode, crouching and staring. To bring him back from the Border Collie planet and to teach him to remain operant around toys, I had done a lot of work including

- Interspersing toy play with shaping sessions, using treats as his reward.
- Making his primary default behavior, which happens to be sit, strong enough to override the instinctive crouching.
- Using the Premack Principle to teach him that a fast response to verbal cues was the way to get back the toy.
- Playing Off-switch games, incorporating tugging and rewarding default behaviors.
- Training him with food while a toy was left on a table in plain sight.
- Training him with food while I held the toy.
- Switching between the food and the toy as his reward.

By the time the article was published, Easy was able to perform a variety of simple behaviors using a toy as his reward without getting stuck. He could sit and place a toy in my hand, play Leave It games with the toy, do circle work exercises and agility obstacles, and target my hand to get the toy in my other hand. Lying down in the presence of toys, however, was still a problem. Sometimes he was able to do it, but I did not have the reliability that I wanted. Lying down was particularly difficult for Easy because when cued to do so, in the process of lying down he crouched—and then he got stuck in his crouch and was unable to make it all the way to the ground. Frozen in position with dreamy eyes, he looked like a blue merle ice sculpture!

I decided that since he was so strongly conditioned to seek out mats and lie down on them, I would mix things up a bit and tug with him next to a mat. I had instant success. I stopped tugging, which is Easy's cue to sit and "hand me" the toy. Easy responded, and I gave him his Go to Place cue, which is *Mat.* He stepped on to the mat readily, then looked longingly at his toy and started to crouch. I remained silent, watching his mind at work. After a couple seconds, he got an "Ah-ha" look on his face as if he were saying, "Oh, I'm on a mat! I get it now. I'm supposed to lie down! Why didn't you say so?" and he slammed down on the mat, causing me to immediately throw his toy for him. The mat was our gateway to getting Easy to lie down, which, pardon the pun, had not been an Easy task! Now Easy lies down lightning fast during Off-switch tug games and other toy-related training.

RECOGNIZING WHEN TO DROP THE LEASH

As the dogs go through various stages of passive and active attention exercises and I see a dog that is actively engaged with his handler, I tell that handler to drop the leash casually and just keep working with the dog as if nothing has happened. Without the sometimes false sense of security that the ring gates provide, many people in class are worried about dropping the leash, but I can help people get a good fix on their dog and know when he is ready for this step.

Sadie appears engaged with her handler. Intrigued by his movement and voice, she watches him intently, ready for the next activity. She is ready to have her leash dropped.

Some of their dogs are ready right away, others need more time to get used to the new environment. Some dogs need a lot of passive attention work because they are so overadrenalized just being in a class situation. Often these dogs are quick to react to other dogs moving, entering the room, exiting crates, and to extraneous noises or other unexpected changes in the environment. They need a lot more time just eating treats, being massaged, and watching from a distance. Others get frustrated with too much passive attention work because they achieve their ready-to-work point much more quickly. Therefore while I move about the class, I point out little things about each dog that help people make the right decision about what activity their dog requires at that moment, and what the optimum balance of activities is for that dog on that day. Handlers need to learn not only to watch their dogs so they can see what "actively engaged with you" *looks* like, they also need to learn what "actively engaged with you" *feels* like. There comes a time when a dog and handler lock in to each other and exemplify the team energetics. That locking-in evolves not from the mechanics of training but from the bond that develops during the training process when a handler really gets to know her dog and his particular needs and honors him. This in turn brings out the best in her dog. Once the team has reached that point, there is so much less worry about leashes, or management, or distractions.

BALANCING ENVIRONMENTAL CHALLENGES AND PERFORMANCE CRITERIA

Just as a student needs to keep tabs on her dog's stimulation level and train the dog to switch easily between states of low and high arousal, the student also needs to learn to adjust her expectations of what her dog can do in a more stressful environment. Dogs do not generalize well. Students and instructors need to keep this fact in mind and adjust their training accordingly. If the *environmental* criteria change, students need to adjust their *performance* criteria.

If something in the environment becomes more distracting or harder to work around and the student has no control over it, she will need to read her dog and decide what to do to help him succeed. She may need to temporarily lower her performance criteria and ask for less from the dog until the dog has adapted. Alternatively, if the dog can somehow manage his changed environment, the handler doesn't have to ask for less. Being able to adjust expectations of a canine partner requires imagination and flexibility. It also requires having an agility instructor who doesn't mind if you're doing your own thing in the background because your dog needs to play a game of Look-at-Those-Running-Dogs-in-the-Other-Half-of-the-Building! before he will be able to accurately nail a contact that is separated from the running dogs by a flimsy, see-through, plastic ring gate.

Whenever I raise a criterion in CU, I point it out to everybody and ask the students if they think they need to adjust what they are doing with their dog in order to get the performance they want. For example, perhaps a dog is doing great off-leash circle work within a closed box of ring gates, with dogs lying on mats on the other side of the gates. At this point I want to take a gate down. Some dogs will be comfortable and savvy enough to keep on working with this change. Others will think, "Oh my! A gate's gone and now I can go see those dogs." So the handler needs to look at how the

In an informal setting after class time, Easy attempts to solicit play from excited Belgian Malinois Rosie. Rosie knew Easy was coming and, as soon as she reoriented to her handler and settled down, she was allowed to play off-leash. Sometimes dogs, loose or leashed, simply "appear" close to your dog. In CU, handlers with excitable, distractible, reactive, or fearful dogs can learn skills not only to help their dog cope when the unpredictable happens, but also to adjust their expectations of their dog's performance when he's faced with environmental challenges.

environment is changing and adjust her criteria to set her dog up for success. Maybe at first she will choose to do the circle work on-leash to remind her dog of the pattern they were engaged in, and then she'll drop the leash as she continues working. Maybe she will choose to keep her dog off-leash but do some stationary active attention exercises that are less stimulating than running. Or maybe she will just heel her dog and gradually work back up to speed. Or, I might suggest, with a dog that showed interest in the dogs lying gateside when the gate was removed, that she choose to play the Look at That! game, if it's already been covered in class, and the dog understands the game (page 122). This game will incorporate the dogs on mats into a rule structure that works for the handler and keeps her dog engaged and interacting with her. Her dog offers glancing at the others and it becomes a behavior to earn a reward rather than glancing because he wants to interact with the other dogs.

Agility students often face the challenge of adjusting expectations of their dog's performance based on the challenges of the environment. The Y2K9s facility, and many others that I know, has a huge open space, large enough to run two agility classes at once, separated only by ring gates. Dogs in one class can clearly see dogs in the other class. Perhaps one class is a structured contacts and weaves class without a lot of running (the kind of class I like to send the CU dogs into), but on the other side of the ring gates there is a sequencing class with dogs running, barking, and tugging. Before rejoining an agility class, I hope the CU dogs will have had enough practice learning to view these running dogs as part of a game they can play with their handler, "I saw a dog running—are we playing a game, mom?" But the handlers are going to need to be aware of their environment and set their dogs up for success within its limitations.

Tools from the CU class that will help include passive and active attention work for grounding and focus, and recognizing when to use barriers. Maybe your dog can perform a certain exercise loose, but he needs an extra ring gate separating him from the others as a reminder. The Look at That! and the Give Me a Break games (pages 122 and 148, respectively) that I'll discuss in the next couple of chapters can help as well. It's hard for students to remember that this type of foundation work is ultimately more important than participating in the agility class or keeping up with the other students. If students don't have the focus or the correct performance and push dogs that are not ready, they're never going to get what they want. Take the cases of "The Lunging Beardie" and "The Poop Connoisseur," both of whom were having problems at agility classes held in a horse barn.

THE LUNGING BEARDIE

Highly aroused by the sight of dogs running, the Bearded Collie screamed, lunged, and lost her mind. It didn't matter that her classes took place in a horse barn; they could have taken place anywhere, and this particular dog would have been over the top.

I had suggested to the Beardie's owner a while back that she bring her dog and her dog's dinner to a different class. I told her to feed her dog dinner in the corner, possibly behind a barrier or in her crate, and leave. This would create a new ritual that would help the Beardie experience being in that environment for a different purpose. Since the Beardie's owner was still enrolled in class, however, she occasionally was feeding her dog in the corner and occasionally was running her dog in the class, which meant putting the dog in a situation where she would be reactive.

I had to tell the owner what I tell my students with pet dogs that are reactive to dogs or people on the street: *Don't mix and match.* A dog that thinks there is a chance of having to interact with his trigger—be it human, canine, or other—is going to be more uncertain (and uncertainty causes reactivity) and react more intensely when he spots his trigger. Reactive dogs that are walked by owners who sometimes stop and chat with a neighbor, or sometimes let their dog meet another dog just to see if they get along, generally take longer to improve than dogs whose owners follow my "No mixing and matching" rule. My rule for a reactive dog is that taking a walk is about playing a game with his person. He should never experience the pressure of wondering, "Am I going to interact with this person/dog? Is he coming up to say hi? What should I do?" If his owner protects him from such interactions and rewards him for playing the game, the dog's triggers thus become an environmental cue that his owner has something good going on. The pressure of an unknown future interaction is off. These reactive dogs do not "meet and greet" on the street. That is a clear rule and takes away a lot of uncertainty. The appearance of a trigger means an interaction or food reward from their person. For dogs that need to improve their social skills, we set up play dates with appropriate dogs and humans that take place in an entirely different context from going for a walk.

It was a slightly different picture with the Beardie but still reminiscent of my reactive pet dog clients. The Beardie was not going to improve if she sometimes ate in the corner and sometimes participated in class where she had a meltdown as soon as other dogs moved. Because her history of lunging and barking in class was strong, she became overstimulated just being in the horse barn that had become connected to these intense feelings. The environment was too challenging for this dog to give anything near the desired performance.

I asked the students what they thought the Beardie's owner should do, aside from taking class somewhere else and starting over in an environment where she could just work on CU exercises first so the dog could learn to think before returning to agility. Everybody was stumped. It's a tough one. What I said to the handler was if she was going to train in that barn, she needed to become a historical revisionist. She needed to create an entirely new history in that place that over time would become strong enough to overcome the old history. I told her she should only use that place to feed her dog dinner and do some CU work in a corner behind gates for maybe 10 or 15 minutes at a time. Eventually she'd build a foundation with her dog that would allow her to participate in class again, if things were adjusted and managed to set her up for success.

Another agility student faced a different sort of environmental problem with her dog but one that demanded equal patience, juggling of criteria, and creating a new history of behaviors at the barn where she took classes.

THE POOP CONNOISSEUR

Although the Vizsla did not have the arousal and impulse-control problems that the Beardie did, she did love horse poop. And, since her handler was training in a horse barn, her turns in agility classes mostly consisted of desperate attempts to call her dog off the horse poop.

Some might argue that she's going to have a lot of distractions at a trial so she needs to just learn to work around the horse poop. But that is not helpful here. There's nothing wrong with the argument itself, but people use that kind of thinking as an excuse for avoiding setting up a class environment so a particular dog can succeed. I am always surprised at the number of people that expect a dog to just get over something. It is our job to teach our dogs, not theirs to figure things out! The dog can't learn to work around the horse poop if over and over again she's allowed to run away during a course and eat it. The handler literally will be training the dog to run away from her on course, and practice makes perfect.

To fix this problem, the dog needed some environmental management and training, and the student needed to substantially adjust her performance criteria. This handler needed a much better foundation on her dog before putting her in a situation that was as difficult for her as the horse barn. That's why she came to CU. If this student could use the horse barn to learn about adjusting her expectations for her dog, lowering criteria, working on focus under threshold, and managing her environment so her dog couldn't learn the wrong thing, then the horse barn would be a great laboratory for her experiments.

My Look at That! game, which makes looking at interesting things in the environment into a game that a dog can play with his handler, is an extremely useful tool for teaching attention to dogs that are easily triggered by distractions. The Look at That! game, which is so useful for so many triggers and distractions, was no help here, however, because the dog not only looked at "that," but she ate "that!" Her owner unwittingly had set up situations during class that allowed her dog to practice running away and eating poop over and over before she arrived at CU. It was a heavily ingrained, highly rewarded behavior. Before even looking at adjusting the handler's training, I looked at how she could change the environment. Could she put the poop behind a solid barrier of some kind, for example? No, that wouldn't work in that facility. But at the least, students could form a human barrier so that if the dog ran over toward the poop, somebody could leash her and foil her dinner plans.

As it was, her dog typically started well enough, but somewhere in the middle of the course, she'd get a good whiff and she'd be off. Since the second half of the sequence usually culminated in the Vizsla running off to eat the poop that was mostly in a far corner, my next suggestion was, rather than doing the entire sequence, the handler should work on the first half of the sequence. She could separate those obstacles near the poop with ring gates and work on her dog's focus and performance away from the poop. The handler could keep incorporating more obstacles and more space into the ring gate barriers until the dog was working close to the poop again. If she could get a successful performance out of her dog within the gated area, she could put obstacles near the gated-off poop area, ask for one or two obstacles, lavishly reward the dog, then leave. She could build up from there, eventually removing the gate just as we do in CU, and the dogs are able to do circle work around dogs lying on mats all over the room. Because of the ingrained nature of the problem, it was going to take ingenuity, historical revisionism, environmental management, and cooperation from this handler's agility instructor and fellow students to fix this problem.

Lightbulb Moment: Conquering Addictions

Sprite (the Vizsla) and I seem to be making genuine progress with her attention. We've gone to class twice at the barn since we finished up CU. I had a plan in mind: spending some time at the beginning of class working on clicking for looking at the other dogs and people and then me; touching/targeting, to remind her what we were there for; taking her out of the crate only when I could be 100% committed to keeping her attention and doing something with her; and keeping our sequences to nine obstacles max to keep her from getting stressed.

The other thing that I did was to introduce peanut butter into our treat regimen at the barn. She is crazy for it. I have actually been successful at calling her off fresh horse manure. This past week there was a new Vizsla in class, which was over-the-top exciting for Sprite. She sat on the start line with the dog just 8' away, glanced at the dog but did not break, and ran the course. People were shocked.

—Sharon

STARTING START-LINE STAYS

I am always amazed at the handlers who enter CU after taking multiple agility classes with dogs that still have no concept of staying at the start line. Coupled with the fact that most of the dogs I get in CU are somewhat reactive to other dogs or have a habit of running off and sniffing, and you can imagine that some of these handlers are doomed before they even get the chance to step to the start line. I love it when I get students who are starting their agility foundation with CU and don't even know what start-line stay means. They are the ones whose dogs will succeed the fastest, because we're starting from scratch. Remember: A start-line stay is just a high-criteria stay.

Some trainers work on motivational stays at the start line to get the dog excited about doing the course. Since most of the CU dogs come in with arousal, reactivity, impulse-control issues, or worry about what's behind or near them, the emphasis for these dogs is on feeling focused and ready to work while also *relaxing* into their stay, just waiting for the next cue. Remember, relaxed does not mean tired or mellow. A dog or person can be alert and ready to work and still feel relaxed. Relaxed is just the opposite of stressed or, if you prefer, tense.

Of course, some of the CU handlers can proceed faster than others, and I adjust criteria based on individual performances. Some handlers have come into class ready to run, point at jumps, and drag tugs on the ground while their dog stays in position. But many of them need to start with baby steps. I set the handlers and dogs up in front of a jump. The dogs that are already jumping occasionally can be released to take the jump as part of the exercise.

Teaching a start-line stay

First, I shock everybody by telling them I don't want them to give a stay cue. What I want is for the dogs to learn that *maintaining a cued position until given a release cue* is more reinforcing than changing position. To that end, once each student has her dog in a sit or a down, I ask the students to start feeding treats rapidly. For some dogs, you can start with counting a few seconds in between treats; with others, you have to "machine gun" treats or the dogs are going to pop up. Then I tell the students to give a release cue (*All Done, That'll Do, Okay*, whatever), and invite their dogs to move. Once the dogs have moved, of course, the treats stop. Right after he has been released, a clicker-savvy dog will start offering the behavior that was working before, hoping to restart the game.

McDevitt begins Easy's start-line stay training by feeding him for maintaining the desired position for increasingly longer periods of time.

So in this initial stage, the dog is learning two things at once:

1. Maintaining a position instead of popping up is good.

2. The release cue means the chance for reinforcement (temporarily) is over. It also means the dog is on break time unless his handler immediately gives another cue.

Usually this is as far as the dogs get doing start-line stays during Night Two. What follows are logical progressions from this basic exercise that we practice during the following nights.

Adding a cue

When students want to add a stay cue, I have them do so after the dog has figured out that good things keep happening until he hears the release cue. Initially, so the dog understands that *Stay* is not a new release cue, I suggest that the handler give the cue and then immediately give a treat as the dog is holding position.

Reading your dog's stay

I tell each student to watch where her dog is putting his weight. Front legs? Back legs? Is he shifting his weight around? People can tell if their dog is thinking about getting up or if he is glued to the ground; they just have to remember to watch his body during stay exercises. I want the handler to read her dog well enough that she can always release him *before* he moves out of position.

TRAINING A RELAXED STAY

If your dog is hyperalert and you want to take his stimulation level down a notch, start rewarding behaviors that are linked with physiologically calm states; for instance, blinking at him, looking at him with heavily lidded eyes, and taking some deep breaths. Mark and reward your dog's reciprocal behavior. You can do the same thing if you feel your dog is too alert during mat work.

Upping the ante

Once you are able to count to at least 10 while the dog remains in position, raise your criteria by taking one step—laterally, so that the dog doesn't think you're cueing him to heel—and immediately return and feed the dog. I tend to click every time I take a step or do something new as long as the dog remains in position. This is not necessary, but it's what works for me. Proceeding gradually, soon you should be able to walk all over the room, do jumping jacks, and so on while your dog stays in position for any length of time.

Upping the ante for the antsy

In my CU classes I get a lot of dogs who hear *1...* or *Ready...* and they pop up because they know enough about that game to get excited, but not enough about it to play it correctly. So for the antsy dog, I ask his handler to start with her dog on either side, and simply bend her knees as if she might dart away, and then feed her dog. This should happen so fast the dog doesn't get the chance to think about moving. Once the dog graduates from that step, the handler can bend her knees and take one step forward, then return and treat. Then she can stick her hand out. Then she can stick her hand out while bending her knees. Then she can stick her hand out, bend her knees, and take a step—the ultimate goal being that she can gesture wildly and run past the jump while her dog is calmly remaining in position waiting for the release cue. If your dog gets up, you went too far too fast. Lower your criteria. Split your movements into even smaller behaviors, making sure your dog can deal with seeing your knees bend and your arms and feet move before putting all these elements together. Then you can add speed, an extra bounce to your step, and a gleam in your eye that communicates *Ready...* before you actually add the word to the picture. I also ask students to walk up to the jumps and touch them, jump over them, and do whatever goofy thing I can come up with that their dogs are ready to handle.

McDevitt raises criteria for Easy's start-line stay by bending her knee slightly as if she is going to move (left), then taking a step away from Easy (middle), then by pointing her finger toward the jump (right).

In a more challenging form of start-line stay training, a handler touches, steps over, and runs by the jump as her Border Collie Flash holds position.

Keep 'em guessing

When practicing start-line stays, it's a good idea to release dogs to a toy or treat *behind* them, or call them to you to play rather than always letting them take the obstacle in front of them. That way they can't always predict what's coming next and will have to think through their excitement in order to succeed. Since in CU the dogs don't jump during their stay exercises, this exercise starts uncoupling the obstacle from the stay.

Border Collie Shiner intently holds her stay, not knowing if she'll be cued to take the dogwalk or released to her get favorite Frisbee behind her. It helps the dog learn to hold his start-line position if he doesn't know where his reward will come from.

Add dogs

Once I am happy with several teams' performances in front of one jump, I place two jumps in a row, then three, and have the dogs do their stays while they can see other dogs staying and other people moving. At first a particularly reactive dog may need ring gates or another barrier separating his jump from the others. Some dogs may need to face the wall before they can face another dog. If the dogs are fine being in a row, I might add dogs lying on their mats on either side of the standards. I might walk or run Snap or a student's dog in between the rows. By this point, since the handlers are proficient at reading their dogs, working under threshold, and raising criteria appropriately, they can start moving past each other, around the jumps, and walk around the room while the dogs are staying in front of the jumps.

Using the start-line-stay box or obstacles

My last modification is the start-line-stay box. I put four jumps in a box formation with the dogs on stays facing each other. By then the handlers are able to run past each other and make all kinds of gestures and movements inside and outside of the box while the dogs remain in place.

Depending on equipment availability, sometimes I also set up a short sequence of jumps, tunnels, tires, whatever is out. As an alternative to the stay box, I have the dogs practice staying in front of obstacles near each other.

In an advanced variation on training start-line stays, students use the start-line-stay box to practice stays with other dogs sitting to the side of and opposite them.

Chapter 5

Night Three

Concepts

- Whistle while you work: Simultaneously building focus and changing attitudes (Look at That! game)
- Giving dogs a task to focus on while working near other dogs (Parallel games)

New Exercises

- Look at That! game
- Parallel games

Reminder: Continue working on passive and active attention and box work at the beginning of each class, raising criteria as appropriate for each dog.

The dogs should be working on their impulse control and focus with the active attention exercises and on feeling calm around the other dogs with the passive attention exercises. Now it is time to add a new element to the mix: changing attitudes toward triggers, the objects, events, or beings that bother each dog.

Whistle while you work: Simultaneously building focus and changing attitudes (Look at That! game)

In 2001, I attended a lecture by Dr. Pamela J. Reid entitled "Untold Secrets of Pavlov's Lab: Getting Rid of Bad Behavior by Rewarding It." Dr. Reid gave the example of counterconditioning a resource-guarding behavior (in this case, a lip-curl) so that the dog associated it with earning a reward rather than with behaving aggressively. She thus turned the lip-curl into a trick the dog could offer her. Dr. Reid discussed the concept of using a simple counterconditioning protocol to change the motivation behind a behavior. She showed us a video of her own highly clicker-savvy dog Eejit who quickly started offering his lip-lifting sneer to Pam as a trick rather than continuing to lift his lip at the dog he had been guarding his toy from.

That lecture inspired my approach to dealing with dogs that are reactive to, or just easily distracted by, other dogs. The idea of clicking a dog for what many people would view as an undesirable behavior was the inspiration behind my trademark practice of clicking dogs for looking at other dogs. By rewarding a dog for looking at a dog he was worried about and turning it into a game, I found the dog relaxed because his reason for looking at the other dog was no longer a defensive one. Looking became a game that he was playing for clicks and treats and therefore decreased his anxiety. *Keep in mind that I work dogs subthreshold.* Once the dog has this new coping skill in his toolbox, it gives him a safe and clear rule structure for what to do when dogs or other triggers are present. He becomes a much more confident and attentive working partner. The same method works well for very friendly dogs that have trouble attending to their handler in class or on the street because they want to interact with every dog that approaches. They too can learn that an approaching dog (or kid, or mailman) is a signal to play the "look game" with their handler.

I first experimented with this concept on my own Tervuren Rumor when he was a teenager.

Rumor, the Adolescent Terv

Soon after I attended Dr. Reid's lecture, adolescence struck Rumor with a vengeance. Much to my dismay, he suddenly wanted to posture and growl at every dog in the training facility. I figured I might as well test my click-for-looking idea on my own reactive dog. It worked so well, I've never looked back.

I knew Ru had gotten the concept when he offered looking at an American Eskimo that he used to growl at in obedience class and turned back to me for a reward. I didn't reward his look right away because I'd been rewarding every time he gave me the behavior of looking at dogs in class, and at that point he was clearly doing it for me rather than doing it because it was the beginning of a reactive-response sequence. So I decided to wait to see what would happen. If I didn't respond quickly, would he turn back to that dog and have a reaction? How much of his feelings about being near that dog had truly changed? If the rate of reinforcement changed, and if I didn't keep interrupting a possible reactive-response sequence by clicking him when he looked at other dogs, would he look at them for a longer period of time rather than turning back to me, and escalate his arousal in the process?

No. Ru looked at the Eskie a couple more times and pointedly turned back to me, as if to say, "Aren't *you* getting it?" Then he offered a sit and next a wave with his paw. Then he put his paw on my knee (another trick we'd been working on). I understood then that he had incorporated looking at other dogs into his tricks-for-treats repertoire, which is exactly what I had been hoping for. Looking at other dogs developed a different meaning, and Ru no longer postured at other dogs. Many dogs have reinforced the Look at That! game for me since that initial attempt, but my big, "doofy" Ru was the first to prove it could be done.

After my experiment with Rumor, and years before CU was even on my radar screen, I used this technique successfully in countless lessons with reactive pet dogs whose owners could barely walk them down the street. It was totally natural to take the technique and create a game out of it for my CU students; I call it the Look at That! game.

A different approach

Both Snap and Poodle Sting have been cued to look at each other at the same time. This photo was very hard to capture because both dogs were glancing for a split second before reorienting to their handlers.

Most often a performance handler with a dog that is reactive to, or overly interested in, other dogs (or anything else for that matter) is told she should make her dog focus on her exclusively. In other words, teaching a behavior incompatible with checking out the environment would solve the problem. I used to teach this concept to my pet clients with reactive dogs. I taught by conditioning the dog to watch the handler and ignore the triggers that cause the reaction. *When trained properly as part of a broader behavior modification program that includes desensitization, counterconditioning, and teaching the dog to relax, the exclusive focus method works well.* The vast majority of handlers, however, aren't using focus as part of a broader behavior modification program. They are just forcing their dogs to watch them as a sort of control Band-Aid. Because teaching dogs to look at their triggers as part of a game they play with you works better than just asking them for their attention, I changed my solution to the problem.

Why do I like this game so much?

The environment is still out there

A dog that is strongly conditioned to watch his handler no matter what doesn't get the chance to learn to cope with his environment. If his handler is not around and has not done any work to address the dog's internal responses to seeing triggers, the dog will still react to his triggers.

How would you like it?

Even if the dog is watching his handler and behaving well, it puts a lot of stress on the dog to worry about what's happening around him that he's not allowed to check out. This stress detracts from the dog's trial performance as well as making him feel bad. If you were walking in a dark forest and kept hearing rustling noises in the bushes, you'd want to see if anything was coming out of those bushes at you. If you were walking with a companion that demanded you constantly watch him, you might comply if you were motivated enough, but a lot of your brain would still be engaged in worrying about what might be in the bushes. Therefore, you would not be able to give your full attention to your companion even if it seemed as if you were.

The "Aggressive" Golden

I worked with a Golden who was reactive to strange dogs, kids, and sudden changes in the environment. He had been trained with prong collar corrections to watch his owner no matter what. At the time I met this Golden he was going to many competitive obedience classes and matches where he felt panicky. His reactivity toward other dogs had escalated to the point that he'd earned himself an undeserved reputation for being aggressive. He even had started growling at practice judges during the stand for exam. To improve his focus, his owner had been taking him to distracting outdoor spaces to do heeling drills and then correcting him every time he looked away from her. This training structure was causing his anxiety to go through the roof.

The Golden needed to know what was happening around him before he could give his handler the kind of focus she needed for the ring. Clearly he understood the behavior of heeling, but when he got into the ring, his demeanor changed. He became hypervigilant and demonstrated what one of my CU students describes as "exorcist head." During the heeling exercises at trials, his body stayed in position but his head swiveled around at every possible angle because, finally, he could look for boogeymen without fear of correction. Not knowing what else to try, his owner worked on heeling outside the ring with even more forceful corrections.

When his owner brought the dog to me for focus work, you could have knocked her over with a feather when I told her we were going to reward him for looking at dogs and other environmental triggers rather than making him look at her. But she quickly became one of my most faithful students.

I pointed out that her dog had a certain level of anxiety about his environment, and the obedience ring had become the only place where he could check things out without the fear of physical punishment. This particular dog was not just looking around because he was distracted. He was experiencing real anxiety about dogs and other stimuli that his owner had never addressed. His handler's behavior, in fact, had accidentally heightened his anxiety. Since corrections aren't allowed in the ring, his handler had unwittingly trained the opposite behavior of the one she wanted. The ring had become the only safe space for her Golden to look around!

We did not work on heeling or any obedience behaviors together. Instead we worked to decrease the Golden's anxiety in a number of ways. We played a whole lot of Look at That Dog! Look at That Kid! Look at That Whatever! on cue. The Look at That! game became the performance warm-up for this Golden. When we turned checking for possible boogeymen into a game he and his handler played outside the ring, the Golden was finally able to give his full focus and his maximum heeling performance in the ring because he wasn't worried about what was happening around him anymore. The game provided great relief for the Golden because (to anthropomorphize for a moment) he had always been in conflict between desiring to work for his handler and worrying about the rustling in the bushes; that is, until we reframed the experience for him as a game. Of course his handler initially got a lot of flak from fellow obedience exhibitors for clicking her dog for looking at other dogs. But once the scoffers realized that the dog was performing better and was calmer in general, they started complimenting her on the change. So far every competition client that I've worked with on the Look at That! game has experienced the same reaction. This Golden is now heeling happily in the ring.

Incompatible behaviors are not always enough

Dogs' feelings about the environment do not change when people just use a *Watch Me!* cue as a Band-Aid. In this scenario, the dogs are giving an incompatible behavior (watching their handlers) to prevent a reactive behavior. But the underlying state that caused the reactivity is still there and, therefore, can come right back if the dog goes over threshold.

THE TENSE SPRINGER

Many moons ago at a flyball tournament, my little mixed breed Maggie and I passed a woman with a Springer Spaniel. As soon as the Springer saw us coming toward her, she gave Maggie a hard eye and every muscle in her body tensed. Her handler immediately asked her to focus and to heel. The Springer complied and heeled past us, watching her owner and ignoring us, without incident. But the whole experience made me nervous for that Springer. I did not like the way her body looked even though she had obeyed her handler so readily.

About an hour later I was lying on the floor snuggled with Maggie in our blanket and pillows (I was not easy to miss at flyball tournaments) when I heard barking and people screaming. I knew it was the Springer. A distressed lady from my club ran into the rest area with her dog; she told me another dog had tried to attack her dog. I asked, "Was it a little black and white Springer?" Yes, it was. This incident reinforced my belief that teaching incompatible behaviors without doing any deeper work to change a reactive or aggressive dog's associations with—or predictions about—his trigger is not enough.

THE REACTIVE BORDER COLLIE

Years ago I was hired to work with a rescue Border Collie who was very reactive to people. Her owner met me in the parking lot outside the facility. As soon as the dog saw me, her owner asked her to sit and to look at her. The Border Collie immediately complied and was the picture of focus. At that point still relatively green to these cases, I approached confidently, thinking, "This dog is okay!" It wasn't until I said, "Hello, Jazz!" that she went over threshold and lunged at me, screaming her head off. I complimented her owner on Jazz's compliance and told her that in order to change Jazz's behavior toward people approaching her, we would need to work on changing the whole picture of what it means when people approach her. Jazz still felt horrified about people approaching, but as long as she was under threshold, she performed her cues perfectly. Although her owner felt Jazz was pretty manageable, to me, a lot of healing needed to take place to help Jazz overcome her fears and truly get better. She needed to learn to relax and feel confident in situations that triggered her. Over time Jazz improved, and her owners were so happy they rescued a second Border Collie, who also turned out to be reactive, but at least this time they knew what to do!

Unlike these two examples of reactive dogs, dogs that are being rewarded for *looking at their triggers* are simultaneously learning that when they see another dog, something nice happens (counterconditioning); therefore their association about what it means when they see another dog changes.

Getting the best of both worlds

When the dog is allowed to look at what he wants or needs to look at (with reorienting to his handler as part of the rule structure), you get the best of both worlds. You free the dog from any possible conflict between being compliant and making sure things are okay. And ultimately the dog is rewarded for attending to you.

Reframe the experience: Change why the dog is looking

When we click dogs for looking at their triggers, we are aiming to change their motivations. Maybe when you started working with your dog, he was looking at other dogs because he was overly aroused, worried, too interested, or challenging. But once the game is in place, he looks because it's a trick to offer you, a game to play with you, and a rule structure for the anxious or reactive dog that helps him feel safe.

Teach the dog to self-interrupt

Dogs that are comfortable within the rule structure of the Look at That! game start reading their triggers (dogs, men with hats, etc.) as "environmental cues" to reorient to their handlers. So when the dog sees a trigger, he interrupts himself after a brief glance, rather than fixating on the trigger, and *turns back to his handler for a treat.* Giving the handler attention is built into the game. The goal is for the appearance of the trigger to elicit a *positive* emotional response in the dog. This is also the goal of Dr. Patricia McConnell's "autowatch" protocol. I learned about the autowatch protocol from Dr. McConnell after she read about my Look at That! game. We had a great discussion about the similarities between our protocols and our shared goal: teaching dogs how to feel better. Since you don't always notice your dog's trigger before he does, reframing a trigger as an environmental cue to reorient to you is very helpful. By creating a structure where the dog self-interrupts at the beginning of a reactive response (noticing a trigger being the first step of the response), we empower the dog to control his own reaction. What a great coping skill to teach!

What actually happens while playing the Look at That! game

The irony with the Look at That! game is that the dogs learn to pay just as much—if not more—attention to their handlers as they would if they were trained solely to watch their handlers. Again, the structure is: Look at an environmental stimulus (in CU, the stimulus is always another dog) as a behavior to give to your handler. After awhile, the dog becomes so engaged with his handler and so nonchalant about the presence of other dogs that he starts looking for shortcuts. He stops taking the time to look directly at the other dog; barely tilting his head or flicking an eye in another dog's direction, he then stares at his handler as if saying, "You saw that, right?"

At this point, many students ask me if that behavior is good enough to reward or if they should reward the dog only for really looking at the other dog. It's a pretty amusing question, considering that most of my students come from the school of thought that the dog always has to watch his handler. The answer to this criterion question depends on the dog and on why you started training the Look at That! game in the first place. If your dog gets distracted because he's friendly and you need him to focus in class, maybe you'd be really happy if he started giving you shortcuts and barely glanced at the other dogs, or stopped glancing altogether. Basically the choice is yours. Reward what makes you happy. Personally, I want the dogs to keep the behavior of looking, even if it's only for a second. Snap has the shortcuts down to an art. I walk him up to another dog and he contorts his face to show me that he's offering the tiniest bit of orienting to the other dog without taking his eyes off me. It makes people laugh, but I'll only click when he takes the time to turn his head toward another dog.

Look at That! helps handlers relax

I have found that students' body language and tone of voice relax when playing this game because the pressure is off of them to notice every trigger and get their dog's attention before the dog has a reaction. Many of my students find themselves in the predicament of noticing an approaching dog after their dog notices him and then asking for their dog's attention once he has begun having the reaction. This is not as efficient as a rule structure that acknowledges that your dog likely will notice a trigger first. With the Look at That! game, even if the dog notices his trigger before you do, when trained properly he will learn to read the trigger as a signal to reorient to you for his treat, so the pressure is off of you to notice everything before your dog does. The pressure is also off of you to keep your dog's attention while he's struggling to watch another dog that is passing by. My students start developing the attitude that "Yeah, there it is. So what?" rather than "Don't you dare look at that!" and that switch allows them to relax. And of course, your dog knows very well if you are feeling relaxed or tense, and this in turn affects his behavior.

Training the Look at That! game

Training the trick of looking at other dogs is easy. Dogs look at stuff. We can click them for it. Remember to work subthreshold. Click the second the dog looks at another dog, and make sure he eats. For a dog that is having a response that is too intense, start with a neutral target, such as a duct tape "X" on the wall. You can click him for looking at the X, then put it on cue, and transfer the behavior to real triggers later. When it's time to transfer the behavior to a trigger (such as a person or dog), you can even tape the X on the trigger at first and then fade it when the dog is comfortably offering the behavior (yet another use for duct tape!). Most dogs don't need that step.

For dogs that might bark, I use cheese in a spray can or peanut butter in a food tube so I can gum up their mouths. For reactive dogs with sensitive stomachs, meat-based baby food in a food tube is a much blander choice. For other dogs, I might throw a handful of food on the ground so they can hunt around for their tidbits. Either way of dispensing treats gives dogs more of a break period from the pressure of looking at other dogs.

When the dog is offering the quick glance behavior, I name the behavior *Look.* Once a dog gets it, he will feel a lot better about being around other dogs. He knows he will be able to look and make sure everything is okay while at the same time giving his handler the rewardable behavior of attention. This is the best of both worlds for the dog.

The dogs quickly start looking at dogs (or other stimuli students are working with) and turning back to their handlers for a reward. Some students worry that the dog will not turn back for his reward but will continue watching the stimulus. Prolonged watching indicates that the dog is going over threshold. In this case the handler has asked for too much, too fast and needs to readjust. If the handler is working sub-threshold and being clear about what she is clicking, the dog quickly understands the structure, which is simply to look at something and reorient to his handler for a reward. The behavior of turning back to the handler automatically gets built in as the dog seeks out his reward, because the reward comes from the handler. The case of Drover, the anxious Whippet, illustrates how you can use the Look at That! game to take the worry out of being around other dogs.

DROVER, THE CIRCUS WHIPPET

Drover, a sweet, black Whippet, got anxious being near strange dogs. At the time I saw him, Drover was pursuing agility, lure coursing, and rally obedience, and his handler did such a great job of managing him that he remained nonreactive around dogs in class. His handler, however, knew that even though she managed Drover well in class, he still felt anxious about other dogs, and he could be quite reactive when he saw loose dogs during walks in the park. She wanted tools to address that part of his training so that he could feel better, but she also needed reassurance that the program would work and that she could do it.

I taught Drover to glance at Snap for a click and treat. Drover's mom worried I would accidentally reward him for staring at Snap, a behavior she did not want to encourage in a sighthound. I explained that I was going to click the second Drover oriented to Snap, which would interrupt the instinctive motor pattern of orient, stare, and chase, and just turn that glance at the other dog into a trick. Though at first Drover needed a lot of distance from Snap to be comfortable, soon he was able to be quite near him and offer little glances; there was no staring. Drover's owner wondered if she might click late, or click the wrong thing. These are the guidelines I gave her:

1. Work subthreshold so the dog is not overly aroused or anxious or having a hard time thinking.

2. Click (or say *Yea* or mark the behavior in some way) before the dog has a reaction or does something undesirable. Glance at Snap, click (motor pattern interrupted), Drover turns to me for the treat.

3. If the dog does have a reaction, do not click after the fact. Instead, if possible, change the picture for the dog by

   • Removing him from the situation that upset him.

   • Increasing the distance between the dog and his trigger.

   • Using your body or a tree or whatever is available as a physical barrier between the dog and his trigger to cut off the visual stimulation.

   When the dog is able, ask for an easy behavior such as a hand target, a sit, or eye contact, and reward him. You can also help him to settle at that point with an ear massage or TTouch.

4. If you're late, don't click. If you're not comfortable with clicking in a certain context or are worried you won't get it right, don't click.

The worst-case scenario is that your dog has a reaction (which is a great indication that you set up a situation where the dog was likely to pass his threshold) and you end up doing damage control as described above. Your goal at that point is to help your dog calm down.

Drover underscored the power of reframing looking at other dogs as a trick to give his owner. Previously he had looked at other dogs because he felt uncertain about their approaching him. His looking turned to staring, and his intensity had increased the longer his handler allowed the stare to continue.

Fortunately, Drover came to me with a repertoire of funny tricks he loved to do, including sneezing, barking, and bowing. His owner liked the result I got when I clicked him for glancing at Snap. He was offering tiny glances at Snap and mostly watching me and had stopped worrying about who Snap was or what he might do, and she wanted to try it. When she took the clicker, Drover immediately started offering her his funny tricks, so I had her add the Look at Snap behavior into his repertoire. Then Drover really brightened up. He sneezed, barked, glanced at Snap, bowed, sneezed, put his head on his handler's knee, and glanced at Snap. He had started out worrying about Snap and now was using Snap's presence as an opportunity to give a new trick to his mom. Drover's case reminds me to tell my students to incorporate tricks their dogs enjoy into the Look at That! game to help get across the concept that seeing a trigger is just part of a game to play, no need to worry.

The Whippet Drover, who was anxious around other dogs, quickly incorporated the Look at That! game into his repertoire of circus tricks. He glances at Snap (left), then offers his target-a-knee-with-your-chin trick close to Snap (middle), and sits pretty in Snap's presence (right).

Like Drover, Maggie Mae, a Jack Russell Terrier, had a lot of anxiety about being around strange dogs, especially loose dogs running or playing in agility class and trials. She had become so reactive that her owner had sadly retired her from agility. Yet the Look at That! game provided her with a structure that made her feel safe and eventually brought her back into the sport.

Miss Maggie Mae, the Stressed-out Jack Russell

Miss Maggie Mae was reactive to other dogs in class and at trials. She shut down, ran away from her handler, sniffed on course, and basically was a nervous wreck. Her handler, an experienced trainer with titles on multiple dogs, had read my article about Snap ("But He Only Plays At Home!" in *Clean Run* magazine,

July 2005), who had issues similar to Maggie's and asked if she could audit a CU course to see what it was all about.

She started observing the course and her eyes lit up whenever she heard something that resonated with her. I could see that I was reframing a lot of concepts for her that were helping her make sense of her dog's needs. She was particularly intrigued by the Look at That Dog! game because she'd been doing the opposite, not allowing Maggie to watch her environment (especially other dogs) as Maggie became increasingly reactive.

She wanted to sign up for the next session and was starting to entertain hopes of getting Maggie back into agility. She asked if she could bring Maggie to class while she was auditing and just leave her in her crate, and I said fine. Although I had not let a reactive dog audit CU from a crate on the sidelines before, it turned out to be a wonderful idea. Maggie's handler sat next to the crate and shaped Maggie to watch the other dogs doing their exercises. The crate took pressure off Maggie. Since she knew she did not have to interact with other dogs or perform in any way, it gave her a boundary she trusted. And Maggie, who had been taught that it was only acceptable to watch her handler and never anything else, started visibly relaxing as she figured out that she could survey the class environment for boogeymen without fear of reprisal. In fact, she was actually being treated for it!

The first night after she tried training Maggie in her crate, Maggie's handler came to me and hugged me. I thought she was going to burst into tears! She said Maggie had never looked that relaxed around other dogs before. She had watched Maggie's muscles, particularly in her face, literally soften as she taught her the Look at That! game in the safety of her crate. Being a savvy clicker trainer, she was able to mark and reward the softening of her dog's features. And we realized another benefit for Maggie. Although she had a long history of being crate aggressive, not once had she reacted during the class to the dogs moving near her crate. Even though her handler hadn't been focusing on that aspect of training, Maggie was being counterconditioned to accept having dogs around her crate!

The last night of that class, we moved to a different room in the facility so we'd have more space to play with obstacles. A dog from class ran in through the front door ahead of her handler, got loose, and ran right up to Miss Maggie Mae's crate. This was quite a different context from the one in which Maggie had been nonreactive in previous classes. Having just arrived herself, Maggie's owner was not engaged with her dog yet, and Maggie was not operating in a structure where dogs running at her crate could be incorporated into a game. Maggie faced a startling sudden environmental change (a highly aroused new dog rushing into the building), the instant proximity of the dog to the crate, and the intensity of the other dog's behavior (he was shrieking into Maggie's crate).

Maggie's handler was unsure what to do. Asking for a behavior wouldn't have been helpful since Maggie's immediate reaction to the loose dog already had put her over the top. I put the loose dog in a crate and selected a dog from class that gave out friendly signals and was under control. I told Maggie's handler that sometimes the situation calls for counterconditioning—changing associations— rather than asking a dog that's already over threshold to perform an incompatible behavior. To give an example to the whole class, I brought the friendly dog near Maggie's crate, clicking the nanosecond the dog was near the hot zone *before Maggie could react*. I threw a ton of food through the top of the crate so it landed all over Maggie. In this context, both the click and the sudden tidal wave of food acted as interrupters. Maggie primed herself to react the first time I brought the dog close, but the click and food helped her think through her upset. Then Maggie was able (in nonclinical terms) to get a grip on herself and eat the food.

The second time I brought the dog over, the scenario repeated itself, with Maggie primed to react but easily interrupted. The third time, we got one "Woof" from Maggie, and then she looked up at the top of her crate, waiting for treats to fall from the sky. The fourth time, Maggie immediately looked up for the treats. I went through this process several more times as Maggie started quietly offer- ing sits and expectantly waiting for the downpour of food. At that point, I removed myself from the picture, standing far away from Maggie's crate and having the friendly dog's handler walk her toward the crate. The second the dog hit the zone I clicked from a distance and ran to shower food on Maggie. I wanted her to know that the structure remained in place even if I wasn't right next to her.

Once Maggie was comfortable with the structure and was in working mode, she offered multiple behaviors when she saw the other dog approaching. "I'm looking at her! I'm looking at you! I'm lying down! Where's the food?" The last thing I did was to bring the dog right up to the crate, then click and throw one piece of food in the far corner of the crate, so that Maggie not only had to turn away to get the treat, but then, purposely, had to walk up to the dog on the other side of the crate to get the next click.

Bringing the tester dog right up to the crate is something that I instinctively knew would work for Maggie, but I don't use the same strategy for every dog. I have good instincts for what will work with a certain dog in a certain context. Moreover, *the principles behind desensitization and counterconditioning are always in my mind when working with a reactive dog.* For a dog that has a serious resource-guarding problem that hasn't been addressed, for instance, food falling from the sky in the presence of another dog might only have escalated his anxiety. Then I would have had to come up with a different strategy in order to make my point about counterconditioning in that class. You have to know the dog you're working with!

Lightbulb Moment: Look at That!

The moment of insight for me was when I saw Maggie starting to relax after I not only gave her permission to observe her environment and other dogs, but even rewarded her for doing so. When Maggie actually lay down and just watched the activity in front of her (two dogs heeling around obstacles and passing each other periodically), and I saw her whole expression change to one of relaxation, I almost cried. This experience clearly was a turning point for Maggie. She has progressed rapidly now and is far less reactive than she used to be. She has even offered to play with a couple other dogs—a Corgi and a Border Collie—and really enjoyed the interaction. She no longer is reactive to dogs running past her, which used to be an immediate trigger. She prefers that uninvited dogs stay out of her face but tolerates them being far closer than in the past. I truly am proud of how she has progressed through this unique system that seems to have been developed just for her benefit. Her changing behavior is clearly making me calmer as well.

—Sandy

While in CU we practice the Look at That! game by using other dogs, it's also a splendid tool for reframing a dog's experience of other triggers. This next student describes the Look at That! game as a way to cope with other events that made his dog uncomfortable.

Lightbulb Moment: Look at the Horses!

I used to avoid the horse paths in our local park because of my dog's extreme reaction to the beasts, but one day on our walk we encountered some horses. Without thinking I started to click and treat my dog for looking at the horses as I was taught in our CU class. She has been playing the Look at That! game since she was a puppy. My dog was still upset but she did not have her usual over-the-top reaction. I decided to continue working my dog around horses. The next time she saw horses, she made uncertain vocalizations but did not lunge and bark at them. Instead, she continued to look at the horses for a click and turned back quickly to me for cheese. Then I noticed a really big improvement. The third time we trained, she saw a horse and happily sneezed and looked at me for cheese. I continued to click and give her cheese for looking at horses. I was thrilled with the success. Amazingly the next time we encountered horses, she casually looked at them, I clicked and treated, but she walked past the horses without seeming to care. My dog now offers looking at things that used to make her nervous, like skateboarders and joggers, rather than having a negative reaction. Of course, I remember to reward and praise her. This program truly has been a lifesaver.

—Mark

It turns out that the Look at That! game also has an unexpected side benefit for the up-and-coming agility dog, as my dog Easy taught me.

AN EASY GENERALIZATION

When it came time to teach Easy about obstacle focus, I was pleasantly surprised to discover that, without any help from me, he immediately generalized the Look at That Dog! behavior to looking at obstacles. Easy had been looking at dogs on cue in CU classes since he was five months old. When I put him in front of a jump or tunnel to teach him about obstacle focus, I expected to wait a bit for him to stop staring at me and glance at the obstacle. Since Easy was so focused on me and had made staring at me his hobby in early puppyhood, people had warned me that he would be too handler-focused in agility. Yet I had never worried about that possibility, knowing I could easily train him to switch his focus as needed. What I didn't realize was that teaching him the Look at That! game had given him the rule structure for what to do when obstacles are in front of you—how convenient for both of us!

As soon as I put Easy in front of a jump or a tunnel, he immediately offered looking at it in the same manner that he offers glancing at other dogs. As soon as he
looked, I rewarded him by cueing him to take the obstacle. And that was it for
obstacle-focus training. Sometimes Easy lives up to his name.

GIVING DOGS A TASK TO FOCUS ON WHILE WORKING NEAR OTHER DOGS (PARALLEL GAMES)

The CU games that pair dogs with each other are what I call "parallel games." I was
inspired by the concept that infants reach a certain stage of development where they
are not quite ready to interact directly with each other but are preparing to interact
by playing alone while near or next to each other. This phenomenon is called "parallel play." For dogs that are uncomfortable working near other dogs, CU's parallel
games give them a job to do or a game to play and focus on while they are near other
dogs, without any pressure to interact directly with another dog.

In multi-dog households where the dogs have tiffs, I have found that parallel activities can foster a spirit of teamwork that encourages the dogs to become more tolerant
of each other. This occurs when the dogs are taught that they have a highly rewarding job to do that they can only perform in the presence of the other household dog.
Therefore the dogs are not pressured to interact directly, but are learning to enjoy
being in each other's presence within a clear rule structure that provides a fun job for
both dogs, such as targeting objects, going to mats, stay exercises, or heeling exercises
(one dog on each side of the handler).

In CU, the parallel games focus on helping an uncomfortable dog learn to work
comfortably near other dogs. Of course, using targets plays a role here by giving the
dog something to focus on. You can also use parallel games to desensitize and coun-
tercondition a reactive or easily aroused dog to tolerate dogs running, tugging, or
otherwise being exciting near him. In the case of Parallel Racing, my beginning-level
parallel game, I try to match the dogs as evenly as possible.

Note: Sometimes a pair of dogs comes into the CU class as friends or even housemates.
I use these dogs as racing partners for each other since they are most comfortable with
each other, then change to Snap or another class dog as appropriate. I want to create a
template for the games that it's not a big deal to be around other dogs running. I start
by using whichever dog will be the least stressful or threatening to the dog learning the
game. This holds true as well for the There's a Dog in Your Face! game (page 166).

PARALLEL RACING

Among its other benefits, this exercise is great for beginner flyball dogs since it can recreate under very controlled circumstances the flyball rule structure of racing with other dogs as well as—in its more advanced form—passing other dogs head-on.

I put a straight line of ring gates down the center of the working area and several ring gates at one end of the line to make a "T" shape. The T shape is good because (with an assistant, if necessary) it can prevent a dog that gets to the end of the line from visiting the dog on the other side of the gates. I ask a pair of handlers to put their dogs in sit-stays on either side of a gate opposite the T and lead out a few feet. If the dogs need more help, I have the handlers stay with their dogs. The handlers can stand between the dogs and the gate if the dogs need more distance from each other, or they can stand on the outside so the dogs are next to each other. Then the handlers either start running with their dogs on the count of three, or, if they are leading out, call their dogs and run on the count of three. Some handlers may need to keep their dogs on a leash or a long line the first few times they run; others can start immediately with the dog off leash. When the dogs get to the T, the handlers reward them with a treat (or a toy, if both dogs doing the exercise are ready for the possible extra excitement of a toy being introduced).

At left, Snap and Weimaraner Bruiser set up for a low-level parallel race with handlers on the inside of the gates to provide a further barrier between their dog and the other dog. The only modification is that the dogs are both unleashed. At right, Snap and Sheltie Boing! prepare for a more advanced form of parallel racing. Here the two handlers have moved laterally away and to the outside of their dogs, which are now only separated by a ring gate. The middle gate has been removed.

Once the dogs are comfortable racing parallel to each other along the line of ring gates, I raise criteria in the following ways, one step at a time, until I get the end result of dogs running loose, parallel to each other, then passing each other head on, without gates:

- By increasing proximity (having dogs move closer to their side of the dividing ring gate; then having dogs work on the inside of the gate if their handlers were on the inside before).

- By increasing speed.

- By folding up the middle gate so the dogs move past each other without part of their barrier (dogs are on leash while getting used to moving past each other without the whole barrier). I fold up the middle gate first so the dogs still have a barrier at the beginning and end of the run. When they are ready, I fold up the end gate and finally the start gate.

- By having the handlers drop the dogs' leashes with the gates in place.

- By folding up the middle gate and having the handlers drop the dogs' leashes. When the dogs are ready we fold up the end and then the beginning gate with leashes still dropped.

Once the dogs have become comfortable racing unleashed to the end of the line of ring gates, raise the challenge by removing the middle ring gate. Note here that both dogs are focused ahead.

When the dogs are able to run parallel to each other, loose and without the barriers, I start the passing exercise. I put the gates back up and place the dogs at opposite ends of the line of ring gates so that they will be running head-on past—rather than parallel to—each other.

Note: Every time I raise one criterion, handlers may need to decrease another criterion to keep their dogs subthreshold. For example, if I take a gate away, a handler may need to walk at a brisk pace (or even at a slow heel) with her dog the first race and build back up to running at full speed. It totally depends on the team. Many teams won't need to decrease speed at this point, but the teams with more sensitive dogs might.

When the dogs are passing each other at full speed, ignoring each other and totally engaged with their handlers, I start taking the gates down one by one. Again, I first remove a middle gate so that the dogs start and end with a barrier, but have a chance to be free in the middle. Then I take down the end gate and, finally, the beginning gate.

Working with motion-triggered dogs

I've had many dogs in CU that could not watch another dog running without going ballistic. For them, this exercise is extremely helpful, as long as you work at a level where they are set up for success. For the dogs that need some prep work before starting parallel racing, you could

- Sit with them at a distance from the gates and play Look at That!

- Simply feed them the whole time another dog is moving.

- Cue them to lie on their Go to Place mats and do some soothing bodywork while the other dogs run in the distance.

If you cannot manage the environment so that your dog is under threshold, and if he will scream the entire time the class is playing parallel games, then do *not* let the dog watch the other dogs race. Crate your dog where he cannot see the dogs running, unless you've set up the situation specifically to help him learn some coping skills. Wait until it's his turn, when you can set him up for success. Never just stand there with him without giving him a clear structure to work with. Make sure he has enough distance to feel comfortable and feed him for watching the racing dogs briefly and turning back to you. Again, I use tubes of peanut butter or squeeze cheese to gum up the dogs' mouths and reduce barking.

Note: If a dog doesn't want to eat, it's often an indication that he is stressing and near or over his threshold, so he isn't in a great state for learning. Look for ways to bring him back rather than making him stay in a situation that could cause a reaction.

I have found—thanks to Deva, the Belgian Sheepdog (see "Deva, The Hair-trigger Belgian," page 144) that for some reactive dogs a crate makes a huge difference in training coping skills with other dogs in motion around them. The first couple of races Deva watched from her crate, while I kept throwing food into her crate the entire time the dogs were moving. When I felt she was ready, I started waiting for her to look at the dogs, then I clicked and treated her, and thus the exercise turned into a Look at That! game. Having Deva crated seemed to take a lot of pressure off both dog and handler. And the handler got to practice her timing and rate of reinforcement without worrying that her dog was going to lunge on her leash.

When Deva was totally quiet, looking at the dogs on cue, and whipping back to me for her reward, I told her handler that we should raise criteria by taking her out of the crate. Deva was ready for this step, but her handler was really enjoying having her in that crate! Nevertheless, her handler sat in a chair with Deva out of her crate and continued to play the game.

Training a reactive dog to watch other dogs in motion

To give a reactive dog the skills to watch other dogs in motion calmly and with self-control, I use Snap (who has done this exercise a million times) or I pick the calmest, least-stimulating dog in the class.

1. I put the calm dog on one side of the line of gates and the reactive dog on the other side at whatever distance is needed to keep both dogs comfortable. I may have the reactive dog on his mat getting some bodywork.

2. I make sure the reactive dog is comfortable while the calmer dog sits quietly next to his handler on the other side of the gates. The Look at That! game comes in handy here.

3. When appropriate, the handler with the calmer dog slowly and quietly heels him down the line of gates. The reactive dog gets fed nonstop as long as the calmer dog is moving; he can watch the heeling dog quietly while he is eating.

4. When the reactive dog is ready for the next step, I ask the handler of the calmer dog to put him in a sit-stay a couple of feet away and call him. The reactive dog gets fed the instant the calmer dog begins to move. To start, the calmer dog could be called from just a couple of feet away to a controlled sit-in-front rather than an all-out *Come!* with the dog running to the handler at speed.

5. If the reactive dog is handling this trigger well, I start playing the Look at That Dog! game with him as the calmer dog starts moving faster and faster. The calmer dog's handler heels him to one end of the line of gates while the handler plays the Look at That! game (or, alternatively, rewards direct, sustained eye contact if that is what her dog is choosing to offer), always using a high rate of reinforcement. Then I ask the calmer dog's handler to turn around and keep going in the other direction, with every lap moving a little faster until they are moving at the pace that initially caused the reaction in the other dog.

6. When the reactive dog can tolerate that level of motion, he gets to join the game. Both handlers will then start by heeling their dogs slowly, parallel to each other, pausing for occasional sits if necessary. Each time they hit the end of the line of gates, they turn, head in the other direction, and pick up speed.

7. Eventually the reactive dog is running alongside the calmer one, and then we can start raising criteria such as removing gates, doing passes, and so on. We can further raise criteria by adding motivational cues, such as *Reaaaaady,* or agility obstacles into the parallel racing area, keeping in mind that each time we raise criteria, we may need to increase distance or use a barrier or find some other way of helping the reactive dog stay calm and focused in the face of this new excitement.

Labrador Retriever Ranger remains calm and stationary while watching Snap get silly. Next steps include gradually increasing Snap's speed and, once Ranger shows good impulse control watching Snap in motion, removing the gate and starting over with an initially calmer Snap. Bringing Ranger closer to Snap would also raise the challenge.

Using crates: Some reactive dogs in CU settle in their crates and can watch other dogs jumping, and so on, without any sort of reaction, even if they react to the same commotion when outside of their crates. For these dogs, we can move the crates closer and closer to "the line of fire" where the other dog is working. When teaching a dog to truly relax in and enjoy his crate I like to use Dr. Overall's Protocol for Relaxation, going through the steps while the dog is in his crate (the door can be open for this). Make sure to use a Go to Place mat inside the crate for the protocol. You can also shape and reward any calm behavior your dog gives you while he's in his crate, aiming for a sleepy-eyed, floppy look.

When the reactive dog is just hanging out in his crate no matter what is going on next door, his handler can release him from his crate. He may need to be taken farther away from the moving dog and gradually brought closer. Remember that exiting the crate should cue the reactive dog to reorient to his handler (following the CU crate rule). Then the handler can start the Look at That! game (or reward sustained eye contact instead, depending on the dog and the situation), or cue the dog to lie on his mat for a massage.

As long as the reactive dog is not reacting, the handler can gradually decrease the distance between him and the calmer dog. If the dog reacts, the handler can put him back in his crate to settle again. The return to the crate is not being used as a consequence; the crate in this scenario is a tool to help the dog recover and feel more comfortable.

Barrier Training For Reactive Dogs

Often I work with dogs that are highly reactive at the mere sight of another dog or a dog in motion. These dogs are clearly not appropriate for CU, but certainly the same basic principles apply to them, too. CU handlers can use the barrier training technique whenever they feel their dog needs to calm down and refocus, or needs a break from visual stimulation.

I ask the reactive dog's handler take him behind one of my high tarp-and-PVC barriers. Often I make a gated area around the barrier. I let out one of my dogs, (usually my veteran helper Maggie) and ask her to lie down and stay at the opposite end of the yard. Then I go behind the barrier to start working with the reactive dog. If the dog already knows how to relax in a crate, I incorporate a crate into the exercise and have him in a crate behind the barrier. I walk the dog outside the barrier for a nanosecond, click, and jackpot the dog with multiple treats. While he's still chewing, I walk him back behind the barrier (or into his crate). Sometimes I do this routine several times before letting out one of my dogs, to teach the reactive dog the pattern of leaving the barrier/eating/going back behind the barrier.

When the dog is comfortable with this pattern and is expecting his jackpot on leaving the barrier, I start increasing the amount of time we stay outside the barrier, by nanoseconds. Since the reactive dog already knows the Look at That! game, I start asking him to look at my dog and click his glance, jackpot, and go back behind the barrier. The dog will be able to stay outside of the barrier for longer periods of time, noticing that my dog is out there at a distance and looking at me expectantly for his treat. Once the dog understands how the barrier game works—we come out, see stuff, eat, and go back in—I can raise my criteria by

- Asking Maggie to move closer to the barrier and lie down again.
- Having an assistant, or the dog's own handler, heel Maggie at gradually decreasing distances from the barrier.
- Removing the barrier, possibly leaving the crate and continuing the exercise with the dog coming in and out of his crate, if the dog needs a transitional step between barrier and no barrier. The dog can also go to a mat as a transitional step.

Note: I use this same barrier structure for an advanced version of the parallel racing game where the dogs run through tunnels and over jumps parallel to each other, but separated by the gates. This level of activity is much more difficult for some dogs to experience, so the barrier training can be very helpful.

Adding motivational cues

When the dogs are ready, we can add what are popularly known as "motivational cues," such as *1... 2... 3... Go!* into the exercise. In the end we are aiming for dogs that are in a reasonable state of arousal, passing right next to each other at top speed, and not even noticing each other.

Adding motivational cues for the overmotivated

I have had many dogs in CU that went so wild with barking and lunging on hearing the words *Ready, Three,* or *Go* (even when a handler was saying these words to another dog) that their handlers were unable to control them. These are dogs whose owners—like Deva's below—unwittingly have spent a lot of time classically conditioning their dogs to lose their minds when they hear motivational cues, even ones not meant for them.

DEVA, THE HAIR-TRIGGER BELGIAN

My favorite example of a handler who was so focused on using a motivational cue that she didn't realize the effect it was having on her dog occurred during my first CU seminar. The parallel racing exercise was the first time I worked Deva, the hair-trigger Belgian, around other dogs. We went through a long period conditioning her to just watch the other dogs quietly. She got to a point where she could handle heeling parallel to another dog with the ring gates in between them, so I allowed the two dogs to move a little faster. When they moved faster, she became aroused and veered a little toward the other dog, and her owner responded by making this Xena Warrior Princess *Lalalaalalalallaallala!* sound deep in her throat. The second Deva heard this sound, I saw her entire body change. She went into overdrive and ran at the gate screaming and trying to get at the other dog.

Once we got Deva settled, I asked her owner, "What ever did you make that noise for?" She replied that she makes that noise when Deva gets excited because it's a motivational sound that's supposed to get the dog to pay attention to her. I pointed out that since she made that sound every time Deva started going over threshold, she had classically conditioned her dog to have a reactive response on hearing that particular sound. Pavlov triumphs again. I told her, "No more Xena Warrior Princess battle cries!"

Deva became excited when hearing the warrior princess noise because of a learning structure called "classical conditioning," in which dogs make associations between two unrelated stimuli. The examples here were Deva's feeling of arousal and her owner's battle cry. We can use this structure to our advantage by noticing when a certain feeling or response occurs naturally in our dogs, and naming it, so that our words evoke that feeling or response in the dog through association.

For example, when Snap gets into a silly, playful mood he bounces around with his whole body teasing "Come and get me if you can!" When he's in this mood, I tell him he is being a weasel because he looks like a crazed ferret to me. I did not condition the response on purpose, but because whenever he felt silly I told him he was a weasel, he associated hearing the word *Weasel* with feeling silly. So now whenever I want to elicit play from him, I tell him he is a weasel and he starts bouncing around. An added benefit is that if Snap is worrying about something, telling him he is a weasel is an effective strategy to cheer him up.

We don't have to set up situations to use classical conditioning to our advantage; we can just observe our dogs, notice their moods and behaviors, and sneak in a word or sound association. Dogs learn through making associations all the time, so we just need to be aware of this potential and use it to our benefit.

To help a dog like Deva learn to think when exposed to motivational cues, I play the game Ready... Set... Eat! or 1... 2... 3... Eat!, depending on which cue makes the dog lose her mind.

1. I place the reactive dog on one side of the ring gates with a dog on the other side of the gates that reliably stays through the motivational cues until released.

2. The reliable dog's handler goes through the cues in a *neutral* voice while the reactive dog's handler feeds his dog. Again, the reactive dog needs to remain under threshold, that means, he needs to be quiet and able to learn. If he's shrieking, that's a clue you need to modify the exercise. That's all I do until the reactive dog understands that unless his own handler or teacher is directly communicating a motivational cue to him, other cues he may hear people give their dogs nearby him are not meant for him and are actually signals to reorient to his own handler.

3. The next step is for the reliable dog's handler to give the cues while the reactive dog's handler waits through *1... 2... 3...* and only feeds at *Go*.

4. Then the handler giving the cues can start saying them in a more realistic tone of voice.

5. Repeating this exercise several times coupled with the steps above to desensitize dogs to other dogs running past them has been enough to fix this problem in class, so far. This work goes quickly because of the groundwork the dogs have already done in class before we get to this exercise.

When some of these dogs return to the context of a real agility class, their handlers will have to continue this work, reframing motivational cues meant for other dogs using barriers, distance, massaging on mats, the Look at That! or Ready... Set... Eat! games as cues to reorient to handler. The end result will be that their dogs can handle both hearing the cues and seeing other dogs run without losing their minds.

Chapter 6

NIGHT FOUR

CONCEPTS

- Whistle while you work: Increasing both enthusiasm and focus in a distracting environment (Give Me a Break game)
- Sniffing is not a crime!
- Teaching the dog to think through his arousal (The Off-switch game)
- Combining the Off-switch game with other games
- Close encounters (Campfire Circle game)

NEW EXERCISES

- Give Me a Break game
- The Off-switch game
- Campfire Circle game

Reminder: Continue working on passive and active attention and box work at the beginning of each class, raising criteria as appropriate for each dog.

By this point the dogs are able to behave calmly around each other, can focus on the active attention exercises, and relax on mats in close proximity. They are starting to be able to work loose, in structured contexts (start-line stays, box work, parallel games). Dogs are watching other dogs as an offered behavior, not out of excitement or excessive interest They are ready to do more challenging focus training, in the form of two games critical to the CU program: Give Me a Break game and some version of The Off-switch game. One uses the concept of the Premack Principle to increase the dog's enthusiasm and focus in a distracting environment; the other enables him to better cope with fluctuating levels of stimulation—and, more important, teaches him to think through his arousal so that he can perform even when very excited. The combination of these games teaches excitement to work and the ability to think through arousal so that the dog can work once we've gotten him excited about working.

WHISTLE WHILE YOU WORK: INCREASING BOTH ENTHUSIASM AND FOCUS IN A DISTRACTING ENVIRONMENT (GIVE ME A BREAK GAME)

Whenever I train a dog who needs help with focus or motivation, I use what I call the Give Me a Break rule structure. Give Me a Break is about giving the dog frequent breaks (using what I call the "quick dismissal") from short, highly rewarding, training sessions and then resuming the session as a reward for the dog's *choosing* to ask, "Can we keep working?" The goal is to increase the dog's attention and eagerness to work with you. Give Me a Break is simple and powerful.

Note: Remember that CU is a fluid program and that I tailor to suit the students; although I have given a general outline of the progression of exercises that I teach throughout the course, I may change the order depending upon what is needed in a certain class. This is especially true with the Give Me a Break game. *Often I find myself playing this game even on the first night of class.* If there is a dog so "sucked in" by everything around him that he is having a lot of trouble focusing, I may play the Give Me a Break game with him myself to help the dog get his mind back. Then I'll coach the dog's handler through playing the game.

Teaching Give Me a Break

1. Have a clear plan in your mind of what you want to train before getting your dog out.

2. Start the game in a controlled environment without a lot of distractions—in an empty basement or a small ring-gate box, for instance, with a chair nearby.

When your dog is playing the game reliably, he is ready to play in a more challenging environment.

3. Count out 10 treats and put them in your hand.

4. Follow your training plan: Ask for a behavior, or a game of tug for dogs whose play drive you wish to intensify, or whatever. (Go To Place is a popular choice to start with in CU class. The dogs already understand the behavior, so the student can focus on getting into the rhythm of the Give Me a Break structure rather than worrying about the dog's performance. And it's easy to reward on the mat and release the dog while being clear about maintaining criteria. After releasing the dog, students using Go To Place will pick up their mats so the dog has to "ask" to get the mat back. Another popular game choice to start with is heeling or circle work. The students move with the dogs, rewarding attention in rapid-fire fashion and then dismiss the dogs.)

5. Use a super-high rate of reinforcement—like 10 treats in 5 seconds, or tugging while counting down from 10 (or 20 or 30, depending on how long the dog stays really engaged in playing).

6. Give a verbal dismissal cue (one that is different from your release cue), turn away from your dog, and go sit in the chair. Your cue and body language should always be the same to show the dog that you are disengaging from the game and dismissing him to go take a break.

7. Allow the dog to do what he wants for up to a minute while you sit in the chair. At the end of the break period, re-engage your dog and start another short, highly rewarding session followed by another break.

During each break, look for signs of reorienting from a dog that is checking out his environment; if the dog comes up to you before his break period is up, immediately reward his attention by starting the game again. This is the goal of using the Give Me a Break training structure: creating a dog that asks to keep working, that doesn't want to take a break because he is so engaged in the training process.

Note: If your dog disengages *before you have released him* to take a break, go sit in the chair as if you had given the release cue. When the dog reorients to you, immediately restart the game.

As you progress, you can make the training sessions last longer, but do it in increments of seconds. You *never, ever* want the dog to disengage *before* you give your verbal release, so for a highly distractible dog, this game will keep you on your toes. I often have students count out several treats for the last behavior they are going to reward before giving their dismissal cue; that way, they have an extra second to say their cue as the dog finishes swallowing, and the dog has no opportunity to take off before being released.

Clicker trainers use a similar structure to allow "latent learning" to take place. Latent learning describes what happens during the dog's timed break period. His brain is processing what he just did, and his understanding will improve with each subsequent session. I started the quick dismissal game with latent learning in mind but quickly found that the dogs were choosing to cut their break short and ask for more work, and I had to reward that! So what has evolved into the Give Me a Break game became one of the most powerful tools I have to increase a dog's enthusiasm and focus to work.

Building Enthusiasm to Work

Snap was the first dog that I trained using this technique. My other dogs hadn't needed such a structured approach to learning; they had more stamina for training and never had the attention issues that Snap experienced. In retrospect, my behavior consults also always operated within this structure in a less formal way, since I switched between briefly working with a dog and then giving him something to chew on or play with as I talked to the human side of the equation. When I adopted Snap he had no attention span and no focus, he stressed under the pressure of learning something new, and he was easily sucked in by the floor, disengaging from any interaction with me to go away and sniff. Offering a highly rewarding, extremely brief training session with a one-minute break made great sense for him. My dismissal accommodated his short attention span and allowed him to go do what he wanted within a structure that would accomplish my goal of increasing his attention span in the long run.

An unexpected phenomenon occurred as we started training this way: Snap became so invested in the training game that when I released him to go take a break, he started choosing to stick around me, offering behaviors in an attempt to get me to keep on training. Since I wanted to reinforce him for preferring to continue training rather than leaving to go do his own thing, I found myself starting a new session before his minute break was up. At this point I decided that, for my purposes, rewarding Snap for choosing to keep going was more important than giving him latent learning time. As our sessions progressed, he became more focused and keener to work. He started ignoring the floor and got swept up in the pattern of training, refusing to take a break and training more, more, and more. This method of short, intense training bouts was also the most effective technique that I found for building Snap's play drive. Tug hard for a couple seconds. "Okay, go away and sniff the floor. Oh, you have no interest in the floor?" Tug hard for a couple more seconds then, "Okay, now really, this time go away, we're done here. Oh, you demand more tugging? Well, I suppose..."

Can you see how this technique will take pressure off a dog that stresses as opposed to forcing a dog to keep training that instead wants to sniff and disengage? Which style is going to help the dog learn better? Which one will teach handler focus faster? One way, you are demanding the dog continue working while his mind is drifting away. The other way, *the dog* is demanding that he continue working.

Setting up the Game in Class
The Give Me a Break exercise is built around

- Quick, highly reinforcing sessions of whatever the students want to work on (toy play, targeting, lying on a mat, circle work, looking at dogs).

- A cue that tells the dog you are disengaging and that he is dismissed.

- Waiting for the dog to reorient to owner and say, "I'm not done yet!"

So, latent learning isn't the part being emphasized in CU. *The dog's choosing to work instead of sniff around or disengage is what we're aiming for. This choice comes once the dog has become invested in the pattern or "feedback loop" of the game.*

Hoping to get his mat back, Snap offers McDevitt a down during his break time.

During this exercise, I put one dog and his handler, loaded with treats, in a box of ring gates and start counting down from 10 (or less—of course, it all depends on the dog) as she clicks and treats her dog for whatever behavior she has chosen to work on. I have a chair within the ring gates so that when the handler gives the release cue, she can sit in the chair and wait it out. At that point, the dog is free to sniff around within the box. The nanosecond the dog reorients to the handler, I want the handler to leap out of the chair and start the next session. As soon as I see that reorientation, I start counting down from 10 again. When doing this exercise I sometimes act like a cheerleader, jumping and clapping and counting down loudly. I like the energy to be high, and I like people to laugh and have fun with it because otherwise some students start feeling bad that their dogs go off and sniff when released instead of acting like Snap who, when he demos the exercise, flat out demands to continue training and won't leave me. I always tell the students not to feel badly if the dog leaves—after all, he was dismissed, and maybe he really needed a break. But after a few sessions, all the dogs end up more focused and start choosing to ask for more training instead of sniffing around.

Note: It is important to have two release cues, one used to dismiss during the game, and a definitive, final release cue when you actually want to stop training and don't want to be pestered!

Switching off the Overaroused

This exercise is particularly hard for dogs with a significant arousal problem. When the owner interacts with the dog, he gets aroused. When the owner dismisses his dog and sits in a chair, the dog is left overstimulated and unable to take a break. Typically he flies at his handler, barking, pawing, and so on. During the Give Me a Break game, these dogs need a lot of structure; being dismissed to go be a dog is not enough information for them. One solution is to put a mat next to the handler's chair and treat the Give Me a Break as an Off-switch game (page 154). In this case, the handler is not going for latent learning or for reinforcing attention, but is just letting her dog get a little excited and then engaging in calming bodywork as he lies on his mat. Three reps per session are plenty for these dogs.

SNIFFING IS NOT A CRIME!

CU operates within my philosophy of getting the best of both worlds. Training is a dance with two partners. You must meet your dog's needs in order to get the performance you want from him. Dogs need to sniff. Dogs need to greet other dogs. Dogs need to look at things. Dogs need to be *normal*. The CU exercises offer a structure in which the dogs can be dogs and still learn to be focused, working partners with you. You do not have to sacrifice your dog's "dogness" to create a great performance partner. Yet I work with so many people who have created or encouraged weird behavior problems in their dogs by raising them with the notion that they won't be good performance dogs if they're allowed to sniff around, interact with other dogs, look at anything but their handlers, and so on. A dog has to know how to be a good *dog*, before he can be a good *performance dog*.

I've seen people get so upset when their dog sniffs the ground. If a dog is sniffing instead of paying attention, it's time to rethink your training plan, not to correct your dog. If your dog is sniffing, is he distracted? Is he stressed? Is he just done for the moment? Dogs have good reasons for sniffing. That doesn't mean I want my dogs sniffing all around when I'm training them, but they don't, because I adjust my training plans to suit them and give each the training structure that he needs. My first agility and flyball dog, Maggie, could go for hours and she never lost focus. She was the ultimate natural partner and she spoiled me. Fast forward to Snap.

Border Collie Blitz communicates that Doberman Jynx's teenage intensity is a bit much for him by turning his back on Jynx and sniffing the ground. Blitz demonstrates two of what many trainers call "calming signals," indicating that he does not want to engage with Jynx.

When Snap came to live with me, he could go for less than a minute before losing focus. So everything I did with him, I did within the Give Me a Break structure. A few seconds of training, a lot of break. Gradually he got to the point where he didn't want or need the break. But when teaching him something new, since he has such a low frustration threshold, I always read him carefully to assess whether he needs to return to the old rule structure. The more we train, the fewer breaks he needs, and the more easily he can handle the frustration that comes with learning and work through it happily instead of turning off. The Give Me a Break game was instrumental for Snap in a variety of ways.

After several months of my getting Snap to the point where he could focus for 5 to 10 minutes without turning off or running away, I started taking private agility lessons. I signed Snap up for half an hour and worked him for 5 to 10 minutes at a time and then gave him a 10-minute break. Then I'd bring him out for another 5 to 10 minutes. That was last year. This year, we are taking hour-long, private agility lessons. He can focus for the entire time and doesn't need even one break. Go Snap!

During lessons, many dogs want or *need* to sniff or run off to do their thing while the instructor gives the handler feedback. To prevent a dog from doing his own thing, handlers usually leash their dogs, pick them up, or crate them. Yet, that minute of instructor feedback provides a good break period for your dog to blow off some steam. When I first started lessons with Snap and it was time to talk to my instructor, I dismissed him with a verbal cue. He was going to go off and sniff anyway and I wasn't going to stop him. Do you see that this is just an advanced version of the Give Me a Break game? Snap did. He started offering me downs as soon as the instructor began talking, asking to continue his lesson. Sometimes I can tell he truly needs a break, so I dismiss him when it's time to talk to my teacher and he sniffs around the building. Snap is allowed to be a dog. If he weren't allowed to be a dog, he'd be a nightmare!

TEACHING THE DOG TO THINK THROUGH HIS AROUSAL (THE OFF-SWITCH GAME)

The purpose of this game is to allow a dog to reach a certain level of arousal and then reward him for calming down before resuming activity. This game helps the dog learn to think through arousal by setting up a situation where he can practice being high and low over and over again—and learn to switch from one to the other with ease.

Here are some examples of how to play:

1. Tug or throw a ball or spray your dog with the garden hose, whatever turns your dog on, for 30 seconds (or until he looks as if he is about to go over the top—you want to stop the exciting activity before he loses it).

2. Then ask your dog to sit or lie down, or wait for him to offer you a default behavior.

    a. If he has a strong default behavior, he will offer it to you when you release him from the game as a way of asking for a continuation. My preference is to condition a default behavior to be so strong that it can override high arousal or instinctive behaviors (page 70). To me this is an essential component of impulse-control training.

b. For dogs that need help thinking through arousal or settling down when they start to get too excited, incorporate biofeedback into the game: take some deep breaths, blink, and look at your dog softly. Watch your dog's eyes, ears, tail—every signal that you can. Give him a food reward for blinking and having soft eyes, droopy ears, a tail that swishes slowly rather than whacking the ground—any sign of softening.

3. Resume the activity.

There should be a clear pattern of get excited, settle, get excited, settle. The more comfortable your dog becomes with this pattern, the better his coping skills will be in stimulating situations. You can be very creative with your off-switch games; for example, if your dog enjoys playing with other dogs in the park, you can incorporate the Off-switch game structure into their play. Send your dog to go play, call him back after a brief period and ask for a settled, calm sit or down, then send him back to play some more. Not only is this exercise an Off-switch game, helping the dog come out of an aroused state, but it also is a smart use of the Premack Principle for recall training.

Snap on. Snap off. Snap offers his default down (right) hoping to get the game of tug started again. His quiet, self-controlled behavior gets the game going again.

Impulse control and agility must go hand in paw

Agility, like other competitive dog sports, puts certain dogs into a state of hyper-arousal that sometimes results in handler casualties (I know so many people who are chronically black and blue from being grabbed during agility and flyball training). The excitement of both the class and trial environment—running, barking, and tugging dogs—can easily send a dog with a low arousal-threshold and poor impulse control over the top.

THE FRESH SHELTIE

I will never forget the fresh Sheltie. While waiting my turn at a trial, I watched a handler NQ because she could not detach her Sheltie from her pants leg. During his run, the Sheltie had gotten increasingly aroused with each obstacle and, somewhere in the middle of the course, he flew at the pants leg and would not—could not—let go. His handler hobbled out of the ring with the dog still attached. I heard somebody sitting nearby me say, "That Sheltie is always so fresh!" Although freshness is not exactly a clinical description for dogs with low arousal-thresholds and poor impulse control, it is the description I will always think of when I see dogs leaping at their handlers, nipping them, or grabbing their clothing on course. I see these dogs often.

When I listen to discussions about dogs that nip and grab on course, the usual responses I hear from people are

- Give time-outs.

- Down the dog the second he gets fresh.

- Apply aversives (anything from a verbal reprimand to a spritz with a water bottle to a physical correction of some sort) because being fresh is unacceptable.

These suggestions all describe actions the handler can take to deal with the dog *after* he has lost it. While asking for a down (if the dog is able to think through his arousal and respond to a cue at all) or giving a time-out can help a dog calm down after the fact, my personal preference would be to teach the dog skills to cope with feeling aroused and to exercise self-control, so that the handler can nip the nipping in the bud rather than get nipped and then respond. Where possible, *be proactive, not reactive.*

Others advise that you need to become a better handler so that you don't frustrate your dog into a state of frenzy with your poor timing and handling. This suggestion encourages a handler to be aware of how her behavior may be affecting her dog. And since it is a handler-oriented suggestion, the frenzied dog in question is not in danger of receiving an unfair aversive as punishment for unacceptable behavior that was out of his control. Moreover, it's common sense: as your handling—and sense of communication with your dog—improve, the agility "picture" becomes clearer for your dog. He starts to understand the rule structure of agility and his role within that structure so his frustration level drops markedly. For some dogs that clarity may be all that is needed to fix their impulse-control problem.

But, because this suggestion takes the dog out of the picture, it does not address the dog's arousal threshold. You can take a dog with a high arousal-threshold (in other words, one that doesn't get excited easily and is one of those slow-but-steady-wins-the-race dogs) and the greenest handler and never see any sign of loss of control. You can take a dog with a low arousal-threshold (hair-trigger, overstimulated-at-the-drop-of-a-hat dogs) and an experienced handler and still get some loss of control because the underlying inhibition- and impulse-control problems have not been addressed. So, my caveat is: I don't want a handler to feel that if she has a dog with impulse-control issues it's all her fault because she's a lousy handler. While her handling may contribute to the dog's frenetic behavior, the dog's behavior is also saying something about the dog: therefore, we need to look at each case of overarousal on course individually, and the handler should be aware if her dog needs some foundation work for learning impulse control.

Dealing with poor impulse control on the agility course

For those dogs that do need some foundation work for learning impulse control, I designed a little program that can be modified as needed to fit your dog. Please note that while some dogs keep their loss of impulse control to the course, others exhibit more general impulse-control problems that manifest themselves in various ways in daily life.

Teach a Default Behavior

Use the guidelines on page 71. A truly strong default behavior is essential for my style of Off-switch games because this behavior enables dogs to think through arousal and control their impulses.

Play Off-switch games

Once the dog is immediately offering the default behavior you chose every time he wants or needs anything from you, you can start playing Off-switch games as described on page 154. The point of these games is to raise the level of stimulation just enough to get your dog excited without going over the top, then give him the chance to think through the stimulation and bring himself back to a more settled state. The better your dog gets at switching between high and low arousal states, the higher you can raise the level of stimulation. You want the dog to succeed, so if your behavior elicits too much of an excited response—such as jumping up on you or barking—you'll know that you need to take your behavior down a notch or two. *For dogs that get jacked up by toy play, make every toy interaction an Off-switch game.*

OFF-SWITCH GAME FOR THE BALLISTIC

> For a dog that easily flies off the handle, you might just bend your knee as if you're going to run, or take one quick step, or say *Ready,* or even just get a look on your face that says, "I'm about to do something crazy." Then stand perfectly still and ignore the dog until he goes into default mode. Use a food reward while the dog is in default position, and then start the game again, gradually raising criteria until you can yodel, playfully shove the dog around if he likes that kind of interaction, run as fast as you can, do jumping jacks, spray him with a hose, or tug hard, and expect him to immediately drop down, sit, or calmly look at you as soon as you cue "game over" by standing still. Eventually you can fade the food reward and use continuation of the game as its own reward.

Incorporate Circle Work into the Game

When you're happy with your basic Off-switch game, add circle work. Start slowly and gradually build up your speed, interspersing the running with toy play and default downs. Then add in crosses or anything else you want to take the opportunity to work on.

If the Dog Gets Fresh

Keep a chair nearby and if the dog at any point starts to fly off the handle, put his leash on and go sit in the chair. During this break time, you could

- Give him nothing to do and wait for him to settle.

- Give him something to chew on if he has so much nervous energy that he can't calm himself if he's doing nothing.

- Massage his jaws (a good idea for barky and nippy dogs).

- Cue him to lie on a Go to Place mat if he needs a more structured break time.

When Shelties attack: An overaroused Whisper grabs her handler's jacket on course (left). By playing an Off-switch game, Whisper learns that she gets rewarded for automatically sitting when her handler stops moving (middle). Whisper then is able to resist the lure of the jacket and move, unattached and in sync with her handler (right).

After a minute or two of settle time, remind him how good he's become at controlling himself by doing some of the old familiar moves, such as cueing *Ready* and waiting for him to offer his default behavior, that let him know he's playing the Off-switch game. Then sneak increasingly faster circle work back in.

Incorporate Obstacles into the Game

Once you've achieved all your criteria on the flat, you'll be ready to incorporate some obstacles into the game. Start with doing Off-switch game circle work around the obstacles without sending your dog to any obstacles. Then add one obstacle at a time into the circle work. For instance, you could build on the sequence:

1. Tunnel, wait for a default down.

2. Tug, wait for default down. Then tunnel, tug, default down.

3. Then jump, tunnel, tug, default down.

4. Increase activity until your dog can do a short sequence without getting to the point where he feels the need to get fresh.

5. Go for a slightly longer sequence.

Recognize Your Dog's Threshold

Remember that if your dog gets fresh, you raised your criteria too quickly. If your dog is doing so well running short sequences that you've stopped playing the Off-switch game and you want to progress to a longer sequence, return to the rule structure of the game. We have created this rule structure to remind the dog to keep his wits about him when he starts feeling too excited. When you raise criteria by asking for a more difficult or longer sequence, you'll need to operate within this structure to maximize your dog's chances of success. Don't push too hard, too fast, and eventually you will be able to do longer sequences and entire courses without the game at all, which is the goal. Make sure you work in short sessions and give your dog plenty of breaks so he doesn't become overloaded. That is key for a dog with a low arousal-threshold that needs some impulse-control work.

COMBINING THE OFF-SWITCH GAME WITH OTHER GAMES

Once a dog has the foundation work in place and is perfect with both games you can combine an Off-switch game with the Look at That! game to increase coping skills and ability to self-calm in a dog that is stressed or aroused by other dogs.

RIPCORD, THE TUGGING PULI

I had a student with a Puli named Ripcord who was reactive to other dogs and felt very stressed around them. He enjoyed tugging greatly and felt happy and comfortable while doing it. When other dogs got too close, however, his tugging style changed to a shake-and-kill movement, and his grip became much more intense. He was using the tug as a displacement tool for his aggression. His handler always knew that if his tugging style changed, it was time to move Ripcord away from other dogs.

There are some dogs with aggression or arousal issues that I do not want to see tugging in group situations, period. But tugging was a connecting activity for Ripcord and his handler. I wanted Rip to continue to benefit from his favorite game, but he needed some coping skills around other dogs so that he stopped reaching the point where the tugging switched from being an enjoyable game to displaced aggression.

I gave Rip a rule structure that enabled him to tug near other dogs without getting too wound up. Rip already knew the Look at That! game, and he was familiar with Snap. So I put Snap in a sit-stay about 10' from Rip, and asked his handler to play the Look at That Dog! game, rewarding him for quickly glancing toward Snap and then reorienting to her. I did not use a barrier because Rip and Snap already were comfortable operating within this structure. Next I had Rip's handler initiate a tug game for about three seconds, and then tell Rip to let go and to look at Snap. He let go, looked at Snap, and then turned back to his handler for his reward. She rewarded him with food. We repeated this pattern a few times, building up to a point where Rip's handler was tugging for a few seconds longer before asking Rip to let go and look at Snap, and then continuing the tugging when he turned back to her instead of using a food reward. Rip already knew an Off-switch tug game, and he felt safe around other dogs when he was working within the look-at-that-dog-for-a-click structure. Combining the two already familiar structures allowed him to experience tugging near another dog without the usual anxiety.

I wanted to add obstacles into this mix, so I put Rip in front of a tunnel and Snap in front of a tire. After Rip was happily offering little glances at Snap and then whipping back to play with his handler, I sent Snap through the tire as his handler clicked and treated Rip for watching Snap move and then reorienting to her. Rip was immediately comfortable with Snap's jumping through the tire and moving quickly because he had already worked with Snap and he already knew all the CU exercises.

Next, I asked Rip's handler to send him into the tunnel while Snap sat in front of the tire. When he came out of the tunnel, his handler rewarded him with food, then asked him to look at Snap, putting him back into the old familiar pattern. After repeating this pattern a couple of times, I let Rip's handler reward his tunnel performance with a tug for about three seconds. Then she asked him to let go and resumed the Look-at-Snap game. Instead of giving a food reward for reorienting to her, she used the tug, again just for a few seconds, then asked Rip to let go and look at Snap again. At this point Rip was comfortable with the rule structure we were operating in and was able to integrate the more arousing activities of tugging and running through a tunnel into the structure.

We then increased proximity, moving Snap closer and closer to Rip. Each time Snap came closer to Rip, his handler cued Rip to play the Look at That Dog! game again, then sent him into the tunnel and rewarded him with a game of tug. We got Rip to a point where he could tug for between 5 to 10 seconds in his happy, playful manner, interspersed with glancing over at Snap about 5' away, without once going into kill mode. This entire process took place in one session; if we had kept working on this particular issue, I know we could have gotten the dogs much closer.

I thought of this structure of tug, look and settle, tug for Rip and have successfully used it for other dogs since. For a dog that has serious dog/dog issues or serious arousal issues, I think tugging near other dogs just jacks up his nervous system too much, so I would avoid it. But it all depends on the dog, his level of self-control, and the emotional responses that tugging brings out in him.

In class Ripcord reached the point where he was able to tug, get highly aroused and run courses squeaking his head off in anticipation, then immediately settle down, lying on his side in a state of satisfied relaxation on his mat, or offering brief glances at the other dogs and checking back with his handler to make sure she saw what a good boy he was being. Since he came into class with a history of being highly reactive, he is truly a CU poster dog. Recently I encountered him and his handler at an agility trial. When first I had met his handler, she had thought she would never feel comfortable enough to trial her dog, but there she was walking him around happily as he offered brief glances toward dogs they passed and turned back to her in delight awaiting his treat. She even felt comfortable enough to hand him to a friend of hers when she went to check in. He attempted to play his Look at That Dog! game with the friend, but since she didn't have any treats he was getting frustrated. Finally, he heaved a sigh at her and gave up, waiting for his mom, who understood the rules. He Qd with a first placement that day, but his biggest accomplishment was just being at the agility trial without getting stressed or reactive. He loves agility, and his handler is a gifted and accomplished agility instructor and competitor. Now that he is in an emotional place where he not only can handle being in a trial environment but also actually can feel happy and confident, they are ready to seriously rock and roll.

CLOSE ENCOUNTERS (CAMPFIRE CIRCLE GAME)

This is a simple variation on the Look at That Dog! game that offers a structure where the dogs take turns being casually brought near each other while everybody sits in a circle. It is a game I use only if there is extra time. I place the dogs and handlers in a large circle and start by walking Snap up to each dog and having each handler click her dog for looking at Snap. Then, depending on the particular mix of dogs, I may let some or all of the handlers take their dogs around the circle. The dog moving around the circle is getting clicked for looking at each dog (and turning quickly back to his handler for the reward). Each dog in the circle is also being clicked for looking at the dog that's come up to him. The dogs by this point barely want to glance at each other and are mostly watching their handlers.

An alternative to the campfire circle is to have the handlers and their dogs stand in a line behind ring gates and run the demo dog or an appropriate student dog parallel to the line. The handlers can click their dogs for watching the moving dog. Obviously if the student dogs are not ready to watch a dog running yet, they can watch a dog heeling and gradually increasing speed as in the basic parallel racing game. You can continue to modify this game until it resembles the agility trial experience of dogs waiting for their turn to run a course and watching the dog ahead of them run.

Chapter 7

NIGHT FIVE

CONCEPTS

- Working up to working loose: Increasing challenges
- Prepping for even closer encounters (There's a Dog in Your Face! game)
- Targeting tasks to perform loose around other moving dogs (Get Outs around jump standards)
- Making it personal: Customizing the CU approach
- "But he only plays at home"

NEW EXERCISES

- There's a Dog in Your Face! game
- Get Outs around jump standards

Reminder: Continue working on passive and active attention and box work at the beginning of each class, raising criteria as appropriate for each dog.

WORKING UP TO WORKING LOOSE: INCREASING CHALLENGES

Some dogs will be ready to work loose sooner than others. When assessing which dogs are ready to have their leashes dropped for an exercise, always err on the side of caution and use barriers, long lines, and assistants as necessary. I have used a long line in CU exactly once, at a student's request, so that she could give her dog a wider range of movement in the parallel games without worrying. My feeling is if you think you need a long line, chances are your dog isn't ready for what you are asking of him yet without more foundation work. On the other hand, if it makes a student more comfortable and it's appropriate for her dog, using a long line is fine with me. Tell your students to crate their dogs if a particularly reactive dog is going to take a turn doing an exercise unleashed. Use any insurance policy you have to prevent a problem.

I have not had any trouble with CU dogs interacting inappropriately. In the past three years of teaching this course, there have been three or four instances of class dogs barking reactively at each other in passing. In each case, the dogs were easily redirected and recovered quickly. I am always vigilant and mindful about which modification will be appropriate for each dog. Keep in mind that the entire CU program is about teaching dogs that their triggers are *no big deal* and that they can feel calm, safe, happy, and enthusiastic about learning in the face of what used to set them off. Some dogs go through the entire class on leashes and repeat the class with the goal of working off-lead the next time around. Some handlers can drop their dogs' leashes right away.

When the dogs are more comfortable with being off-leash and working near each other, it's time to raise our criteria by

- Inducing excitement or speed in the demo dog working near the class dogs.
- Starting the Dog In Your Face! game, whatever shape that takes for each dog to succeed.
- Teaching Get Outs around jump standards in preparation for the Out 'n Mats game, a more advanced parallel game that uses targeting to keep the dogs focused on going ahead amid the distraction of other dogs and people moving nearby.

PREPPING FOR EVEN CLOSER ENCOUNTERS (THERE'S A DOG IN YOUR FACE! GAME)

This game is another favorite among CU students. Its purpose is to provide a rule structure for dogs that teaches them that if a dog runs near or straight at them it means two things:

1. A dog running toward them is an environmental cue to orient to their handlers for a treat.

2. They are under no pressure to interact with loose dogs running toward them and the situation will be taken care of without their having to react.

The game involves running a demo dog or appropriate class dog up to another class dog with whatever modifications initially are needed to make this a nonstressful event (barriers, distance, or a demo dog at first moving at an angle or parallel rather than head-on). Reframing this potentially uncomfortable event for the dog makes it just another neat game to play with his handler.

I made this game up because I kept getting complaints from agility students that dogs were getting loose and running up to other dogs on course. When jumping over the apex of the A-frame, many dogs get upset if they suddenly see a loose dog rushing at them. I've had a couple of private clients whose dogs were kicked out of classes for being "aggressive" because they barked reactively when a class dog got away from his handler and rushed them on the A-frame.

Starting the game

I put a dog and handler behind a ring gate, giving them as much distance as I think that team will need to feel comfortable. By the time I start this game in class, the dogs are ready for me to run Snap straight at them up close to the gate. If a dog wasn't ready, I would increase distance, angle my approach, and heel Snap slowly—whatever it took to keep the dog comfortable and happy while he learned. As soon as the dog sees Snap approach, the handler clicks while saying something that will come to mean "Yep, a dog is approaching!" and, depending on the situation, either feeds her dog from her hand or throws a handful of treats

Ranger learns that when Snap approaches the gate, she gets a jackpot.

on the ground. I used to tell people to say *There's a dog in your face!* as they tossed treats, but they complained that the phrase was too long; now we usually say *Incoming!* In many cases, tossing a small avalanche of treats on the ground acts to interrupt a dog's thinking about whether or not to react. Just be aware that if you opt for the treat toss, you don't want to throw treats on the ground in situations where you don't have total control. In some cases other dogs would want the treats, or your dog might decide to guard them. When in doubt, always feed from your hand.

After Ranger has associated Snap's running up to the gate with her jackpot, McDevitt removes the gate, and Ranger gets a jackpot as Snap approaches (left). As she raises one criterion (no gate), she lowers another (Snap is heeling, not running). Ranger ignores Snap in closer proximity with no gate; Snap is loose and walking in a natural manner around Ranger (right).

I run Snap closer and closer and since each dog gets so used to Snap being in his face doing Look at That! games, parallel games, and in other situations, it doesn't faze him that Snap is running up to the gate. When the dog reaches the point that every time he sees Snap coming, he automatically looks at his handler expectantly, "He's coming; where's the food?", I remove the gate. To make it easier now that I've removed the gate, I add a little distance and decrease Snap's speed. Remember, if you raise one criterion, lower another one to help your dog get it right. I work back to the point where I am literally running Snap right into the dogs' faces and they are watching their owners asking, "Where's the food?"

Next, just as in the parallel race, I start adding motivational cues that make Snap bark and pick up speed. I say, *One…* and Snap says "WOOF!" Snap gets more interesting, but at this point the dogs are so engaged in the game and already so used to Snap being interesting, they don't care about him anymore.

In classes where the dogs are more advanced, I incorporate obstacles into the rule structure of this game, just as I would do for the parallel racing game.

A-frame version

Once the class dogs are nonchalant about Snap running right up to them (they are literally staring at their owners and eating happily while I am teasing *1... 2... 3...* to get Snap vocal and running right at them with speed), I start adding obstacles to the exercise. If the dog already does the A-frame and has a contact behavior that involves stopping and staying on the contact, I put him on the down contact of an A-frame with a ring gate in front of the contact. I go through the whole game again, running Snap up to the other dog first with the gate, then without, while the dog practices his contact behavior. Then I let the dog actually complete the A-frame. (It should not be so high that the dog can't see the in-your-face dog for the first couple of repetitions.) The dog then gets rewarded for stopping on his contact, and then gets fed some more because Snap suddenly is in the picture again.

Tunnel version

If the dog doesn't have a contact behavior, I use a tunnel. A-frames are challenging because the dog doesn't see a loose dog coming before he hits the apex, so there is that element of surprise. Tunnels are challenging because of the dog's momentum running through them and because, in a curved tunnel, the dog can't see a loose dog at the exit until he rounds the bend. Station the in-your-face dog at the tunnel exit. You can curve tunnel openings away from each other so the dog exits away from the in-your-face dog. I angle a ring gate from the tunnel exit so the dog doesn't run smack into the gate. The handler sends her dog through and, as he is exiting, I take Snap up to the ring gate. When the dog is ready, I remove the gate, allowing Snap to be in clear view of the dog coming through, always careful not to put Snap in the line of fire. Each time Snap approaches, the handler gives her

At left, Sheltie Boing! ignores Snap as she zooms through the tunnel. Snap watches Boing! on cue and remains in a sit-stay. This way both dogs learn during the exercise. After McDevitt increases the challenge by removing the gate (middle image), Boing! continues to ignore Snap. Snap offers eye contact to McDevitt. In a similar fashion at right, Snap walks near Poodle Gwennie while she practices her teeter contact; Gwennie remains unfazed.

Incoming cue and feeds her dog. Eventually the dogs are able to race through tunnels with Snap standing right at the exit and totally ignore him. I've also run up with Snap as dogs slam the teeter.

If your dog gets uncomfortable during this game, he's letting you know you've set the criteria too high. If you feel uncomfortable about the game, your dog will be affected. So far I've been able to guide all my students through the game, using Snap or other appropriate dogs from class as the in-your-face dog. My students really like the game because it gives them an opportunity to practice worst-case scenarios while having control of the situation. The dogs learn to enjoy playing a game without feeling stress that another dog is moving around near obstacles while they are working. By this point the dogs have learned to trust that "weird stuff" happens in the context of CU class and it means a fun game. The students' challenge is to interpret real-life weird stuff for their dogs within the CU framework so that the dogs no longer need to worry or react in contexts outside of class.

Applying There's a Dog in Your Face! to real life

Now will that same nonchalance that my students' dogs show to Snap generalize to every obnoxious dog that runs up to them on a course in the future? I wish I could say yes. On the bright side, it's given each handler a template to work with so that she can practice with different dogs when she *is* in control of the situation. And, if a dog does get loose and approaches her on course or on the street, she will have tools to normalize the event for her dog. She'll be able to present it as part of a familiar game, not something to get upset about. That is, if she can react fast enough!

The problem in a real-life situation is that if a loose dog is running toward your dog while you're on course or on the street, initially you might forget to put the event into the jolly rule structure of "Ha. It's coming right at you. Isn't that nice!" and feed your dog while moving the other dog out of the way. Therefore I have some alternative suggestions:

- Keep a crate on the periphery of the course (obviously this is for class, not trials), teach a rock-solid *Go to your crate* cue, and send your dog to his crate while you are dealing with the loose dog.

- Use fellow behavior consultant and agility instructor Sue Sternberg's idea of teaching your dog to stick his head between your legs on cue to get treats from behind your back. That way, when you see a loose dog, you can set up the situation so your dog doesn't have to meet the loose dog face to face while you are dealing with the situation. (Thanks for a great idea, Sue!)

- If your dog is small, pick him up and turn your back to the loose dog. Then pray he's a *nice* loose dog.

- I also tell people who worry about loose dogs rushing their reactive dogs when walking on the street to carry a canister of Direct Stop citronella spray (available at www.cleanrun.com). The spray can stop a fight before it starts and give you the opportunity to get your dog out of the situation. Please note that the spray is never a training tool; it is an *emergency* tool to stop a dogfight without risking getting hurt by trying to separate the dogs yourself.

Lightbulb Moment: Singing is Believing

There's a Dog in Your Face! is the exercise for Jack and me. Saying those words to your dog and actually believing them is what is working for me. We have only been practicing for six to seven months. Staying calm when there is an actual event about to happen is the hard part. Jack tended to sense my uneasiness when I said, *There's a dog in your face!* Recently I started putting a little tune into *There's a dog in your face!* I sing it to him with a soft inflection in my voice, and Jack's body language seems softer to me. Before I learned this exercise, inviting the other dogs in my house into Jack's and my space had been a problem because of Jack's reactivity. Now he turns his head away from the other dog or looks to me for his cookie.

What I have noticed is that singing the phrase keeps me relaxed, which then channels down to Jack, keeping him relaxed. Yelling, pulling, or yanking didn't work for Jack and me. The new skill, however, is a real lifesaver. Practicing it is important so that it becomes second nature. It is a commitment for a better life.

—*Carol*

The Dog in Your Face! game also was extremely helpful in giving my formerly reactive Belgian Malinois friend Rosie the confidence to relax about her space, even around kids.

Lightbulb Moment: Rosie, the Diamond in the Rough

I got Rosie, my three-year-old Belgian Malinois rescue, from the Brooklyn, New York, shelter when she was two. Having had just one dog previously (a laid-back, mixed breed) I had no idea what I was in for. Rosie came with lots of issues. She was either extremely reserved around other people or exceedingly reactive to environmental changes. She barked violently and/or bared her teeth and charged.

When I took Rosie to meet my niece and nephew (Sydney and Kyle, then ages 10 and 7), they walked into her space and past her just a little too fast for her liking. She immediately started barking and lunging, which intimidated the kids. I knew we were going to need some help if they were ever going to feel comfortable around her.

Rosie especially benefited from two CU exercises: There's a Dog in Your Face!, with other dogs running into and around her space, and the parallel games, which taught her that she could run side by side with another dog. Both games helped Rosie focus more on me rather than on external stimuli and increased her confidence and attention span. Consequently she is a much more relaxed and likable dog. While she still has moments where it's hard for her to control herself, she no longer needs to be in constant "on" mode. We've worked hard on her training, and she has settled into her life with me. She now readily and eagerly approaches people to solicit attention. Sydney and Kyle now adore her and are no longer fearful of her. They ask to have her visit and love to put her through her repertoire of tricks. At a recent visit, Kyle had some friends over. He stopped his friends from running over and very clearly explained to them that you could not run up to her, but that you had to greet her with her name first and walk slowly up to her. She was perfect for his friends.

Rosie is a work in progress, but now we have a great foundation to build on. I got the best compliment from my brother: "That dog is your diamond in the rough. She's going to be phenomenal one day." Funny—I already know that she is!

—Carolyn

TARGETING TASKS TO PERFORM LOOSE AROUND OTHER MOVING DOGS (GET OUTS AROUND JUMP STANDARDS)

I teach this game in preparation for the Out 'n Mats game, my intermediate-level parallel game that I introduce somewhere around nights five or six. Out 'n Mats is a targeting exercise in which the handler sends her dog through a maze around jump

McDevitt shapes Easy to Get Out around a jump standard.

standards to lie on his mat. I give each student a jump standard and show her how to train her dog to move laterally away from the handler to go around the standard. Students can either shape the dog (in other words, click and reward any small increment that will lead to the desired end behavior) or use a hand target or target stick to get the behavior from the dog.

CU assistant Brown's Doberman Jynx learns Get Out by following a target stick and getting rewarded. Brown will soon fade the target stick.

When using a hand target to teach the Get Out, the handler stands with the dog in between her and the standard. She uses the hand that's farthest from the dog as a target placed on the far side of the standard; so if the dog was at her left side, she'd use her right hand as the target. The dog moves around the standard in order to touch her hand (or a target stick), and she clicks his movement around the standard. For students using their hand as a target, I tell them to fade the hand quickly. After the dog gets clicked as he moves around the standard a few times, he gets it.

It's cleaner to shape this behavior by standing with your dog at your side and the standard to the left or right side of your dog. Any lateral motion the dog gives is clickable; and, if your dog is used to being shaped, he will quickly figure out to move around the standard. Remember when shaping, the dog is figuring out what gets rewarded on his own, so you shouldn't be using your hand or body to cue him to move.

Once your dog understands the lateral behavior, you can start adding distance. Every time your dog moves around the standard and returns to you for his reward, take another step to the side so that when he performs his next Get Out he has to move a little farther laterally to find the right place to move around the standard. Since the dogs already have a similar structure for going to their mats, they quickly pick up on the distance aspect (and, of course, some of them already know a Get Out before attending CU).

As a dog gets more comfortable with being sent around the jump standard, the handler can increase her dog's distance from the standard or send him to his mat after his Get Out. Here Easy flies to his mat after completing a Get Out. Sending the dog to his mat is preparation for the Out 'n Mats game.

MAKING IT PERSONAL: CUSTOMIZING THE CU APPROACH

At this point in the course, the dogs truly should be learning to relax in the face of their triggers. Remember, Night Five is an arbitrary structure. It may take 11 nights to get the dogs to this point in the course; or it may truly take 5. It all depends on the dogs. There is both science and art behind this course. Knowing how to apply learning theory to modify behavior is the science. The art is in understanding which aspects of the CU program to apply and when, and how to combine them for the best result. As an example of combining—and personalizing—aspects of this course to help a distracted, stressed, or reactive dog succeed, I've included Snap's story here. Snap had complex issues that required creativity (what clicker trainers call "lateral thinking") and a multifaceted approach. This story was originally published as an article in the July 2005 issue of *Clean Run* magazine.

This tale may superficially appear to recount how I got Snap to tug in class, but in the context of this book, you will see that the story is actually about combining CU principles to build Snap's confidence to a level where he was able to play in the training center among other dogs. His inability to play in that context was merely a symptom of his underlying issues, and I used his willingness to play as one barometer of our progress in increasing his comfort level at school. He felt happy tugging, so if I could get him tugging around dogs and other triggers that worried him, I could also bring that happy feeling he gets when tugging into situations that were worrisome. Here I'm talking about the emotional component of play for Snap. There are other dogs that get too aroused or too predatory when tugging so I would have designed a different program for them. This is Snap's story. Remember as you read it that I am always adjusting for each dog as an individual.

"But he only plays at home"

In Agilityland, tugging has become an emotionally charged issue because many feel it reflects on your relationship with your dog. When a dog is unable to tug under the stress of class or a trial, his handler is made to feel that she has a bad relationship with her canine partner. It can be a humiliating experience. For dogs that would actually benefit by being able to tug or play in a class environment, we need to look at why dogs that appear to have play or prey drive to spare at home shut down outside the home. In Snap's case, it was a combination of two major issues: distractibility and stress. I could tell when he was distracted versus stressed. Distracted meant that he ran off to find something more interesting to do, and he looked happy while doing it. Stressed meant that he had a meltdown, couldn't think clearly, and engaged in displacement behaviors such as sniffing and wandering.

Snap is an extremely athletic, fast little guy, who seemed to have moderate drive to tug and to play ball and Frisbee. As I began working with him, however, I saw how easily he could turn off. It was dramatic—I'd have him swinging in the air tugging and growling like a maniac and suddenly the heating system in the basement (which is where I train at home) would make a sound, and he couldn't think anymore. He disengaged from me and the toy, wandered off to sniff, and appeared concerned. As we began to play in different places, I learned it wasn't just noises from the heating system that caused stress. Any unexpected noise could cause a meltdown.

Moreover, Snap could not play if another dog was nearby. If he was happily playing with a toy and saw another dog, he instantly dropped the toy, had a stress-sniffing fiesta, and refused to so much as look at the toy again until the other dog was gone. After having Snap for a few weeks and observing his behavior, I invited a friend and her dog over for a play date in my backyard, thinking this dog would be a good match for Snap. He was, and they raced around happily for a while. Then, while my friend's dog checked out my yard, Snap stayed close to us. Snap spied a Frisbee in the grass and he picked it up triumphantly and carried it to me. My friend and

I held our breath in excitement as I began to tug with him—could this be a breakthrough? Suddenly, at the other end of the large yard my friend's dog looked in our direction and took a step toward us. Snap dropped the Frisbee as if it had caught fire. "You see what I'm talking about?" I said to my friend.

Now, six months later, Snap and his other dog friends all race around the training facility with toys in their mouths, and Snap, who initially was fearfully barking and lunging at strange dogs in class, is now enjoying class, tugging and playing ball near other dogs, and generally showing a lot more confidence. He also has become focused on me. I would say he is about 95% where I'd like him to be, meaning his comfort level is high enough for his toy drive to overcome his stressors. How did we do it?

Snap's distractibility factor was high. He could not sit still, had the attention span of a fly, and was constantly checking out the environment for interesting stuff that had nothing to do with me. To address his lack of focus, I used the Premack Principle. Simply put, this learning theory states, "Give 'em what they want." The amazing thing is, the more you give them what they want, the less they want it. The reverse psychology component is strong here; as the environmental attractions become less interesting, you automatically become more interesting.

A squirrel tale: Premack to the rescue

When I adopted Snap, it was not quite squirrel season yet and we were having fun playing Frisbee in the backyard. He was focused on me and excited about the toy. It was a wonderful bonding experience for us. A month later, when the squirrels returned, Snappy said, "Game's over, Mom," and his terrier nature took over.

I took some deep breaths and made a plan. I was not about to be outdone by squirrels in my own yard. I put the Frisbee in one pocket, treats in another, let Snap into the yard, and told him to go chase squirrels. He of course ran toward our tree line barking madly. I followed along behind casually and called him—I felt comfortable enough in our relationship at that point to take that risk. He instantly turned toward me, and I clicked and gave him a food reward. As he was still chewing, I told him to go chase the squirrels again.

When using the Premack Principle, you never want the dog to take the opportunity to dismiss himself. You are always the one sending him away to go see or do what he wanted to in the first place. Therefore you are creating a structure where the dog still gets what he wants but you have sneakily put yourself in charge of access to it. The dog suddenly finds himself in a conditioned pattern where he interacts with you, then is sent back to the distraction, and then interacts with you some more. Thus it is no longer you vs. the environment. And at this point, if you are using a high enough rate of reinforcement and being entertaining enough, most dogs will start choosing to continue interacting with you rather than returning to the distraction to self-reward.

Snap figured out my pattern of come away from a squirrel/go to a squirrel in two clicks. Then he started offering me behaviors for a click. He sat, he lay down, and he made eye contact—all of it right under the trees that were ripe with squirrels. I rewarded all offered behaviors around squirrels and after every reward—before he could disconnect from me and leave without my permission—I sent him to go check out the squirrels. He totally started losing interest in the squirrels, so I shaped him to offer looking up at squirrels in the trees for a click and food reward. Snap quickly figured out that looking up in the trees was getting clicked, so squirrel watching became just another behavior in his small tricks-for-clicks repertoire.

Snap chooses to focus on his Frisbee instead of squirrels in the trees.

It was at this point that I decided to take a leap of faith and see if I could get Snap to tug on his Frisbee, even for a second. If I could get him to even look at the Frisbee, my plan was to send him to see the squirrels if that's what he wanted. I mentally crossed my fingers and produced the favorite Frisbee from my pocket. He perked up and looked interested so I took another leap of faith and threw it! As I was berating myself for pushing him too much and for being a sloppy trainer, he brought the Frisbee back to me, wanting a game of tug, and from that moment on we have been able to play under the trees without a problem. I accomplished this step in one afternoon.

When I let Snap and my other dogs into the yard just to do their own thing, Snap still chases the squirrels, but squirrel chasing has not affected his motivation to play Frisbee with me in the yard.

Stress!

Stress around other dogs greatly dampened Snappy's toy drive. Snap had grown up with several intact male Border Collies and had adopted a "pre-emptive apology" strategy to deal with them. Whenever he saw one, he flung himself on his back, squirmed like a worm, and urinated. He was too intimidated to play with me if Border Collies were close by, a challenge since the training facility was full of them. At the facility and on the street, Snap had a different strategy for dogs that were "foreign"—that is, dogs he was not used to seeing. Dobermans, Boxers, Standard Poodles, Portuguese Water Dogs, and Labrador Retrievers were high on his list. He responded to these breeds with shrieking, snapping, and airborne lunging. One of the ways I dealt with his reactivity to these foreign dogs was by playing the Look at That! game. This game reframed seeing strange dogs in a structure Snap felt comfortable operating within, and he started offering looking at dogs and turning back to me expectantly waiting for "payment." In addition, at home we were working hard on relationship building and impulse control. Many layers of training were happening simultaneously, all designed to encourage Snap to feel secure, learn to think through his excitement and stress, and bond with me.

The first two seven-week agility sessions I took with Snap, I used food rewards since I mostly was focused on getting him used to being in a class situation and feeling more confident with strange dogs close by. The few times I dared take a toy out, he looked at me as if I were insane to suggest such a thing, and I despaired that I would ever get him to play in class! By the third agility session, Snap was ready and willing to play, even quite close to other dogs. To get to that point, I had to address Snap's issues with motivation, trust, and relaxation, which I detail in the next paragraphs.

Motivation: Making associations

Some dogs cannot eat when they're stressed. Fortunately, I haven't yet found a stressor that would diminish Snap's appetite. I wanted to see if I could pair food with toys in Snap's mind. My thought process was, since he can eat in front of strange dogs, if I can condition him to associate toys with food, he'll be able to play in the same situations. I considered starting over from scratch and clicker training Snap to offer playing with toys for food—which is what I would have done if he had not had any play drive at all. But since he did have a healthy dose of play drive, my instinct was to skip that step and instead just teach him that playing with his toy was a predictor of a really good snack.

Access to the garden hose is one of Snap's primary motivators.

Aside from food, Snap loves attacking the garden hose. Therefore, at the end of a tugging or retrieving session, if we were inside I'd jackpot him (give him several treats instead of just one), and if we were outside, I'd let him engage the garden hose in battle. Outside, Snap was able to ignore the "dead" garden hose and play Frisbee with me until I released him from the Frisbee and made the hose come to life. Inside, Snap was not able to think about a toy if there were treats within visual range. So I put the treats in my pocket, played with him, and fed him afterward. After about a week I was able to put treats out on the shelf and he would tug with me and ignore the treats. When he was ready, I started alternating tugging and feeding, rather than just jackpotting at the end of a play session. Sometimes I used tugging as a reward, sometimes I gave him a food reward.

"But I wasn't done yet!"

Once Snap had made the association between toy play and a food reward, I started using the Give Me a Break game that we learned in Night Four (page 148) to increase his interest in play. Give Me a Break employs a concept I call the "quick dismissal" that many agility trainers use when teaching an obstacle. You engage the dog in an activity (training contacts, tugging, and so on) for a brief period of time and then dismiss him well before he is ready to quit. That way, the dog is always left wanting more. In addition (as I mentioned in the squirrel story) you are putting yourself in charge of telling the dog when he has finished performing a certain behavior rather than allowing him to disengage from you and go find something better to do. Re-engaging in the activity with you thus becomes the reward for the dog's enthusiasm about it in a cycle or feedback loop that builds even more enthusiasm to continue playing the game.

To apply the quick dismissal technique, a friend came over with a stopwatch and we timed the play sessions and the breaks in between play sessions. Initially, the tugging lasted from 10 to 20 seconds; then I verbally dismissed Snap with an *Okay*, and sat in a chair and ignored him for exactly one minute. During the first two or three sessions, Snap spent his break period sniffing around the floor and when it was over I had to call him back to restart the game. Quickly, however, he became so interested in the game that, when I said *Okay* and sat on my chair, he started offering a down in front of my chair and stared at me intently, wanting to continue playing. At that point, I stopped timing his break periods and restarted the game based not on the stopwatch, but on his behavior. The more intense he looked, the faster I restarted the game.

A sample training session went like this:

- 10 seconds of tugging, one minute of break.
- 20 seconds of tugging, one minute of break.
- 30-40 seconds of tugging, end session.

If your dog wanders away during the break period, that is "legal," but it's more effective to do this exercise in a controlled environment that your dog does not find very seductive. We did these sessions in my empty basement, which I only use for dog training. If your dog disconnects from you and goes off to do his own thing before you dismiss him, simply go sit in the chair as if you had actually dismissed him and wait for him to notice that you've removed yourself from the picture. When he notices and comes over to you, immediately restart the game as his reward.

Snap got so into the pattern of tugging, then staring at me to restart the game, then tugging some more, that he completely stopped noticing the sounds of the heating system as well as the sounds of my other dogs moving around upstairs (another distraction). This method was not just reserved for skill training. Every single time I played with Snap, I did it in the spirit of the Give Me a Break game. I made sure to play the game in different parts of the house, in my backyard (during the break periods I would tell him to go look at squirrels and I would lean against a tree; he always just watched me for signs of restarting the game), in a field near our home, and ultimately at the training building.

I believe the Give Me a Break game was so effective in building Snap's play drive not just because he was being released when he wasn't ready, but also because he was being patterned to play, then wait, then play. The forced wait is a great anticipation builder, and his default break period behavior is the lie-and-stare. Now when we are playing near other dogs in class and I dismiss him, if he sniffs the floor rather than staring at me to restart the game, it's a clear signal to me that he's feeling some stress and that I need to modify the situation for him.

I needed a two-pronged approach to make Snap comfortable enough to play around his stressors. First, I needed to increase his drive to play (the Give Me a Break game solved that problem). Second, I needed to decrease his anxiety. Somewhere in the balance lay my answer.

Relaxation

Snap's nervous system was so tweaked when I got him that he jumped at an unexpected touch or sound, spun repetitively in tiny circles until he made us all dizzy, and couldn't sit still for a nanosecond. I started Dr. Karen Overall's Protocol for Relaxation with him immediately (see page 37 for a description). I use it on all my dogs because I have found that it not only helps them relax but also is effective both for building a relationship and for teaching focus. The dogs become very intent on you as you move through the exercises.

I like to add a Go to Place mat or bed to the relaxation exercises so that the dog has a specific place that reminds him of how he feels when experiencing the protocol. Repeat the protocol in various locations. Taking along a mat or bed helps the dog generalize and gives him an added sense of structure and security. As soon as the dog sees his mat, he understands, "Oh—we're playing that relaxation game now!" If you have a dog that gets nervous when crated in class or at trials, you can also do the exercises while your dog is in a crate. Or you could put the dog's special relaxation mat in his crate during those times.

Snap was doing well with the protocol on his mat—concentrating on me, feeling relaxed, and demonstrating self-control even with the front door wide open, a can of tuna in front of his mat, my cats picking at the tuna, and my other dogs moving around close by—when a thought struck me. What if I incorporated toy play into the relaxation exercises? Would Snap's confidence and happy attitude within the structure of the relaxation protocol allow him the mental space he needed to be able to play when stressors were present? For example, the sound of barking dogs normally caused Snap to shut down and be too worried to play. If I tried tugging with Snap while he was relaxing on his mat, would he be able to play while my friend's Sheltie barked in a nearby room? My instinct was that pairing relaxation exercises with brief tug sessions would further increase Snap's confidence to play. This was a new application of the protocol, and I emailed Dr. Overall (a wonderful source of support and inspiration to me) to ask what she thought.

With a green light from Dr. Overall and with much anticipation I sent Snap to his mat and began the protocol. After several exercises I called him off his mat to play ball with me. He tugged on the ball, so I threw it. He retrieved it happily, and tugged on it some more. Then I sent him back to his mat and continued with the relaxation work. He immediately assumed the heavy-lidded look that dogs get during the protocol. I did a couple more of the relaxation exercises and then played ball again. The idea was working, and the protocol plus playtime had an extra, unforeseen benefit. Snap was suddenly switching back and forth from ball to treats without any problem. I started this protocol at a time when Snap was still having problems concentrating on his toy while in the basement and in the presence of food. One session of protocol interspersed with play time and he has been able to switch between food rewards and toys ever since.

The next day I decided to encourage my friend's Sheltie to bark during the relaxation-play protocol. For the first time, Snap was able to ignore barking, do the relaxation work, and retrieve his ball with gusto. Success!

Snap learned to trust that McDevitt will not let another dog bother him while he's playing with a toy.

An ounce of prevention: McDevitt started teaching Easy at eight weeks that it is safe to play with her in close proximity to other dogs.

Trust

I have an exuberant Belgian Tervuren, Rumor, who intimidated Snap when he came to live with us. Rumor was dying to play with Snap, and whenever Snap showed any interest in a toy, Rumor tried to initiate a game by taking the toy and asking to be chased. This ploy failed miserably and Snap didn't want anything to do with toys when he was around Rumor.

I figured that before I could get Snap to show interest in toys around strange dogs at our facility, I had to get him to play around Rumor. So I created a new game.

I had Rumor sit and wait while I initiated tugging with Snap. I then allowed Rumor to move about *behind* me and try to get to Snap. I kept body-blocking Rumor so he never got too close to Snap. Rumor found this game entertaining, and Snap started feeling safe enough to play with toys around my big Belgian boy. At some point I faded myself out of this game and Snap and Ru started tugging with each other and finally learned how to play together. I believe this experience really built up Snap's trust that he could play with me and I wouldn't let other dogs either take his toy or bother him.

As time passed, I saw a consistent level of improvement, resulting in a dog that felt safe enough to tug his heart out in class. Though Snap still notices if a dog is barking hysterically or if something unexpected happens around him, he is able to recover and continue working rather than shutting down.

Postscript: Since the publication of this article, Snap has ceased noticing other dogs barking and other sudden environmental changes when he is in happy play mode with me. More important, one of the reasons I knew he was feeling super-comfortable and delighted to be at our third agility trial was that he started lobbing a ball at me and merrily initiating play in an environment filled with his former stressors.

Chapter 8

NIGHT SIX

CONCEPTS
- Raising criteria: More fast, more furious, still under threshold

NEW EXERCISES
- Out 'n Mats game
- Car Crash game

Reminder: Continue working on passive and active attention and box work at the beginning of each class, raising criteria as appropriate for each dog.

At this point the dogs are comfortable working around each other in close proximity in a variety of situations and are able to be thoughtful and calm in arousing situations such as watching other dogs run. Now they are ready for more advanced distance work.

RAISING CRITERIA: MORE FAST, MORE FURIOUS, STILL UNDER THRESHOLD

The name of the game now is to continue raising criteria where appropriate and to keep the dogs feeling comfortable while building excitement and speed into two new parallel games. One game emphasizes working away from you; the other creates a rule structure where the dogs perform a task in extremely close proximity to other dogs—so close that occasionally they might even touch as they pass. At this point in the course most of the leashes are off for these games, but many students prefer to start the game with the leash on to give the dog the idea of it before taking it off.

DISTANCE WORK (THE OUT 'N MATS GAME)

The Out 'n Mats game is my intermediate-level parallel racing game using jump standards and Go to Place mats as targets the dogs can interact with *at a distance from you*. Distance is a new criterion here.

Once the dogs have an understanding about getting out around standards, you can start the Out 'n Mats game. I put a jump standard, a mat, and a standard in a line 5' to 10' apart. Parallel to that line I put a mat, a standard, and another mat. Parallel to that I put a standard, a mat, and a standard, and so on, alternating the pattern. I start with a good deal of distance between the lines (roughly 10') and, of course as the dogs progress, I decrease distance between their working areas. The idea is simply

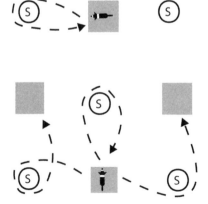

The Out 'n Mats game allows handlers to send their dogs around jump standards (S) and to mats (the shaded squares) in a variety of patterns, with other dogs working nearby.

to have the dogs Get Out around the standards and lie on the mats. By the time we play this game the dogs are loose. If there is a dog having difficulty, I separate his mat and standard area with ring gates, maybe just letting him watch the others for a while before asking him to play the game.

When the dogs are comfortable racing around, I start changing the patterns. Rather than having dogs simply working parallel to each other, I have dogs pass each other on their way to standards or mats. I let it get as chaotic as it can get while still maintaining focus and control. This game is just a more advanced form of using targets to help dogs work loose near each other. It can get pretty silly, almost like a game of Twister.

The Out 'n Mats game is an advanced targeting game that allows dogs to practice working at a distance among other dogs. Border Collie Flash happily performs a Get Out while Snap and Australian Terrier Sadie wait to be released from their mats (left). Flash's handler lines him up for his next Get Out while Snap starts a Get Out (right). Distractible Australian Terrier Sadie gets rewarded for remaining on her mat through all the activity around her.

WORK IN TIGHT QUARTERS (THE CAR CRASH GAME)

Once the dogs are doing well with the Out 'n Mats game, the next class they can try my advanced-level parallel game, the Car Crash game. It is the last exercise I teach in the course. I've included it here to show the progression more clearly. With two or more dog-handler teams turning right or left through a maze of jump standards, the dogs gradually build up speed so that the Car Crash game becomes a fast-paced exercise with lots of "crashes" (dogs moving past each other in close proximity, not actually crashing into each other) between the dogs in tight quarters. By the time the dogs are crashing, they should think it's no big deal to be passing close to each other. If they do think it's a big deal, they're telling you that they're not ready for this game.

This particular game was inspired by Linda Tellington Jones's TTouch exercise of using labyrinths for reactive dogs. TTouch practitioners set up a labyrinth of barriers that twist and turn for one handler to move her dog through while another handler guides her dog through a parallel labyrinth. This exercise gives a reactive dog a job to focus on—following his handler's movement and negotiating a series of turns and possibly walking over bars or other obstacles on the ground—while getting used to working near another dog. The Car Crash game provides a similar rule structure but is set up so that two dogs are performing the same job at once. If you are working with a dog that is not ready for the Car Crash game, you can create two jump boxes and let that dog work in a separate box without sharing space with his parallel partner, or you can work a dog on the periphery of the box, playing Look at That! while he watches other class dogs crashing.

I put four sets of jump standards, without the bars, into a jump box formation roughly 10' to 15' apart. The standards are far enough apart so that both handler and dog can comfortably walk through them. Then I divide the class into As and Bs. I walk the A pattern (all right turns) through the standards. Then I walk the B pattern (all left turns) through the standards. I put an A team and a B team at their starting points. The A and B teams both complain that they don't know their pattern yet, and I laugh an evil laugh and say *Go!* The dogs are leashed at first. When they are ready, their handlers can let the leashes drag or take them off.

When team A passes through a set of standards at the same time as team B and the dogs pass close by each other, that is a car crash—not as violent as it sounds! I encourage car crashes. When dogs crash, the handlers do not stop; they give their dogs a treat while they continue walking on as if nothing happened. When every-

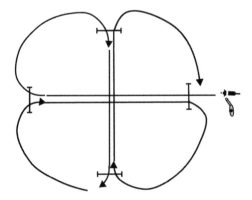

In the Car Crash Game, handlers and their dogs trace a path through a jump box, making either all right turns or all left turns. Dogs and handlers both pass through the wide-set stanchions. With two or more dog-handler pairs in the box at the same time, traffic is congested and the dogs pass very close to each other (a "crash"). When that happens, the dog gets a treat for passing the other dog. This schematic shows the path of one right-turn dog and handler team.

body is working smoothly, I start asking for speed. Depending on the class, I may have just two teams in the jump box at a time. If I have a precocious class, I keep adding new teams into the mix without dismissing the old teams. My record is six teams, dogs unleashed, running past each other through the standards. That was a real blast!

Trixie's handler quietly talks to her and rewards her for watching calmly as Snap's and Rosie's paths begin to intersect during a Car Crash game. Snap and Rosie remain focused on their handlers and are comfortable moving close to each other.

Chapter 9

Night Seven

Concepts
- Next steps: Applying CU to agility contexts
- Think inside the box
- Guidelines for integrating CU games into daily life
  - Dealing with the distracted
  - Coping with stress
  - Combining games to reduce stress
- Help for the CU handler: Dealing with real life

New Exercises
- Continue to raise criteria as appropriate for the exercises already covered. If there hasn't been enough time to introduce the Car Crash game, it's a good grand finale exercise.

Reminder: Continue working on passive and active attention and box work at the beginning of each class, raising criteria as appropriate for each dog.

After six weeks of class (keep in mind this is an arbitrary amount of time) students are familiar with the games and have practiced applying them to their dogs. They are learning to combine the games for maximum benefit. Now, on graduation day, each student needs to mull over how the lessons she and her dog have learned in CU will operate in real life, whether in an agility class or during a walk in the park. This final night we

- Review the basic principles behind the class.

- Discuss how the exercises have already influenced the handlers and dogs in various situations (you'll get some good stories).

- Discuss how handlers can use various CU exercises to help their dog find the right level of stimulation in order to maximize training success.

- Discuss principles for mixing and matching games for the greatest effect.

- Specifically show how handlers can manage the agility or other class environment to create a space where their dog can enjoy learning.

- Discuss how handlers can integrate what they have learned into everyday life.

There are many applications for the tools in this book. For instance, even if a student is on her own and can't do the pairs exercises, with some creative thinking she can take all the principles here and modify them into exercises that will suit her environment. I tell my students to

- Generalize the games by getting creative and using each of the games out of its original context.

- Creatively combine the games to personalize them.

The CU program provides tools for anybody who wants to teach her dog about impulse control, focus, off-lead attention, and relaxing around triggers. I have taught a fun CU-style seminar for reactive pets. It was easy to modify the CU course for this audience; after all, the learning theory behind CU is the same one I used to help my private clients with reactive pet dogs years before I created the course for my agility club. Both the general concepts and the specific exercises in this book can be integrated into the realities of daily living whether you have a pet dog or a performance dog (and the majority of what we call "performance dogs" are primarily pets anyway). So far in my classes, however, the typical CU students have been people who either are starting their dog in agility or who have run into behavior issues while training their dog in agility classes or running them at trials. For agility competitors who seek out my course, the next step is to use the new tools in their toolbox in an agility context. The following tips are based on my experience guiding my students through the experience of integrating CU principles into agility training.

NEXT STEPS: APPLYING CU TO AGILITY CONTEXTS

Recently I began my first advanced CU course, mixing CU games and Open-level agility sequencing. It was a pleasure to see former students excited about our next experiment together.

I watched my students enter my yard without giving them any instruction. They all left their dogs in the car and set up little stations with folding chairs and crates and mats. They then got their dogs, watchful of space issues around my gate, and each handler rewarded her dog for reorienting to her after stepping through the gate. They walked their dogs over to their respective stations, cued them to lie on their mats, and began massaging them. It was a quiet, organized entrance.

Warm-up

We then warmed up with some familiar old games: crate manners and active attention exercises. They played the Give Me a Break game within a ring-gate box, and the dogs fervently chose not to take their breaks. As I took the gates down, we briefly played Look at That Dog! As I walked six-month old Easy up to the class dogs, they barely glanced at him and whipped back to their handlers. Then my friend Jacky Judd (who was teaching the agility portion of the class) brought in her Sheltie that none of the CU dogs had seen before. Jackie asked the class dogs to play There's a Dog In Your Face with her Sheltie. The dogs recognized that the new dog was part of their comfortable rule structure. They offered looking at the dog and looking at their handlers and remained relaxed and happy to be in class again.

Very pleased, I handed the reins over to Judd, who showed the students the sequence she had set up. Here is where things got interesting.

Running the sequence

A few of the dogs in class smoked the sequence; nothing else existed in those moments for them but the course and their moms. It was thrilling to see their progress! Two dogs got stressed during the sequence, ran away, and sniffed the ground.

Their handlers felt lost and frustrated as they often did in agility class and at trials. Now what were they supposed to do?

Seeing my students in this new context really drove the point home to me that it's difficult for people to apply CU principles to agility without coaching within an agility context. That's precisely why I had decided to create the advanced class.

The two stressed dogs that had run away and sniffed during the sequence had just performed beautifully in the CU warm-ups, giving full attention and the appearance of complete connection. Both of these dogs—a retriever and a terrier mix—struggle with anxiety that manifests as a shut-down reaction. Their coping mechanism is to go off by themselves and sniff, the way somebody who is upset at work might go outside and smoke a cigarette. I had not seen that reaction in these dogs after the first couple of nights in CU because, as I got to know them, I found ways to raise their comfort level. With each class they got happier and more focused. Now I was experiencing them in a context where they continued to feel stress.

Sniffing is a typical strategy dogs use to cope with stress on the agility field.

Generalizing CU

Just as dogs frequently have a hard time generalizing newly learned behaviors to different situations, these students were having a hard time generalizing lessons learned in CU in a context where they were surrounded by agility obstacles and sequences to run. Just being in a yard filled with obstacles had primed some of my students and their dogs to feel, "Oh no, it's agility class." For some, this alone was a situation in which both handlers and dogs were used to getting frustrated and confused. My students had mastered the tools; they just didn't know when to use them. How could I help my students generalize what they had learned in CU so they could use the games and the perspective in a variety of contexts and environments? First, I reminded the students of their dogs' excellent performance during the warm-ups, pointing out in particular their rapt attention within the ring gates. Then I discussed a concept that is essential in applying CU to other contexts.

THINK INSIDE THE BOX

The ring-gate box is a *template* for agility—and for real life. When used to its maximum benefit, the ring-gate box offers you a framework where your dog pays attention even when unleashed and in the face of various distractions, even without ring gates. We start our attention work within a small ring-gate box so that the dogs can't wander far. As we raise our criteria, we no longer need the ring gates. If you find yourself in a quandary, put those gates back up and start again, if not in reality, then in your imagination. This will help you think of ways to get your dog's focus back. If your dog wanders off while running agility courses, put the obstacles into an *imaginary* ring-gate box. Think about what agility in a trial context looks like: a bunch of obstacles inside a huge ring-gate box, with various people and dogs moving outside the box while your dog stays connected with you and focused on work inside the box. Sounds like a high-criterion version of the CU box games to me! This concept enables you to reframe any experience for both your dog and you so that you can both be successful.

Photo Credit: Craig Lizotte/CL Photography

Thinking of an agility ring full of equipment as a giant ring-gate box gives a handler a framework for working her dog in sync and off-leash. The same CU principles apply as in the small ring-gate box used in CU class

While watching Sophie, the Golden Retriever, I noticed that she could take three obstacles in a row before she started stressing. She was getting overloaded around the fourth obstacle and then running off for a break. I watched this pattern several times and then made the handler aware of it. The game I showed them allowed Sophie to move about the yard and take obstacles without experiencing the fourth-obstacle meltdown.

Sophie felt happy and comfortable doing close circle work or heeling with her handler. So we went back into the middle of the sequence, surrounded by obstacles, and I had her handler play the "We don't need no stinkin' leashes" game, heeling with a high rate of reinforcement. We began on-leash, continued with the leash dragging, then finally off-leash. Sophie was back in a rule structure she felt happy with and was not feeling any pressure or performance anxiety. The obstacles just happened to be close by. I had her handler move with her around the entire yard in this manner, then incorporate a tunnel followed by a treat, and more movement. Then Sophie got a break. I wanted her handler to see how a simple game with which her dog was comfortable would decrease Sophie's anxiety and therefore get back her attention. By *reframing* what it meant to that dog to be around obstacles, I wanted to change her attitude from, "Now I'm supposed to do all this and it's too much" to "I like it when I get to run with Mom. Oh there's a tunnel. Okay, I'll take it." And "Oh, there's a jump, okay. I'll take that too." This was a simple but effective solution for Sophie. Gradually this retriever will be able to perform more obstacles in sequence without needing to take a break. I don't expect it to take long for her to run entire sequences now that we've reframed the experience for her.

For Target, a terrier mix, the Give Me a Break game had been a mainstay of his training program. I started playing the game with him in the middle of the sequence, again ignoring the obstacles. My instinct here was to run with him for five steps, click at the fifth step while he was in position at my knee, and treat. I repeated this pattern several times and gave him his release cue to sniff the grass. A funny character, Target looked down at the grass and bobbed his head back up at me, so I immediately responded by running another five steps. We repeated this pattern, and I raised criteria quickly by running more steps, and covering larger distances without clicking and treating. I then started incorporating an obstacle at a time into the pattern. I was still operating within the Give Me a Break structure, but he was choosing not to take breaks, so we just kept going, and suddenly he was doing a brief sequence without realizing it!

A common place where dogs experience stress is at the start line, and Target's handler had struggled for a long time trying to teach a reliable start-line stay before coming to CU.

RECREATING THE START-LINE EXPERIENCE

When Target's handler walked him up to the start line, he automatically disengaged and sniffed. He was already in "Oh no, the start line" mode. Being left in a sit at the start line caused him to initiate all sorts of displacement behaviors, including sniffing, yawning, and muzzle-licking. He looked very uncomfortable even if he wasn't breaking his stay.

I had his handler play the leash game at the start line rather than leaving him in a stay. We had already played this game with success in our regular CU class, but when faced with a real sequence, his handler went into her old walk-your-dog-to-the-start-line mode and her dog went into his "Oh no!" mode. I had her run with her dog on leash, then off-leash, near the first obstacle. He was attentive and engaged in playing a game with no bad associations. Then I asked her to run her dog past the first obstacle and take the second one. After a few repetitions, I had her return to the start line, play the leash game, unleash her dog and take the first obstacle, again without a stay at the start line. The start line was reframed; the picture had changed. Target felt comfortable, and he took that first obstacle without any stress-related behavior. Since Target is quite fluent in running to mats and relaxing comfortably on them, another start-line remedy I had tried success-fully with this dog in CU was to put a mat on the start line. His handler had not thought to do either of our start-line interventions before trying the sequence, because in her mind she was separating CU from agility class. I needed to help her integrate CU and agility class into one big picture.

GUIDELINES FOR INTEGRATING CU GAMES INTO DAILY LIFE

To help integrate CU games into other classes and life in general, I've briefly summarized some core exercises helpful for dealing with typical issues that motivate handlers to bring their dogs to my class, including being distracted, stressed, reactive, or shutting down.

If the dog appears to have agility ADD, first determine whether he is distracted because he is stressed or merely because he needs help learning to focus. Remember, always observe the dog in context, looking for common displacement behaviors that indicate stress (page 37).

If the dog is performing at less than an optimum level, make sure you can change the picture for him so that he can succeed. Give him the distance and/or the barriers he needs and use passive attention, biofeedback, Dr. Overall's relaxation protocol, or any other tools you have to help him relax and cheer up.

Dealing with the distracted

The general CU cornerstones for dealing with a distractible dog are:

1. Shape attention. Always notice and reward any attention your dog pays you.

2. Use the Look at That! game (page 122) to teach focus while allowing your dog to feel comfortable knowing what's in his environment.

3. Remember to use the Premack Principle. Pattern your dog to attend to you as part of his interacting with the environment. Reward your dog by releasing him to what he wanted to do in the first place (for instance, greet somebody or sniff the grass) after he attends to you. Use the Give Me a Break game (page 148) to build concentration, focus, and enthusiasm to work with you in distracting situations.

4. Use creative targeting exercises to give your dog something tangible and specific to focus on in distracting situations.

By using a high rate of reward for paying any sort of attention, putting looking at "other stuff" on cue, and using the Premack Principle in conjunction with the Give Me a Break game, handlers can transform distracted dogs into very engaged partners, that is, *unless* there is a medical reason that the dog has agility ADD, or the dog is suffering from behavioral pathology (acute anxiety, for example). See "Nuts & Bolts" (page 19) for advice if you think your dog's distractibility has a medical basis or if he suffers from behavioral pathology.

One of my students combined the Look at That! and Give Me a Break games with targeting to help her highly distractible Jack Russell Terrier focus. This student definitely came up with a personalized solution to her dog's lack of attention.

JUNIOR, THE TARGETING MANIAC

Junior, the Jack Russell Terrier, wandered off and sniffed a lot during agility class. Because of Junior's interest in sniffing the grass in my backyard one of the first exercises I taught him was the Give Me a Break game. I either asked for his attention or simply clicked whenever he oriented to me on his own, rewarding multiple times, and verbally dismissing him to go sniff the grass. I expected the game to be helpful, but Junior started doing something that no other student's dog ever had done: he literally started targeting the grass as a trick for me. When I saw what he was doing, I doubled over in laughter. Who had ever heard of such a thing? Here was this tiny spotted terrier, very purposely and carefully doing nose touches to blades of grass and quickly looking up at me, as if to say, "Did you see what I just did?" After a while, he was paying attention and ignoring the grass.

I later found out Junior loved to target anything and everything. So it was natural that he incorporated this behavior into the Give Me a Break game. A few months later, (after Junior became a star in CU class, learned to be very connected to his handler, and worked off-leash in my yard around various dogs and wonderful-smelling grass and dirt), I found out something that blew my mind. Junior was one of those dogs that took agility lessons in a horse barn that often had horse poop in or near the agility area. He had a long history of running away to eat the poop. Thinking creatively as I encourage my students to do, Junior's handler had walked him up to the poop and played the Give Me a Break game the same way I showed her how to do with the grass. A bold move, but it yielded an amazing result. Junior started targeting the horse poop in exactly the same way as he had targeted the grass! Any interaction with horse poop became a funny trick for Junior to give his owner. The poop had been reframed for Junior as an opportunity to give his mom a trick, it lost its original lure, and he was able to focus in class.

Junior helped me to clarify the connection between the Give Me a Break game and the Look at That! game. In the Give Me a Break game we send our dogs away to do what they want and we reward them for choosing to work with us. In the Look at That! game we click or mark our dogs for looking at something else, not us, then ask them to reorient to us for their reward as part of the game. Within the rule structures of both games the dogs are learning that what triggers them or just interests them "out there" is not a big deal. They also learn that engaging with "stuff" is part of a pattern connected to engaging with us. There is no conflict about grass or poop vs. the handler, or looking at an approaching dog vs. looking at the handler. It's all connected. Ultimately the dogs are able to give their handlers full attention around triggers that distracted them in the past. They start offering the behaviors of going away and sniffing grass as part of a behavior chain in which they return for a treat. In a similar fashion, the dogs offer the behavior of looking at other dogs or other triggers so that they can turn back to their handlers for a reward.

When you train in new environments you may need to play these games initially to remind the dog about the rules and how to interact with the environment during training time. When the light goes on and the dog, rather than being distracted, is offering looking around as a behavior to give you, then you can start rewarding him for sustained eye contact (when desired) or for offering whatever behavior you want. At that point the dog is fully engaged in giving behavior to you, because the patterns he learned from the games reframed his biggest distractions into *opportunities* to offer behavior you can reward. The stuff around him is just not a big deal anymore. You can then let the dog know which behavior is going to work best for you in that moment. In Junior's case, he started interacting with grass as a trick for me rather than because he found the grass to be all-consuming. I started clicking him for watching me, and then moving with me in a slow circle, off-lead. As he moved with me, his head never turned toward the ground again. That single session lasted maybe 10 minutes.

A friend who teaches pet obedience classes came up with a group application of the Look game to deal with a class of overaroused, adolescent dogs.

Lightbulb Moment: Helping Excited Dogs Focus in Obedience Class

I am a pet dog trainer in New York City and often use Leslie's Look at Stuff game for reactive dogs that need to learn to walk down the street without reacting. It works beautifully and my clients can easily execute the game. Recently, when I was teaching an adolescent pet dog class, several dog-and-owner teams were late, the weather was lousy, and the dogs had not been properly exercised. They were unfocused, barking, and just unruly. I knew I wasn't going to be able to follow my lesson plan. Instead, I asked the handlers to click and treat their dogs for looking at the other dogs in the room. Within minutes my class was under control. The dogs were offering to look at the other dogs rather than barking and lunging at the end of their leashes. The owners were happy to have another tool to help their distracted young dogs. Thank you, Leslie.

—Dawn

Of course every dog is different, but if you are clear in your own mind about how to play the Give Me a Break game and you can manage your environment enough so that your dog can't just wander off and fail to return, it should not take long to teach a dog the concept behind the game. That is unless you have a dog whose serious anxiety makes him hypervigilant about the environment. In Junior's case I taught him the game within a small square of ring gates while he was loose. He could leave me and sniff grass after I dismissed him, but he could not wander around my entire yard. When he was ready for me to raise the criteria, I took the gates down.

In the following example, I incorporated the Give Me a Break game into agility sequencing to help a dog focus on obstacles in a distracting environment.

THE CHALLENGE OF OUTDOOR AGILITY

A CU student came to me privately to work on focus for outdoor agility with her cute West Highland Terrier, Niles. Since the Westie already had the foundation from the Give Me a Break game, I showed his handler how to use that game to give her what she wanted. "It works for terriers!" one of my CU alumni likes to tell people.

First I casually walked with Niles off-leash around my unfamiliar yard. I walked at his side as he enjoyed sniffing around. Every time he oriented to me, I clicked and fed him 5 to 10 little treats. I then verbally dismissed him as I walked a few steps away from him. He quickly got into the pattern of the game and started following me around, his initial excitement about the yard waning.

I started some simple circle work, using a high rate of reinforcement (every few seconds a click and a jackpot), and he happily ran with me. After the jackpot I dismissed Niles again and walked away. His interest in continuing the game had won over his enthusiasm for the yard by this point. Every time I walked away he followed me. When he came up to me, I immediately restarted the game.

He was doing well so I had his handler start from scratch. She walked around the yard and clicked when he oriented to her. She needed to work on her dismissal. I asked her to use a neutral tone instead of her singsong voice when dismissing her dog, since she also used that singsong voice when calling his name and asking him to watch her. I told her, "We're not asking him to watch us; we're telling him to go away. And we're rewarding him for asking if he can continue playing with us instead of going away!" I made her pick one dismissal word and stick with it. It was hard for her to stick with one dismissal cue. She also needed to make it clear that she was disengaging by using her body language as well as her voice.

I coached her through clarifying the dismissal aspect of the Give Me a Break game until Niles was giving her his full attention. Then I let her start the circle work. Her dog was brightly racing at her side, so I added in a jump. After the jump, I had her jackpot and then dismiss him. When Niles reoriented to her, I had her immediately start the circle work again, incorporating the jump.

In this manner, we continued to add obstacles until the Westie was doing a sequence of three jumps to a tunnel to weaves. One time during this session, Niles lost his focus and she started to call him in her singsong voice. He continued sniffing the grass, so I asked her to say his dismissal word in a neutral voice and go sit in a chair that I had strategically placed near the obstacles. She sat in the chair and Niles ran right over to her. The second he got there, I told her to jump up and send him into the tunnel, the obstacle closest to the chair. Since during the Give Me a Break game, the students sit in a chair during break time, sitting in a chair becomes a cue to the dog to reorient to his handler. Reframing "doing agility outside" as a new version of the Give Me a Break game allowed this CU student to get the level of focus from her dog that she had wanted.

Postscript: In 2006 Niles ranked as the #1 West Highland Terrier competing in AKC Novice B (both events) and the #3 West Highland Terrier in AKC Open Standard.

"Sirius Targeting" is a story about a targeting application I made up for a Belgian Sheepdog that couldn't function in agility class when another dog was running. He screamed uncontrollably at the sight of other dogs moving. At the time CU had not been created and I wanted to work Sirius near other dogs doing agility. I was able to try this application in the background of a friend's agility class. It offers an example of taking a behavior that is familiar and comfortable to many of us—targeting—and putting a twist on it.

Sirius Targeting

To help Sirius learn to focus in class, I devised a strategy of gradually moving ring gates, in a structured way, toward the distraction of dogs running. This solution essentially is a targeting exercise.

Initially, I put Sirius in the facility's obedience area, which is separated from the agility area by a folding wooden partition that the dogs cannot see through. He could still hear the agility class, which was exciting enough for him. I suggested that his owner do all kinds of circle work and focus exercises within ring gates in the corner of our obedience area farthest from the wooden partition. Every time she moved Sirius closer to the gate near the agility ring, I asked her to jack up her rate of reinforcement immensely, so Sirius kept driving to get back to that gate, while remaining focused on her.

I kept moving that gate closer to the partition without adjusting the other gates to keep the box structure. Sirius was only focused on the gate nearest the agility ring, and it didn't matter to him that he wasn't staying within a box anymore. He was doing his circle work and staying engaged with his owner, knowing that if he played this game she would eventually take him back to that gate where the rate of reinforcement would shift dramatically and they would have a serious party. Eventually I moved the gate so that it was touching the wooden partition. I then opened the partition a crack and put the gate in the crack. Rather than continuing the movement-oriented work, I asked Sirius's handler to play Look at That! and click him for watching the other dogs. He watched them, for the first time ever, without barking or screaming. So I had his handler return to her circle work game, and I continued opening up the partition until it was folded and Sirius could see the entire class. He remained quiet and stayed in the pattern of working with his owner so he could get back to that gate. If he started getting distracted, we played the Look at That! game until he lost interest.

I continued moving the gate closer and closer until we were on the periphery of class. My friend's Jack Russell Terrier was running a course 15' away, and Sirius just stood there and quietly watched. All that separated them was one flimsy, see-through plastic gate. This was the most success Sirius had ever had when dealing with a charged agility environment. A lot of it had to do with targeting— compare the gate to my red van story. This progress happened during a single lesson, but obviously Sirius would need a lot more work before being ready to rejoin a class. His owner was doing other foundation work with me privately.

Coping with stress

Often dogs are brought to CU because stress or anxiety causes them either to behave reactively or to flat out shut down. These dogs have issues that need to be resolved at deeper levels than the dogs that are merely happily distracted. Dogs that become reactive (or catatonic, depending on their personality) when triggered by something that upsets them improve when their handler reads and acknowledges their stress signals, teaches them how to relax, and provides a consistent rule structure that communicates to the dog that he is safe. For example, if a dog is in a new class and new classes worry him, his handler can provide trusted and well-rehearsed structures that will lend an air of the familiar and comfortable to the new situation. She can bring the dog's Go to Place mat and start passive and active attention, or biofeedback, or targeting games, or the Look at That! game.

The general CU cornerstones for dealing with a dog that becomes reactive or shuts down as a response to stress in class are:

1. Learn how to read your dog and recognize and acknowledge his stress symptoms.

2. Teach your dog how to relax using the relaxation protocol, mat work, and passive attention exercises.

3. Determine your dog's optimum arousal point through Off-switch games.

4. Know your dog's triggers and play Look at That! or other games to teach him a new response.

To reframe the picture for a shutdown or reactive partner, teach your dog to relax, to comfortably modify his arousal levels, and to view worrisome triggers as opportunities to earn rewards. Reducing a reactive or shutdown dog's stress is a prerequisite to getting his focus. The first step is to pay attention to what your dog is telling you.

At an agility seminar Snap provided a nice example of the importance of paying attention to your dog, noticing when he is uncomfortable, and addressing the cause of his discomfort.

THE CASE OF THE COMPROMISE STAY

At a workshop with former USDAA World Team member Donna Rohaus, it was Snap's turn to do a sequence, and I placed him in a stay in front of the first jump. While keeping his butt on the ground, he wheeled himself in a semicircle so that he was facing my knee rather than the first jump. This is what I call the "compromise stay," the dog isn't actually getting up, but he is moving. I have found that dogs always have a good reason for compromising the stay this way. I asked Snap to return to his original position, which he did, all the while looking extremely uncomfortable. Immediately he reverted to his compromise stay.

Many handlers correct their dogs for the compromise stay, physically pulling them back into place and reprimanding them. What I do is note where the dog is looking when he compromises his stay position. I always see something interesting that I hadn't noticed before and that is demanding the dog's attention. In the case of Snap at Donna's seminar, I followed his line of vision and saw a friend's Border Collie (who happens to closely resemble a dog that Snap feared) watching Snap from the sidelines, straining at the end of his leash in full Border Collie crouch. His handler was holding him and there was no chance he was going to go anywhere. Even if he did break free, he's a friendly dog that poses no real threat. But from Snap's perspective—if I may speak for him—the dog was a serious threat. The crouching dog had zeroed in on Snap and was eyeing him intensely. If you didn't know he was leashed, it certainly would look as if he were about to explode from stalk to chase in the sequence of predatory behaviors that all dogs instinctively know.

I acknowledged to Snap that I saw this dog and what he was doing. I told him conversationally that it was cool, the dog wasn't going to bother him, and we could run the course without worry. Snap got back into the correct stay position and ran the course confidently. He just needed to know that I, too, saw the dog and that I clearly felt he wasn't a threat. From that point, Snap could trust me that he was safe.

Snap hasn't compromised a stay since then, but if he does, I will respond in the same manner, checking out things from his perspective as best I can, acknowledging his needs, and letting him know things are okay.

Lark, an adorable Nova Scotia Duck Tolling Retriever that worried about the proximity of other dogs, was queen of the compromise stay when we practiced start-line stays in class. When we acknowledged her insecurity and played a Look at That! game before asking her to stay, however, she could see which dogs were close to her within a comfortable rule structure. She then was able to remain in the correct position. Her insecurity played out more generally in a lack of focus. Like many CU dogs, Lark needed a ritual to help her feel comfortable before she could perform complex behaviors and succeed at the games. Letting her see who was where, doing relaxing mat work near other dogs, and finding the right balance for her between letting her look around and asking her to focus helped her gain confidence.

The Worried Toller

When Lark entered a box of ring gates, she wasn't ready to start cold with circle work or the Give Me a Break game as the other dogs in her class could. I took her into a ring-gate box and did some passive attention work, massaging her ears a bit and stroking her. Then I invited her to sniff around, on-leash, and followed her lead as she sniffed the periphery. She needed to check out the space she was in. Then she needed to see what was nearby, so I clicked her for looking around at the other dogs that were on mats relaxing nearby. She understood the game, and she was reorienting to me after looking around. Once she knew who was where outside her box, I started clicking her just for orienting to me. I wanted to underscore to her that her focusing on me was the big thing now. This was the last piece for her before she would be ready to start moving at my side successfully. It was important that I find the right balance for her between looking around and watching me. I needed to know when to switch from a Look at That! game structure to reinforcing sustained direct attention. I found this balance for her and she happily gave her full attention to me. At that point I started the actual circle work game and worked her off-leash. She gave me the nice performance I knew she had in her.

Maggie, the Border Collie, was what I call a "space case." She experienced anxiety when other dogs got too close, and behaved reactively. Hers is another situation where an underconfident dog needed to know that her handler was paying attention to what the dog was telling her, recognized signs of stress, and would keep her safe. A combination of relaxation exercises, Look at That! games, and particularly training her owner to read (and act on) Maggie's stress level, turned her into a relaxed, confident companion that now enjoys agility classes.

Maggie, the Formerly Misunderstood Border Collie

In agility class at Y2K9s, a beautiful Border Collie named Maggie clearly had much potential, but from what I could see, she always looked stressed. What was stressing her was the lack of rule structure about the proximity of other dogs. Maggie did not want dogs to invade her space, and the class environment was chaotic for her, with lots of strange dogs that sometimes got too close. When this happened, Maggie barked and lunged. Maggie's handler attempted to get her attention with tennis balls, but it was a temporary fix. Maggie focused on the ball until she felt uncertain about a dog, then lunged at that dog. This ritual of ball-focus/freak-out, ball-focus /freak-out kept playing out until Maggie joined a CU class.

Throughout CU we watched Maggie blossom into the dog she was meant to be— confident, relaxed, and ready to work. Maggie needed her handler to acknowl-edge her anxiety when other dogs got too close. Maggie needed her handler to let her know that she "had Maggie's back" and was not going to allow other dogs to bother her. Only then could Maggie concentrate on working without wasting energy worrying about other dogs. To work on Maggie's reactivity her handler had taken her to an obedience class where the instructor had put the dog in a down-stay and paraded dogs around her. Being obedient and terribly bright, Maggie was able to maintain the down-stay, but in light of what we know about Maggie, imagine what this exercise did to her nervous system. Having dogs all around her moving unpredictably when she was not allowed to move was her worst nightmare.

There were no down-stays for Maggie in CU! We spent a lot of time giving her the message that her handler recognized when she felt worried and that her handler would take care of the situation. When we placed her parallel to other dogs separated by ring gates, I pointed out the signals she was giving to help her handler gauge her state of anxiety in that moment. If Maggie was worrying about another dog, I had her handler move her farther away until we could see her body relax. When Maggie figured out that her mom had finally gotten it, the whole class could see her body language change.

All the exercises, especially the ones geared toward helping Maggie relax, did a great deal to boost her confidence about being around other dogs. By the end of class she was able to lie limply on her mat, enjoying a massage as other dogs ran by her on the other side of a ring gate. She was able to focus on her mom without worrying. As a trick for her handler she offered glances at dogs that ini-tially bothered her. She no longer cared about the dogs, knowing that her handler would take care of her needs. And she was wiggling and wagging and happy instead of looking as if she were ready to jump out of her skin.

After Maggie graduated, one of her old instructors came up to me and said she had observed Maggie walking through Y2K9s, and remembered it had been difficult for her before her CU class because of the many dogs that she'd had to worry about. The instructor said Maggie looked like a different dog, walking through the building in a self-contained and confident manner, no longer vigilant about which dog was where. She had the acknowledgement she needed and was finally ready to have fun learning agility.

Maggie's handler clearly understands her role in reducing her dog's stress and keeping her comfortable and is proud of their success. Maggie and her handler are now enjoying group agility classes at Y2K9s.

Lightbulb Moment: Maggie, the Space Case

I never thought I would see the day when Maggie could share her space in a civil manner with a dog she didn't know. Not only has that day come, but now she even can cope with my sister's adolescent Golden, a dog Maggie used to attack. Because of CU, I know how to address Maggie's concerns about being near other dogs in a positive manner and reduce her stress.

—Maureen

Combining games to reduce stress

In a stressful situation, you can combine the Give Me a Break game with the Look at That! game to get the focus you want.

TEMPERING SNAP'S ANXIETY

I took Snap to a heeling seminar. Ironically, he's at a point where he's totally used to the chaos of agility classes and seminars and can operate fine within that structure, but when he walked into an obstacle-free space and saw a bunch of dogs just standing quietly with their people, *it looked different and alarmed him.* He started sniffing the floor and his energy was scattered. It was Snap's typical, worried response.

Asking for focus as a way to deal with Snap's "driftiness" was only going to put more pressure on him and result in more sniffing. So instead, I dropped his leash, knowing he wasn't going to go more than a few feet away from me, and started asking him to look at the other dogs. This put him immediately into a structure he feels comfortable with, and he briefly glanced at the other dogs and turned back to me for his treat. When he was engaged with this game, I started playing Give Me a Break. I asked him for some hand targeting as he moved around with me. I used a high rate of reinforcement and had him turning in different directions and moving with me on both sides while I counted down from 15 in my head. I then gave him a verbal release and disengaged from him. He was loose this entire time, because I knew that would work for him. On being released he offered a down, his way of asking for a continuation of the game.

If, instead, he had gone off and sniffed the floor some more, I would have known that he was still stressed. I could have gone back to his Look at That! game, done bodywork on the floor, or created his own space with gates—whatever my instinct told me would help him feel comfortable. But I knew he was ready to work because of his response to being released: "No, I don't want to be released, it's time to work!" So we joined the class (we'd arrived late and the other dogs had started heeling exercises throughout Snap's warm-up), and I didn't get any floor-sniffing or driftiness for the remainder of the seminar. In fact, the little weasel enjoyed himself and decided heeling was fun.

HELP FOR THE CU HANDLER: DEALING WITH REAL LIFE

Many CU handlers, as well dogs, need a warm-up to get themselves in the proper mindset to work. There are several key aspects of the CU program that handlers sometimes forget.

1. When dealing with reactive dogs, you not only need to fine-tune your ability to read dog body language but also to reduce your reaction time. Be timely, clear, and consistent with your signals.

2. Remember that ultimately CU is about connecting with your dog. It's not just about doing exercises.

3. You are working on behavior modification with your dog, not merely training obedience skills. Rather than simply teaching new behaviors, CU is usually more about using the techniques of counterconditioning and reframing the picture to give your dog a new perspective and create a space where he can feel safe and confident enough to focus and succeed.

4. You need to keep the rate of reinforcement far higher for far longer than you would if you were simply training an obedience exercise. The CU exercises are the means to a happy, confident, and focused dog. Train yourself to look for tiny steps to reward, and reward generously.

Be clear

With reactive or fearful dogs, it's more necessary than ever to be clear, timely, and consistent in how you signal your dog. With a reactive dog, you may have a nanosecond to manage a situation before you find yourself resorting to emergency damage control. With a sensitive, soft, or fearful dog, your miscommunication can reverse weeks of progress, as the next case illustrates.

THE SHY WEIMARANER

Once we were doing a Campfire Circle, where the dogs take turns looking at other dogs, and one of my students, the handler of the painfully shy Weimaraner Arial, was trying to get Arial to look at the next dog. Arial, who had started to really come out of her shell in class, only wanted to look at her mom. So my student pointed a finger in the other dog's direction in an attempt to get Arial to look at the dog. Arial read the pointed finger as a target cue and she obediently touched the finger. "Uh-Uh!" exclaimed her handler, defaulting to her old behavior of verbally correcting Arial. Not knowing what she had done wrong, Arial retreated into her shell.

Focus on the dog, not the exercise

In the case study above, Arial was more comfortable making sustained eye contact with her handler than she was with looking at the dogs around her. There are two ways I would suggest handling such a situation:

- Let the dog choose the behavior she feels best about, as long as she is calm and subthreshold. If she wants to just look at you, let her look at you. If she wants to look at other dogs but you need her attention, then put the looking away on cue so that you can easily get her to refocus.

- Examine the possible reasons for the dog's avoiding the cued behavior. In Arial's case, she was not concerned with the proximity of the other dogs and therefore did not need more distance or other adjustments to raise her comfort level. She simply had not done the Campfire Circle exercise before and had not generalized her Look at That! behavior to this new set-up.

The case of Lark the Nova Scotia Duck Tolling Retriever is another illustration of the importance of reading your dog and adjusting your training structure to set her up for success in a difficult situation.

Lark seemed so distracted in part because her handler had been focusing on doing obedience exercises to teach her to pay attention rather than taking a good look at Lark and thinking in terms of how to help her succeed when she was stressed. I needed to switch her handler from exercise focus to Lark focus. I needed to help him think about what sort of prep work Lark as an individual needed before she was ready to do an actual exercise. I also needed to point out indicators in Lark's behavior that would help him understand what she was feeling. This understanding helped the handler switch to Lark focus and gave him an entirely different perspective on how to experience taking your dog to a group class.

When in doubt, raise your rate of reinforcement

I am never in a hurry to treat my own dogs less, and I haven't had any trouble with making the transition from an extremely high rate of reinforcement to taking them into a ring where I can't use treats or toys. They trust me, they trust the process, they understand what's expected, and they can predict that a reward is coming. Moreover, the work itself is rewarding to my dogs because that's built into how they learned it. I keep my dogs on a high rate of reinforcement forever. I mix up the rewards between toys, treats, and environmental rewards such as *Go outside* and *Go play with that other dog*, and *Go pee on that tree*, and *Come out of the crate*, and *Jump!*, but I'm always rewarding my dogs' behavior with *something*.

Reinforcement is communication. Initially, most beginning trainers don't reward their dogs often enough. The longer the interval between rewards, the more confused and discouraged the dog gets and the quicker he is to disengage. The Toller Lark was a good example.

An obedience instructor had told Lark's handler to wean her off treats as soon as she learned a behavior but had not provided him with the definition of when a behavior was "learned." If a dog cannot perform a behavior on cue anytime and anywhere, he hasn't achieved what is called "fluency" in that behavior. Lark was not ready for any of her behaviors to be put on a random schedule of reinforcement (or no reinforcement at all), and the concept of randomizing food rewards had not been introduced to her handler in his obedience class. As a consequence, he went from a ratio of one treat for one behavior to no treats, and Lark lost her behaviors.

When Lark's handler joined CU, he needed to dramatically raise his rate of reinforcement. I told him he didn't have to give a treat for each sit he asked for at home or at school if Lark was comfortable and confident responding to that cue in those environments, but if he asked her for a sit in a different environment—Piccadilly Circus, for instance—he would have to raise the rate of reinforcement again, because he had raised criteria by asking for that behavior in a highly distracting, novel place. In addition, since Lark had a tendency toward insecurity and CU for her primarily was about finding her confidence and helping her feel comfortable around strange dogs, the rate of reinforcement for the work we were doing needed to stay super high. We were not just *reinforcing* her behavior, we were creating *positive associations* through counterconditioning. So in CU, weaning off treats should never have been a blip on her handler's radar screen.

Lark's handler did an excellent job of raising his rate of reinforcement (improving his timing and precision in the process) and learning to watch his dog and assess what type of work she needed to succeed in the various exercises. Lark's confidence, happiness, and attention span increased tremendously. Her handler learned to understand Lark on a deeper level and learned to focus on her needs in a particular situation rather than focusing on making her do a certain behavior. He and Lark became a great team and a great example of what happens when my students embrace the shift in perception that CU offers.

Chapter 10

REAL LIFE:
SNAP'S PROGRESS REPORT

Agility has been such a gift to Snap and me. Both of us enjoy it so much. It has given our relationship a special feeling of connection, accomplishment, and pride. Here is Snap's progress report, to give you an idea of our process.

When I first adopted Snap, I knew he had started learning about agility equipment in his previous home, so I enrolled him in a class that was supposed to be at his level. After the first night, I pulled him from class, knowing we would not return until Snap was able to focus, feel comfortable around other dogs, and control his impulses. Snap had run off from me while doing a sequence, he looked ready to bounce off the walls, and being near strange dogs stressed him out. He just wasn't ready to handle all of the variables that made class at once both an overstimulating and a challenging environment for him. Unfortunately I see dogs in group classes all the time that remind me of the old Snap. These dogs are not yet ready to participate in a group class environment.

While I was teaching Snap how to process information in a way that would not overwhelm him, I was also doing agility foundation work. Snap got to the point after about six months of working with me at home and in our training facility where I felt he had enough focus to start private lessons with one of our agility coaches, Barb DeMascio. During the privates I worked him for up to 10 minutes at a time and gave him lots of breaks. Also during this time I continued taking Snap to the Y2K9s facility (when it was empty) to play the Give Me a Break game to help him continue acclimating to the excitement of being in the facility. He was learning how to pay attention in what for him was a distracting, all-consuming place. This game allowed him to explore the building within a rule structure that enabled him to pay attention to me for increasingly longer periods of time. I also used this structure to get Snap comfortable with playing with toys in the building, first without other dogs around, and then with them. This was the period of the "But He Only Plays at Home" article, which detailed various ways I enabled Snap to prepare for the road ahead. Eventually Snap was taking hour-long, fairly demanding private lessons without needing a break. He was staying focused and remaining happy to work with me. *It was only at that point that I took Snap back to group class.*

When we returned to group class, I used CU exercises to help Snap get comfortable and focus around the strange dogs and other stimuli that would make it more difficult for him to keep his wits about him. I used a combination of

- Passive attention exercises at our working station.

- Active attention exercises increasingly closer to the other dogs.

- Playing Look at That! to help Snap assimilate information about the other dogs while reinforcing him for attending to me.

- Playing more Give Me a Break games to continue building his ability to work and focus for longer periods of time.

In the agility group class environment, until I got the level of concentration, self-control, and comfort that I wanted from the spotted weasel, doing CU exercises with Snap was far more important than doing agility with him. I was lucky to be able to take classes taught by my heart friend Alexa Karaoulis, so I was able to use the class environment to work with Snap without running into conflict with an instructor.

We took roughly five seven-week sessions of group classes before Snap evolved into a dog that could just enter the facility and start class cold without any CU exercises. He was focused, happy, and always tried his hardest. At the same time, of course, we continued with the private lessons and were becoming a good working team.

At that point, I entered Snap in a match. This is where we begin the progress report. Keep in mind that my goal with Snap, no matter what context we are in, is for him to feel happy, confident, and safe. When he's feeling good, I get the focus and connection I need to do well in the ring. I love agility, and what's more, I love that Snap loves agility, and I enjoy it when we do well. But my goal is for my boy to have a good time without worry.

THE MATCH

At Snap's first agility match, I entered him in one Novice Standard run. We got there early and spent time hanging out on the periphery. I talked to some students and said hello to various dog friends, all the while rewarding Snap for any signs of calm and focused behavior. When dogs walked by, he automatically offered his trademark so-brief-you-almost-missed-it glance and then stared at me. He relaxed to the point that he lay down on his side as people and dogs passed close by, busy and excited, preparing for their turns.

I moved him near the ring gate and his status did not change. He lay on his side and looked very comfortable with his surroundings. Suddenly a German Shepherd ran out of the ring and right at us. My friend Jen swooped down upon the dog and stopped it in its tracks before it got any closer, before my mind could even formulate a strategy. I thought this was going to be a major trauma for Snap, but he settled right back down and I decided not to leave our ringside seats. When the next German Shepherd ran, Snap jumped in my lap—his safe haven—and watched.

I played the Look at That! game for a few clicks, told him he was safe, and he lay back on the floor.

When it neared our turn, I walked him up to a line of waiting, excited dogs (all strangers) that were pulling at the ends of their leashes. He started sniffing the floor. I called him and he was able to immediately reorient to me, so I rewarded that behavior and then told him to sniff the floor again. After the fourth repetition of this little cycle, he lost all interest in the floor and just watched me. The floor sniffing itself, as a stress reliever, would have been fine, but I wanted to see how easily he could come out of it as an indicator of whether he was truly ready to take his turn in the ring.

He had to stand in the line of dogs and did a great job of remaining self-contained. When it was our turn, he walked into the ring happily with a confident attitude: no sniffing, no interest in anything but doing the course with me. I was beyond proud of him. I decided to ask for a start-line stay as another gauge of his inner state and I got a confident, uncompromised stay. He did everything I asked of him on the course; of course, not everything I asked of him was right! But that was of much, much less importance than his mood at the match.

THE FIRST TRIAL

It was Snap's first trial, and though I should have devoted all my energy to him, I couldn't resist bringing along eight-week-old Easy. I was so wrapped up in Easy's experience of the trial environment that Snap spent more time in a crate than I'd planned.

When I walked Snap around, however, he seemed totally at ease. I thought he was doing fine—until I took him over to the practice jump. As soon as we got there, his eyes glazed over and I could see his mind was gone. I moved him away from the jump and massaged his ears and tried my best to avoid feeling frustrated. When he started to come back to earth, I asked him for fun, simple behaviors, which he was able to do, and gave him tons of treats. I then returned to the jump and his eyes weren't glazing over. I asked him to sit and he was able to do it. I asked him to stay, and then jump, and he was able to do that as well. Whatever it was, the spell of the practice jump had been broken.

Waiting for his turn in the ring, Snap was a little sniffy but mostly settled and was able to think and focus. His stress in this context had significantly decreased since the match. He was more distracted entering the ring than he was at the match, where he had been completely focused on his job, because the match had been held at Y2K9s, (our home away from home) and he had never before been to this trial location. Here he needed to know who was behind the ring gates, but he was focused enough that I decided to run him. He was overaroused by running the course and had a little trouble thinking at warp speed—an issue I knew we would continue to work on for future shows—but he remained clear-headed enough to qualify in both his runs and to get a third place.

THE PET EXPO

At his first pet expo, Snap really shone. Y2K9s had been hired to do agility demos, and I decided to see if Snap would be up to participating. Not only did he do the demo beautifully, (even though the staging area offered no separation between the course and the audience and there were little kids literally sitting in the course). He was able to walk around an incredibly stimulating pet expo and stay totally focused on me.

In fact, I felt he was too focused. I was proud that all manner of strange dogs approached Snap and a hundred kids ran up and petted him, and he happily stared at me the entire day. I wanted him to experience the expo like a regular old dog, walking around, sniffing stuff, meeting people, but he wouldn't stop watching me. I brought him up to horses, pigs—you name it—and he thought we were playing the Look at That! game, so my pleas to look around at stuff "for real" fell on deaf ears.

It is easy to overdo training, especially when you have a reactive dog with whom you want to be able to compete. I went home wondering if Snap didn't have a normal enough experience at the pet expo of just walking around like a dog. Had I had cheated him of something by overtraining? But maybe Snap had a better experience focusing on me than he would have had if he had really looked around at the chaos. Maybe that would have been too much for him. Maybe that level of focus was the only way that Snap could have succeeded in his pet expo experience. Every handler needs to find the right balance of art and artifice to allow her dog-with-issues to be as normal as possible while still being able to succeed in trying situations.

THE SECOND TRIAL: WE GOT HIM JUST WHERE WE WANT HIM

At Snap's second agility trial, I was curious to see changes in his behavior as he got more accustomed to the trial structure. The Keystone USDAA Northeastern Regional was a star-studded affair with a stunning array of the most competitive teams. It was thrilling to watch some of my favorite teams live and in Technicolor.

We had to get there early to get Snap measured, and I'd only entered him in Jumpers to assess his ability to perform, focus, and relax in a major trial environment. Of course Novice Jumpers was the last event of the day, so we had to wait 10 hours for our first run!

When his class began, I set up a station near the ring, with my folding chair next to Snap's crate, ready to do whatever work I needed to help Snap assimilate the staggering amount of information the environment was throwing at him. I was prepared to do passive or active attention work, play Look at That Dog Run a Jumpers Course! or some basic counterconditioning ("Yea! There's an Aussie sniffing your rear end!").

Snap is perched like a cat on his favorite vantage point.

Snap didn't need much work. He was content to hang out quietly and mostly lay cat-like on top of his crate, a favorite vantage point. In fact our work with relaxing around triggering stimuli had gone so well that Snap was literally sound asleep and snoring when it was his turn to run and I had to wake him up and walk him, groggy-eyed, to the ring! I did not think that boded well for our performance!

Once Snap was on the start line, however, he woke up and adopted an "I-know-what-to-do" expression on his pointy, weasel face. His entire body (from his expression to his level of muscle tension and overall animation) looked as prepared to work as I'd ever seen it. And he was clearly comfortable staying at the start line.

All these signals told me that Snap had reached his optimum stimulation level. He was operating confidently in the middle of that stimulation continuum instead of at either extreme as he used to do. When I had first started training Snap, he had been either in a high frenzy and unable to think or he totally shut down and was unable to think. Returning to our Goldilocks analogy, Snap had bounced around from "too hot" to "too cold," and had finally gotten to "just right!" I knew we were going to have a great run.

And we did, though we failed to qualify due to handler error. But that didn't matter. I had never felt so connected with Snap on a course. We were truly aware of each other, experiencing that joyous energetic teamwork that had been my goal all along. Not once during that run did I experience a loss of that special connection I was feeling with Snap. And in that sense, we were winners.

THE THIRD TRIAL: TAIL OF A BRAVE LITTLE MUNCHKIN

At the time that I was tying up loose ends for this book, Snappy and I went to our third agility trial. I was very excited and a bit nervous, because it was a local trial where many of my students and my friends would be watching us. I had a wonderful time walking Snap around the trial site and observing students of mine enjoying interacting with their dogs.

Snap felt happy and confident in the trial environment. This was the first trial where he asked me to play ball with him. He no longer needed to do CU games such as Look at That! and Give Me a Break to help him focus and tolerate being around strange dogs. He wanted to play ball, and he wanted to do agility. I threw his ball for him in a field adjacent to the site and he ignored the dogs, people, and kids walking around and was thrilled to be playing. This was a tremendous benchmark for him. It indicated how confident and safe he felt in an environment that once would have been too much for him to handle without becoming reactive or shutting down, depending on his mood and the situation. He also was happy to do the practice equipment without signs of stress. Watching him leap for his ball with his tail wagging and a big smile on his face, I saw that the inner Snap, (the dog I knew was in there somewhere when I adopted him) had finally emerged.

Snap's first run was a Novice Standard course. As I listened to the excited cheering of my students watching us on the sidelines, I knew that we were going to come in first. I felt electricity between us. When my heart friend Dawn Prentiss started jumping up and down and calling to me from the score-posting area, I was not surprised, but I had a feeling of peace and pride and connection with Snap that goes beyond words.

© Barry Rosen/Ain't MuttsBehavin'

At the Kruisin' Kanines trial, Snap was a picture of joy, focus, and connection.

I collected Snap's placement and Q ribbons and he was just as excited as I was. He was dancing in his little merry way and flipping balls at me. I decided to take him to a vendor to buy him a victory present. I walked him into a vendor's tent so he could pick out his present. There were toys and treats in every corner and both he and I were glowing. And that is when the attack occurred.

The vendor next door had stopped by to talk to the treat vendor and had taken her dog along, a black mixed breed slightly larger than Snap. As we shopped, Snap ignored the little black dog. Suddenly the dog lunged and screamed at Snap, and the rest was a crazy blur. Her owner lost control, and Snap tried to avoid a fight by attempting to leap into my arms. Snap was making a sound of sheer terror and pain that I had never heard before. The vendor finally got her dog back and she sent her friend to pet Snap and make a fuss over him while he continued to scream. I was in shock. It was like watching the scene through a fog even as Snap shivered in my lap. The vendor gave me a free keychain as an apology (I found out later she was giving away keychains to everybody at the trial).

I walked off with Snap toward my tent, both of us very much shaken. He was no longer screaming but he was crying and carrying his tail so low it touched his belly, which he had never done before. Suddenly I saw flecks of blood on his haunches and I started searching through his fur for wounds, but could not find any. It took me a couple minutes to realize that the flecks of blood had come from his tail and had sprayed onto his haunches. His tail was a mess. It took a few minutes for the blood to seep through all that fur to the surface, but now his tail was drenched.

I returned to the vendor and showed her Snap's tail and she acted apologetic and surprised that he'd been bitten that badly. I walked away in a daze and found the trial secretary and asked if there was a vet on site or a first aid kit. Most people at the trial knew Snap and started coming over to see what was wrong. It turned out there was a vet there trialing her own dog, and another competitor who was a vet tech. They rushed over to examine Snap. Trying to assess the damage, they poured water on his tail as he screamed.

The trial secretary went to talk to the vendor who was packing up to leave, not even halfway into the day. I was in absolute disbelief when she denied that her dog had bitten Snap.

The vet said Snap needed to go to the ER, where I was planning to take him anyway. My friend Dawn dropped everything and rushed us to the ER. The ER vet shaved Snap's tail, so that his appearance temporarily went from weasel to rat. There were three big punctures in his tail, the lowest one being particularly nasty. She put Snappy on antibiotics, gave him a booster shot (because we had no information about the dog that attacked him), gave him Rimadyl for the pain, and put the dreaded plastic cone over his head so he could not chew his tail.

By then everybody in the hospital, tech, office personnel, and client, had heard of our incredible day of highs and lows. When the ER vet returned Snap to me, she said, "I love your dog. He is such a brave little munchkin." In fact she was so touched by his story and by his sweetness, she called twice the next day to find out how he was feeling.

By the next day, Snap was feeling pretty good. He was maneuvering around with the plastic cone and seemed generally pleased with himself. But I was a mess. People who know me well emailed me and urged me not to let this incident set me back. They knew how depressed and miserable I was feeling and they knew that I was anxious that Snap would be too traumatized to continue competing. Emails kept pouring in, most of them from people asking how Snap was doing. I was truly surprised by the number of people who said they loved Snap and knew he was a special dog. I had not realized how many lives he had touched.

Those people were right! I was terrified that Snap wouldn't want to do agility anymore. I'd worked for two years on many facets of behavioral and agility training to get him to the point where we could trial together. I'd helped him overcome his anxieties about working and playing near strange dogs and tried very hard to teach him that he could trust me to watch his back so he wouldn't have to worry. I felt that I'd let him down. And the five-year-old-child in me kept saying, "It's not fair! Why did this have to happen at an agility trial of all places? Why did this have to happen to Snap of all dogs? It's *not* fair!"

A wise person told me that I should replay the trial in my mind as if it were a movie and end it before I walk Snap to the vendor to get his present. She pointed out, as a few others had, that I was letting my worry and anger override the joy of the day— that I should still be celebrating with Snap about how far he had come. Instead, by focusing on our traumatic experience, I was taking that joy away from us. I saw the importance of this message and resolved to keep the good images of Snap at the trial in my mind and stop stewing over the attack.

Freed of his plastic cone, Snap shows off his winning ways.

A couple weeks later, when Snap was given the okay to be active again (the vet was worried he would bang his tail against something so I had greatly curbed his activity), I took Snap to an outdoor agility class. He had not been to this location before and did not know the dogs. When he saw the equipment he squeaked in anticipation, and when it was his turn, he squeaked as he ran the course. He was so happy that the cone was off and he was doing agility again. He did not worry about the other dogs; he did not even look at them. He wanted agility, and he wanted to be with me, and he was filled with joy. I knew everything was going to be okay.

When we ran in the first trial since the attack, Snap was exactly as I always envisioned he could be one day: just right. He walked in cold with the happy attitude, "Oh, a trial!" and took everything in stride. We did not need CU exercises. He did not have to "Look at" anything, he did not need to relax, he did not need help focusing. He walked around all the strange dogs and people in the way that I wished he could have at the pet expo: he was just hanging out at the show. I was so thrilled by his nonchalance at everything around him and his happiness and readiness to do his thing that I renamed him Snap 2.0! And I started telling people his nervous system had gotten an upgrade. I truly feel it has.

And that, my friends, was the biggest victory of all. No matter how Snap and I do in competition, Snap had faced his worst nightmare and conquered it. He showed me that he had come so far on his path that he was not going to let a little adversity set him back. He showed me, once again, his strength, courage, and spirit. The old memories of Snap are fading fast and the details of Snap's transformation are blurring. He came into my life as

- A wind-up toy dog that could not think.

- A dog that was too intimidated to play near other dogs.

- A dog that launched himself in a pre-emptive strike when certain dogs approached.

- A dog whose nervous system caused him to be either way too aroused or to shut down under pressure—without any balance.

- A dog that many people felt would be too hard to train.

All I see now when I look at the little spotted one is a master teacher, a wise spirit, my partner. I see a dog who is totally comfortable with who he is: a balanced, peaceful, joyful being. I now see the inner Snap, whose door I worked hard to open. And all the while that I thought I was opening a door for him, he was opening one for me.

Recommended Resources

Behavioral Protocols

Manual of Clinical Behavioral Medicine for Dogs and Cats by Karen Overall, Ph.D. (2007) Elsevier

"Humane Behavioral Care for Dogs: Problem Prevention and Treatment," DVD by Karen Overall, Ph.D. (2007) Elsevier (sold both separately and with the *Manual* above)

Reading Canine Body Language

On Talking Terms with Dogs: Calming Signals, 2nd Ed., by Turid Rugaas (2006) Dogwise Publishing

For the Love of a Dog: Understanding Emotion in You and Your Best Friend by Dr. Patricia B. McConnell (2006) Ballantine Books

"The Bite-O-Meter" and "Yowser! A Guide to Defensive Handling Techniques," DVDs by Sue Sternberg, Great Dog Productions

Training for Reactive Dogs

Click to Calm: Healing the Aggressive Dog by Emma Parsons (2004) Sunshine Books

Scaredy Dog: Understanding and Rehabilitating Your Reactive Dog by Ali Brown (2004) Tanacacia Press

Bodywork

Getting in TTouch With Your Dog: A Gentle Approach To Influencing Behavior, Health, and Performance by Linda Tellington-Jones (2001) Trafalgar Square Publishing

"How to Massage Your Dog: A Hands-On Guide to Health & Wellness," DVD by Marie Duthie (2005) Annisage Inc.

Clicker Training

"Know Way, Know How! The science and art of clicker training," DVD by Kathy Sdao, M.A. (2006) Tawzer Dog Videos

"The How of Bow Wow: Building, Proofing, and Polishing Behaviors," DVD by Virginia Broitman and Sherri Lippman (2003) Take a Bow… Wow!

Please check out the articles and other resources on Karen Pryor's website, www.clickertraining.com.

Training and Learning Theory

The Power of Positive Dog Training by Pat Miller (2001) Howell Book House

The Culture Clash by Jean Donaldson (2005) James and Kenneth Publishers

Excel-erated Learning by Pamela J. Reid, Ph.D. (1996) James and Kenneth Publishers

"Cujo Meets Pavlov! Classical Conditioning for On-leash Aggression," DVD by Kathy Sdao, M.A. (2004) Tawzer Dog Videos

Feisty Fido: Help for the Leash-Aggressive Dog by Patricia B. McConnell and Karen B. London (2003) McConnell Publishing

Everything
for the
Agility Enthusiast
www.cleanrun.com